# Mastering the Craft of Typescript Programming

*Unraveling the Secrets of Expert-Level Programming*

Steve Jones

Published by Walzone Press

For permissions and other inquiries, write to:
P.O. Box 3132, Framingham, MA 01701, USA

# Contents

# Introduction

In the realm of modern software development, TypeScript has emerged as a transformative technology, bridging the gap between traditional scripting languages and full-fledged programming paradigms. With its robust static typing system, enhanced tool support, and seamless integration capabilities, TypeScript offers developers the tools to create maintainable and scalable applications. This book, "Mastering the Craft of TypeScript Programming: Unraveling the Secrets of Expert-Level Programming," aims to equip experienced programmers with advanced skills and insights necessary to harness the full potential of TypeScript.

As software projects continue to grow in complexity and scale, the demand for typed languages that can offer both flexibility and safety has increased. TypeScript not only meets these demands but also augments JavaScript's expressive power. By introducing a type layer on top of JavaScript, TypeScript allows developers to catch errors at compile time, reducing runtime errors and vastly improving code reliability. Moreover, with TypeScript's growing popularity among large-scale systems and applications, understanding its nuances is increasingly vital for modern developers who wish to stay ahead of the curve.

This book is organized methodically into ten comprehensive chapters, each addressing a critical aspect of advanced TypeScript programming. Readers will embark on an exploration of sophisticated topics, ranging from TypeScript's intricate type system to the deployment of optimized, high-performance applications. Chapters are meticulously structured to provide insights into advanced operational techniques, encompassing modularization, asynchronous programming, and integration with powerful frontend libraries such as React and Redux. Additionally, significant attention is devoted to tooling and practices that are essential for maintaining high standards of code quality and efficiency in professional development environments.

Each chapter is designed to stand alone, focusing on key technical aspects and offering pragmatic code examples to illustrate core concepts. As readers progress, they will find detailed discussions that delve into decorators, metadata, robust API construction, and innovative testing methodologies. Furthermore, they will discover strategies for embracing TypeScript within the broader ecosystem via modules and namespaces, as well as how to effectively harness its robust features in real-world scenarios.

In crafting this book, the objective is to provide actionable knowledge and frameworks that enable developers not only to grasp the theoretical underpinnings of TypeScript but also to apply these concepts practically to enhance their coding practices. By the conclusion of this book, readers will possess a deepened understanding of TypeScript, equipping them to tackle advanced technical challenges with confidence and precision.

This publication stands as a testament to the importance of mastering TypeScript for any developer serious about advancing their skills in contemporary programming environments. As the scope of software development continues to expand, acquiring proficiency in such versatile tools poses a significant competitive advantage, affording developers the capability to innovate and deliver solutions that are both resilient and scalable.

# 1

# Chapter 1: Deep Dive into TypeScript's Type System

*This chapter explores the intricate features of TypeScript's type system, enhancing code precision and reliability. It covers static typing, union and intersection types, and advanced type inference. Readers will learn about conditional and mapped types, type guards, assertions, and the practical use of type aliases, interfaces, literal types, and enums. Mastery of these concepts supports the development of robust and maintainable TypeScript applications.*

## 1.1 Understanding TypeScript's Static Typing

TypeScript introduces a compile-time type system that fundamentally differs from JavaScript's runtime dynamic typing. This section examines the technical intricacies of static typing in TypeScript, categorizing the system's behavior, precision, and error detection capabilities to em-

power experienced programmers to write robust, maintainable code
with stronger guarantees at compile time.

TypeScript's type system is integrated into the compilation process,
executing exhaustive checks that bridge the gap between JavaScript's
permissiveness and the rigor of static languages. Whereas JavaScript
variables can assume any type at runtime due to its dynamic typing,
TypeScript requires, either explicitly or through contextual inference,
that variables conform to predetermined types. The resulting static
contracts enable early detection of errors and encourage disciplined
software architecture.

TypeScript supports explicit type annotations as well as type inference.
Explicit annotations allow the developer to precisely dictate the intended type, for example:

```
let count: number = 42;
let userName: string = "Alice";
```

In cases where explicit types are omitted, TypeScript employs sophisticated inference algorithms to deduce types from the context.
Advanced scenarios might leverage function return types, parameter types, and even complex generics in order to ensure consistency
throughout the codebase. This static approach contrasts markedly
with JavaScript's approach, where the type of any variable can mutate
unexpectedly, introducing potential runtime anomalies.

Central to TypeScript's static type system is the concept of gradual
typing. Instead of forcing all variables to be typed, TypeScript allows
gradual adoption of its type system, meaning segments of code can
remain untethered from static contract constraints through the use of
the any type. However, reliance on any defeats many advantages of
static typing, as it effectively disables compile-time type-checking for

14

that variable. Developers must exercise caution and prefer unknown when invoking untyped external libraries, thus ensuring that any subsequent type narrowing is explicitly handled.

```
function process(data: unknown): void {
    if (typeof data === "string") {
        console.log(data.toUpperCase());
    } else {
        console.error("Unsupported type");
    }
}
```

The distinction between the static (compile-time) and dynamic (runtime) aspects becomes especially important when considering union and intersection types. Static typing in TypeScript concretizes the types of expressions during compilation, but at runtime, the resultant JavaScript code is not safeguarded by a type system. This dichotomy requires the programmer to ensure that validation or runtime type guards are in place while still enjoying the compile-time benefits. Advanced patterns often involve creating specialized type guard functions that produce narrow types by performing explicit checks, thus merging the safety of static analysis with the flexibility of runtime checks.

Error detection at compile time is not merely a courtesy but an enforced contract in TypeScript. For example, consider a function utilizing a numeric operation:

```
function addNumbers(a: number, b: number): number {
    return a + b;
}
```

A call such as addNumbers("5", 10) would be flagged during compilation, preventing potential runtime errors that would have occurred in JavaScript. This enforcement of constraints is a primary advantage

of static typing. Furthermore, when dealing with complex data structures, interfaces and type aliases allow static contracts to extend to object shapes. Advanced developers are encouraged to design their systems using these constructs to capture invariants that persist throughout their applications.

TypeScript's static type system also shines in scenarios that involve
complex generics. Generics permit functions and classes to remain
abstract with respect to types, enforcing compile-time contracts even
when the specific type is unknown. This is highly advantageous when
designing libraries or frameworks where flexibility is paramount. Consider the following generic function:

```
function identity<T>(value: T): T {
    return value;
}
```

Here, T is inferred from the parameter provided, ensuring that the
function returns a result that matches the input type. When used in
more complicated contexts, advanced type inference in conjunction
with generics can aid in building type-safe APIs that both abstract and
preserve the expected constraints.

A notable feature is TypeScript's support for nullable types. In
JavaScript, null and undefined may be passed around with little
compile-time reshuffling. TypeScript, however, allows developers to
denote optional values using the union type construction T | null
| undefined or by leveraging the strict null checking mode. This
comprehensive handling of absence of value improves the overall
reliability of data structures and functions when used in production
systems.

```
function safeDivide(a: number, b: number): number | null {
```

```
if (b === 0) {
    return null;
}
return a / b;
}
```

The technical depth of TypeScript's compiler includes the analysis of control flow for narrowed types. For instance, after a type guard check, the type system refines the type of a variable within subsequent code blocks. Such refinements are achieved using sophisticated algorithms that analyze the control flow graph of the function, thereby eliminating impossible code paths and reducing erroneous assumptions.

The type system also enables function overloading with precise signatures. Through multiple declarations, a single function can gracefully encapsulate several possible type patterns, making it versatile at compile time while remaining executable in the untyped JavaScript target. Advanced developers will find the combination of static contracts and run-time polymorphism within these overloads to be a robust tool when interacting with heterogeneous data sources.

TypeScript's static analysis capabilities can be extended via custom type definitions, particularly when integrating third-party libraries. By writing ambient declarations (`declare module`) or leveraging the DefinitelyTyped repository, developers impose accurate static contracts on otherwise untyped libraries. This not only enhances the safety of the code but also broadens the scope for advanced refactoring strategies, where automated changes across the codebase are possible with minimal risk of runtime discrepancies.

```
declare module 'legacy-lib' {
    export function legacyFunction(input: string): number;
}
```

17

The compiler options provided by TypeScript further tailor the static analysis process. The `strict` mode, for instance, activates a series of flags that enforce rigorous type checks, ensuring that the developer is immediately aware of any potential discrepancies between declared types and inferred types. Advanced programming techniques often involve fine-tuning these flags for performance optimization and a higher degree of correctness, particularly in large-scale applications.

Integration patterns with existing JavaScript projects illustrate additional static typing techniques. When migrating legacy code from JavaScript to TypeScript, developers can iteratively add type annotations, converting dynamic code into a statically certified codebase. This transition is facilitated by TypeScript's compatibility with plain JavaScript, empowering experts to incrementally annotate and modernize existing systems while preserving execution semantics.

The underlying design of TypeScript's type system includes mechanisms to balance usability and type safety. The interplay between explicit annotations, gradual typing, and sophisticated inference algorithms ensures that coding is not hampered by verbosity while still enforcing a strong contract. Advanced usage often involves the careful design of type hierarchies that mimic domain models, thereby embedding business logic into compile-time validations.

TypeScript's static typing can be further extended through utility types such as `Partial`, `Required`, and `Readonly`. These enable the construction of advanced type transformations, facilitating code reuse and maintaining invariants in mutable or immutable contexts. The developer is given full control over how types are projected and manipulated, which is a significant departure from JavaScript's inherent dynamism.

```
interface User {
    id: number;
    name: string;
}
type PartialUser = Partial<User>; // All properties optional
type ImmutableUser = Readonly<User>; // All properties immutable
```

Static analysis tools provided with TypeScript also contribute to the extended capabilities of this type system. Linters and integrated development environments leverage TypeScript's language server to provide robust error checking and real-time feedback, streamlining the development process. For advanced programmers, integrating these tools into continuous integration workflows reinforces code quality and reduces technical debt from improper type handling.

The deliberate separation between TypeScript's compile time and JavaScript's runtime implies that what is checked statically is never enforced automatically at execution. As such, expert developers often implement runtime validations that complement compile-time checks, ensuring that external interactions remain secure even if they bypass the compiler's safety net. To maintain this balance, advanced type strategies advocate using static types for internal invariants and explicit runtime checks when interfacing with external data sources.

Mastering static typing in TypeScript involves not only comprehending the language's nuances but also adopting an architecture that leverages its strengths across the entire development lifecycle. Diligent application of explicit type annotations, coupled with advanced type inference, ensures that complex systems are both robust and amenable to refactoring. The static contracts enforced by TypeScript facilitate a level of discipline and foresight that is absent in purely dynamic languages, forming a cornerstone of expert-level TypeScript programming.

## 1.2   Mastering Union and Intersection Types

Union and intersection types are advanced mechanisms in TypeScript
that facilitate the construction of flexible yet strongly-typed code archi-
tectures.  Union types, denoted by the | operator, allow a variable to
assume one of several specified types.  In contrast, intersection types,
expressed via the & operator, combine multiple type definitions into a
single compound type that satisfies all constituent constraints.  These
constructs not only serve to articulate complex domain models but also
enable rigorous compile-time checking while retaining the dynamic
versatility intrinsic to JavaScript.

TypeScript's union types enable developers to represent data that may
conform to one of several type alternatives.  For experienced practitioners, a key utility of unions is the ability to formulate discriminated unions—an advanced pattern whereby each member of the
union contains a unique literal property that effectively discriminates
between the variants.  This pattern is deeply integrated with Type-
Script's control flow analysis, allowing type narrowing based on conditional checks. Consider the following example:

```
interface Circle {
    kind: 'circle';
    radius: number;
}

interface Square {
    kind: 'square';
    side: number;
}

type Shape = Circle | Square;

function calculateArea(shape: Shape): number {
    switch (shape.kind) {
```

```
        case 'circle':
            return Math.PI * Math.pow(shape.radius, 2);
        case 'square':
            return Math.pow(shape.side, 2);
    }
}
```

In the above discriminated union, the property kind acts as a literal type that distinguishes between Circle and Square. TypeScript's control flow analysis leverages this discriminant to narrow the union down to its specific member in each branch of the switch statement, thereby preserving type safety without additional run-time type checks.

Intersection types, on the other hand, allow multiple types to be merged into one composite type. When two or more types are intersected, any variable of the resultant type must satisfy all the constraints simultaneously. This proves particularly useful when constructing types that represent entities possessing amalgamated properties of disparate objects. For instance:

```
interface Loggable {
    log: () => void;
}

interface Serializable {
    serialize: () => string;
}

type LogSerializable = Loggable & Serializable;

const entity: LogSerializable = {
    log() { console.log("Logging data"); },
    serialize() { return JSON.stringify({ key: "value" }); }
};
```

Here, the type LogSerializable is a composite type that demands

21

both logging and serialization capabilities. The intersection type enforces that objects of this type adhere to both contracts, ensuring that
any variable declared with LogSerializable can be seamlessly used
in contexts requiring either interface.

Advanced programming techniques with union and intersection
types often involve their interplay with generics and conditional
types.    Generics by themselves provide abstraction over types,
but when combined with union or intersection types, they yield
exceptionally versatile utilities.   A sophisticated use-case involves
overloading functions based on union types to support multiple
method signatures with differing internal behaviors. For example:

```
function processValue(value: string): number;
function processValue(value: number): string;
function processValue(value: string | number): string | number {
    if (typeof value === 'string') {
        // Logic for string: return length of string
        return value.length;
    } else {
        // Logic for number: return string representation
        return value.toString();
    }
}
```

In this overload scheme, TypeScript enforces that calls to processValue
adhere to one of the defined signatures. It is crucial for advanced developers to recognize that union types in overloads can constrain input
parameters in such a way that the function's behavior is determined by
the type narrowing applied in the implementation.

Another useful pattern that showcases the power of union types is the
construction of safe API endpoints where response types may vary.
When an API might return a success object or an error object, the union
type representation allows for precise type-checking prior to process-

ing the response:

```
interface SuccessResponse {
    status: 'success';
    data: any; // Replace with actual data type
}

interface ErrorResponse {
    status: 'error';
    error: string;
}

type APIResponse = SuccessResponse | ErrorResponse;

function handleResponse(response: APIResponse): void {
    if (response.status === 'success') {
        // The type of response is narrowed to SuccessResponse here.
        console.log("Data: ", response.data);
    } else {
        // The type of response is narrowed to ErrorResponse here.
        console.error("Error: ", response.error);
    }
}
```

This pattern not only clarifies the contract for API consumers but also embeds runtime guarantees into the codebase through compile-time checks.

Intersection types extend beyond simple combinations of objects. They also facilitate the construction of types that simulate multiple inheritance. In codebases that require high levels of modularity, intersection can be used to amalgamate mixins or augment objects with additional behaviors. Developers may define a base entity type and then intersect it with various behavior interfaces, ensuring that the final type has a complete set of required functionalities. Moreover, intersections can be combined with union types to describe a broader set of valid outcomes, particularly in state management or complex domain models.

23

Consider the following example involving state transitions:

```
interface LoadingState {
    status: 'loading';
}

interface SuccessState {
    status: 'success';
    data: any;
}

interface ErrorState {
    status: 'error';
    error: string;
}

type DataState = LoadingState | (SuccessState & { timestamp: number
    }) | ErrorState;
```

In this example, the SuccessState is extended via an intersection with
an object that adds a timestamp. This design ensures that whenever a
state is marked as successful, the presence of a timestamp is mandated.
Such patterns are particularly useful in reactive or event-sourced systems where state augmentation is a common requirement.

Utilizing union and intersection types in conjunction with conditional
types further amplifies TypeScript's static analysis capabilities. Advanced programmers can write utility types that extract or manipulate
parts of existing types based on conditional expressions. For instance,
one might define a utility that conditionally adds properties to a type
based on boolean flags:

```
type WithTimestamp<T> = T extends { status: 'success' }
  ? T & { timestamp: number }
  : T;

type DataStateExtended = WithTimestamp<SuccessState>;
```

Here, the conditional type `WithTimestamp` intelligently intersects the `timestamp` property with the type T only if T conforms to the `SuccessState` interface. This mechanism provides a fine-grained, declarative approach to type transformations, crucial for building scalable APIs where type relationships evolve over time.

Working with union and intersection types also means understanding and mitigating potential pitfalls. One common challenge arises from excessive use of union types which might lead to overly complex type inference that can confuse both the developer and the compiler. In such scenarios, it is beneficial to explicitly annotate variables or decompose unions into smaller, more manageable types. Conversely, intersection types, if not carefully managed, can become unwieldy when compounded; ensuring that the intersected types are truly orthogonal and do not conflict is paramount to maintaining code clarity and compiler performance.

A pragmatic trick for advanced users is to leverage type aliases to create semantically meaningful combinations. This transparency in your codebase aids both in maintenance and in presenting intuitive APIs for end consumers. For example:

```
type Configurable = BasicConfig & AdvancedConfig;
```

By defining clearly named type combinations, developers not only make their intent explicit but also enable easier refactoring later. Additionally, the use of intersection types in module augmentation supports extending third-party libraries without altering the original definitions, thereby embedding custom behavior while preserving type safety.

Another advanced consideration is the role of union and intersection

types in function parameter definitions. A function that accepts parameters defined via union or intersection types can be designed to handle
a multitude of cases while still enforcing specific invariants. When two
objects with disparate shapes need to be merged for processing, using
intersection types ensures that both sets of properties are present for
downstream operations:

```
function mergeConfigs<T, U>(base: T, extension: U): T & U {
    return { ...base, ...extension };
}

const baseConfig = { debug: false, version: 1 };
const extConfig = { endpoint: "https://api.example.com", timeout:
    5000 };

const fullConfig = mergeConfigs(baseConfig, extConfig);
```

In this code, the function `mergeConfigs` returns an intersection of the
types of both arguments, providing a statically-typed composite that
satisfies the contracts of each input. Such techniques are indispensable
when designing systems that require intensive configuration management and runtime composability.

For expert programmers, a deep understanding of union and intersection types informs the design of robust and maintainable code structures. Employing discriminated unions to resolve ambiguous API responses, leveraging intersections to enforce multiple contracts, and
combining these with generics and conditional types collectively elevate the codebase's type-safety and expressiveness. Each technique,
when applied judiciously, minimizes runtime errors and clarifies the
intended behavior of complex systems. Mastery of these constructs is
a significant step towards advanced type-driven development in Type-
Script.

## 1.3  Advanced Type Inference

TypeScript's type inference mechanism is a cornerstone of its design, empowering developers to write code that is both succinct and robust. The compiler applies sophisticated algorithms to deduce types without explicit annotations, ensuring that type safety is maintained even when type declarations are omitted. Advanced developers can leverage these mechanisms to build generic, highly reusable libraries and APIs that capture subtle, context-dependent behaviors at compile time.

At the foundation of type inference in TypeScript is the concept of contextual type inference. When a variable or parameter is declared without an explicit type, the compiler examines its initializer or usage context to deduce an appropriate type. For example, in the following code snippet, the type of the variable `result` is automatically inferred to be number based on the literal value provided:

```
let result = 42;
```

While this elementary inference is straightforward, the advanced capabilities emerge when inferring types in more complex scenarios. When functions are defined without explicit return types, the compiler infers the return type by analyzing the code paths taken by the function. However, advanced patterns involve inferring not only the return type but also generic type parameters that depend on the shape of the input. This feature allows for writing highly abstracted functions that adapt their behavior based on the provided arguments.

Consider a generic identity function where TypeScript infers the type parameter from the argument:

```
function identity<T>(value: T): T {
```

27

```
    return value;
}

const output = identity("TypeScript");
// output is inferred as string
```

In this example, even though the type parameter T is not explicitly provided, the compiler successfully deduces that "TypeScript" is a string. The potency of this mechanism is amplified in scenarios where functions manipulate data structures of varying complexity.

A particularly noteworthy aspect of advanced type inference is its interplay with conditional types. Conditional types allow the compiler to compute a type based on a condition. For instance, consider a type transformation that conditionally adds a property based on an input type:

```
type WithTimestamp<T> = T extends { status: 'success' }
  ? T & { timestamp: number }
  : T;

interface ApiResponse {
    status: 'success' | 'error';
    data?: any;
}

type ExtendedResponse = WithTimestamp<ApiResponse>;
```

In this example, the WithTimestamp conditional type examines whether the input type extends a particular structure. The inference mechanism computes the resulting type at compile time, merging additional properties through an intersection type when the condition is satisfied. This capacity to combine conditional checks with inference affords advanced developers fine-grained control over type transformations.

In addition to conditional types, recursive type inference plays an essential role in processing nested data structures. When dealing with deeply nested objects or arrays, the compiler must recursively apply inference rules to determine the type of each layer. This process is crucial in scenarios such as parsing JSON objects or working with abstract syntax trees (AST), where the shape of the data can be complex and dynamically constructed:

```
type DeepReadonly<T> = {
    readonly [P in keyof T]: T[P] extends object
    ? DeepReadonly<T[P]>
    : T[P];
};

interface Config {
    database: {
        host: string;
        port: number;
    };
    cache: {
        enabled: boolean;
    };
}

const config: DeepReadonly<Config> = {
    database: {
        host: "localhost",
        port: 5432
    },
    cache: {
        enabled: true
    }
};
```

The recursive utility type DeepReadonly applies inference to each level of nested properties, ensuring that the entire structure becomes immutable. Such patterns are indispensable in large-scale applications where safeguarding against unintended mutations is critical.

Type inference is also prominent in handling function overloads. Advanced programmers often define multiple overload signatures for a single function to cater to different types of inputs while centralizing the implementation. The compiler must reconcile these overloads with a unified implementation that consistently infers the correct return type based on the input type. Consider the following example:

```
function parseInput(input: string): number;
function parseInput(input: number): string;
function parseInput(input: string | number): string | number {
    if (typeof input === 'string') {
        return input.length;
    } else {
        return input.toString();
    }
}

const parsedNumber = parseInput("example");
const parsedString = parseInput(123);
// Correctly inferred as number and string respectively
```

Within the overloaded function, the inference mechanism ensures that the type returned corresponds precisely to the type of input, capitalizing on the union type defined in the implementation signature.

Advanced type inference extends into the realm of contextual typing within callbacks and higher-order functions. When a function is passed as an argument, the context in which it is used often provides clues regarding its expected type. This contextual inference simplifies generic programming, as the type parameters of the callback are automatically derived from the surrounding structure. This behavior is commonly observed in array methods or functional paradigms:

```
const numbers = [1, 2, 3, 4];
const doubled = numbers.map(n => n * 2);
// The type of 'n' is inferred as number
```

Here, the callback function for `map` leverages the context of the array's element type, resulting in type safety without redundant type annotations. For advanced programming tasks—such as designing custom higher-order functions—explicitly controlling the inferred types can be critical. In these cases, explicitly specifying generic parameters or using helper types can steer the inference engine in the desired direction.

Another advanced application of TypeScript's inference engine involves the use of default type parameters and type constraints. By defining constraints on generic parameters, developers can ensure that only specific shapes of types are permitted, while still enjoying the benefits of type inference:

```
function mergeObjects<T extends object, U extends object>(obj1: T,
    obj2: U): T & U {
    return { ...obj1, ...obj2 };
}

const merged = mergeObjects({ a: 1 }, { b: "text" });
// The return type is inferred as { a: number } & { b: string }
```

Specifying constraints via `extends object` ensures that non-object types are excluded from the merge, while the inferred return type is a precise intersection of the input object types. This technique is particularly useful in building composable APIs and libraries where type transformations are a recurring theme.

Advanced developers also encounter scenarios where the inference engine requires augmented assistance to resolve complex type relationships. In some cases, explicit type annotations cannot be completely eliminated for clarity or to guide the compiler in ambiguous contexts. Techniques such as leveraging helper functions, applying type assertions, or decomposing complex types into simpler, inferable units can significantly improve type resolution accuracy. For instance, when

31

working with polymorphic functions that require explicit type guards
or disambiguation, careful structuring of code ensures that the compiler can infer types with minimal manual intervention.

An instructive pattern involves deep integration of type inference with
conditional logic, particularly in state management for asynchronous
operations. Consider a scenario where state transitions in a promise-
based API need to be captured in the type system. By combining advanced inference with discriminated unions, one can accurately model
various states and transitions:

```
interface LoadingState {
    state: 'loading';
}

interface SuccessState<T> {
    state: 'success';
    data: T;
}

interface ErrorState {
    state: 'error';
    error: string;
}

type AsyncState<T> = LoadingState | SuccessState<T> | ErrorState;

function updateState<T>(prev: AsyncState<T>, next: AsyncState<T>):
    AsyncState<T> {
    // Advanced inference enables precise control flow refinement
    if (prev.state === 'loading' && next.state === 'success') {
        return next;
    }
    return prev;
}
```

In this example, the type parameter T is dynamically inferred based
on the usage of the state management function. The interplay between
union types, generics, and conditional inference permits the compiler

32

to maintain a coherent understanding of the state, ensuring that transitions adhere to defined contracts.

Performance considerations also arise in advanced type inference scenarios. When complex types and recursive conditional types are combined, the compiler's type-checking performance can degrade. Expert programmers should be aware of techniques to mitigate these issues by reducing excessive nesting, modularizing type definitions, or explicitly annotating critical sections. Analyzing compiler performance in large codebases and refactoring type-intensive modules can prevent slow compilation times without sacrificing the benefits of static analysis.

Expert users of TypeScript are encouraged to explore the less-documented corners of the type inference engine, such as inference in mapped types. Mapped types facilitate the transformation of types by iterating over the keys of an object type. Advanced patterns often involve combining mapped types with conditional types to generate highly adaptable utility types:

```
type Nullable<T> = { [P in keyof T]: T[P] | null };

interface Person {
    name: string;
    age: number;
}

type NullablePerson = Nullable<Person>;
// Inferred as { name: string | null; age: number | null }
```

The compiler's ability to infer types over property mappings without explicit annotations is a powerful tool in the construction of domain-specific models, allowing for rapid prototyping and robust type safety.

In meta-programming, advanced type inference facilitates the creation

of self-adaptive types that modify their shape based on operations
performed on them. Mastery of these techniques unlocks significant
potential for refactoring and evolving codebases over time. By leveraging inference in combination with union, intersection, and conditional types, developers create type systems that are both expressive
and dynamic—capable of accurately modeling complex, real-world domains while maintaining the rigidity necessary to prevent runtime errors.

The deep understanding of TypeScript's sophisticated inference engine
equips advanced programmers with the tools to build scalable, maintainable, and highly resilient systems. The strategic use of generics,
conditional types, and recursive inference not only reduces verbosity
but also embeds rigorous compile-time guarantees into every aspect of
the code, ensuring that advanced architectures remain robust as they
evolve.

## 1.4   Utilizing Mapped and Conditional Types

Mapped and conditional types represent some of the most powerful
features of TypeScript's type system, allowing for dynamic transformation and adaptation of types at compile time. Advanced programmers leverage these constructs to create highly reusable utility types
that encapsulate common type transformations, reduce redundancy,
and enforce rigorous invariants across large codebases. This section
delves into the mechanisms and applications of mapped and conditional types, providing in-depth analysis and illustrative examples to
demonstrate how these techniques enhance code reusability and expressiveness.

Mapped types provide a declarative syntax to transform each property of an existing type through a mapping function. The typical syntax employs the [K in keyof T] construct, where T is an object type and K iterates over its keys. Such constructions enable developers to create variants of a type by modifying its properties systematically. For example, consider a utility to make all properties of a given type optional. The built-in Partial<T> type is defined as follows:

```
type Partial<T> = { [K in keyof T]?: T[K] };
```

In this definition, each property in T is mapped to an optional version of itself. Similar patterns exist for other transformations, such as making a type completely read-only using:

```
type Readonly<T> = { [K in keyof T]: T[K] };
```

By modifying the mapped type with the optional modifier ?, advanced developers can tailor these constructs to capture more complex invariants, such as recursively making a type read-only. The recursive nature of mapped types can be harnessed to build deep transformations:

```
type DeepReadonly<T> = {
    readonly [K in keyof T]: T[K] extends object ? DeepReadonly<T[K]>
      : T[K];
};
```

In this implementation, each property is checked using a conditional type to determine whether it is itself an object. If so, the transformation is applied recursively. Such patterns are essential in libraries where state immutability is enforced across deeply nested structures.

Conditional types extend the power of mapped types by introducing logic to inspect and transform types based on compile-time conditions. The basic syntax uses the keyword extends within a ternary-like structure:

```
type Conditional<T> = T extends U ? X : Y;
```

In this form, if type T is assignable to U, the type resolves to X; otherwise, it resolves to Y. The conditional type operator is distributive by default when applied to union types. A canonical example is the built-in Exclude<T, U> utility type, which filters out from T those types that are assignable to U:

```
type Exclude<T, U> = T extends U ? never : T;
```

In this construct, if each constituent of the union T extends U, it is replaced by never, effectively removing it from the union. This distributivity property provides deep insights into how TypeScript handles union types, and understanding it is pivotal when designing custom transformations.

A further advanced utility is the use of the infer keyword within conditional types. When combined with conditional checking, infer allows the extraction of subtypes from complex types. For instance, to obtain the type of the elements from an array type, one might define:

```
type ElementType<T> = T extends (infer U)[] ? U : T;
```

If T is an array type, ElementType<T> extracts the element type U; otherwise, it resolves to T. Such mechanisms are particularly useful in generic programming and when writing APIs that need to adaptively transform input types.

Advanced usage often involves combining mapped and conditional types to create flexible, declarative utility types. For example, constructing a type that conditionally makes properties nullable based on

36

a given criterion can be achieved with:

```
type NullableProperties<T, U> = {
    [K in keyof T]: T[K] extends U ? T[K] | null : T[K];
};
```

Here, each property of T is checked; properties that extend type U are augmented with null, while other properties remain unchanged. Such transformations allow developers to dynamically adjust type constraints based on specific conditions without affecting unrelated properties.

One of the more challenging aspects when combining these concepts is managing the complexity that arises from deeply nested and interdependent types. Advanced codebases may require creating custom wrappers that iterate over a type's properties, apply conditional logic, and then reassemble the results into a cohesive type. Such techniques are central when modeling external data sources whose types evolve over time. Consider a transformation for deep partial updates:

```
type DeepPartial<T> = {
    [K in keyof T]?: T[K] extends object ? DeepPartial<T[K]> : T[K];
};
```

This recursive structure ensures that every level of the type T is made optional, a transformation particularly useful when creating patch operations for immutable data. In similar fashion, a deep required type can enforce that certain optional properties become mandatory:

```
type DeepRequired<T> = {
    [K in keyof T]-?: T[K] extends object ? DeepRequired<T[K]> : T[K
    ];
};
```

The -? modifier explicitly removes the optional attribute from each property, demonstrating how mapped types can be fine-tuned to address very specific transformational requirements.

Another advanced trick involves the interplay of mapped types and union distribution. When dealing with union types, mapped types can sometimes produce unexpected results if the designer does not account for distributivity. For example, consider a transformation that should only apply when the type is a specific object type rather than a union. In such cases, wrapping the type parameter in a tuple can prevent unwanted distribution:

```
type NoDistribute<T> = [T] extends [object] ? { [K in keyof T]: T[K]
    } : T;
```

By using a tuple wrapper, the conditional check circumvents TypeScript's default behavior of distributing unions, allowing for more controlled type transformations. Such patterns are essential to reduce ambiguity and ensure that type transformations yield predictable, maintainable outcomes.

Integration of mapped and conditional types is also crucial when extending or augmenting third-party library types. For instance, suppose the need arises to enforce an additional layer of validation on an external API response type. By combining mapped and conditional types, the process of type augmentation can be automated. Consider:

```
type ValidateResponse<T> = {
    [K in keyof T]: T[K] extends string ? (T[K] extends "" ? never :
    T[K]) : T[K];
};

interface ApiResponse {
    id: string;
    content: string;
    metadata?: object;
}
```

```
type ValidatedResponse = ValidateResponse<ApiResponse>;
```

In the example above, each property of `ApiResponse` is inspected; if a property is a string, an inner conditional type ensures that an empty string is replaced with `never`, thereby enforcing stricter validation rules at compile time. Such nuanced control over type behavior is indispensable when dealing with dynamic data that must conform to rigid standards.

Another area where these techniques shine is the creation of utility types that perform type filtering and extraction. Built-in types such as `Extract` and `NonNullable` are based entirely on conditional types:

```
type Extract<T, U> = T extends U ? T : never;
type NonNullable<T> = T extends null | undefined ? never : T;
```

Extracting subtypes from complex unions or filtering out undesired types can be critical in ensuring that functions receive only valid inputs, thus reducing potential runtime errors. By defining custom filtering types, advanced developers can construct APIs that are not only safe but also self-documenting through type constraints.

The optimization of mapped and conditional types is also relevant when considering compile-time performance. Deep recursive mappings and complex conditional evaluations can sometimes lead to increased compile times. Experts often mitigate these issues by caching common type patterns in intermediate type aliases or by breaking down deeply nested type calculations into more manageable components. Such practices ensure that while the type system remains expressive and robust, it does not negatively impact developer productivity.

Finally, the combined use of these constructs opens avenues for innovative type-driven design patterns. By employing both mapped and
conditional types, advanced programmers can create type utilities that
adapt to a variety of contexts, ranging from dynamic form validations
to intricate state management solutions in reactive systems. The key
is to view the type system not as a static set of rules, but as a flexible, programmable layer that operates alongside the application logic,
ensuring that invariants are preserved and that the codebase remains
both scalable and robust.

The mastery of mapped and conditional types represents a significant
leap in type-level programming in TypeScript. By dynamically transforming types, developers can enforce strict contracts, reduce code
duplication, and create highly resilient and adaptable systems. The
techniques and patterns discussed in this section empower advanced
programmers to take full advantage of TypeScript's static analysis capabilities, transforming abstract type logic into concrete, maintainable
implementations.

## 1.5   Exploring Type Guards and Type Asser-
tions

Type guards and type assertions are critical mechanisms in TypeScript
that enhance both the guarantees provided by the type system and
the robustness of code execution. These constructs enable developers
to refine types at runtime and assert certain type behaviors when the
static analysis may be insufficient. Advanced programmers leverage
these techniques to ensure that the correct types are being handled,
particularly in complex scenarios involving unions, intersections, and

40

conditional types.

Type guards are functions or expressions that perform runtime checks to narrow down the type of a variable. While TypeScript supports many built-in type checks—such as typeof and instanceof—advanced use of type guards often involves custom guard functions. A custom type guard function has a return type in the form value is T, guaranteeing that within a branch guarded by the check, the type of the variable is narrowed appropriately. For example, consider a function that refines a variable to ensure it is a non-null object with a particular structure:

```
interface User {
    id: number;
    name: string;
}

function isUser(obj: any): obj is User {
    return obj !== null && typeof obj === 'object' &&
        'id' in obj && typeof obj.id === 'number' &&
        'name' in obj && typeof obj.name === 'string';
}

function processUser(data: any) {
    if (isUser(data)) {
        // Within this block, 'data' is inferred as User.
        console.log(`Processing user ${data.name} with ID ${data.id
    }`);
    } else {
        throw new Error('Invalid user data');
    }
}
```

In this example, the custom type guard isUser explicitly refines the type of data so that subsequent operations involving data.name and data.id are subject to rigorous compile-time checking. This pattern is essential in codebases that interface with external or loosely typed sources.

Beyond custom guards, the use of discriminated unions in conjunction
with type guards enables precise control flow analysis. When each
member of a union has a distinguishing literal property, conditional
checks can narrow the union to a particular variant. For instance:

```
interface Square {
    kind: 'square';
    size: number;
}

interface Circle {
    kind: 'circle';
    radius: number;
}

type Shape = Square | Circle;

function area(shape: Shape): number {
    if (shape.kind === 'square') {
        return Math.pow(shape.size, 2);
    } else {
        return Math.PI * Math.pow(shape.radius, 2);
    }
}
```

In the above code, the literal property kind is used as a discriminant
in the union Shape. The conditional check refines the type in each
branch, allowing the appropriate properties to be accessed with confidence. This technique eliminates the need for redundant runtime
verifications in every branch, further securing the logic flow against
improper access.

Type assertions, commonly known as type casts in other languages, allow developers to override or refine the compiler's inferred type. They
are syntactic directives that not only assure the compiler but can also
serve as documentation for other developers. The two syntaxes avail-

able are the angle-bracket syntax and the as syntax. In advanced programming scenarios, type assertions are frequently used when integrating with untyped code (for instance, a legacy JavaScript module) or when the developer has contextual information that the compiler does not possess.

Consider a scenario involving retrieval of DOM elements in a browser context. Although TypeScript can infer types from established APIs, there are cases where the developer is certain that a retrieved element is non-null. In such cases, a type assertion can be used:

```
const button = document.getElementById('submit') as HTMLButtonElement
    ;
button.disabled = false;
```

Here, the assertion as `HTMLButtonElement` informs the compiler that `button` is of type `HTMLButtonElement` despite the possible `null` return from `getElementById`. Nevertheless, advanced programmers must exercise caution since erroneous assertions may bypass type safety and lead to runtime errors.

Moreover, type assertions are indispensable when dealing with complex control flows. For instance, a function that processes a heterogeneous array may require asserting specific types based on the programmer's domain knowledge. When combined with custom type guard functions, assertions can further refine the logic flow:

```
type ApiResponse = { status: 'ok'; data: unknown } | { status: 'error
    '; error: string };

function processResponse(response: ApiResponse) {
    if (response.status === 'ok') {
        // Here, we know the structure of response.data, but if
    necessary,
        // a type assertion may be applied.
        const data = response.data as { id: number; payload: string
```

43

```
    };
        console.log(`Response received with id ${data.id}`);
    } else {
        console.error(`Error occurred: ${response.error}`);
    }
}
```

Although the discriminated union model inherently provides type narrowing, there are instances where external data does not guarantee
such structure and a type assertion helps reconcile the static type with
the runtime data.

Another advanced pattern involves using type assertions in combination with the non-null assertion operator ! to signal that a variable is
not null or undefined. This is particularly useful in scenarios where
variables are temporarily nullable due to asynchronous data flows or
sloppy initializations, yet the subsequent logic depends on a firm guarantee:

```
function getUserName(user: Partial<User>): string {
    // The non-null assertion operator '!' is used to assert that
    user.name is defined.
    return user.name!;
}
```

Although this pattern circumvents compile-time checks, it requires
careful reasoning to ensure that the variable is indeed non-null.
Overuse or misuse can compromise the stability of the program,
so advanced programmers often combine non-null assertions with
runtime checks or fail-safe defaults.

Advanced developers may also implement composite type guards that
combine several checks into a single function. Such functions can be
generic and even infer types based on the value examined. Integrating
conditional types with type guard functions further strengthens type

guarantees. For example, a generic type guard might be designed to verify that each element of an array conforms to a given predicate:

```
function isArrayOf<T>(arr: any[], predicate: (elem: any) => elem is T
    ): arr is T[] {
    return arr.every((elem) => predicate(elem));
}

function isNumber(elem: any): elem is number {
    return typeof elem === 'number';
}

const values: any[] = [1, 2, 3, 4];
if (isArrayOf<number>(values, isNumber)) {
    // 'values' is now inferred as number[].
    const sum = values.reduce((acc, value) => acc + value, 0);
    console.log(`Sum is ${sum}`);
}
```

In this instance, isArrayOf uses a generic predicate to refine the array type. This flexible pattern permits advanced type checking in custom frameworks, where data structures may be highly polymorphic and require methodical validation.

Sometimes, certain properties in an object may undergo dynamic transformation that is not fully representable with static types. In these cases, type assertions become necessary to tell the compiler that the outcome of a complex operation is safe. For example, while handling JSON data returned from an API, which lacks strict typing, an advanced developer might write:

```
const rawData: unknown = fetchDataFromApi();
const parsedData = JSON.parse(rawData as string) as { records: any[]
    };
```

This double assertion—first asserting that the raw data is a string and then asserting a specific structure after parsing—demonstrates how as-

45

sertions can be layered to provide adequate type safety when dealing
with data of uncertain origin.

Type guards and assertions are not mutually exclusive; they often coexist in complex type transformations. A robust pattern involves using
type guards to initially filter or refine data, and then applying type
assertions once sufficient runtime validation is complete. This two-
step approach ensures that the compiler's static analysis is reinforced
rather than bypassed. Careful structuring of type guard functions,
combined with contextual type assertions, provides a resilient framework in which advanced applications can operate without sacrificing
type integrity.

Expert users must also consider the implications of using assertions
when evolving codebases. As APIs converge and external libraries receive updated type definitions, assertions and type guards should be
revisited to ensure they remain accurate. Refactoring opportunities
often arise when the underlying assumptions behind an assertion or
guard change, and advanced programmers routinely use automated
tools and comprehensive test suites to verify that these type-level contracts continue to hold.

Type guards and type assertions are indispensable in scenarios where
static analysis of the type system must be supplemented with dynamic
runtime checks. Mastery of these techniques enables advanced programmers to maintain rigorous type safety in complex, real-world applications. By constructing custom type guard functions, integrating
discriminated unions, and judiciously applying type assertions and
non-null operators, developers create powerful safeguards against runtime errors while preserving the clarity and robustness of their code.
This disciplined approach to type refinement ensures that even when
interfacing with loosely typed data, applications remain reliable and

maintainable.

## 1.6 Getting the Most from Type Aliases and Interfaces

Type aliases and interfaces are fundamental constructs in TypeScript that allow advanced programmers to define custom types and enforce structural contracts in a scalable, maintainable manner. Although both constructs share common capabilities, such as describing the shape of objects and combining types with unions and intersections, their nuanced differences have important implications in large-scale system design and type-driven development. This section provides an in-depth exploration of advanced patterns, best practices, and techniques for leveraging type aliases and interfaces to their fullest potential.

Type aliases provide a mechanism to assign a type expression to a new identifier. This capability is particularly useful for complex types that incorporate unions, intersections, or mapped and conditional types, thereby encapsulating intricate type logic in a reusable fashion. Consider the following example, where a type alias is used to define a composite type that captures multiple possible states of an operation:

```
type OperationStatus =
  | { status: 'loading' }
  | { status: 'error'; message: string }
  | { status: 'success'; data: unknown };
```

In this alias, the series of unioned object types creates a discriminated union, which can be effectively employed with type guards to streamline control flow analysis. Advanced techniques often layer these constructs, combining type aliases with conditional types to derive new

47

types from existing ones. For instance, one might define a type that extracts the data payload from a successful operation, while gracefully excluding error and loading states:

```
type ExtractData<T> = T extends { status: 'success'; data: infer D }
    ? D : never;
type OperationData = ExtractData<OperationStatus>; // Inferred as '
    unknown'
```

In contrast, interfaces are designed to define an explicit contract for object shapes. They are particularly powerful in describing API contracts, class implementations, and complex object compositions. One salient advantage of interfaces is the ability to extend themselves via inheritance, which facilitates the development of scalable type hierarchies. For example:

```
interface BaseResponse {
    timestamp: number;
}

interface SuccessResponse extends BaseResponse {
    status: 'success';
    data: any;
}

interface ErrorResponse extends BaseResponse {
    status: 'error';
    error: string;
}

type ApiResponse = SuccessResponse | ErrorResponse;
```

Here, the BaseResponse interface encapsulates shared properties and is extended by more specific response interfaces. This hierarchical structure enhances clarity and ensures that common properties remain consistent across different type variants.

Merging declarations is another critical capability that sets interfaces apart from type aliases. Interfaces support declaration merging, allowing multiple declarations with the same name to be unified by the compiler. This feature is particularly beneficial when augmenting external libraries or adding metadata to existing types. For example, when modifying the built-in Window interface for custom global properties:

```
interface Window {
    customSetting: boolean;
}
```

By merging with the default declaration, advanced developers can safely integrate custom properties without modifying the original library definitions. In contrast, type aliases do not support merging; instead, they require careful composition via intersections, necessitating that each modified alias is redeclared in full.

While both type aliases and interfaces can represent object structures, a common question arises regarding when to use one over the other. Advanced programming principles suggest that interfaces are preferred when designing APIs or public contracts due to their extensibility and merge capabilities, while type aliases excel at expressing more abstract compositions and complex type transformations. In situations where union types or mapped types are involved, type aliases are indispensable, as demonstrated by the following example that iterates over the keys of an object type to create a new alias:

```
type Nullable<T> = { [K in keyof T]: T[K] | null };

interface User {
    name: string;
    age: number;
}

type NullableUser = Nullable<User>;
// Result: { name: string | null; age: number | null }
```

By leveraging mapped types within a type alias, developers can suc-
cinctly create new variants of an existing interface without modifying
the original definition. This approach is especially effective in transformation functions and state management scenarios.

Generics play a pivotal role in both type aliases and interfaces, enabling
the creation of reusable, parameterized types. Advanced usage often
involves the careful application of type constraints and default type
parameters. For example, a generic interface might be crafted to define
a repository pattern:

```
interface Repository<T, ID = number> {
    findById(id: ID): T | null;
    save(entity: T): void;
}

interface Product {
    id: number;
    name: string;
    price: number;
}

const productRepository: Repository<Product> = {
    findById(id) {
        // Implementation details...
        return null;
    },
    save(product: Product) {
        // Persist product...
    }
};
```

In this example, the interface Repository is generic over the entity type
and identifier type, promoting reuse across various domain models.
The use of a default type parameter for ID demonstrates how interfaces can elegantly handle common patterns while remaining flexible
for edge cases.

50

Advanced programming also requires careful management of compatibility between type aliases and interfaces. Although both can often be used interchangeably to describe a type, subtle differences in their behavior—especially during union, intersection, and conditional operations—can impact overall type safety. When combining types from disparate sources, interfaces are recommended for public-facing APIs, while type aliases are best suited for internal type manipulations and transformations. Strategies such as creating a base interface for common properties and then generating multiple type aliases via intersection can yield robust types. For example:

```
interface BaseEntity {
    id: number;
    createdAt: Date;
    updatedAt: Date;
}

type UserEntity = BaseEntity & {
    username: string;
    email: string;
};

type ProductEntity = BaseEntity & {
    name: string;
    price: number;
};
```

This pattern leverages the strengths of interfaces for common properties and uses type aliases to extend these definitions with additional attributes. It ensures that updates to the base contract propagate automatically to all extended types.

Maintaining clarity in large projects often necessitates the separation of internal and external type definitions. Advanced programmers commonly employ a dual-layer approach, wherein public interfaces dictate the external API while type aliases work behind the scenes to model

the internal state with transformations such as normalization, filtering,
or computed properties. This separation allows developers to safely
refactor the underlying implementation without disrupting the public
contract, as the interface layer remains stable over time.

One advanced trick involves using type aliases to create conditional
mappings between different types. For instance, consider an alias that
converts all string properties of an interface to uppercase literal types
to enforce a specific naming convention at compile time:

```
type ToUpperCase<T extends string> =
    T extends "a" ? "A" :
    T extends "b" ? "B" :
    T;

type UpperUserName = ToUpperCase<"a">; // Resolves to "A"
```

By extending this idea with mapped types and template literal types
(introduced in recent versions of TypeScript), developers can create
sophisticated type transformations that enforce naming conventions
or other domain-specific rules without runtime overhead.

Interoperability with external libraries often necessitates augmenting
existing types. Advanced techniques involve using interface merging
to extend third-party modules, ensuring that custom behaviors are
seamlessly integrated with imported types. For instance, when integrating with a popular framework where certain components require
additional properties, an interface may be augmented as follows:

```
declare module 'some-framework' {
    interface ComponentProps {
        customProp?: string;
    }
}
```

This approach allows the application code to benefit from type safety while expanding the framework's inherent capabilities. In cases where type aliases are used, similar outcomes can be achieved through intersections, though with the added complexity of manually composing multiple type definitions.

Best practices for advanced type design dictate that type aliases and interfaces should be chosen based on their intended usage and the evolution metrics of the codebase. Interfaces, with their inherent extensibility and merging capabilities, are preferable for designing public contracts and APIs. Type aliases, due to their flexibility and powerful combination with generics, conditional, and mapped types, excel in constructing complex internal types and dynamic transformations. Skillful application of these constructs enables advanced programmers to create expressive, maintainable type systems that safeguard against common runtime errors while facilitating large-scale refactoring.

The interaction between type aliases and interfaces also extends to tooling and IDE support. Modern TypeScript development environments offer intelligent suggestions, type inference, and seamless integration with language servers. Leveraging these capabilities can lead to cleaner code and faster development cycles. Advanced programmers optimize their development workflow by combining well-structured interfaces with strategic type aliases, ensuring that type definitions are both comprehensive and intuitive.

Ultimately, the key to mastering type aliases and interfaces lies in understanding their individual strengths and recognizing the contexts in which one is favored over the other. Through a combination of inheritance, composition, merging, and transformation, developers have at their disposal a robust toolkit for managing type complexity in modern TypeScript applications. By adopting these advanced patterns and best practices, one can construct type-safe, scalable code architectures that effectively bridge the gap between dynamic JavaScript fundamentals and the precision of a statically-typed language.

## 1.7 Empowering Code with Literal Types and Enums

Literal types and enums are powerful tools in TypeScript that enable developers to write code with increased expressiveness and robustness. These constructs allow for the restriction of possible values to a particular set, enabling compile-time checking, improved type narrowing, and more transparent code semantics. For advanced programmers, the interplay between literal types and enums facilitates the creation of domain-specific languages and state machines within a type-safe context.

Literal types extend the type system by allowing values to be specified as types. The most common use cases involve string and numeric literals. When a variable is declared with a literal type, its value is fixed to that specific literal. For instance, consider a scenario where an application defines a fixed set of modes for a workflow. By using union literal types, one can enforce that only the allowed strings are assignable, thereby reducing potential errors:

```
type WorkflowState = 'pending' | 'inProgress' | 'completed';
function updateWorkflowState(state: WorkflowState) {
    // Process based on the specific workflow state.
}
updateWorkflowState('inProgress'); // Valid
// updateWorkflowState('canceled'); // Compilation error
```

This explicit declaration results in a self-documenting API where each possible value is evident at compile time. Advanced scenarios often involve using literal types as discriminants in union types. When combined with type guards, discriminated unions allow the compiler to narrow the type of a variable based on the value of its literal property. This technique sufficiently streamlines control flow, ensuring that each branch of logic is exhaustive and type-safe:

```
interface Pending {
    status: 'pending';
    reason?: string;
}
interface InProgress {
    status: 'inProgress';
    startedAt: Date;
}
interface Completed {
    status: 'completed';
    completedAt: Date;
}
type TaskStatus = Pending | InProgress | Completed;
function handleTask(task: TaskStatus) {
    switch (task.status) {
        case 'pending':
            // task.reason is available if provided.
            break;
        case 'inProgress':
            // Access task.startedAt confidently.
            break;
        case 'completed':
            // Use task.completedAt for finalization.
            break;
        default:
            // The compiler ensures this case is unreachable.
            const _exhaustive: never = task;
            return _exhaustive;
    }
}
```

The enforcement of such constraints significantly reduces potential

runtime errors by catching invalid states during compilation. Beyond
simple usage, literal types can be combined with conditional types to
create utilities that transform or extract parts of types based on literal
values. For example, a utility that maps a literal to another related
literal value can be designed as follows:

```
type ResponseType = 'success' | 'error';
type ResponseMessage<T extends ResponseType> = T extends 'success'
    ? 'Operation completed successfully'
    : 'Operation failed due to an error';
const successMessage: ResponseMessage<'success'> = 'Operation
    completed successfully';
const errorMessage: ResponseMessage<'error'> = 'Operation failed due
    to an error';
```

This pattern leverages literal types to implement type-level logic, enabling a high degree of precision when defining APIs and aligning
compile-time validation with business logic.

Enums, on the other hand, provide a mechanism to define a set of
named constants. They come in various forms, including numeric
enums, string enums, and even heterogeneous enums. Enums enhance
code readability and maintainability by replacing magic numbers or
strings with semantic identifiers. Unlike unions of literal types which
exist purely at the type level, enums are present at both compile time
and runtime, offering a dual benefit. Consider the following numeric
enum definition:

```
enum Direction {
    Up,
    Down,
    Left,
    Right
}
function move(direction: Direction) {
    // Directional logic based on enum values.
}
```

```
move(Direction.Up);
```

In this example, the enum Direction provides a clear and maintainable set of identifiers that correspond to integer values. Because enums are compiled to objects in JavaScript, they also enable reverse mapping, allowing retrieval of the key name from a value:

```
const dirName = Direction[0]; // 'Up'
```

For cases where string values are more suitable, string enums provide additional clarity:

```
enum LogLevel {
    Debug = 'DEBUG',
    Info = 'INFO',
    Warn = 'WARN',
    Error = 'ERROR'
}
function log(level: LogLevel, message: string) {
    console.log(`[${level}]: ${message}`);
}
log(LogLevel.Info, 'This is an informational message');
```

String enums are particularly beneficial in contexts where the values must be human-readable or when interfacing with external systems that expect string literals. Advanced usage of enums also includes the utilization of const enums, which are inlined at compile time, thereby reducing the runtime footprint:

```
const enum Status {
    Active = 1,
    Inactive,
    Archived
}
let currentStatus = Status.Active;
```

Const enums, due to their removal during code emission, are ideal for performance-critical code where minimizing bundle size is crucial. However, developers must exercise caution with const enums when debugging, as these values do not exist at runtime in the emitted code.

Integrating enums with literal types often enables the design of hybrid patterns that exploit the strengths of both. For instance, one might define a function whose parameter accepts either a literal type or an enum value, allowing flexibility while preserving type safety. This can be achieved by unifying the two constructs into a discriminated union:

```
enum AnimationState {
    Running = 'RUNNING',
    Paused = 'PAUSED',
    Stopped = 'STOPPED'
}
type AnimationAction = 'start' | 'pause' | 'stop';
type AnimationControl = AnimationState | AnimationAction;
function controlAnimation(control: AnimationControl) {
    // Combine handling by comparing against enum values and string
    literals.
    if (control === AnimationState.Running || control === 'start') {
        // Start animation.
    } else if (control === AnimationState.Paused || control === '
    pause') {
        // Pause animation.
    } else if (control === AnimationState.Stopped || control === '
    stop') {
        // Stop animation.
    } else {
        // This branch is unreachable.
        const _exhaustive: never = control;
        return _exhaustive;
    }
}
```

Such patterns allow the API to evolve over time while supporting both legacy literal strings and new enum-based constants, affording backward compatibility without sacrificing the benefits of strong typing.

Furthermore, literal types and enums can be combined with advanced type features such as mapped and conditional types to create sophisticated domain models. For example, consider a system that maps string-based commands to specific enum values. A mapped type can enforce this relationship throughout the codebase:

```
enum CommandEnum {
    Launch = 'LAUNCH',
    Abort = 'ABORT',
    Retry = 'RETRY'
}
type CommandMap = {
    [key in CommandEnum]: () => void;
};
const commandHandlers: CommandMap = {
    [CommandEnum.Launch]: () => { /* launch procedure */ },
    [CommandEnum.Abort]: () => { /* abort procedure */ },
    [CommandEnum.Retry]: () => { /* retry procedure */ }
};
```

This approach ensures that every command defined in the enum has a corresponding handler, a pattern that is particularly valuable in finite state machines or command dispatch systems. Unit tests that iterate over the enum members verify that no command is left unimplemented, thereby closing potential gaps in the application logic.

Advanced programmers also benefit from using literal types and enums for exhaustive pattern matching. In scenarios where an application must perform distinct actions based on a finite set of conditions, leveraging these constructs minimizes the risk of unhandled cases. The combination of literal types in discriminated unions, as previously discussed, with enums further refines the control flow and enhances static analysis. This results in code that is not only correct by construction but also easier to maintain, as any addition of new literal values or enum members triggers compile-time errors in areas that have not been updated.

Moreover, enums can be augmented or merged through declaration
merging techniques, much like interfaces. This functionality allows
developers to extend enums declared in external libraries or to add
metadata for customized processing. While not as common as interface merging, this technique provides additional flexibility in situations where the type system must be extended post hoc. For example,
one may add helper properties to an existing enum by redeclaring it
and appending supplementary members or functions.

In performance-sensitive applications, advanced techniques such as
using const assertions (the `as const` syntax) can lock down literal
types within arrays and objects, thereby improving type inference and
reducing accidental assignment. For instance, defining an array of command strings with const assertions ensures that its contents are inter-
preted as literal types rather than simply as strings:

```
const commandList = ['start', 'stop', 'pause'] as const;
type Command = typeof commandList[number];
// 'Command' is a union of 'start' | 'stop' | 'pause'
```

This guarantees that the accepted values conform precisely to the predefined set, reinforcing the integrity of the interface between different
parts of the application.

Ultimately, literal types and enums empower advanced TypeScript applications by providing a structure that is both expressive and resilient.
They transform the type system from a static check into a dynamic
framework for enforcing business rules and domain constraints at compile time. Mastery of these constructs not only reduces runtime errors
but also enhances developer productivity by making the code more
self-documenting and easier to reason about. By strategically combin-

ing literal types with enums, developers create a cohesive type land-
scape that accurately reflects the intricacies of the application domain
and fosters maintenance and scalability over time.

# 2

# Chapter 2: Advanced Functions and Generics

*This chapter delves into advanced function techniques and generic programming in TypeScript to improve code flexibility and reusability. It covers function overloading, generic constraints, and creating utility types. Readers will explore complex function types, such as variadic and currying functions, and the power of higher-order functions, preparing them to craft efficient and sophisticated TypeScript solutions.*

## 2.1  Deep Comprehension of Function Overloading

Function overloading in TypeScript represents an advanced technique by which a single function implementation is equipped with multiple signatures, thereby enhancing the flexibility and specificity of function calls. This mechanism allows the developer to define multiple type-safe interfaces for a function, enabling it to behave differently based on the types and numbers of arguments provided. By utilizing function overloading judiciously, expert programmers can not only improve the expressiveness of their APIs but also maintain robust compile-time type checking, ultimately reducing the risk of runtime errors.

At its core, function overloading in TypeScript entails the declaration of several function signatures preceding a single implementation signature. The compiler uses these signatures to resolve the appropriate call signature during static type checking. It is important to note that only the implementation signature may contain the function body, while all preceding overload signatures exist purely for compile-time validation. Thus, the overload signatures serve as contracts that guarantee the relationship between input parameters and output types.

A typical scenario involves a function that is required to operate on inputs of disparate types. Consider a generic `combine` function that might append arrays, merge objects, or concatenate strings based on the input type. An advanced programmer can define multiple overloads for such a function, ensuring each overload explicitly documents the expected types. The following code snippet demonstrates an overload pattern where different input types yield different return types:

```
function combine(a: string, b: string): string;
function combine(a: number[], b: number[]): number[];
function combine(a: object, b: object): object;
function combine(a: any, b: any): any {
    if (typeof a === "string" && typeof b === "string") {
        return a + b;
    } else if (Array.isArray(a) && Array.isArray(b)) {
        return a.concat(b);
    } else if (typeof a === "object" && typeof b === "object") {
        return { ...a, ...b };
```

```
    }
}
```

In the above example, the function `combine` is overloaded with three distinct signatures. Each signature corresponds to a specific combination of argument types and a specific return type. The implementation signature that follows these overloads uses runtime type checks (such as `typeof` and `Array.isArray`) to determine which logic to execute based on the actual input values. This pattern exemplifies the utility of function overloading when constructing APIs that need to accept varied types while preserving type safety.

When designing overloaded functions, one must take the order of overload signatures into careful consideration. The order is significant because TypeScript resolves the overload signatures in a top-down manner. Hence, the most specific overloads must precede more general ones so that the most concrete match is recognized. Failing to order these overloads correctly may lead the compiler to choose an unintended signature, resulting in a non-intuitive or erroneous type inference. Thus, expert developers must arrange overload signatures from the most specific to the least specific to ensure type resolution works as intended.

Moreover, function overloading is particularly powerful when combined with conditional types and advanced type inference. By leveraging sophisticated conditional logic in type definitions, programmers can refine overload signatures to accurately model complex scenarios. Consider a function that behaves differently when provided with a callback function versus when it operates directly on value types. Expert programmers can define overloads that discriminate based on whether the second parameter is a function, thereby enforcing additional constraints:

```
function process<T>(input: T[], processor: (item: T) => T): T[];
function process<T>(input: T[], processor: undefined): T[];
function process<T>(input: T[], processor?: ((item: T) => T) |
    undefined): T[] {
    if (typeof processor === "function") {
        return input.map(processor);
    }
    return input.slice();
}
```

This example illustrates the benefit of overloads in permitting a singular function name (process) to accommodate both functional transformation and simple array copying. Such versatility is achieved without compromising type safety and facilitates the development of more concise, self-documenting code.

Advanced techniques also involve the integration of function overloading with generic parameters to create more adaptable APIs. The combination permits the definition of overloads that are both type-safe and highly reusable. With overloads parameterized by type variables, functions can adapt to a broad spectrum of input types while enforcing constraints on their relationships. Consider the overloaded function for a generic transformation that adapts its output based on the structure of its input:

```
function transform<T, U>(input: T[], transformer: (item: T) => U): U
    [];
function transform<T>(input: T[], transformer: undefined): T[];
function transform<T, U>(input: T[], transformer?: ((item: T) => U) |
    undefined): (T | U)[] {
    if (typeof transformer === "function") {
        return input.map(transformer);
    }
    return input.slice();
}
```

Here, the function `transform` is overloaded to handle the cases where a transformer function is provided and where it is not. The generic parameters T and U allow for a precise articulation of the transformation process, ensuring that the return type is correctly inferred from the type of the transformer. Combining generics with overloads significantly enhances code expressiveness and enforces strict type contracts, which is a critical requirement in large-scale applications.

Another sophisticated utilization of function overloading revolves around integrating with union types and discriminated unions. In certain advanced scenarios, a function may accept a union of several types, yet the processing logic needs to diverge entirely based on the actual type received. In such cases, overloads can be used to enumerate all potential union constituents as discrete signatures, thus allowing the code to leverage exhaustive type checking. This is particularly useful in libraries where function behavior differs sharply between distinct input types.

Error-prone areas to be aware of include ambiguous overload resolution and the inadvertent use of overly general implementation signatures. Developers should avoid having an implementation signature that is not a subset of the declared overloads, as this can circumvent the compiler's strict checking mechanism. Additionally, the reliance on runtime type assertions within the implementation must be minimized to preserve the integrity of type safety provided by the overloads. Expert-level usage involves carefully balancing the granularity of overloads with the clarity of runtime checks, ensuring that every conditional branch satisfies the contract specified by the overload signatures.

Furthermore, the interplay between overloaded functions and their integration within larger systems necessitates awareness of module boundaries and API stability. In a complex project, various parts of the system might invoke an overloaded function with different expectations. Ensuring that the overloads are correctly documented and that their intrinsic relationships are clear is paramount to prevent misinterpretation by other developers or even automated tools. Utilizing code comments in conjunction with precise overload signatures can serve as an internal form of documentation that reinforces the intended usage.

While TypeScript's function overloading provides a robust mechanism for creating adaptable, type-safe functions, it also imposes certain limitations. The implementation signature must be carefully managed to avoid exposing its more liberal type definition externally. Consequently, the technique demands a disciplined approach to function design, where the overload signatures are the primary interface while the implementation remains an encapsulated detail. Expert programmers often encapsulate overloaded functions within modules or classes where internal consistency is enforced, further promoting maintainability in large codebases.

The practical application of function overloading also extends to scenarios that demand polymorphic behavior without strictly adhering to classical object-oriented paradigms. For instance, overloaded functions can serve as a bridge between procedural and functional programming techniques, allowing for the creation of APIs that fluidly adapt to different programming contexts. This duality is instrumental in libraries that provide a wide range of functionalities, from simple data transformations to complex asynchronous operations. In such cases, using overloads aids in delivering clear boundaries between synchronous and asynchronous function signatures, thereby reducing inadvertent misuse.

In environments where backward compatibility is a concern, particularly during API evolution, function overloading offers a pragmatic solution. By incrementally adding new overloads while preserving existing ones, developers can extend functionality without breaking existing contracts. This strategy ensures that the API remains robust and type-safe across multiple versions, a crucial aspect for enterprise-level codebases where stability is paramount.

Function overloading in TypeScript ultimately represents a deliberate design technique that marries flexibility with stringent type enforcement. By carefully orchestrating multiple function signatures, experts can create versatile and precise interfaces that reduce runtime errors and improve code clarity. The nuanced control over function behavior achieved through overloading—when combined with generics, conditional types, and discriminated unions—empowers developers to construct APIs that scale with the complexity of modern applications.

## 2.2 Harnessing Generic Functions for Reusability

Generics in TypeScript are a foundational mechanism that provide both type safety and adaptability, enabling developers to formulate functions that remain agnostic to specific types while enforcing strict type constraints. This section delves into advanced techniques for designing generic functions that are both reusable and robust, focusing on patterns and practices that leverage the power of TypeScript's type system to its fullest extent.

Generics enable functions to encapsulate behavior independent of concrete types by parameterizing types through type variables. This parameterization allows the function logic to remain consistent while ensuring that operations on the generic parameters are type-safe. Consider a simple generic function that manifests this concept: a function that returns the identity of its input. Although elementary in its behavior, it serves as the cornerstone for more sophisticated abstractions.

```
function identity<T>(arg: T): T {
    return arg;
}
```

In the above example, the generic parameter T represents a placeholder for any type. When invoking `identity`, the compiler infers or explicitly specifies the actual type for T, ensuring that type consistency is maintained throughout the function call. This pattern forms the basis for reusability, as the function does not commit to any specific type until the moment of invocation.

Advanced applications of generics frequently involve the orchestration of multiple generic parameters and the exploitation of type inference to significantly reduce boilerplate while enhancing code expressiveness. A common scenario is the transformation of value types whereby input and output types differ. Consider a generic transformation function that not only maps each element of an array but also changes their type:

```
function mapArray<T, U>(array: T[], transform: (item: T) => U): U[] {
    return array.map(transform);
}
```

Here, T and U are two separate generic parameters: one representing the type of the array elements and the other representing the type after transformation. The compiler's ability to infer these types ensures that no runtime type mismatches occur, provided that the transformation function adheres to its signature.

In scenarios requiring more nuanced type relationships, advanced pro-

grammers can further enhance generic functions by incorporating conditional types and type inference from function parameters. Such
strategies are invaluable when designing APIs that mirror functional
programming paradigms or when constructing libraries that must handle a variety of data shapes. For example, consider a generic function
pipe that composes a sequence of functions into a single function, ensuring that the output type of each function aligns with the input type
of the next:

```
function pipe<T, U>(input: T, f1: (x: T) => U): U;
function pipe<T, U, V>(
    input: T,
    f1: (x: T) => U,
    f2: (x: U) => V
): V;
function pipe<T, U, V, W>(
    input: T,
    f1: (x: T) => U,
    f2: (x: U) => V,
    f3: (x: V) => W
): W;
function pipe(input: any, ...fns: Array<(x: any) => any>): any {
    return fns.reduce((acc, fn) => fn(acc), input);
}
```

The above implementation leverages overloads in tandem with generics to enforce type compatibility across a variable number of functions.
By defining explicit overloads for each arity, the function pipe maintains a rigorous contract such that improper sequencing or incompatible types between functions is caught at compile time.

Generic functions can also be designed to accommodate more complex
data manipulations, particularly when dealing with structures like tuples, arrays, or even objects with dynamic keys. Consider a generic
function that extracts a subset of properties from an object. Utilizing
key remapping and mapped types, the function can be typed to ensure

71

that only valid property names are permitted:

```
function pick<T, K extends keyof T>(obj: T, keys: K[]): Pick<T, K> {
    const result = {} as Pick<T, K>;
    keys.forEach(key => {
        if (key in obj) {
            result[key] = obj[key];
        }
    });
    return result;
}
```

In this example, K extends keyof T, ensuring that the keys provided are valid in the context of T. The function returns an object whose type is precisely the subset picked from T. This design pattern is instrumental in crafting APIs that facilitate safe and predictable manipulation of data objects.

When designing extensive codebases, the reuse of generic functions becomes a strategic asset. Generic abstractions not only reduce duplication but also enhance code consistency by encapsulating common patterns into a single, reusable, and type-safe unit. Advanced developers often compose libraries of generic utility functions that provide core functionalities such as deep cloning, merging, and validation of various data structures. For example, a generic deep clone function can be implemented by recursively traversing the object graph while preserving type information:

```
function deepClone<T>(obj: T): T {
    if (obj === null || typeof obj !== "object") {
        return obj;
    }
    // Handle arrays
    if (Array.isArray(obj)) {
        return obj.map(item => deepClone(item)) as unknown as T;
    }
    // Handle objects
    const clonedObj = {} as T;
```

```
    for (const key in obj) {
        if (Object.prototype.hasOwnProperty.call(obj, key)) {
            clonedObj[key] = deepClone((obj as any)[key]);
        }
    }
    return clonedObj;
}
```

This recursive function is typed generically and can handle deep cloning of arrays and objects while ensuring that type integrity is preserved across recursive calls. The methodology here demonstrates how generics can drive reusability in scenarios where data structures are arbitrarily nested or complex.

Beyond single-function implementations, the true power of generic functions is realized when they are composed into higher-order constructs. Higher-order functions that accept other functions as parameters can be made generic to add cross-cutting concerns such as logging, error handling, or memoization. For instance, a generic memoization function can be employed to cache results of any pure function, dramatically reducing computational overhead for expensive operations:

```
function memoize<T extends (...args: any[]) => any>(fn: T): T {
    const cache = new Map<string, ReturnType<T>>();
    const memoizedFn = (...args: Parameters<T>): ReturnType<T> => {
        const key = JSON.stringify(args);
        if (cache.has(key)) {
            return cache.get(key)!;
        }
        const result = fn(...args);
        cache.set(key, result);
        return result;
    };
    return memoizedFn as T;
}
```

This memoization technique exploits generics to ensure that the memo-

73

ized function adheres precisely to the signature of the original function. By basing the cache keys on the serialized arguments, the function effectively remembers previous computations, offering potential performance optimizations in scenarios involving expensive or frequently called pure functions.

Expert programmers may further refine generic function patterns by incorporating advanced type constraints, such as using intersection types or union types to describe more complex relationships between type parameters. For example, one might design a generic function to merge two inputs, ensuring that both inputs share overlapping keys while also enforcing that the result comprises the union of these keys:

```
function mergeObjects<T, U>(obj1: T, obj2: U): T & U {
    return { ...obj1, ...obj2 };
}
```

Here, the return type is an intersection of T and U, mandating that consumers of `mergeObjects` treat the result as containing all properties from both source objects. This pattern is particularly useful in scenarios where multiple sources of configuration data or state information must be combined to form a cohesive interface.

Another advanced use case pertains to enforcing invariants across asynchronous flows and promise chains. Generic functions can be extended to work seamlessly with promises, applying transformations and validations on eventual values while utilizing the type system to track asynchronous operations. A generic promise mapper may be implemented as follows:

```
function mapPromise<T, U>(promise: Promise<T>, transformer: (value: T
    ) => U): Promise<U> {
    return promise.then(transformer);
}
```

By abstracting asynchronous behavior into generic functions, code-bases can remain DRY (Don't Repeat Yourself) and maintain a uniform approach to managing promise resolutions and rejections. Incorporating generics ensures that transformations are both composable and type-safe across diverse asynchronous contexts.

The cumulative benefits of harnessing generic functions extend beyond individual applications. They facilitate the construction of modular code that abstracts away type-specific details, thereby simplifying maintenance and enabling scalability. Advanced refinement of generic functions may involve conditional type logic, where the type output depends on conditions evaluated at compile time. For instance, using conditional types to infer return types based on input constraints ensures that functions are not only generic but contextually accurate:

```
type Nullable<T> = T extends null | undefined ? never : T;
function filterNonNullable<T>(array: (T | null | undefined)[]): Array
    <Nullable<T>> {
    return array.filter((item): item is Nullable<T> => item != null);
}
```

This example employs a conditional type `Nullable` to exclude null or undefined types from the resulting array. The filter predicate is typed to refine the type guard, ensuring that the function both filters and narrows the type, which is critical for advanced type manipulations in complex systems.

Expert-level usage of generic functions involves not only understanding their theoretical underpinnings but also mastering implementation details that unlock their full potential. Techniques such as recursive types, utility type mappings, and algorithmic-complexity-aware generic implementations distinguish advanced code from basic type-safe code. By embracing these strategies, developers create building

75

blocks that are both highly reusable and capable of interfacing with a broad range of application domains. The careful integration of generics with functional paradigms, asynchronous patterns, and advanced type constraints yields code that is robust, maintainable, and aligned with modern software engineering practices.

## 2.3   Building Custom Utility Types with Generics

Custom utility types in TypeScript represent a potent mechanism for constructing expressive type transformations tailored to complex application needs. By leveraging generics, advanced developers can design utility types that extract, reshape, and enforce constraints on object types, arrays, and function signatures. These constructs augment the core TypeScript language while preserving type safety and enhancing code reusability.

At its essence, a custom utility type operates as a type-level function that takes one or more types as parameters and returns a modified type. This transformation is achieved through generics combined with conditional types, mapped types, and key remapping. A rudimentary example is a custom version of the built-in Partial type, which makes all properties of a given type optional. The following snippet demonstrates one's own implementation:

```
type MyPartial<T> = {
    [P in keyof T]?: T[P];
};
```

This construction uses a mapped type to iterate over each property P in T and appends the optional modifier. The advanced programmer can extend such patterns by incorporating additional logic. Consider

76

a utility type that selectively makes properties optional based on a condition; for instance, making properties of a string type optional while retaining the original required status for other types.

```
type OptionalStrings<T> = {
    [K in keyof T]: T[K] extends string ? T[K] | undefined : T[K];
};
```

In the above utility type, OptionalStrings evaluates each key K in T and uses a conditional type to determine if the property type extends string. If the condition holds true, the property type is augmented with undefined, effectively making it optional in practice. This nuanced control highlights the flexibility generics offer when creating custom type transformations.

Beyond optionality, custom utility types can encapsulate more sophisticated operations such as key filtering. For instance, when designing APIs, it is often necessary to derive subsets of properties that satisfy specific constraints. A utility type to extract properties of a certain type from a given object may be expressed as follows:

```
type FilterProperties<T, U> = {
    [K in keyof T as T[K] extends U ? K : never]: T[K];
};
```

Here, FilterProperties leverages key remapping with the as clause to conditionally include or exclude keys based on whether T[K] extends the target type U. This process yields a new type that contains only keys whose associated values conform to the specified constraint. Such a custom utility type is invaluable when dealing with objects that mix disparate data types and need to be partitioned for distinct processing routines.

The concept of excluding properties is equally significant in advanced type manipulations. A custom implementation of the `Omit` utility type, typically used to exclude specified keys from a type, can be constructed using generics and conditional mappings:

```
type MyOmit<T, K extends keyof T> = {
    [P in keyof T as Exclude<P, K>]: T[P];
};
```

In this version, the `Exclude` helper is employed to subtract the keys present in K from the overall set of keys P. The resulting type represents T without the omitted properties. This pattern demonstrates the composability of native utility types when crafting custom solutions.

Advanced scenarios may require dynamically transforming object types. For example, when dealing with readonly configurations that need to be mutable during certain phases of an application lifecycle, a custom utility to remove the `readonly` modifier might be necessary. This can be achieved using mapped types along with property modifiers:

```
type Mutable<T> = {
    -readonly [P in keyof T]: T[P];
};
```

The minus sign before the `readonly` modifier effectively removes it for each property in T. Such techniques are essential when designing systems that require both immutable and mutable representations of the same underlying data structure.

Another area where custom utility types shine is in the establishment of deep type transformations. Common utility types like `Partial` or `Readonly` operate on a shallow level; they do not affect nested properties. A deep version of these utilities traverses the object recursively, applying the transformation at every level. Consider the following generic deep partial type:

```
type DeepPartial<T> = {
    [P in keyof T]?: T[P] extends object ? DeepPartial<T[P]> : T[P];
};
```

This utility uses a recursive conditional type to check whether each property is itself an object. If so, DeepPartial is recursively applied, otherwise the type remains unchanged. Such constructs are indispensable in situations where objects with nested structures must be partially updated or optionally specified, such as in configuration management or state updates in complex applications.

Advanced control over index signatures is another frontier for custom utility types. When working with collections or records, it may be necessary to transform keys and values. For instance, consider a utility that inverts an object's keys and values. The following implementation assumes the values are of type string or number, suitable for use as keys:

```
type InvertObject<T extends Record<string, string | number>> = {
    [P in keyof T as `${T[P]}`]: P;
};
```

By utilizing template literal types, the value T[P] is converted into a string and used as the key of the new type. This inversion is particularly effective when the objective is to create bidirectional maps within type definitions.

Composite utility types can also integrate multiple transformations in a single construct. For instance, a powerful pattern is to selectively mark properties as nullable and then remove certain fields, all in one operation. The following example demonstrates a two-step transformation applied within one utility type:

```
type NullableAndOmit<T, K extends keyof T> = {
    [P in keyof T as Exclude<P, K>]: T[P] extends object ?
    NullableAndOmit<T[P], never> : T[P] | null;
};
```

Here, every property is made nullable, and properties specified in K are omitted. The recursive call with never for nested objects ensures that the omission logic is only applied at the top level, while still transforming nested properties to be nullable. This pattern is particularly useful when preparing data for serialization where specific fields must be excluded and nullability is enforced.

When crafting custom utility types, consideration must be given to the interplay between performance and type system complexity. Although the TypeScript compiler is highly optimized, complex conditional and mapped types may result in slower compile times or increased cognitive load during maintenance. Advanced techniques, such as breaking down overly complex utilities into smaller helper types, can mitigate these issues. For example, one could refactor a deep transformation into auxiliary types that handle specific aspects of the transformation, thus modularizing the logic and improving readability.

Another trick for advanced usage involves combining these utilities with branded types to enforce nominal typing patterns. By intersecting utility transformations with unique symbols, it is possible to create types that are structurally identical yet semantically distinct. This allows for fine-grained control and prevents inadvertent mixing of logically separate data types. An example is as follows:

```
type Brand<K, T> = K & { __brand: T };

type UserID = Brand<number, "UserID">;
```

```
type OrderID = Brand<number, "OrderID">;
```

Utility types that transform or manipulate these branded types must preserve the branding, ensuring that contracts remain intact throughout the codebase. This guarantees that even after multiple utility transformations, the resulting types retain semantic identifiers that distinguish them from one another.

In advanced scenarios such as API design or library development, custom utility types can also work in tandem with discriminated unions and intersection types to model complex domain states. For example, a utility type that maps over a union of result types and extracts error messages can be constructed by first filtering the union and then mapping over the error type:

```
type ExtractError<T> = T extends { error: infer E } ? E : never;
```

This type evaluates a union and extracts the error type from members that contain an `error` property. Such utilities prove invaluable in constructing type-safe error handling mechanisms in asynchronous or server-side code.

By methodically constructing these custom utility types with generics, advanced developers can encapsulate recurring type transformations into concise, reusable components. This modularity not only reduces code duplication but also enforces consistency across large-scale projects, ensuring that type operations adhere to predetermined patterns and standards. The interplay between custom utility types and other advanced features—such as overloads, generics in functions, and intricate type inference—creates a robust framework for static type checking and composes a critical area of mastery for expert-level programming in TypeScript.

81

## 2.4    Leveraging Generic Constraints

Generic constraints in TypeScript provide a powerful means to enforce type compatibility at compile time by limiting generic type parameters to a subset of types that satisfy specific structural requirements. Advanced developers can utilize these constraints not only to ensure the correctness of type operations but also to impose design policies that guide the structure of APIs and libraries. By employing the `extends` keyword in generic definitions, one can narrow the acceptability of types to those that exhibit required properties, methods, or interfaces, which is critical in complex systems where maintainability, predictability, and scalability are paramount.

The most straightforward application of generic constraints involves restricting a generic type parameter to types that possess specific members. For example, consider a common pattern that requires access to a `length` property. By enforcing this constraint, the function is guaranteed to work only with arrays, strings, or any type that provides a `length` member. The following code snippet illustrates this usage:

```
function logLength<T extends { length: number }>(arg: T): T {
    console.log(arg.length);
    return arg;
}
```

In this function, the constraint `T extends  length: number` ensures that only types which include a numeric `length` property are accepted. This method of type restriction guarantees that the `length` property can be safely accessed without resorting to runtime checks or type assertions, thus preserving type safety and code quality.

More sophisticated scenarios involve designing constraints based on

82

custom interfaces. When developing APIs, it is often necessary to create functions that operate on objects with predetermined properties. Defining an interface to serve as a constraint allows for precise control over the structure of accepted types. For example:

```
interface Identifiable {
    id: string | number;
}

function getId<T extends Identifiable>(entity: T): T["id"] {
    return entity.id;
}
```

Here, the `Identifiable` interface serves as a constraint, ensuring that any object passed to `getId` implements an `id` property. The return type `T["id"]` further leverages TypeScript's indexed access types to precisely infer the type of the `id` property from the input parameter, thereby preserving consistency across diverse implementations.

Generic constraints can be further refined by combining multiple interfaces into intersection types. This approach can enforce more complex contracts in situations where multiple structural requirements must be satisfied simultaneously. For example:

```
interface Timestamps {
    createdAt: Date;
    updatedAt: Date;
}

interface SoftDeletable {
    deletedAt?: Date;
}

function mergeMetadata<T extends Timestamps & SoftDeletable>(entity:
    T): T {
    // Business logic that utilizes timestamps and optional deletion
    date.
    return {
        ...entity,
```

```
        updatedAt: new Date()
    };
}
```

The intersection `Timestamps` & `SoftDeletable` in this definition ensures that T must satisfy both contracts. Such composite constraints are
frequently employed in data modeling within domain-driven designs
and complex state management systems, where objects must adhere to
multiple standards simultaneously.

When working with generic constraints, developers can exploit conditional types and mapped types to create patterns that adapt based on
the presence or absence of certain properties. This is particularly useful
in cases where a function must handle types differently depending on
their structural composition. For instance, consider a utility function
that conditionally applies transformations only if an object has a certain
flag:

```
interface Transformable {
    transform: () => any;
}

function conditionalTransform<T>(obj: T): T extends Transformable ?
    ReturnType<T["transform"]> : T {
    if (typeof (obj as any).transform === "function") {
        return (obj as Transformable).transform() as any;
    }
    return obj as any;
}
```

In this example, while the generic parameter T is unconstrained, the
function uses a conditional type to determine the returned type based
on whether T satisfies the `Transformable` interface. Although this pattern differs from exclusive constraints by allowing a union of valid
types, it underscores the application of advanced type logic to provide

84

flexible yet type-safe function outcomes.

A further level of sophistication is achieved when constraints guide the interplay between function parameters or between input and output types. Consider the scenario where the function's logic must verify that both parameters share a common structure. Generic constraints can enforce this pairing by linking the types of multiple parameters:

```
function copyProperty<T, K extends keyof T>(source: T, key: K): T[K]
    {
    return source[key];
}
```

In the copyProperty function, the constraint K extends keyof T ensures that the key parameter is one of the property names of T. This constraint prevents accidental misuse where a key not present in the source is provided, effectively establishing an invariant between the object and its property access.

Generic constraints also play a vital role in polymorphic function design, where the same function must operate over a detailed hierarchy of types while ensuring that only valid operations are performed. For example, when implementing a caching mechanism that operates on entities with a unique key, one can define the function to accept only entities that implement a getKey method:

```
interface Cacheable<K> {
    getKey: () => K;
}

function cacheEntity<T extends Cacheable<K>, K>(entity: T, cache: Map
    <K, T>): void {
    const key = entity.getKey();
    cache.set(key, entity);
}
```

The constraint `T extends Cacheable<K>` tightly couples the generic type T with the generic key type K and ensures that caching logic is applied uniformly across different entity types. Such constraints are especially valuable in large-scale applications where entities originate from various modules but share common behaviors.

Additionally, it is beneficial to consider generic constraints in the context of library design and API evolution. As a library evolves, maintaining API stability while introducing new type capabilities becomes challenging. By constraining generic parameters to adhere to established interfaces, library authors can extend functionality without compromising type safety. For instance, in a library providing transformation functions over data streams, one might design generic constraints that enforce the presence of certain stream-related properties:

```
interface Stream<T> {
    read(): T;
    write(data: T): void;
}

function processStream<T, S extends Stream<T>>(stream: S, processor:
    (data: T) => T): void {
    const data = stream.read();
    stream.write(processor(data));
}
```

Here, the generic constraint `S extends Stream<T>` demands that any type passed as `stream` conforms to the `Stream` interface. This ensures that the processor function, together with the stream's read and write operations, aligns with the strategy adopted by the library. Such disciplined use of constraints fosters a robust API that gracefully handles future extensions while preventing misusage by consumers.

Advanced techniques also involve employing generic constraints in tandem with default type parameters to offer fallbacks when explicit types are not provided. In many cases, complex systems benefit from presets that simplify generic function usage while preserving type accuracy. For instance, consider a generic factory function that generates instances of classes with default constructors:

```
interface Constructor<T> {
    new (...args: any[]): T;
}

function createInstance<T, C extends Constructor<T>>(ctor: C): T {
    return new ctor();
}
```

In this scenario, the constraint C extends Constructor<T> ensures that the constructor provided is valid for creating an instance of T. Generic constraints in this context not only maintain type safety but also enable developers to specify default behaviors that reduce boilerplate when explicit type annotations might be omitted.

Moreover, integrating generic constraints with discriminated unions can enhance the precision of API contracts. When designing functions that need to operate on unions of types but enforce certain properties in some cases, constraints can dynamically narrow down the acceptable types. For example, consider a function that processes a union of object types with an optional configuration:

```
interface Configurable {
    config?: object;
}

function initialize<T extends Configurable>(item: T): T {
    if (!item.config) {
        item.config = {};
    }
    return item;
}
```

The constraint `T extends Configurable` ensures that every object passed into `initialize` contains the optional `config` property. This design reduces the risk of runtime exceptions by ensuring that all processed items adhere to a minimum structural contract.

In complex codebases, it is often necessary to balance the precision of generic constraints with maintainability concerns. Overconstraining generics can lead to verbose type definitions that may be over-specific and resistant to future integration. Expert programmers handle these situations through modular design, abstracting constraints into dedicated interfaces or helper types. This not only localizes constraint logic but also enhances reusability across multiple modules. One approach is to encapsulate common constraints in utility types that can be imported across various parts of an application, thereby standardizing how type policies are enforced.

The strategic use of generic constraints facilitates designing systems where type compatibility is not an afterthought but an integral part of the function's design. By enforcing structural contracts at compile time, developers are better positioned to create scalable, maintainable, and robust codebases. Advanced patterns such as conditional constraints, intersection constraints, and dynamically inferred constraints further empower TypeScript developers to capture complex business rules within the type system itself. Such patterns transform the compiler into a first line of defense against type-related errors and design inconsistencies.

By integrating generic constraints into the development workflow, programmers benefit from improved type inference and enhanced debugging capabilities. When constraints are violated, TypeScript's error messages often provide precise feedback, guiding developers to adjust their design or refactor their types to align with the enforced policies. This methodology not only minimizes runtime errors but also promotes rigorous code documentation through type annotations and interface contracts.

## 2.5 Implementing Advanced Function Types

Advanced function types in TypeScript transcend simple interfaces by allowing functions to be treated as first-class entities with rich type information. By precisely annotating callbacks and function-returning functions, developers can construct complex control flows, enforce rigorous contracts, and facilitate higher-order programming patterns. In this context, advanced function types are defined using a combination of generics, overloads, and conditional types to offer a robust abstraction mechanism that supports diverse programming paradigms.

A central concept in advanced function type implementations is the fine-tuned definition of callback signatures. Callbacks often serve as parameters to higher-order functions, and their types must capture not only the inputs and outputs but also any contextual constraints. Consider a function that accepts a callback for processing a data stream. The type of the callback can be defined to enforce that it receives a precise type of data and returns a processed result:

```
type DataProcessor<T, U> = (data: T) => U;

function processData<T, U>(data: T[], processor: DataProcessor<T, U>)
    : U[] {
    return data.map(processor);
}
```

Here, the DataProcessor type alias encapsulates the pattern of transformation from type T to type U. By abstracting the callback type, subse-

89

quent functions can reuse this signature, ensuring consistency across the codebase. Leveraging generic function types to annotate such callbacks contributes significantly to code clarity and type safety.

Function-returning functions form another domain where advanced function types are indispensable. These functions, which return other functions as values, enable the creation of highly modular and composable systems. One prevalent example is the use of currying, where a function is decomposed into a sequence of unary functions:

```
function curry<T, U, V>(fn: (a: T, b: U) => V): (a: T) => (b: U) => V
    {
    return (a: T) => (b: U) => fn(a, b);
}
```

In this curried version, the returned function itself is strongly typed, ensuring that each successive argument is validated by the compiler. Currying simplifies function composition and partial application, two key techniques in functional programming that promote reusability and composability.

More complex scenarios may require functions that return callbacks with additional type dependencies. Consider a function that dynamically generates event handlers based on runtime parameters. The event handler's type might depend on the event data, and advanced function types can be employed to achieve this dynamic behavior:

```
type EventHandler<T> = (event: T) => void;

function createEventHandler<T>(predicate: (arg: any) => arg is T):
    EventHandler<T> {
    return (event: T) => {
        if (predicate(event)) {
            console.log("Handling event:", event);
        }
    };
```

```
}
```

In this pattern, the type guard predicate not only refines the type but also ensures that the returned event handler is correctly parameterized. Such techniques are particularly useful when integrating with DOM events or custom event systems where the payload structure may vary.

Achieving advanced function types frequently involves the use of overloads to cater for multiple function signatures under a unified interface. Overloading allows different function behaviors to be specified and subsequently selected at compile time based on argument types. This strategy is especially effective when designing functions that need to operate differently depending on the number or types of parameters passed. For example, a versatile function which conditionally generates function callbacks based on input parameters can be defined with several overloads:

```
function createLogger(level: "info"): () => void;
function createLogger(level: "error", retry: boolean): (error: Error)
    => void;
function createLogger(level: string, retry?: boolean): ((error?:
    Error) => void) {
    if (level === "info") {
        return () => console.info("Information log");
    }
    if (level === "error" && retry) {
        return (error?: Error) => {
            console.error("Error encountered. Retrying...", error);
        };
    }
    return (error?: Error) => {
        console.error("Error encountered:", error);
    };
}
```

By defining multiple overloads, the function createLogger conveys distinct type contracts. Consumers are then guided by the compiler to supply the appropriate parameters, and the returned function signature is contextually determined. This approach effectively encapsulates complex behavior within a single, strongly typed interface.

Advanced function types often incorporate generics in combination with callback signatures to enforce detailed relationships between input and output types. For instance, a higher-order function designed to perform asynchronous operations might accept a callback that operates on data once it has been fetched. The function-returning strategy can extend beyond simple synchronous callbacks to support promises and async/await patterns:

```
type AsyncProcessor<T, U> = (data: T) => Promise<U>;

function asyncProcessData<T, U>(data: T[], processor: AsyncProcessor<
    T, U>): Promise<U[]> {
    return Promise.all(data.map(processor));
}
```

In this example, the asynchronous processor function returns a Promise of U, and the encompassing function uses Promise.all to effectively aggregate the results. This design pattern is essential when handling asynchronous data flows and ensures that the entire structure remains type-safe throughout the asynchronous chain.

Closely related to asynchronous patterns are function-returning functions that generate promise-based callbacks. A common use-case involves retry logic for failed asynchronous operations. By designing a function that returns a new function encapsulating retry behavior, advanced developers can abstract repetitive logic while maintaining precise type safety:

```
function withRetry<T>(fn: () => Promise<T>, retries: number): () =>
```

```
    Promise<T> {
  return async () => {
      let attempts = 0;
      while (attempts < retries) {
          try {
              return await fn();
          } catch (_) {
              attempts++;
              if (attempts === retries) {
                  throw new Error("Maximum retries exceeded");
              }
          }
      }
      throw new Error("Should not reach here");
  };
}
```

This withRetry function is a higher-order function that takes an asynchronous function and returns a function with built-in retry semantics. The use of async/await within the returned function ensures that error handling remains consistent, and the overall structure is amenable to intricate workflows in network operations or resource management.

Another advanced aspect of function types involves function composition. The composition of multiple functions into a single operation is a hallmark of functional programming. Advanced TypeScript developers employ function types to define composition operators that ensure seamless type transitions between functions. For instance, consider a generic function composition operator:

```
function compose<T, U, V>(
    f: (b: U) => V,
    g: (a: T) => U
): (a: T) => V {
    return (a: T) => f(g(a));
}
```

In composition, the types of intermediate functions are rigorously checked at compile time, meaning that if function g returns a type incompatible with the expected input of function f, the compiler generates an error. This guarantee provides a high level of confidence in the correctness of composed functions, which is particularly beneficial in pipelines, middleware, and data processing chains.

A more intricate example of composition involves handling functions with multiple parameters. For these cases, advanced developers use tuple types and variadic arguments to capture the exact relationship between input and output parameters. The following example demonstrates a generic function composeMany that composes an arbitrary number of functions:

```
type Func<T extends any[], R> = (...args: T) => R;

function composeMany<T extends any[], R>(...fns: Array<Func<any, any
    >>): Func<T, R> {
    return (...args: T): R =>
        fns.reduceRight((prevFn, fn) => [fn(...prevFn)], args)[0] as
    R;
}
```

While this implementation uses a simplified reduction strategy with variadic types, advanced implementations may require precise type inference along each stage of composition. Such patterns necessitate the use of recursive types and tuple manipulation, illustrating the depth and complexity that advanced function types can achieve.

Dynamic function generation also benefits from advanced type constructs. When functions need to generate other functions based on runtime conditions, it is often necessary to encode these dynamics within the type system. One robust approach is to employ conditional types in conjunction with function signatures. For example, consider a function that returns different function types based on a Boolean flag:

```
function conditionalFunc<T>(
    flag: boolean,
    fn: (x: T) => T
): flag extends true ? (x: T) => T : () => T {
    if (flag) {
        return fn as any;
    } else {
        return (() => fn((undefined as any) as T)) as any;
    }
}
```

Conditional types empower the compiler to distinguish between distinct return types based on the input parameters. Although the above example uses type assertions due to intrinsic limitations in TypeScript's control flow analysis, it demonstrates the potential to encode highly dynamic behaviors into function type signatures.

Advanced function types further extend to optional and variadic parameters. When a function's behavior depends on the number of parameters, TypeScript's ability to handle tuple types and optional parameters becomes crucial. A variadic function can be declared to accept an indefinite number of parameters with a well-defined relation between the arguments and the output:

```
type VariadicFunc<T extends any[], U> = (...args: T) => U;

function invokeVariadic<T extends any[], U>(
    fn: VariadicFunc<T, U>,
    ...args: T
): U {
    return fn(...args);
}
```

This function invokeVariadic maintains type integrity by ensuring that the arguments passed match the expected tuple type T, and that the result conforms to type U. Such patterns are highly valuable in

95

generic libraries that need to accommodate a wide spectrum of function signatures.

By harnessing the full expressiveness of advanced function types, developers can create intricate APIs that precisely capture application logic and enforce strict contracts at compile time. The detailed specification of callback types and function-returning functions leads to more predictable, maintainable, and type-safe code. This depth of type precision not only reduces runtime errors but also promotes a coherent design when composing complex behaviors from simpler building blocks.

## 2.6   Exploring Variadic and Currying Functions

Advanced functional programming in TypeScript has led to the development of highly abstracted coding patterns that allow developers to manipulate and compose functions with remarkable dynamism. Variadic functions and currying are two such techniques that enable the decomposition and flexible reassembly of operations, streamlining complex task flows. These approaches depend heavily on advanced type inference using tuple types, rest parameters, and generics, thereby ensuring rigorous type safety while promoting code reuse.

Variadic functions are defined with an arbitrary number of arguments and are particularly useful when the operation to be performed does not require a fixed number of parameters. In TypeScript, this is enabled by rest parameters which are captured as tuple types. By leveraging tuple inference, developers can design functions that accept any number of arguments while preserving the types associated with each argument. For example, a generic logging function that joins multiple arguments into a string might be implemented as follows:

```
function logVariadic<T extends any[]>(...args: T): void {
    console.log(...args);
}

// Usage:
logVariadic("Error:", new Error("failure"), 404);
```

In the above example, the rest parameter ...args is defined using a generic tuple type T. This design permits TypeScript to infer the correct types for each element passed to the function, ensuring that no information is lost in the process. Furthermore, advanced type techniques can be applied to variadic functions to manipulate these tuples at the type level. For instance, it is possible to define a variadic function that maps over its arguments and applies a transformation, while preserving the tuple structure:

```
type Transformer<T extends any[]> = { [K in keyof T]: (arg: T[K]) =>
    T[K] };

function transformArgs<T extends any[]>(...args: T): T {
    const transformers: Transformer<T> = args.map((arg) => {
        return (x: any) => x; // Identity transformation for each
    type.
    }) as Transformer<T>;
    return args.map((arg, i) => transformers[i](arg)) as T;
}
```

This example illustrates the use of mapped types to create a type-level mapping over a tuple. The Transformer type applies a function type to every element of the tuple, ensuring that the resulting types align with the input tuple. Although the transformation in this case is the identity function, similar strategies can be applied to more sophisticated operations such as type conversion or validation.

Currying is another powerful technique that transforms a function of

multiple arguments into a sequence of unary functions. Currying facilitates partial application and function composition by isolating arguments one at a time. In its simplest form, currying allows developers
to pre-bind certain parameters and generate specialized functions that
are easier to reuse and test. Consider the example of a binary function
that is transformed into its curried counterpart:

```
function add(a: number, b: number): number {
    return a + b;
}

function curryAdd(a: number): (b: number) => number {
    return (b: number) => add(a, b);
}

// Usage:
const addFive = curryAdd(5);
const result = addFive(10); // 15
```

While the above example demonstrates a manually curried function,
advanced programming with TypeScript seeks general solutions that
can curry functions of arbitrary arity. A generic curry type can be constructed by capitalizing on tuple manipulation and recursive type definitions. One common approach is outlined below:

```
type Curried<Args extends any[], R> = Args extends [infer A, ...infer
    Rest]
    ? (arg: A) => Curried<Rest, R>
    : R;

function curry<Args extends any[], R>(fn: (...args: Args) => R):
    Curried<Args, R> {
    return function curried(...args: any[]): any {
        if (args.length >= fn.length) {
            return fn(...args);
        }
        return (...more: any[]) => curried(...args, ...more);
    } as any;
}
```

In this implementation, the `Curried` type recursively decomposes a tuple of arguments into a sequence of unary functions that ultimately produce a result of type R. The function `curry` then leverages this type definition to provide a curried version of an arbitrary function `fn`. By checking the accumulated number of arguments against the original function's length, the implementation dynamically decides whether to invoke the base function or return another partially applied version. This approach results in a highly flexible and expressive currying mechanism that caters to functions with varying numbers of parameters.

The combination of variadic functions and currying allows developers to design libraries that support a wide range of application patterns. For example, consider the case of function composition, where several functions are combined into a single operation. A variadic composition function can be implemented utilizing both techniques:

```
function compose<T>(...fns: Array<(arg: T) => T>): (arg: T) => T {
    return (arg: T) => fns.reduceRight((prev, fn) => fn(prev), arg);
}
```

In this example, the `compose` function takes a series of functions of type `(arg: T) => T` as variadic arguments and returns a new function that applies them in right-to-left order. The ability to compose functions in this manner is central to functional programming and is made robust through TypeScript's advanced type system. For further sophistication, one can generalize composition to functions with heterogeneous types, though doing so involves more intricate tuple transformations and conditionals.

Advanced developers can also utilize variadic tuple types to implement functions that perform type-safe currying for functions with optional parameters or overload signatures. For this purpose, the proposed implementations carefully manage edge cases where the number of supplied arguments may not directly match the expected count. One such pattern involves leveraging helper types to extract subsets from a tuple type:

```
type DropFirst<T extends any[]> = T extends [any, ...infer Rest] ?
    Rest : never;

function curry2<Args extends [any, ...any[]], R>(
    fn: (...args: Args) => R
): (arg: Args[0]) => (...rest: DropFirst<Args>) => R {
    return (arg: Args[0]) => (...rest: DropFirst<Args>) => fn(arg,
    ...rest);
}
```

The type `DropFirst` manipulates a tuple by removing its first element, allowing the curried function to accept the remainder of the arguments as a new tuple. Such helper types are crucial in designing flexible utilities that honor the strict type contracts expected in advanced applications.

Variadic and curried functions not only simplify code modularity but also facilitate techniques like partial application and memoization. Advanced patterns in memoization frequently combine these paradigms to optimize expensive computations. For instance, a memoization utility that supports curried functions can be designed to cache intermediate results for various argument combinations:

```
function memoizeCurry<Args extends any[], R>(
    fn: (...args: Args) => R
): (...args: Args) => R {
    const cache = new Map<string, R>();
    return function (...args: Args): R {
        const key = JSON.stringify(args);
        if (cache.has(key)) {
            return cache.get(key)!;
```

```
    }
    const result = fn(...args);
    cache.set(key, result);
    return result;
  };
}
```

This pattern demonstrates the synergy between currying and memoization, where the curried structure of a function can be preserved
while caching intermediate outcomes. Such utilities are highly beneficial in performance-critical applications where repeated computations
must be minimized without sacrificing readability or type safety.

Further advanced techniques involve chaining currying with function
composition to build complex pipelines. For example, a pipeline that
processes data in stages may leverage currying at every step, allowing each function to be partially applied with configuration parameters
prior to composition. This style of programming not only improves the
modularity of the code but also enhances testability because individual
stages can be isolated and verified separately.

It is also important to address potential caveats in implementing these
advanced patterns. The combination of variadic functions and currying, while powerful, can lead to more complex type signatures that
challenge both the compiler and the reader. As such, when designing API surfaces that expose curried or variadic functions, it may be
beneficial to balance type sophistication with documentation clarity.
Breaking the functionality into smaller, well-typed helper functions
can mitigate cognitive load and foster maintainability without sacrificing expressive power.

Moreover, performance considerations must be taken into account
when using these advanced functional constructs. Though currying

and variadic functions improve code modularity, they may introduce overhead due to additional function calls. Profiling and benchmarking in critical paths are recommended to ensure that the benefits in code clarity and reusability do not compromise runtime performance in production systems.

The integration of variadic functions and currying in TypeScript underscores the language's capacity to support advanced functional programming paradigms. By employing features such as rest parameters, tuple types, and recursive generics, developers can construct utilities that are both flexible and type-safe, enabling the creation of sophisticated abstractions that simplify complex operational chains. These techniques not only enhance maintainability but also provide a foundation for scalable, reusable libraries that integrate seamlessly with modern architectural designs.

## 2.7   Mastering Higher-order Functions

Higher-order functions are a cornerstone of functional programming in TypeScript, empowering developers to abstract control flow, manipulate data transformations, and encapsulate cross-cutting concerns. With TypeScript's robust type system, higher-order functions can be designed to provide compile-time assurances that data and function contracts are strictly maintained. This section demonstrates advanced techniques for creating, composing, and optimizing higher-order functions, with a focus on both design patterns and performance considerations.

At its core, a higher-order function is one that takes one or more functions as arguments or returns a function as its output. This abstraction enables developers to encapsulate recurring behaviors such as logging, error handling, and memoization in a reusable way. A trivial example is a function that applies a given transformer to its input. Consider the following implementation that leverages generics for type safety:

```
function apply<T, U>(f: (x: T) => U, x: T): U {
    return f(x);
}
```

Here, apply is parametrized by T and U. The function f transforms data from type T to type U, and the higher-order function ensures that the transformation adheres to this contract. Although simple, this pattern forms the basis for more sophisticated designs.

A common advanced usage pattern is function composition, which allows multiple functions to be chained together to perform complex operations. To create a robust composition operator, one must guarantee that the output type of one function matches the input type of the next. A basic implementation using generics is depicted below:

```
function compose<T, U, V>(
    f: (y: U) => V,
    g: (x: T) => U
): (x: T) => V {
    return (x: T) => f(g(x));
}
```

This operator serves as a building block for function pipelines. In practice, composing functions with heterogeneous types may require more generalized type manipulation using variadic tuple types and recursive type definitions. Advanced compositions can be implemented by combining multiple function arguments into a single chain, maintaining strict type compatibility across every stage.

Higher-order functions also serve as a meeting point for abstracting

103

control flow. Consider the implementation of a function that provides conditional execution logic. The following implementation accepts two callbacks—a function to be executed if a condition is met and an optional alternative function otherwise:

```
function conditionalExecutor<T>(
    condition: boolean,
    onTrue: () => T,
    onFalse?: () => T
): T {
    if (condition) {
        return onTrue();
    }
    return onFalse ? onFalse() : (undefined as unknown as T);
}
```

The conditionalExecutor pattern encapsulates branching logic while preserving the contract that the returned value is of type T. When designing systems that require complex decision-making processes, this approach allows for building flexible yet type-safe control flows.

In many applications, higher-order functions are used to implement decorators that modify or augment the behavior of existing functions. A decorator is a higher-order function that wraps an input function with additional logic. For example, consider a decorator that adds logging around a target function's execution:

```
function withLogging<T extends (...args: any[]) => any>(fn: T): T {
    return ((...args: Parameters<T>): ReturnType<T> => {
        console.log("Executing function with args:", args);
        const result = fn(...args);
        console.log("Function result:", result);
        return result;
    }) as T;
}
```

This decorator preserves the exact input and output types of the original function through the use of TypeScript's `Parameters` and `ReturnType` utility types. Using generics in this way ensures that changes in the target function's signature automatically propagate to the decorator, reducing maintenance overhead and preventing type mismatches.

Error handling is another domain where higher-order functions prove beneficial. Wrapping functions with higher-order error handlers enables global policies for fault tolerance and logging without cluttering business logic. An example of an error-handling higher-order function is given below:

```
function withErrorHandling<T extends (...args: any[]) => any>(fn: T):
    T {
    return ((...args: Parameters<T>): ReturnType<T> => {
        try {
            return fn(...args);
        } catch (error) {
            console.error("Error during function execution:", error);
            throw error;
        }
    }) as T;
}
```

This pattern ensures that every invocation of the target function is wrapped in a try-catch block, centralizing error management. Such patterns are particularly valuable in asynchronous programming, where higher-order functions can be combined with `Promise` chaining and `async/await` syntax to create robust error propagation mechanisms.

Memoization is a common performance optimization that benefits from higher-order designs. A generic memoization function caches results based on input arguments to avoid redundant computations. An advanced memoization function relies on serializing arguments and careful cache handling to ensure type safety and performance:

```
function memoize<T extends (...args: any[]) => any>(fn: T): T {
    const cache = new Map<string, ReturnType<T>>();
    return ((...args: Parameters<T>): ReturnType<T> => {
        const key = JSON.stringify(args);
        if (cache.has(key)) {
            return cache.get(key)!;
        }
        const result = fn(...args);
        cache.set(key, result);
        return result;
    }) as T;
}
```

Advanced techniques can involve parameterized cache eviction policies, custom key generation strategies, or even integrating with external state management libraries. The key concept remains that higher-order memoization functions decouple computational logic from caching concerns, thereby promoting code clarity and reusability.

In addition to wrapping and transforming functions, higher-order functions can facilitate partial application and currying. Partial application allows pre-binding of a subset of function arguments, resulting in a new function awaiting the remaining parameters. Advanced implementations of partial application leverage variadic tuple types to maintain precise type relationships:

```
function partial<T extends any[], U, R>(
    fn: (...args: [...T, U]) => R,
    ...args: T
): (arg: U) => R {
    return (arg: U): R => fn(...args, arg);
}
```

In this example, the partial application function captures a tuple of arguments T and returns a function that expects the final argument.

106

The use of tuple types and spread syntax preserves the specificity of the function signature, ensuring that the resulting function conforms to the expected input and output types. These techniques are instrumental in building modular APIs and refining complex operations by decomposing them into simpler, reusable parts.

Higher-order functions also empower asynchronous programming by abstracting complexities inherent in handling side effects, timeouts, or retries. A higher-order function that implements retry logic for asynchronous operations demonstrates this approach:

```
function withRetry<T>(fn: () => Promise<T>, retries: number = 3): ()
    => Promise<T> {
  return async (): Promise<T> => {
      let lastError: any;
      for (let attempt = 0; attempt < retries; attempt++) {
          try {
              return await fn();
          } catch (error) {
              lastError = error;
          }
      }
      throw lastError;
  };
}
```

The function withRetry wraps an asynchronous operation with retry logic, ensuring that transient failures are managed transparently. Combining such higher-order functions with comprehensive logging or performance monitoring can lead to robust systems that gracefully handle operational uncertainties.

Composition of higher-order functions itself becomes an area of intensive focus in advanced TypeScript applications. Systematic composition allows for the creation of pipelines where each stage is represented by a higher-order wrapper that encapsulates discrete behaviors. Consider constructing a pipeline that applies both memoization and error handling to a computationally intensive function:

```
const safeCompute = withErrorHandling(memoize((x: number, y: number)
   => {
   // Intensive computation here.
   return x + y;
}));

// Usage:
const result = safeCompute(10, 20);
```

Such composition showcases the power of higher-order functions to seamlessly integrate independent concerns—caching and error management in this case—into a single, well-typed operation. This modular approach not only improves code maintainability but also simplifies testing, as each layer can be isolated and examined independently.

Performance and maintainability are critical considerations when employing higher-order functions, especially in large-scale TypeScript projects. Although higher-order abstractions yield reusable and concise code, excessive function wrapping may introduce minor runtime overhead. Advanced techniques such as inline caching, tail-call optimization (where supported), and thoughtful function inlining can minimize such overhead. Profiling and benchmarking are recommended to strike an optimal balance between abstraction and performance.

TypeScript's robust type system not only enforces contracts on higher-order functions but also aids in debugging by producing informative compile-time errors when types are mismatched. Patterns such as using the `Parameters<T>` and `ReturnType<T>` utility types ensure that function wrappers accurately mirror the signatures they decorate. Furthermore, by employing generics throughout, the higher-order functions become self-documenting, conveying essential behavioral contracts through their type signatures.

Mastery of higher-order functions is essential for designing scalable applications where logic flow and data transformation are abstracted into composable units. Advanced techniques—ranging from sophisticated function composition and partial application to asynchronous error handling and memoization—not only improve code modularity but also provide a framework for building robust, maintainable systems. Through diligent integration of these patterns and a strong focus on type safety, developers can transform application logic into a series of well-composed, declarative modules that are both easy to reason about and resilient under varying runtime conditions.

# 3

# Chapter 3: Mastering Asynchronous Programming in TypeScript

*This chapter examines asynchronous programming in TypeScript, focusing on Promises, async/await syntax, and error handling. It discusses callbacks, streams, and observables, guiding readers through composing asynchronous operations and managing concurrency. These techniques enable developers to build responsive and high-performance TypeScript applications effectively.*

## 3.1 Asynchronous Patterns and Promises

As developers progress to building performance-critical, event-driven applications, an in-depth understanding of asynchronous program-

ming becomes indispensable. The asynchronous paradigm in Type-
Script, underpinned by the Promise specification, necessitates a precise command over its construction and manipulation to address challenges inherent to I/O-bound operations, network latency, and concurrent execution flows. The Promise API, standardized in ES6, provides
a robust mechanism for sequencing asynchronous operations without
compromising the functional purity of the codebase.

In the advanced usage of Promises, it is vital to perceive them not
merely as wrappers for asynchronous computations but as first-class
compositional constructs that allow operators to shape complex execution paths. Each Promise represents a finite state machine with states
including pending, fulfilled, and rejected. Leveraging this invariant, developers can design algorithms that transition between these
states in a controlled and predictable manner, ultimately ensuring consistency and determinism within asynchronous operations.

The fundamental building block is the Promise constructor, which integrates seamlessly with higher-order functions. Advanced programmers must be vigilant in handling race conditions and ensuring idem-
potency in callback execution, especially when chaining several asynchronous calls. The chaining mechanism via the then method allows
for serializing asynchronous tasks, where each subsequent operation
is executed upon the fulfillment of the prior Promise. Consider the
following advanced example where careful error propagation and intermediate value transformation are handled:

```
function fetchData(endpoint: string): Promise<any> {
    return new Promise((resolve, reject) => {
        // Complex asynchronous operation that could involve retries
    or exponential backoff strategies
        const xhr = new XMLHttpRequest();
        xhr.open('GET', endpoint);
        xhr.onreadystatechange = () => {
```

```
                if (xhr.readyState === 4) {
                    if (xhr.status === 200) {
                        try {
                            const data = JSON.parse(xhr.responseText);
                            resolve(data);
                        } catch (error) {
                            reject(new Error(`Parsing error: ${error}`));
                        }
                    } else {
                        reject(new Error(`Request failed with status ${
    xhr.status}`));
                    }
                }
            };
            xhr.send();
    });
}


fetchData('https://api.example.com/data')
    .then(data => {
        // Transform data with synchronous map operations
        return data.map(item => ({ ...item, processed: true }));
    })
    .then(transformedData => {
        // Further asynchronous operations might be chained here
        console.log('Transformed Data:', transformedData);
        return transformedData;
    })
    .catch(error => {
        console.error('Error occurred during asynchronous operations
    :', error);
    });
```

Understanding the intricacies of Promise resolution requires attention to how error propagation is intrinsically coupled with the catch
method. Unlike traditional try-catch blocks in synchronous code, the
asynchronous error handling mechanism in Promises is inherently
chained. A Promise that is rejected bypasses any subsequent then handlers until a catch is encountered, allowing for centralizing error management in complex asynchronous flows. Advanced error handling

113

techniques involve wrapping promises in higher-level functions that standardize error messages and implement retry logic.

A sophisticated pattern involves the use of `Promise.all` and `Promise.race` to manage multiple asynchronous operations concurrently. `Promise.all` waits for the entire collection to fulfill, failing immediately if any single Promise rejects, which is useful in cases where every asynchronous process is critical. Conversely, `Promise.race` initiates several asynchronous operations concurrently and returns the result of the first settled promise, allowing for competitive execution. The intricacy lies in determining the appropriate scenario for each combinator, ensuring that the composed asynchronous flow does not introduce latent race conditions or resource contention issues.

```
const promises = [
    fetchData('https://api.example.com/first'),
    fetchData('https://api.example.com/second'),
    fetchData('https://api.example.com/third')
];

// Using Promise.all to enforce all operations should complete
    without failure
Promise.all(promises)
    .then(results => {
        // Process the aggregated results from all endpoints
        console.log('Aggregated results:', results);
    })
    .catch(error => {
        // If any of the promises fail, the error is caught here.
        console.error('One of the operations failed:', error);
    });

// Using Promise.race to complete as soon as one of the promises
    settles
Promise.race(promises)
    .then(result => {
        // Proceed with the fastest result, useful in fallback
    mechanisms
```

```
      console.log('Fastest response:', result);
})
.catch(error => {
      console.error('Error in the fastest response:', error);
});
```

Advanced patterns also leverage combinators that extend the API for asynchronous sequencing. The `Promise.resolve()` and `Promise.reject()` factory methods facilitate the integration of synchronous results into an asynchronous flow, ensuring a unified interface for both immediate and delayed computations. By wrapping synchronous output with `Promise.resolve()`, developers can chain operations without resorting to conditional branching that can obscure control flow.

When constructing middleware or chaining functions that incorporate both synchronous and asynchronous logic, it is essential to normalize the interface. This is achieved by consistently returning a Promise object, even when the operation is inherently synchronous. Failing to do so may introduce subtle bugs where sequence assumptions are violated. Consider the abstraction of a middleware function:

```
function processData(input: any): Promise<any> {
    // Wrap synchronous logic into a Promise to ensure compatibility
    return Promise.resolve(input)
        .then(data => {
            // Perform a synchronous transformation
            return { ...data, timestamp: Date.now() };
        })
        .then(modifiedData => {
            // An asynchronous call that further processes the data
            return fetchData('https://api.backend.com/process')
                .then(response => {
                    return { ...modifiedData, backendResponse:
response };
                });
        });
```

115

```
}

processData({ id: 1, value: 'test' })
    .then(result => console.log('Processed result:', result))
    .catch(error => console.error('Processing failed:', error));
```

One advanced technique involves constructing custom control flows where Promises are combined with recursive algorithms or loops. In these cases, the iterative pattern must be crafted to avoid unnecessary stack growth and ensure that each iteration returns a Promise that resolves before the next iteration is initiated. This pattern is often crucial in scenarios such as paginated API requests or long-running background computations where each iteration must wait for asynchronous data retrieval. Utilizing self-contained promise chains eliminates the risk of excessive recursion in the call stack.

```
function processPages(page: number, accumulator: any[] = []): Promise
    <any[]> {
    return fetchData(`https://api.example.com/data?page=${page}`)
        .then(data => {
            accumulator = accumulator.concat(data.items);
            if (data.hasNextPage) {
                return processPages(page + 1, accumulator);
            } else {
                return accumulator;
            }
        })
        .catch(error => {
            // Handle individual page failures without silently
    terminating the chain.
            console.error(`Error retrieving page ${page}:`, error);
            throw error;
        });
}

processPages(1)
    .then(allItems => {
        console.log('All paginated items received:', allItems);
    })
    .catch(finalError => {
```

```
        console.error('Failed to process paginated data:', finalError
    );
});
```

Combining asynchronous control with defensive programming techniques is paramount for high-integrity applications. Mastering techniques such as timeouts, circuit breakers, and fallback strategies in
combination with Promises can efficiently manage external service un-
reliability. For instance, implementing a timeout mechanism entails
racing the original Promise with a timeout Promise that rejects after a
specified duration:

```
function fetchDataWithTimeout(endpoint: string, timeout: number):
    Promise<any> {
    const timeoutPromise = new Promise((_, reject) => {
        setTimeout(() => {
            reject(new Error('Operation timed out'));
        }, timeout);
    });

    return Promise.race([fetchData(endpoint), timeoutPromise]);
}

fetchDataWithTimeout('https://api.example.com/resource', 3000)
    .then(result => console.log('Data retrieved within timeout:',
    result))
    .catch(timeoutError => console.error('Timeout/error occurred:',
    timeoutError));
```

A comprehensive command over asynchronous programming also involves understanding the internal behavior of promise queues. Modern JavaScript engines implement the microtask queue to process resolved and rejected promises. This queue exhibits characteristics that
differ from regular event loop tasks, specifically regarding the precision and order of execution. Advanced developers benefit from in-
specting engine-specific optimizations to align promise-based opera-

tions with performance-critical sections of their application. Moreover, performance profiling tools can reveal bottlenecks introduced by an overabundance of chained promises or unhandled microtasks that delay the rendering process in UI-centric applications.

In practice, abstracting promise-handling patterns into reusable modules increases code maintainability and testing efficiency. Patterns such as promise lifting, function memoization, and cancellation tokens illustrate matured techniques. While the native Promise API does not include cancellation functionality, several libraries implement composable counterparts that allow the deactivation of pending asynchronous operations to mitigate resource wastage and control propagation of stale data. Incorporating such libraries may involve wrapping native promises with decorators that expose additional control – such as cancellation and status monitoring – which is especially relevant in reactive programming environments that demand rigorous state management.

Mastering asynchronous programming in TypeScript through an astute application of Promises empowers developers to construct responsive, modular, and error-resilient code.

## 3.2   Utilizing Async/Await for Simplicity

The introduction of `async/await` in TypeScript fundamentally transforms asynchronous programming by linearizing asynchronous control flow. The syntax abstracts underlying Promise chains, reducing syntactic overhead and improving code readability without sacrificing performance or reliability. This section delves into the technical intricacies of `async/await`, exploring advanced patterns, potential pitfalls, and techniques to optimize asynchronous operations in complex systems.

At its core, the `async` keyword designates a function that produces a Promise. Within these functions, the `await` operator pauses execution until the awaited Promise is either resolved or rejected. This syntactic sugar eliminates the need for multiple nested `then` calls, thereby flattening asynchronous control flows. With `async/await`, error handling is integrated via conventional `try/catch` statements, providing a cohesive and uniform mechanism for managing exceptions across asynchronous boundaries. Advanced techniques involve structuring nested asynchronous calls and combining simultaneous asynchronous operations in a maintainable fashion.

An exemplary pattern involves converting complex Promise chains into sequential, synchronous-style code while retaining full asynchronicity. Consider the following pattern where asynchronous HTTP requests are made in sequence:

```
async function fetchResource(url: string): Promise<any> {
    try {
        const response = await fetch(url);
        if (!response.ok) {
            throw new Error(`HTTP error! status: ${response.status}`)
    ;
        }
        const data = await response.json();
        return data;
    } catch (error) {
        // Error propagation is centralized in a try/catch block.
        throw new Error(`Failed to fetch resource: ${error}`);
    }
}

async function processDataSequence(endpoints: string[]): Promise<void
    > {
    for (const url of endpoints) {
        const data = await fetchResource(url);
```

```
        console.log('Processed Data:', data);
    }
}
```

In the above example, sequential processing is straightforward to understand and maintain, but not without performance trade-offs when independent asynchronous operations are available. Advanced developers often seek to maximize concurrency by combining await with Promise.all(). This approach facilitates parallel execution while preserving the clarity of linear syntax:

```
async function processResourcesParallel(endpoints: string[]): Promise
    <void> {
    try {
        // Initiate all asynchronous operations concurrently
        const fetchPromises = endpoints.map(url => fetchResource(url)
    );
        // Await their collective resolution
        const allData = await Promise.all(fetchPromises);
        console.log('Aggregated Data:', allData);
    } catch (error) {
        console.error('Error in processing parallel requests:', error
    );
    }
}
```

A critical insight is that await does not force sequential execution unless used within an iterative structure. It is vital to distinguish between awaiting inside a loop (which is sequential) and initiating multiple asynchronous tasks before awaiting their resolution concurrently. This distinction allows the developer to strike a balance between control flow clarity and optimal performance. Advanced techniques may involve strategically mixing sequential and concurrent processing, such as batching operations or applying dynamic concurrency limits when interfacing with rate-limited external services.

Errors within asynchronous contexts propagate through the promise chain until intercepted by a catch block. When using async/await, errors are treated as synchronous exceptions. This mechanism simplifies error handling, but advanced developers must remain cautious when dealing with nested asynchronous operations. In particular, a try/catch block placed at the outermost level of an async function will capture exceptions arising from any awaited expression. However, when combining multiple independent awaits, isolating specific error types for granular recovery requires multiple nested try/catch blocks or custom error propagation logic.

```
async function processMultiple(endpoints: string[]): Promise<void> {
    for (const url of endpoints) {
        try {
            const data = await fetchResource(url);
            console.log(`Data for ${url}:`, data);
        } catch (error) {
            // Errors are isolated per iteration, allowing individual
        handling.
            console.error(`Failed processing ${url}:`, error);
        }
    }
}
```

Another advanced approach is to deliberately introduce concurrency control within an async function. This technique becomes essential when asynchronous tasks share limited resources or when the uniqueness of response order is significant. In these cases, an advanced pattern involves combining asynchronous sequences with concurrency throttling. One effective method is to use an iterator-based approach, whereby a defined number of asynchronous tasks are executed simultaneously, and subsequent tasks await the completion of previous ones. This pattern helps to prevent resource saturation and ensures controlled execution dynamics.

Cancellation of asynchronous operations, though not natively supported in Promises or async/await, is an area that demands sophisticated design patterns. Advanced applications require the capability
to abort pending operations to avoid performance bottlenecks. Design
patterns such as cancellation tokens or third-party libraries that extend
Promise semantics provide a controlled means of introducing cancellation capabilities. A typical implementation involves encapsulating
asynchronous actions within an abstraction that monitors cancellation
state, as illustrated below:

```typescript
interface CancellationToken {
    isCancelled: boolean;
}

async function fetchWithCancellation(url: string, token:
    CancellationToken): Promise<any> {
    const response = await fetch(url);
    if (token.isCancelled) {
        throw new Error('Operation cancelled');
    }
    return await response.json();
}

async function processWithCancellation(endpoints: string[], token:
    CancellationToken): Promise<void> {
    const results = [];
    for (const url of endpoints) {
        if (token.isCancelled) {
            console.log('Operation cancelled, aborting further
    processing');
            break;
        }
        try {
            const data = await fetchWithCancellation(url, token);
            results.push(data);
        } catch (error) {
            console.error('Error during fetch:', error);
        }
    }
    console.log('Final processed results:', results);
}
```

The power of `async/await` is further amplified through its seamless integration with other language features, such as destructuring and default parameters. In advanced scenarios, this ability facilitates the creation of highly modular and configurable asynchronous workflows. Moreover, leveraging advanced TypeScript types in conjunction with `async/await` reinforces API contracts and eliminates a class of runtime errors. When designing complex asynchronous interfaces, consider the use of generics and type inference to design robust abstractions.

Another notable advanced pattern is the integration of `async` functions within memoization strategies. By caching the output of asynchronous operations, one can avoid redundant network calls or computations. Caching asynchronous results requires caution to ensure that race conditions do not lead to inconsistent states. A skeletal implementation of asynchronous memoization is provided below:

```
const memoCache = new Map<string, Promise<any>>();

async function memoizedFetch(url: string): Promise<any> {
    if (!memoCache.has(url)) {
        const fetchPromise = fetchResource(url);
        memoCache.set(url, fetchPromise);
    }
    return await memoCache.get(url);
}

async function batchFetch(urls: string[]): Promise<void> {
    try {
        const results = await Promise.all(urls.map(url =>
    memoizedFetch(url)));
        console.log('Batch fetch results:', results);
    } catch (error) {
        console.error('Error during batch fetch:', error);
    }
}
```

A particular consideration for advanced usage pertains to resource cleanup and managing long-lived asynchronous operations. Asynchronous loops or intervals can leak resources if not properly terminated. Advanced developers must design lifecycle management strategies within async functions to ensure that open connections, timers, or file handles are correctly disposed when operations complete or are aborted. Finalizers and explicit cancellation patterns can assist in mitigating these issues.

An additional technique involves integrating async iterators with for-await-of loops to process streams of data that arrive asynchronously. Unlike traditional iterations over collections, async iterators allow for consumption of data as it becomes available, aligning with backpressure principles inherent to high-throughput systems. The following example demonstrates the use of async iterators to process a stream of results:

```
async function* generateDataStream(): AsyncGenerator<number, void,
    undefined> {
    for (let i = 0; i < 10; i++) {
        await new Promise(resolve => setTimeout(resolve, 500));
        yield i;
    }
}

async function processDataStream(): Promise<void> {
    try {
        for await (const value of generateDataStream()) {
            console.log('Stream value:', value);
        }
    } catch (error) {
        console.error('Error processing data stream:', error);
    }
}
```

Underlying every advanced async/await workflow is the awareness of the JavaScript microtask queue. Each `await` internally causes subsequent operations to be queued as microtasks. Performance tuning, therefore, may involve careful measurement of microtask saturation and its effect on UI and I/O responsiveness. Advanced applications in environments with mixed rendering and computation tasks must calibrate the frequency and duration of asynchronous pauses to avoid starving higher-priority processing tasks.

By leveraging `async/await`, experienced TypeScript developers can build sophisticated, fully composable asynchronous architectures with enhanced error propagation, efficient concurrency control, and improved code maintainability. The integration of cancellation support, advanced caching strategies, and async iteration patterns into `async/await`-based workflows solidifies its role as a powerful abstraction for modern asynchronous programming. This approach not only simplifies the cognitive load when reasoning about concurrency but also endows developers with a clarity of structure that is critical when designing scalable, robust systems.

## 3.3   Handling Errors in Asynchronous Code

Robust error handling is an essential pillar in building reliable asynchronous systems in TypeScript. Given that asynchronous operations may fail due to various external factors such as network interruptions, unexpected response formats, or resource unavailability, advanced developers must design error handling strategies that not only capture and propagate errors in a coherent manner but also allow for recovery or fallback operations. The nature of asynchronous code, particularly when employing `async/await`, shifts the traditional paradigms of error handling into mechanisms that are inherently compositional and structured around state propagation.

A central concept in error management is understanding that errors propagate through promise chains similarly to synchronous exceptions, yet the timing and order are influenced by the microtask queue. The standardized behavior defines that when a Promise is rejected, the control flow bypasses subsequent then handlers until it is intercepted by a catch or equivalent error handler. In advanced use cases, capturing the granularity of error states becomes important, for instance, when multiple asynchronous operations execute concurrently. In such scenarios, aggregating errors using combinators or custom error wrappers ensures that diagnostic information is preserved and that fallback strategies can be applied selectively.

Consider a prototypical asynchronous operation where robust error management is implemented using async/await. The following example exemplifies standard practices in error propagation within an asynchronous function:

```
async function fetchResource(url: string): Promise<any> {
    try {
        const response = await fetch(url);
        if (!response.ok) {
            throw new Error(`Network response was not ok: ${response.
statusText}`);
        }
        const data = await response.json();
        return data;
    } catch (error) {
        // Wrap and rethrow to include additional context for
        debugging purposes.
        throw new Error(`fetchResource failed for ${url}: ${error.
message}`);
    }
}
```

In this snippet, errors in network or JSON processing are captured and rethrown with enriched context. For applications that involve multiple concurrent requests, the adoption of `Promise.allSettled` enables capturing the outcome of each promise, allowing the system to handle individual failures while still collecting results from successful operations. This pattern is particularly meaningful in scenarios where non-critical failures should not abort an entire batch operation.

```
async function fetchMultipleResources(urls: string[]): Promise<any[]>
    {
    const results = await Promise.allSettled(urls.map(fetchResource))
    ;
    return results.map(result => {
        if (result.status === 'fulfilled') {
            return result.value;
        } else {
            // Log the error and optionally transform it into a
    default object.
            console.error('Error fetching resource:', result.reason);
            return { error: true, message: result.reason.message };
        }
    });
}
```

When designing systems with nested asynchronous operations, it is often desirable to isolate failures without terminating the entire control flow. Using multiple `try/catch` blocks, one can segregate successful paths from error paths within iterative or deeply nested operations. This granular approach to error handling allows developers to apply selective retries or adjust internal state based on partial successes.

```
async function processData(endpoints: string[]): Promise<void> {
    for (const url of endpoints) {
        try {
            const data = await fetchResource(url);
            // Proceed with processing data if the fetch is
    successful.
            console.log('Processing data from:', url, data);
```

```
        } catch (error) {
            // Log error and decide whether to continue or break the
    loop based on criteria.
            console.error(`Processing skipped for ${url}:`, error);
        }
    }
}
```

Advanced patterns require not only the identification and propagation of errors but also the implementation of recovery mechanisms.
Retry patterns, for example, enable developers to automatically reat-
tempt failed operations a finite number of times with optional delays
between attempts. An exponential backoff strategy is a widely adopted
approach that balances load and reduces the risk of overwhelming dependent services.

```
async function retryOperation<T>(
    operation: () => Promise<T>,
    retries: number,
    delay: number
): Promise<T> {
    let lastError: Error;
    for (let attempt = 0; attempt < retries; attempt++) {
        try {
            return await operation();
        } catch (error) {
            lastError = error;
            // Delay before next attempt using a promise-based timer.
            await new Promise(resolve => setTimeout(resolve, delay *
    Math.pow(2, attempt)));
        }
    }
    throw new Error(`Operation failed after ${retries} attempts: ${
    lastError.message}`);
}
```

Combining the retry pattern with error classification is another powerful stratagem. Developers can design custom error classes that encapsulate error metadata and cause chains, facilitating fine-grained con-

128

trol over which error types warrant retries and which should propagate immediately. This approach demands careful type design and consistent usage of error wrappers.

```
class TransientError extends Error {
    constructor(message: string) {
        super(message);
        this.name = 'TransientError';
    }
}

async function fetchWithRetry(url: string, retries = 3): Promise<any>
    {
    return retryOperation(async () => {
        const response = await fetch(url);
        if (!response.ok) {
            // Mark certain failures as transient to enable retry.
            if ([502, 503, 504].includes(response.status)) {
                throw new TransientError(`Transient failure: ${
response.statusText}`);
            }
            throw new Error(`Permanent failure: ${response.statusText
}`);
        }
        return response.json();
    }, retries, 500);
}
```

Error aggregation is critical when dealing with multiple asynchronous operations in parallel. Instead of propagating the first encountered error, developers might seek to collect all error instances and report them collectively. This can be achieved by processing the results of Promise.allSettled and constructing an aggregate error that encapsulates all failure states.

```
class AggregateError extends Error {
    public errors: Error[];

    constructor(errors: Error[]) {
        super(`Multiple errors occurred: ${errors.map(e => e.message)
```

```
    .join('; ')}`);
        this.name = 'AggregateError';
        this.errors = errors;
    }
}

async function aggregateFetch(urls: string[]): Promise<any[]> {
    const results = await Promise.allSettled(urls.map(fetchResource))
     ;
    const errors: Error[] = [];
    const values: any[] = [];

    results.forEach(result => {
        if (result.status === 'fulfilled') {
            values.push(result.value);
        } else {
            errors.push(result.reason);
        }
    });

    if (errors.length > 0) {
        throw new AggregateError(errors);
    }
    return values;
}
```

Integrating cancellation strategies into error handling can also influence the overall architecture for asynchronous systems. Although JavaScript does not provide built-in cancellation semantics, pattern-based solutions such as cancellation tokens can mitigate the propagation of errors resulting from aborted operations. By checking the token state before resolving promises, one can preemptively avoid executing downstream logic when cancellation is signaled.

```
interface CancellationToken {
    isCancelled: boolean;
}

async function cancellableFetch(url: string, token: CancellationToken
    ): Promise<any> {
    const response = await fetch(url);
```

```
if (token.isCancelled) {
    throw new Error('Operation cancelled');
}
return response.json();
}
```

Error handling in asynchronous contexts also requires developers to be cognizant of the potential for "silent failures," particularly when errors are improperly captured or suppressed. It is important to design error handlers that do not inadvertently mask errors. One common pitfall involves catching errors at a high level without proper logging or rethrowing, which may lead to inconsistencies in system state. Thus, logging strategies should include context-aware messages that ensure traceability across the asynchronous call stack. Leveraging structured logging libraries that handle asynchronous log accumulation and consistency can confer significant benefits at scale.

A best practice when handling errors with `async/await` is to avoid redundant error wrappers. Introducing multiple layers of error encapsulation can obscure the root cause and complicate downstream diagnostics. Instead, each error rethrown should add only incremental contextual information, often incorporating a unique error code or trace identifier that is subsequently logged. Developers may also consider centralized error reporting solutions that collect exception data from distributed modules, thereby facilitating robust monitoring and alerting in production environments.

Advanced error handling techniques incorporate the use of finally blocks within `try/catch` structures. The `finally` block guarantees the execution of cleanup logic irrespective of the success or failure of the preceding asynchronous operations. Whether closing file descriptors, releasing network resources, or resetting application state, cleanup op-

erations are indispensable in ensuring that transient errors do not result in resource leakage.

```
async function performOperationWithCleanup(url: string): Promise<void
    > {
    let resource: any;
    try {
        resource = await acquireResource(url);
        // Process resource with guaranteed release on exit.
        await processResource(resource);
    } catch (error) {
        console.error('Error encountered during operation:', error);
        throw error;
    } finally {
        if (resource) {
            await releaseResource(resource);
        }
    }
}
```

For asynchronous operations spanning multiple system boundaries, a
layered error handling strategy is essential. Each layer of the application, from network communication to business logic, should implement its own error resilience measures; however, these layers must expose errors through well-defined interfaces. Such modularity permits
downstream handlers to decide whether to manage specific error types
locally, apply retries, or escalate issues for centralized coordination.

Robust error handling in asynchronous code is achieved not only by
effective exception management but also by enforcing strict adherence
to interface contracts. When employing TypeScript's advanced type
system, developers can define custom error types that tie into annotations across function signatures. This approach provides compile-time
assurances that errors are appropriately handled and helps to mitigate
runtime failures due to unanticipated error states.

The ongoing evolution of asynchronous paradigms in TypeScript necessitates continuous learning and adaptation of modern error handling techniques. By consolidating best practices including error aggregation, retry strategies, cancellation semantics, and resource cleanup, advanced developers create asynchronous systems that exhibit deterministic error propagation and resilience. This meticulous design fosters codebases that remain robust under various failure modes while maintaining clarity and scalability in error resolution workflows.

## 3.4 Working with Callback Functions

Callback functions remain a foundational paradigm in asynchronous programming despite the advent of `Promises` and `async/await`. In advanced TypeScript programming, mastery over callback patterns is indispensable when interacting with legacy interfaces, event-driven architectures, or Node.js-style APIs. The challenge lies in managing inversion of control, ensuring error propagation, and mitigating the complexity introduced by deeply nested callback structures, commonly known as "callback hell." Advanced developers must enforce disciplined patterns for converting callback-based APIs into composable, maintainable components.

At the core, a callback is a function invoked after the completion of an asynchronous operation. Unlike `Promises`, which provide structured methods such as `then`, callbacks require explicit error-first conventions to signal success or failure. This paradigm is best illustrated by the Node.js convention, where the callback signature is typically defined as `(error, result)`, and error handling must manually inspect the first parameter. Carefully validating inputs and standardizing callback

133

interfaces contribute substantially to code reliability and maintainability.

A typical example of a Node.js-style asynchronous function might be as follows:

```
function readFileAsync(path: string, callback: (err: Error | null,
    data?: string) => void): void {
    // Simulate asynchronous file reading
    setTimeout(() => {
        if (path === '') {
            callback(new Error('Invalid file path'));
        } else {
            callback(null, 'File content for: ' + path);
        }
    }, 100);
}
```

Advanced usage requires that such callback-based functions are composed and handled in a manner that preserves error context and allows for elegant extensions. Techniques such as the "waterfall" pattern can be used to sequence operations, yet they often lead to a nested structure which is difficult to maintain. Advanced developers instead prefer to modularize callback functions into reusable units, often wrapping them with Promises for greater composability.

Conversion from callback style to Promises can be achieved manually or through utility functions. The manual approach involves encapsulating the callback logic within a new Promise. This pattern allows developers to write uniform error handling and leverage modern asynchronous control flows:

```
function readFilePromise(path: string): Promise<string> {
    return new Promise((resolve, reject) => {
        readFileAsync(path, (err, data) => {
            if (err) {
                return reject(err);
```

```
        }
        resolve(data as string);
    });
  });
}
```

Advanced programmers may further encapsulate these conversions into generic utilities. For instance, using TypeScript generics, one can construct a helper function that automatically converts any Node.js-style callback function into its Promise-based counterpart:

```
function promisify<T, U>(fn: (arg: T, callback: (err: Error | null,
    result?: U) => void) => void): (arg: T) => Promise<U> {
  return (arg: T) => {
    return new Promise<U>((resolve, reject) => {
      fn(arg, (err, result) => {
        if (err) {
          reject(err);
        } else {
          resolve(result as U);
        }
      });
    });
  };
}
```

This utility enables a seamless transition between paradigms. By applying promisify to a suite of callback-based APIs, one can immediately integrate them with promise-based workflows, thereby reducing the cognitive overhead associated with nested callbacks.

Another advanced technique involves error segmentation and isolation within callback flows. Developers must design callback handlers that not only capture errors but also propagate them in a manner that preserves context. In deeply nested structures, contextualized error objects allow downstream handlers to enact conditional recovery strategies. Instrumentation of callbacks with metadata, such as operation

135

identifiers or timestamps, facilitates granular logging and debugging:

```
function extendedCallback(err: Error | null, result?: any, context?:
    { operation: string, timestamp: number }): void {
  if (err) {
      console.error(`[${context?.timestamp}] Error in ${context?.
  operation}: ${err.message}`);
  } else {
      console.log(`[${context?.timestamp}] Success in ${context?.
  operation}:`, result);
  }
}
```

In many high-performance systems, callback functions are combined
with event emitters and observers. When channeling asynchronous
events, developers must compose observers that can manage multiple
simultaneous callback invocations. This calls for an understanding of
the event loop and microtask queue to design non-blocking, reactive architectures. Advanced patterns include using publish/subscribe mechanisms to decouple the source of events from their handlers, thereby
managing dependencies more effectively.

Consider an example where an event emitter is used to notify multiple
subscribers about the completion of an asynchronous task:

```
import { EventEmitter } from 'events';

class AsyncOperationEmitter extends EventEmitter {
    executeOperation(data: any): void {
        // The asynchronous operation simulated with a delay
        setTimeout(() => {
            try {
                // On successful processing, emit success event
                const result = processData(data);
                this.emit('success', result);
            } catch (error) {
                // On error, emit error event
                this.emit('error', error);
            }
        }, 200);
```

```
        }
}

function processData(data: any): any {
    if (!data) {
        throw new Error('Invalid data provided');
    }
    // Complex processing logic
    return { processed: true, data };
}

const emitter = new AsyncOperationEmitter();
emitter.on('success', (result) => {
    console.log('Operation succeeded:', result);
});
emitter.on('error', (err) => {
    console.error('Operation failed:', err);
});

emitter.executeOperation({ payload: 'sample data' });
```

When applying callback functions in event-driven frameworks, it is essential to address potential pitfalls such as callback reentrancy and memory leaks. Improperly detached event listeners can cause modules to remain active longer than necessary, resulting in excessive memory consumption and degraded performance. Advanced developers should systematically implement weak references or explicit deregistration methods to mitigate these risks.

Another nuanced aspect of callbacks in asynchronous programming lies in the orchestration of parallel and sequential operations. Callback-based functions can be composed into pipelines where each step relies on the previous operation's outcome. However, if these steps are interdependent and not adequately isolated, a single failure may cascade across the pipeline. Advanced strategies involve using control flow libraries or custom frameworks that implement waterfall, series, or parallel processing patterns while preserving a clean separation of concerns:

```typescript
function series(tasks: Array<(callback: (err: Error | null, result?:
    any) => void) => void>, finalCallback: (err: Error | null,
    results?: any[]) => void): void {
    const results: any[] = [];
    let index = 0;

    function nextTask(err: Error | null, result?: any): void {
        if (err) {
            return finalCallback(err);
        }
        if (result !== undefined) {
            results.push(result);
        }
        if (index === tasks.length) {
            return finalCallback(null, results);
        }
        const task = tasks[index++];
        task(nextTask);
    }

    nextTask(null);
}

series([
    (cb) => readFileAsync('path/to/file1.txt', cb),
    (cb) => readFileAsync('path/to/file2.txt', cb),
    (cb) => readFileAsync('path/to/file3.txt', cb)
], (err, results) => {
    if (err) {
        console.error('Series execution failed:', err);
    } else {
        console.log('Series execution complete:', results);
    }
});
```

Maintaining such orchestration libraries requires careful consideration
of asynchronous error propagation, context binding, and debugging.
Advanced error reporting in series or parallel orchestration should
include details about which task failed and why. This involves instrumenting each task with context identifiers and employing logging

strategies that capture the state of the system at the time of the error.

Another effective technique for managing callbacks is to adopt inversion of control patterns, such as dependency injection. By designing modules that require callback functions as explicit parameters, developers can substitute mocks, logging mechanisms, or error handlers during testing and production. This modularity enhances testability and decouples application logic from callback management concerns.

```
interface AsyncOperation {
    execute(callback: (err: Error | null, result?: any) => void):
    void;
}


class NetworkRequest implements AsyncOperation {
    execute(callback: (err: Error | null, result?: any) => void):
    void {
        // Simulate network request
        setTimeout(() => {
            // Injecting potential error for demonstration
            if (Math.random() > 0.5) {
                callback(new Error('Network failure'));
            } else {
                callback(null, { data: 'Response Data' });
            }
        }, 100);
    }
}


function runOperation(operation: AsyncOperation, callback: (err:
    Error | null, result?: any) => void): void {
    // Dependency is injected, allowing for different operation
    implementations
    operation.execute(callback);
}


runOperation(new NetworkRequest(), (err, result) => {
    if (err) {
        console.error('Operation failed:', err);
    } else {
        console.log('Operation succeeded:', result);
    }
```

```
});
```

Managing callback functions in advanced asynchronous programming requires continual refinement of techniques to combat callback inversion, error opacity, and resource mismanagement. By encapsulating callback patterns into well-defined abstractions, employing systematic conversion strategies, and adopting orchestration libraries, developers can build robust modular code that interfaces correctly with both legacy callback-based APIs and modern Promise-based paradigms. This sophisticated approach ensures that asynchronous workflows remain clean, maintainable, and resilient in the face of unexpected runtime behavior, thereby reinforcing the robustness of large-scale TypeScript systems.

## 3.5   Implementing Streams and Observables

In advanced TypeScript applications, handling data sequences that evolve over time necessitates the use of streams and observables. These paradigms extend asynchronous programming beyond single-event resolutions by introducing a continuous push model that supports dynamic and potentially infinite data sets. Streams and observables are particularly essential in scenarios such as real-time data processing, UI event handling, and complex network protocols, where traditional Promise-based approaches lack the expressive capacity to model temporal sequences.

Streams are abstractions that model data that can be read in chunks over time. They provide efficient handling of large data sets by allocating memory dynamically and ensuring that operations such as filtering, transformation, and aggregation can be performed in a resource-efficient manner. In Node.js environments, streams are a fundamental building block with utilities for reading from files, network sockets, and other sources. Advanced developers leverage streams by composing pipelines where every transformation stage is itself a stream, and proper error propagation ensures that failures in any stage terminate the pipeline gracefully.

In TypeScript, streams are often implemented as instances of the Readable, Writable, or Duplex classes. For example, when processing large JSON files, a Readable stream can be used to asynchronously parse incoming data, and a Transform stream can convert or filter the data as it flows. Consider the following advanced example that demonstrates constructing a custom transform stream to filter data before further processing:

```typescript
import { Transform, TransformCallback } from 'stream';

class FilterStream extends Transform {
    constructor(private readonly predicate: (chunk: any) => boolean)
    {
        super({ objectMode: true });
    }

    _transform(chunk: any, encoding: BufferEncoding, callback:
    TransformCallback): void {
        try {
            if (this.predicate(chunk)) {
                this.push(chunk);
            }
            callback();
        } catch (err) {
            callback(err);
        }
    }
}

// Usage in a pipeline
import { pipeline, Readable, Writable } from 'stream';
```

```
const source = Readable.from([{ value: 1 }, { value: 2 }, { value: 3
    }], { objectMode: true });
const filter = new FilterStream((data) => data.value % 2 === 1);
const sink = new Writable({
    objectMode: true,
    write(chunk, encoding, callback) {
        console.log('Processed chunk:', chunk);
        callback();
    }
});

pipeline(source, filter, sink, (err) => {
    if (err) {
        console.error('Pipeline encountered error:', err);
    }
});
```

Observables, popularized by the Reactive Extensions (RxJS) library, extend the stream model by incorporating operators that allow sophisticated manipulation of event streams. While streams focus on I/O-bound data flows, observables generalize the push-based data model to include events and arbitrary asynchronous data sequences with rich combinatorial and filtering operators. In RxJS, an observable is a function that sets up an observer and returns a cleanup function, thereby providing fine-grained control over subscription lifecycles.

For advanced applications, observables provide a unified interface to handle asynchronous events through a fluent API. The operators available in RxJS, such as map, filter, merge, and debounceTime, empower developers to express complex logic in a declarative manner. Advanced practitioners often compose operators in pipelines that create deterministic flows, enforce backpressure, and offer robust error handling. The following example illustrates a scenario where an observable is used to process a stream of events, applying multiple operators to transform and filter the sequence:

```
import { Observable, fromEvent } from 'rxjs';
import { map, filter, debounceTime, catchError } from 'rxjs/operators
    ';

// Create an observable from DOM events (e.g., keyup events)
const keyup$ = fromEvent<KeyboardEvent>(document, 'keyup');

const processed$ = keyup$.pipe(
    debounceTime(300), // Avoid rapid-fire events by smoothing out
    bursts
    map(event => (event.target as HTMLInputElement).value),
    filter(text => text.length > 3),
    map(text => text.toUpperCase()),
    catchError((error, caught) => {
        console.error('Stream error:', error);
        return caught;
    })
);

const subscription = processed$.subscribe({
    next: value => console.log('Processed value:', value),
    error: err => console.error('Observable error:', err),
    complete: () => console.log('Observable completed')
});
```

A key advanced concept in observables is the management of subscription lifecycles. Unlike Promises that resolve once, observables represent ongoing sequences that must be explicitly managed to release resources. Cancellation of observables is performed by unsubscribing, and advanced applications may incorporate composite subscriptions to manage complex interdependencies among multiple data streams. It is critical to ensure that subscriptions are terminated appropriately, particularly in long-lived applications like single-page applications (SPAs) or server applications, to prevent memory leaks and unintended side effects.

```
import { Subscription, interval } from 'rxjs';

const timer$ = interval(1000);
```

143

```
const sub1 = timer$.subscribe(val => console.log('Timer 1:', val));
const sub2 = timer$.subscribe(val => console.log('Timer 2:', val));

// Combine subscriptions and later unsubscribe collectively
const compositeSub = new Subscription();
compositeSub.add(sub1);
compositeSub.add(sub2);

// After a defined period, unsubscribe from all timers
setTimeout(() => {
    compositeSub.unsubscribe();
    console.log('All timer subscriptions cancelled');
}, 5000);
```

Advanced observables also incorporate error propagation and transformation at various stages in the pipeline. Utilizing error-handling operators like catchError or retryWhen, developers can implement fallback strategies, log detailed error metrics, or trigger alternative asynchronous workflows. This approach ensures that downstream operators operate on valid, sanitized data even when the source observable encounters intermittent failures. It is important that the design of the observable pipeline adheres to a consistent error contract to allow seamless integration with other asynchronous components.

The interoperability between streams and observables remains a critical subject for advanced programmers. Although both paradigms share the core concept of providing data asynchronously, their operational semantics differ. Streams in Node.js are predominantly pull-based or push-based models that interface with system-level I/O, whereas observables provide a more functional-reactive approach. Converting between streams and observables is a common requirement, and specialized adapters exist for such purposes. For instance, in RxJS, one can create an observable from a Node.js stream:

```
import { fromEvent, Observable } from 'rxjs';
```

```
import { createInterface } from 'readline';
import { createReadStream } from 'fs';

const rl = createInterface({
    input: createReadStream('largefile.txt')
});

// Create an observable that emits one line at a time
const line$ = new Observable<string>(subscriber => {
    rl.on('line', (line) => subscriber.next(line));
    rl.on('close', () => subscriber.complete());
    rl.on('error', (err) => subscriber.error(err));

    // Teardown logic
    return () => {
        rl.close();
    };
});

line$.subscribe({
    next: line => console.log('Line:', line),
    error: err => console.error('Error reading file:', err),
    complete: () => console.log('Finished reading file')
});
```

The integration of custom operators in observables further enhances
the expressiveness of data processing pipelines. Advanced programmers often extend RxJS operators to encapsulate domain-specific logic.
This can involve creating higher-order operators that merge, buffer, or
combine multiple event sources based on intricate conditional logic.
The design of such operators should emphasize reusability, composability, and adherence to the observable contract. For example, a custom operator that buffers events until a condition is met might look
like the following:

```
import { Observable, OperatorFunction } from 'rxjs';

function bufferUntil<T>(predicate: (buffer: T[]) => boolean):
    OperatorFunction<T, T[]> {
    return (source: Observable<T>) =>
```

145

```typescript
        new Observable<T[]>(subscriber => {
            let buffer: T[] = [];
            const subscription = source.subscribe({
                next(value) {
                    buffer.push(value);
                    if (predicate(buffer)) {
                        subscriber.next(buffer);
                        buffer = [];
                    }
                },
                error(err) {
                    subscriber.error(err);
                },
                complete() {
                    if (buffer.length > 0) {
                        subscriber.next(buffer);
                    }
                    subscriber.complete();
                }
            });
            return () => subscription.unsubscribe();
        });
}

// Usage of the custom operator
import { interval } from 'rxjs';
import { take } from 'rxjs/operators';

interval(500).pipe(
    take(10),
    bufferUntil<number>(buffer => buffer.length >= 3)
).subscribe({
    next: buf => console.log('Buffered output:', buf),
    complete: () => console.log('Buffering complete')
});
```

Performance considerations are paramount when working with
streams and observables in demanding environments. Efficient
memory management, backpressure handling, and non-blocking
pipeline designs contribute to scalable implementations. Techniques
such as batching, debouncing, and throttling are essential in

146

controlling resource utilization and ensuring that data producers do not overwhelm consumers.

Advanced debugging and profiling tools that visualize the flow of observable events or stream data are invaluable.  Utilizing such tools, developers can inspect operator execution, measure latency between transformations, and detect potential bottlenecks or memory leaks within complex pipelines.  Instrumenting observables with logging and metrics aggregation further allows real-time monitoring and debugging of live systems.

A disciplined approach to testing is also required when developing applications that rely on streams and observables.  Deterministic tests should emulate asynchronous data flows and simulate edge cases like sudden terminations or delayed event emissions.  Frameworks that support virtual time or mock schedulers provide avenues to validate the behavior of reactive streams reliably, ensuring that each operator adheres to its contract under various timing conditions.

The sophistication of streams and observables in TypeScript unlocks a powerful model for reacting to continuous changes, external events, and complex data transformations.  By mastering these paradigms, advanced developers can architect resilient, scalable systems that seamlessly integrate synchronous and asynchronous operations while maintaining clarity in design and consistency in error handling.  This approach affords extensive flexibility for tailoring data flows to application-specific requirements, thereby ensuring that systems remain robust and performant as they scale.

## 3.6 Composing Asynchronous Operations

Advanced asynchronous programming in TypeScript requires the ability to combine multiple operations into cohesive workflows that can gracefully handle complex dependencies, conditional execution paths, and error propagation. Building upon earlier discussions of Promises, async/await techniques, and orchestration patterns, this section explores sophisticated strategies for composing asynchronous operations. Developers are encouraged to employ a combination of sequential chaining, parallel processing, and mixed concurrency models to construct robust architectures that meet performance and scalability goals.

A fundamental approach to composing asynchronous operations involves the careful selection and combination of Promise combinators. The `Promise.all` method is effective when several operations are independent but require aggregation. However, advanced scenarios may demand fine-tuned control over the ordering of operations. In sequential compositions, operations are invoked one after the other, each dependent on the successful resolution of the previous result. For instance, consider the case where a configuration fetched from a remote server informs subsequent requests. Utilizing `async/await` to structure these operations yields a more linear and maintainable flow:

```
async function initializeApplication(configUrl: string): Promise<void
    > {
    try {
        const config = await fetchConfig(configUrl);
        // Configuration is required for database initialization
        const dbConnection = await connectToDatabase(config.
    dbSettings);
        // Further operations using established database connection
        const initialData = await loadInitialData(dbConnection,
    config.initialQuery);
```

148

```
        console.log('Application initialized with data:', initialData
    );
    } catch (error) {
        console.error('Initialization failed:', error);
        throw error;
    }
}
```

In contrast, scenarios where multiple operations can be executed concurrently may benefit from parallel composition. The Promise.allSettled and Promise.race combinators provide mechanisms to handle varying levels of dependency. When operations are independent but require a combined result, it is essential to manage error states accordingly. The following example demonstrates parallel execution with error resilience by aggregating results, even in the presence of failures:

```
async function fetchMultipleResources(urls: string[]): Promise<any[]>
    {
    const results = await Promise.allSettled(urls.map(url =>
    fetchResource(url)));
    return results.map(result => {
        if (result.status === 'fulfilled') {
            return result.value;
        } else {
            // Log error and assign a fallback value
            console.error('Resource fetch error:', result.reason);
            return null;
        }
    });
}
```

For complex workflows, it is common to encounter mixed execution patterns where batches of operations run concurrently, followed by sequential processing of aggregated outcomes. Consider an advanced scenario involving data enrichment: multiple sources are queried in parallel for raw data, and once the data is aggregated, subsequent sequential transformations are applied to integrate and normalize the results. The orchestration of such a pipeline requires careful management of state and error conditions. The following example illustrates a composite operation that blends concurrency with sequential transformation stages:

```typescript
async function enrichData(dataIds: number[]): Promise<any[]> {
    try {
        // Stage 1: Parallel fetching of raw data from multiple
    sources
        const rawDataPromises = dataIds.map(id => fetchRawData(id));
        const rawResults = await Promise.all(rawDataPromises);

        // Stage 2: Sequential data enrichment, where each step may
    depend on previous transformations
        let enrichedData = [];
        for (const rawItem of rawResults) {
            // Each rawItem is further processed
            const cleanData = await cleanDataItem(rawItem);
            const extendedData = await extendDataWithMetadata(
    cleanData);
            enrichedData.push(extendedData);
        }
        return enrichedData;
    } catch (error) {
        console.error('Data enrichment process failed:', error);
        throw error;
    }
}
```

Another advanced technique employs higher-order functions to encapsulate asynchronous control flow patterns. Rather than writing boilerplate code repeatedly, developers can abstract common composition patterns into reusable functions. A frequently encountered pattern is the conditional branching of asynchronous operations based on intermediate results. For example, a function might need to decide whether to retry an operation, use a fallback path, or continue with subsequent operations based on computed metrics. The following generic function

150

demonstrates a compositional pattern where an asynchronous operation is conditionally retried or passed through:

```
async function conditionalRetry<T>(
    operation: () => Promise<T>,
    shouldRetry: (result: T) => boolean,
    maxRetries: number
): Promise<T> {
    let attempt = 0;
    while (attempt < maxRetries) {
        try {
            const result = await operation();
            if (!shouldRetry(result)) {
                return result;
            }
        } catch (error) {
            console.error('Operation error on attempt', attempt + 1,
        ':', error);
            // Optionally inspect error to decide retry eligibility
        }
        attempt++;
    }
    throw new Error('Operation failed after maximum retries');
}
```

This compositional pattern is further extensible when combined with cancellation or timeout strategies, ensuring that a long-running operation does not stall the entire workflow. For instance, combining a promise race with a timeout promise allows asynchronous operations to fail fast, enabling higher-level orchestration logic to decide on alternative strategies. Advanced composition often includes the interleaving of cancellation tokens to allow for the graceful shutdown of sub-operations when the overall context is no longer relevant:

```
async function fetchWithTimeout(url: string, timeout: number):
    Promise<any> {
    const timeoutPromise = new Promise((_, reject) =>
        setTimeout(() => reject(new Error('Timeout exceeded')),
    timeout)
    );
```

151

```
    return Promise.race([fetchResource(url), timeoutPromise]);
}

async function executeBatch(urls: string[], timeout: number): Promise
    <any[]> {
    const batchPromises = urls.map(url => fetchWithTimeout(url,
    timeout));
    return Promise.all(batchPromises);
}
```

For highly dynamic systems, it often becomes necessary to compose asynchronous operations in a way that elegantly handles dependencies among operations that may not be known at design time—dynamic composition. Using factories and registries for asynchronous behaviors allows developers to add, remove, or modify individual operations at runtime. This pattern is particularly useful in microservice architectures where orchestration may depend on runtime discovery of service capabilities or load balancing across multiple endpoints.

```
interface AsyncOperation {
    (input: any): Promise<any>;
}

class OperationRegistry {
    private operations: Map<string, AsyncOperation> = new Map();

    register(name: string, op: AsyncOperation): void {
        this.operations.set(name, op);
    }

    async executeSequence(initialInput: any, sequence: string[]):
    Promise<any> {
        let current = initialInput;
        for (const name of sequence) {
            const operation = this.operations.get(name);
            if (!operation) {
                throw new Error(`Operation ${name} not found in
    registry`);
            }
            current = await operation(current);
```

```
        }
        return current;
    }
}

const registry = new OperationRegistry();
registry.register('fetchData', async (input) => await fetchData(input
    ));
registry.register('transformData', async (input) => {
    // Example transformation logic
    return { transformed: true, ...input };
});
registry.register('validateData', async (input) => {
    if (!input.transformed) {
        throw new Error('Invalid data format');
    }
    return input;
});

registry.executeSequence('https://api.example.com/data', ['fetchData
    ', 'transformData', 'validateData'])
    .then(result => console.log('Final result:', result))
    .catch(error => console.error('Sequence execution failed:', error
    ));
```

Error propagation in composed asynchronous operations requires careful orchestration to ensure that failures in one part of the pipeline do not inadvertently cascade into unrelated operations. In such cases, adopting error isolation techniques—such as wrapping individual promises with error handlers or using combinators that return all results with status tags—enables selective handling and logging. Aggregate error objects, as shown earlier, can encapsulate multiple failure scenarios in a single exception that provides detailed insights into which specific sub-operation did not succeed.

Another aspect of composing asynchronous operations is leveraging design patterns such as the orchestrator or mediator when the interactions between various components become too complex to be man-

aged by simple chaining. An orchestrator pattern centrally manages
the flow of asynchronous tasks, determining the sequence based on
dynamic conditions, external triggers, or resource constraints. This
pattern is particularly effective in distributed systems where individual components operate asynchronously and must coordinate state
changes. Implementing an orchestrator often entails a state machine
that triggers asynchronous transitions based on the completion of operations and received events.

```typescript
enum OperationStatus {
    Pending,
    InProgress,
    Completed,
    Failed
}

interface OperationState {
    name: string;
    status: OperationStatus;
    data?: any;
    error?: Error;
}

class AsyncOrchestrator {
    private state: OperationState[] = [];

    async execute(operations: { name: string; operation: () =>
      Promise<any> }[]): Promise<OperationState[]> {
        for (const op of operations) {
            const opState: OperationState = { name: op.name, status:
        OperationStatus.Pending };
            this.state.push(opState);
            try {
                opState.status = OperationStatus.InProgress;
                const result = await op.operation();
                opState.status = OperationStatus.Completed;
                opState.data = result;
            } catch (err) {
                opState.status = OperationStatus.Failed;
                opState.error = err as Error;
                // Optionally decide whether to continue with
```

```
        subsequent operations
            }
        }
        return this.state;
    }
}


const orchestrator = new AsyncOrchestrator();
orchestrator.execute([
    { name: 'Operation1', operation: async () => await fetchData('
    https://api.example.com/one') },
    { name: 'Operation2', operation: async () => await fetchData('
    https://api.example.com/two') },
    { name: 'Operation3', operation: async () => await fetchData('
    https://api.example.com/three') }
]).then(finalState => {
    console.log('Orchestration state:', finalState);
}).catch(error => {
    console.error('Orchestration failed:', error);
});
```

When composing asynchronous operations, diligent attention must be paid to performance optimizations, particularly in high-load scenarios. Batching similar requests', debouncing operations to avoid redundant calls, and applying backpressure techniques are crucial in preventing resource exhaustion. Developers should employ profiling tools to monitor asynchronous execution timelines and ensure that orchestrated chains do not introduce unexpected latency.

In summary, mastering the composition of asynchronous operations empowers advanced TypeScript programmers to develop sophisticated, resilient, and scalable applications. By judiciously combining sequential and parallel patterns, abstracting common workflows into higher-order functions, and orchestrating dynamic operation sequences, developers can overcome the challenges associated with asynchronous dependencies and error propagation. Such skills are imperative for modern applications that must handle complex, real-world

155

interactions in distributed or event-driven environments.

## 3.7   Concurrency Management in TypeScript

Concurrency in TypeScript applications is a complex topic that requires a comprehensive strategy to avoid race conditions, optimize
performance, and efficiently allocate limited resources. A deep understanding of the JavaScript event loop, microtasks, and the asynchronous runtime is imperative for designing systems where multiple asynchronous operations operate concurrently without interfer-
ence. Managing concurrency effectively involves strategies such as
throttling, debouncing, mutexes, semaphores, and lock-free designs to
ensure that shared data is accessed in a controlled manner.

Advanced applications frequently confront race conditions when
several asynchronous operations attempt to access or update
shared state simultaneously. Even though JavaScript is inherently
single-threaded in the browser, asynchronous operations can still
lead to non-deterministic behaviors as a result of the interleaving
of microtasks and event callbacks. For example, two asynchronous
operations might fetch and update a shared resource, with one
update inadvertently overwriting the other. A fundamental principle
is to minimize side effects and encapsulate state transitions. When
shared state is unavoidable, it is critical to implement mechanisms
that enforce mutual exclusion.

A common concurrency control mechanism in asynchronous programming is the use of a mutex. Implementing a mutex in TypeScript involves the creation of a promise-based locking mechanism that allows
only one asynchronous function to execute a critical section at a time.

Consider the following implementation of a simple mutex:

```
class Mutex {
    private mutex = Promise.resolve();

    lock<T>(fn: () => Promise<T>): Promise<T> {
        // Chain a new operation to the current mutex promise
        this.mutex = this.mutex.then(() => fn().catch((err) => {
            // Ensure the error does not break the chain
            throw err;
        }));
        return this.mutex;
    }
}


// Usage example for a shared counter update
let counter = 0;
const mutex = new Mutex();

async function updateCounter(): Promise<void> {
    await mutex.lock(async () => {
        const current = counter;
        // Simulate asynchronous delay
        await new Promise(resolve => setTimeout(resolve, 100));
        counter = current + 1;
    });
}


Promise.all([updateCounter(), updateCounter(), updateCounter()])
    .then(() => console.log('Final counter value:', counter))
    .catch(err => console.error('Error:', err));
```

This mutex implementation serializes operations that update a shared variable. In scenarios requiring a more fine-grained control, semaphore patterns can be applied to limit concurrency to a given number of parallel processes. A semaphore controls access to a resource that can be shared by multiple tasks simultaneously but within a fixed bound. The following example implements a simple semaphore:

```
class Semaphore {
```

```typescript
    private tasks: Array<() => void> = [];
    private counter: number;

    constructor(private readonly max: number) {
        this.counter = max;
    }

    async acquire(): Promise<() => void> {
        if (this.counter > 0) {
            this.counter--;
            return () => {
                this.counter++;
                if (this.tasks.length > 0) {
                    // When a slot frees up, execute the oldest
queued task.
                    const nextTask = this.tasks.shift();
                    if (nextTask) nextTask();
                }
            };
        }
        return new Promise(resolve => {
            this.tasks.push(() => {
                this.counter--;
                resolve(() => {
                    this.counter++;
                    if (this.tasks.length > 0) {
                        const nextTask = this.tasks.shift();
                        if (nextTask) nextTask();
                    }
                });
            });
        });
    }
}


// Example usage to throttle concurrent API calls
async function throttledFetch(url: string, semaphore: Semaphore):
    Promise<Response> {
    const release = await semaphore.acquire();
    try {
        return await fetch(url);
    } finally {
        release();
    }
}
```

```
const semaphore = new Semaphore(3); // Limit concurrency to 3
const urls = [
    'https://api.example.com/data1',
    'https://api.example.com/data2',
    'https://api.example.com/data3',
    'https://api.example.com/data4',
    'https://api.example.com/data5'
];

Promise.all(urls.map(url => throttledFetch(url, semaphore)))
    .then(responses => Promise.all(responses.map(res => res.json())))
    .then(data => console.log('Fetched data:', data))
    .catch(err => console.error('Fetch error:', err));
```

When operations rely on user input or external events, techniques such as debouncing and throttling are essential to reduce unnecessary processing. Debouncing postpones execution until a period of inactivity is observed, while throttling ensures that an operation is executed at most once per specified time interval. These patterns, though simple, are critical for avoiding performance bottlenecks in environments with high-frequency events. The following example demonstrates a debounce function implemented in TypeScript:

```
function debounce<T extends (...args: any[]) => void>(fn: T, wait:
    number): T {
    let timeout: ReturnType<typeof setTimeout>;
    return function(this: any, ...args: any[]) {
        clearTimeout(timeout);
        timeout = setTimeout(() => fn.apply(this, args), wait);
    } as T;
}

// Example: Debounced input handler
const processInput = (value: string) => {
    console.log('Processing input:', value);
};

const debouncedProcessInput = debounce(processInput, 300);
```

159

```
// Simulate rapid input events
['a', 'ab', 'abc', 'abcd'].forEach((val, index) => {
    setTimeout(() => debouncedProcessInput(val), index * 100);
});
```

Beyond classic concurrency control, optimizing performance in asynchronous TypeScript applications also pertains to reducing lock contention and designing lock-free algorithms. In some cases, immutable data structures, functional programming approaches, and state isolation can eliminate the need for locks entirely. By adopting an immutable design, shared state becomes inherently thread-safe, which is particularly beneficial when operations are divided across multiple web workers or in server-side environments using Node.js clusters.

When using web workers to manage CPU-bound tasks off the main thread, concurrency is achieved through message passing rather than shared memory. Advanced developers may design a worker pool that dynamically allocates tasks and aggregates results, thereby leveraging multicore processing environments to avoid blocking the event loop. A basic worker pool implementation is shown below:

```
// WorkerPool.ts
export class WorkerPool {
    private availableWorkers: Worker[] = [];
    private busyWorkers: Set<Worker> = new Set();

    constructor(private workerScriptUrl: string, private poolSize:
    number) {
        for (let i = 0; i < poolSize; i++) {
            const worker = new Worker(workerScriptUrl);
            this.availableWorkers.push(worker);
        }
    }

    async runTask<T, U>(taskData: T): Promise<U> {
        const worker = await this.acquireWorker();
        return new Promise<U>((resolve, reject) => {
```

160

```typescript
            worker.onmessage = (event) => {
                this.releaseWorker(worker);
                resolve(event.data);
            };
            worker.onerror = (error) => {
                this.releaseWorker(worker);
                reject(error);
            };
            worker.postMessage(taskData);
        });
    }

    private async acquireWorker(): Promise<Worker> {
        if (this.availableWorkers.length > 0) {
            const worker = this.availableWorkers.shift() as Worker;
            this.busyWorkers.add(worker);
            return worker;
        }
        return new Promise(resolve => {
            const interval = setInterval(() => {
                if (this.availableWorkers.length > 0) {
                    clearInterval(interval);
                    const worker = this.availableWorkers.shift() as
    Worker;
                    this.busyWorkers.add(worker);
                    resolve(worker);
                }
            }, 50);
        });
    }

    private releaseWorker(worker: Worker): void {
        this.busyWorkers.delete(worker);
        this.availableWorkers.push(worker);
    }
}
```

This worker pool design helps in managing concurrency by limiting
the number of active workers and ensuring efficient task distribution
among available threads.

Another aspect of concurrency management involves the correct scheduling of asynchronous tasks to optimize CPU usage and I/O responsiveness. Utilizing microtask management through `Promise.resolve()` or `queueMicrotask()`, developers can enforce immediate execution of high-priority tasks without preempting the main execution thread excessively. Understanding when to use macrotasks versus microtasks is critical; for instance, UI updates should not be delayed by heavy computations running in microtasks, lest they block the rendering cycle.

```typescript
function scheduleMicrotask(task: () => void): void {
    queueMicrotask(task);
}

function heavyComputation(): Promise<number> {
    return new Promise(resolve => {
        // Simulate non-blocking heavy computation using microtasks
        scheduleMicrotask(() => {
            let result = 0;
            for (let i = 0; i < 1e6; i++) {
                result += i;
            }
            resolve(result);
        });
    });
}

heavyComputation().then(result => console.log('Computation result:',
    result));
```

In scenarios that require combining both concurrency management and composition of asynchronous operations, orchestrating global state updates becomes more challenging. Techniques such as transactional updates with optimistic concurrency control can mitigate race conditions by verifying state consistency before committing changes. Advanced designs utilize versioning, conflict detection, and rollback mechanisms to ensure that even if multiple operations attempt to update shared state, only consistent changes are finalized.

162

Performance tuning in concurrent environments also necessitates continuous monitoring and profiling. Instrumenting critical sections of code with performance metrics, such as timing measurements and error rates, can reveal contention points and guide optimizations. Tools like Chrome DevTools, Node.js profiling, and logging frameworks that support asynchronous trace correlation are essential for diagnosing bottlenecks.

Concurrency management in TypeScript further intersects with API design and modularity. Designing libraries and modules that inherently support concurrent operations simplifies client code and reduces the risk of race conditions. It is advisable to expose APIs that internally manage locks, queues, and cancellation behaviors rather than requiring consumers to implement these mechanisms ad hoc.

By integrating these strategies—promise combinators, mutexes, semaphores, debouncing, throttle controls, worker pools, microtask scheduling, and optimistic concurrency controls—advanced TypeScript developers can build highly performant, scalable, and robust applications. Such architectures ensure that even under intense loads and simultaneous operations, data integrity is protected and responsiveness is maintained, thereby aligning with the stringent requirements of modern, event-driven software systems.

# 4

# Chapter 4: Effective Use of Decorators and Metadata

*This chapter explores the use of decorators and metadata in TypeScript, covering class, method, property, and parameter decorators. It delves into metadata reflection capabilities and the creation of custom metadata using the reflect-metadata library. Additionally, it discusses combining decorators with dependency injection, enabling the development of flexible and modular applications.*

## 4.1  Understanding Decorator Patterns

The decorator pattern in TypeScript serves as both a syntactic and semantic mechanism to extend class functionality in a modular and declarative fashion. Its integration into TypeScript leverages the experimental metadata reflection API to enable behavior augmentation at runtime, allowing developers to enforce cross-cutting concerns such as logging, validation, and authorization directly at the declaration site. This section examines the foundational principles underlying decorators and explores sophisticated strategies for combining multiple decorators, optimizing runtime performance, and ensuring type safety in extensive codebases.

Decorators in TypeScript are implemented as higher-order functions operating upon class declarations, methods, properties, or parameters. They provide a mechanism to transform or extend the behavior of the annotated constructs without modifying the underlying implementation. The power of this pattern lies in its ability to capture and manipulate metadata, such as the types of method arguments or property descriptors, which supports advanced techniques such as dependency injection and aspect-oriented programming.

When designing decorators at an advanced level, it is essential to understand the composition of decorator factories versus direct decorator functions. A decorator factory is a higher-order function that returns a decorator function. The factory approach introduces configurability while encapsulating enhanced semantics alongside static type annotations. It is particularly useful when parameterization is paramount for enabling conditional behavior transformations or advanced logging mechanics. Consider the following example, which demonstrates a simple class decorator factory that logs instantiation details:

```
function LogClass(prefix: string) {
    return function<T extends { new (...args: any[]): {} }>(
    constructor: T): T {
        return class extends constructor {
            constructor(...args: any[]) {
                console.log(`${prefix} - Creating instance of ${
    constructor.name} with arguments:`, args);
                super(...args);
```

```
            }
        };
    };
}

@LogClass('DEBUG')
class SampleService {
    constructor(public dependency: string) {}
}
```

In the snippet above, the `LogClass` function is a decorator factory that accepts a prefix string for logging. The returned decorator function then intercepts the class instantiation process by extending the original class, thereby injecting logging behavior without altering the original business logic. This technique of wrapping classes via extension is robust and leverages polymorphic behavior, which is a key advantage of decorator patterns in object-oriented programming.

Beyond class decorators, similar patterns apply to methods, properties, and parameters, each with unique challenges. Method decorators allow the interception of function calls, providing hooks for pre-execution, post-execution, or even conditional execution based on runtime parameters. When working with method decorators, it is critical to manage the method bindings and context carefully to preserve the original method's intended behavior. Advanced implementations often require wrapping the method while preserving the original signature for compatibility with higher-order functions. An example that demonstrates a method decorator intended for performance measurement is provided below:

```
function MeasureExecutionTime(target: any, propertyKey: string,
    descriptor: PropertyDescriptor) {
    const originalMethod = descriptor.value;
    descriptor.value = function (...args: any[]) {
        const startTime = performance.now();
```

```
        const result = originalMethod.apply(this, args);
        const endTime = performance.now();
        console.log(`Execution time for ${propertyKey}: ${endTime -
    startTime}ms`);
        return result;
    };
    return descriptor;
}

class ComputationallyIntensive {
    @MeasureExecutionTime
    compute(data: number[]): number {
        // Complex computation
        return data.reduce((acc, val) => acc + Math.sqrt(val), 0);
    }
}
```

In this code, the `MeasureExecutionTime` decorator intercepts method calls to calculate and log the duration of the execution window. Notice that the original method is preserved, and its context is bound via `apply(this, args)`. This pattern safeguards the integrity of the method's logic while providing performance insights in production scenarios.

Property decorators introduce additional complexity as they do not natively expose the underlying property value. Instead, they provide access to the property descriptor during declaration time. Advanced property decorators are often combined with a backing store mechanism to intercept property access and assignment. This approach facilitates lazy instantiation, caching, or even validation. An illustrative example is given below:

```
function ValidateRange(min: number, max: number) {
    return function(target: any, propertyKey: string) {
        let value: number;
        Object.defineProperty(target, propertyKey, {
            get: function() {
                return value;
```

```
            },
        set: function(newValue: number) {
            if (newValue < min || newValue > max) {
                throw new RangeError(`Value of ${propertyKey}
    must be between ${min} and ${max}`);
            }
            value = newValue;
        },
        enumerable: true,
        configurable: true
    });
    };
}


class Sensor {
    @ValidateRange(0, 100)
    public reading: number;

    constructor(initialReading: number) {
        this.reading = initialReading;
    }
}
```

The ValidateRange decorator ensures that the value assigned to the property falls within a specified numeric range. By redefining the property descriptor via Object.defineProperty, the decorator enforces constraints while maintaining standard property access semantics.

Parameter decorators, although less common in everyday applications, provide a means to modify or inspect parameters passed to a method. They can be used for runtime injection of metadata, crucial in frameworks that rely on dependency injection or custom parameter parsing strategies. When using parameter decorators, the target method's metadata is augmented, enabling rigorous analysis or transformation before the function execution context is established. An advanced use case involves injecting configuration data or coupling parameters to external metadata repositories.

The order of execution for decorators is non-trivial. During the class definition phase, decorators are applied in a bottom-up fashion, meaning that for multiple decorators affecting the same member, the decorator that is closest to the method or property in the source file is applied first. This ordering can have a profound impact on the final behavior and requires careful consideration when layering multiple decorators. In complex systems, decorators may be chained to accomplish various interdependent tasks. Developers should design these chains to be commutative wherever possible to avoid subtle bugs arising from non-deterministic execution side effects.

An effective strategy for combining multiple decorators is to ensure separation of concerns. Each decorator should fulfill a single responsibility to maximize reusability and to mitigate the risk of hidden dependencies between decorators. For instance, separating logging logic from error handling allows each decorator to operate independently, thereby easing the debugging and maintenance process. In performance-critical applications, it is equally important to measure the overhead introduced by decorator layers. Profiling tools and static analysis can be used to detect and quantify any runtime penalties.

From a type-safety perspective, modern TypeScript versions provide advanced static type inference that can be extended to decorator factories. However, decorators can occasionally break the type inference chain if not meticulously applied. It becomes essential to use generic typing in decorator implementations to maintain type fidelity. This is particularly crucial when decorators are used to modify class constructors or methods with complex signatures. Advanced type constraints and conditional types can be leveraged to ensure decorators do not inadvertently widen or narrow types, which may result in hard-to-diagnose errors during compile-time.

Managing metadata within decorators is another advanced technique that has profound implications for reflective programming. Type-Script's experimental support via reflect-metadata allows developers to define custom metadata on class elements that can be retrieved at runtime to interconnect disparate modules in a loosely coupled manner. This capability is vital for building frameworks that require dependency injection or runtime type checks. Utilizing metadata effectively can provide a robust reflection system that improves modularity and integration testing.

A sophisticated application of metadata can be observed in scenarios where decorators contribute to a dependency injection framework. Here, metadata is used to annotate class constructors and properties with dependency tokens, which are then resolved at runtime. The dynamic registration and instantiation of dependencies require a thorough understanding of both the decorator and metadata APIs to ensure correctness. In such systems, decorators not only augment functionality but also serve as documentation, providing insight into dependency graphs that can be statically validated.

Advanced programming with decorators demands careful consideration of execution context, memory management, and performance overhead. The dynamic wrapping of methods and properties may introduce subtle inefficiencies if not designed with optimization in mind. Developers are advised to conduct rigorous benchmarking, employ lazy initialization techniques, and utilize inline caching where feasible. Many performance pitfalls arise from repeated metadata lookups or redundant logging operations, which can be alleviated through the careful structuring of decorator composition.

One optimization trick involves minimizing the number of times metadata is queried by caching results within the decorated function's
closure. This caching mechanism can be employed to store results
from `Reflect.getMetadata` calls, thereby reducing overhead during
repeated accesses. Another technical consideration is to utilize property descriptors to enforce immutability in areas where repeated assignment is unnecessary—to this end, marking properties as non-
configurable or non-writable at runtime can provide both safety and
performance gains.

```
function CacheMetadata(target: any, propertyKey: string, descriptor:
    PropertyDescriptor) {
    const metadataKey = `__cached_metadata_${propertyKey}`;
    const originalMethod = descriptor.value;
    descriptor.value = function (...args: any[]) {
        if (!this[metadataKey]) {
            this[metadataKey] = Reflect.getMetadata('design:type',
    target, propertyKey);
        }
        // Optionally perform operations using cached metadata
        return originalMethod.apply(this, args);
    };
    return descriptor;
}
```

This example of `CacheMetadata` demonstrates an advanced optimization where metadata is stored locally within the instance, thereby reducing repetitive calls to the reflection API. Such optimizations become crucial when deploying applications at scale or in performance-
sensitive environments.

The decorator pattern, when properly leveraged, provides a robust
framework for implementing aspect-oriented programming within
TypeScript. Its effective use requires mastery of both JavaScript's pro-
totypal inheritance model and TypeScript's type system. Through

careful design of decorator factories, rigorous adherence to separation of concerns, and thoughtful composition of multiple decorators, advanced developers can exploit this paradigm to write clean, modular, and highly extensible code.

## 4.2 Creating and Using Class Decorators

Class decorators in TypeScript provide a mechanism to systematically extend or modify the behavior of classes at the time of declaration. This technique allows for dynamic wrapping of constructors, enabling cross-cutting concerns to be injected in a centralized manner. Class decorators are executed when the class is defined, and a decorator function receives the class constructor as its primary input, permitting modification or the creation of a new constructor function while preserving the prototype chain. Advanced usage demands strict adherence to both the static type system and a deep understanding of JavaScript's execution model.

In defining a class decorator, one typically chooses between invoking a simple decorator function or creating a decorator factory— the latter enables parameterization. The following example shows the structure of a decorator factory that logs instantiation and supports conditional property injection:

```
function Injectable(prefix: string) {
    return function<T extends { new (...args: any[]): {} }>(
    constructor: T): T {
        return class extends constructor {
            constructor(...args: any[]) {
                console.log(`${prefix} - Instantiating ${constructor.
    name} with arguments:`, args);
                super(...args);
                // Additional injection or initialization logic can
```

```
be inserted here.
        Object.defineProperty(this, 'injectedProperty', {
            value: "InjectedValue",
            writable: false,
            configurable: false
        });
    }
  };
};
}
```

In this example, the decorator factory `Injectable` returns a new constructor that wraps the original class constructor. By extending the class, the decorator provides access to both the instance and constructor logic, while ensuring that any new behavior is appended without altering the base class. The code leverages the `Object.defineProperty` method to inject critical metadata or configuration in a controlled manner. It is imperative to ensure that the extended class preserves the prototype chain so that any instance method or inheritance structure remains intact, a practice supported by the use of the `extends` keyword.

When employing decorators to modify class behavior, a critical consideration is the handling of constructor arguments. Unauthorized modifications or assumptions about argument structure can lead to inconsistencies, especially in complex dependency injection frameworks. Therefore, it is useful to encapsulate any logic such as argument validation or sanitization within the decorator, decoupling this functionality from the business logic of the class. Access control, policy enforcement, or even error handling can be embedded seamlessly within the decorator.

Advanced techniques involve maintaining type safety across decorator boundaries. In TypeScript, ensuring that decorator modifications do not inadvertently widen or alter type signatures requires explicit generic constraints. For instance, one can define decorators that extend classes while preserving constructor signatures by using generic constraints to bind the types:

```
function WithTimestamp<T extends { new (...args: any[]): {} }>(
    constructor: T): T {
    return class extends constructor {
        public readonly createdAt: Date = new Date();
    };
}

@WithTimestamp
class DomainEntity {
    constructor(public id: number) {}
}
```

Here, the `WithTimestamp` decorator extends the class definition by introducing a read-only property `createdAt`. The generic constraint ensures that the extended class maintains a compatible instantiation signature. This method not only augments the class at runtime but also provides compile-time guarantees regarding the class structure, fostering robust and scalable application design.

Developers must also consider decorator composition. When multiple class decorators are applied, the order of execution follows a bottom-up sequence on the class declaration. Therefore, subsequent decorators must be carefully designed to either anticipate or verify the state applied by prior decorators. A useful trick involves using composition techniques where the functionality of multiple decorators is merged into a single cohesive unit. One approach is to design a higher-order decorator that accepts an arbitrary number of decorator functions and applies them sequentially. A sample implementation can be seen below:

```
function ComposeDecorators(...decorators: Function[]) {
    return function<T extends { new (...args: any[]): {} }>(
```

175

```
    constructor: T): T {
        return decorators.reduce((prevConstructor, decorator) => {
            return decorator(prevConstructor);
        }, constructor);
    };
}


function Fallback<T extends { new (...args: any[]): {} }>(constructor
    : T): T {
    return class extends constructor {
        public fallbackMethod() {
            console.log('Fallback method executed.');
        }
    };
}


function Audit<T extends { new (...args: any[]): {} }>(constructor: T
    ): T {
    return class extends constructor {
        constructor(...args: any[]) {
            super(...args);
            console.log(`Audit: ${constructor.name} instantiated.`);
        }
    };
}


@ComposeDecorators(Fallback, Audit)
class BusinessService {
    constructor(public serviceName: string) {}
}
```

With ComposeDecorators, the decorators Fallback and Audit are applied in a predictable sequence to the BusinessService class. This composition ensures that each decorator operates with full knowledge of the prior modifications, thereby enabling more complex layering of responsibilities. Advanced usage of such techniques demands rigorous testing and static analysis to avoid unforeseen side effects.

The use of class decorators also extends to facilitating dependency injection frameworks. In such contexts, decorators annotate classes

176

to signal that they are candidates for service resolution within an inversion-of-control container. This marks a departure from manual service instantiation and helps manage the lifecycle of objects in large systems. The decorator can embed metadata required by the container, such as identifiers or scope indicators, using the experimental `reflect-metadata` API:

```
import "reflect-metadata";

function Service(identifier: string) {
    return function<T extends { new (...args: any[]): {} }>(
    constructor: T): T {
        Reflect.defineMetadata("service:identifier", identifier,
        constructor);
        return constructor;
    };
}

@Service("UserService")
class UserService {
    constructor(private readonly repository: any) {}
}
```

Employing metadata in this manner creates a clear contract between the class definition and the dependency injection container. The container can retrieve the metadata with `Reflect.getMetadata("service:identifier", target)` and dynamically resolve instances. For advanced systems, combining such patterns with lazy loading, scoped injection, and circular dependency resolution becomes critical. Developers can extend the basic pattern by including error handling and fallback strategies if the service resolution fails or if metadata is incomplete.

Error handling and diagnostics are an area that benefits from integrating decorators. For example, when constructing a new instance or modifying class methods, runtime errors may be intercepted earlier.

177

Class decorators can wrap constructors within try-catch blocks or incorporate logging to capture instantiation anomalies. It is advisable to design decorators that do not obscure underlying errors; rather, they should supplement the error stack with additional contextual information to aid debugging. An optimized approach involves creating decorators that sanitize input parameters before propagating them to the actual constructor logic, thereby reducing the risk of inconsistencies:

```
function SanitizeInput<T extends { new (...args: any[]): {} }>(
    constructor: T): T {
   return class extends constructor {
       constructor(...args: any[]) {
           const sanitizedArgs = args.map(arg => {
               return typeof arg === 'string' ? arg.trim() : arg;
           });
           super(...sanitizedArgs);
       }
    };
}
```

This SanitizeInput decorator exemplifies the integration of validation logic at the class level. When combined with other decorators within a composition, the overall class definition becomes significantly more resilient to malformed input without cluttering the business logic.

Performance considerations also command an advanced approach in designing class decorators. While the layering of decorators enriches the functionality, each additional layer imposes a slight overhead at runtime. A proven strategy to mitigate this impact is to apply caching mechanisms or employ conditional logic that bypasses decorator logic when not needed. Profiling and benchmarking become essential tools to ensure that the benefits of abstraction do not incur unacceptable performance costs. For example, in performance-sensitive modules, one might cache metadata or precompute invariant values:

```
function OptimizedService<T extends { new (...args: any[]): {} }>(
    constructor: T): T {
    let cachedMetadata: any = null;
    return class extends constructor {
        constructor(...args: any[]) {
            if (!cachedMetadata) {
                cachedMetadata = Reflect.getMetadata("custom:info",
    constructor) || {};
            }
            super(...args);
            // Utilize cached metadata for additional initialization.
        }
    };
}
```

In this code snippet, the OptimizedService decorator demonstrates a rudimentary caching mechanism that minimizes redundant metadata lookups. Such design considerations are crucial when deploying decorators on classes that are instantiated frequently, ensuring that the performance trade-offs remain minimal.

Designing class decorators to support extensibility and reusability requires careful documentation and rigorous type testing. Advanced patterns incorporate extensive unit tests and static type validation—techniques that help detect any divergence from expected behaviors at compile-time. Utilizing TypeScript's powerful type inference system allows developers to design decorators that guarantee input and output types remain consistent. Combining these features with tools such as tslint or eslint, along with type-checking configurations, is a standard practice among expert programmers.

The integration and composition of class decorators in a TypeScript environment reflect a paradigm shift towards highly modular and scalable software architectures. By embedding key responsibilities such as logging, validation, dependency injection, and error handling directly

179

into class definitions, decorators bridge the gap between declarative design and dynamic runtime behavior. When used correctly, class decorators offer an elegant solution that minimizes boilerplate, encapsulates cross-cutting concerns, and delivers robust, traceable code.

This integration of class decorators significantly enhances maintainability. Advanced programmers are thus equipped to harness the full potential of decorator-based designs, ensuring that large-scale TypeScript applications remain flexible, testable, and efficient.

## 4.3   Method and Property Decorators

Method and property decorators in TypeScript offer precise control over the behavior of class member functions and properties. They intercept member definitions, enabling transformation, instrumentation, or validation at runtime. Advanced usage of these decorators takes advantage of reflection metadata, dynamic descriptor manipulation, and closure-based state caching to ensure efficient augmentations without violating encapsulation or type safety.

Method decorators in TypeScript receive three parameters: the target object, the property key, and the property descriptor. The property descriptor represents the underlying method definition and enables the decorator to override, wrap, or extend the original function. A common approach in method decoration is to wrap the original method while preserving its signature. This approach is used to insert pre- and post-execution logic, for cases such as logging execution time, managing transactions, or enforcing security measures. A detailed transformative example is provided below:

```
function Transactional(target: any, propertyKey: string, descriptor:
```

180

```
    PropertyDescriptor) {
    const originalMethod = descriptor.value;
    descriptor.value = function (...args: any[]) {
        console.log(`Transaction started for ${propertyKey}`);
        try {
            const result = originalMethod.apply(this, args);
            console.log(`Transaction committed for ${propertyKey}`);
            return result;
        } catch (error) {
            console.error(`Transaction rolled back for ${propertyKey
    }`, error);
            throw error;
        }
    };
    return descriptor;
}


class DatabaseService {
    @Transactional
    public executeQuery(query: string): any {
        // Simulate query execution with potential error handling
        if (query.trim() === '') {
            throw new Error('Query cannot be empty');
        }
        return { data: 'Result Data' };
    }
}
```

In this example, the Transactional decorator wraps the
executeQuery method, adding logging and error handling semantics
that are crucial in enterprise applications. By intercepting the method
call, the decorator encapsulates transaction control mechanisms
without altering the underlying business logic.

For performance-critical applications, it is important to ensure that
the overhead introduced by these wrappers is minimized. Techniques
such as caching function results or conditionally bypassing instrumentation when in production mode can be layered into decorators. For
instance, a method decorator may cache the result of computationally

expensive operations:

```
function Memoize(target: any, propertyKey: string, descriptor:
    PropertyDescriptor) {
    const originalMethod = descriptor.value;
    const cacheKey = Symbol(`__cache_${propertyKey}`);
    descriptor.value = function (...args: any[]) {
        if (!this[cacheKey]) {
            this[cacheKey] = new Map();
        }
        const argKey = JSON.stringify(args);
        if (this[cacheKey].has(argKey)) {
            return this[cacheKey].get(argKey);
        }
        const result = originalMethod.apply(this, args);
        this[cacheKey].set(argKey, result);
        return result;
    };
    return descriptor;
}

class IntensiveComputation {
    @Memoize
    public calculate(value: number): number {
        // Emulate heavy computation process.
        let result = 0;
        for (let i = 0; i < value; i++) {
            result += Math.sqrt(i);
        }
        return result;
    }
}
```

This `Memoize` decorator employs a map stored in the instance to cache computed results, thereby reducing redundant executions. Advanced developers must consider serialization overhead when using JSON.stringify for key generation and may explore custom hash functions to improve performance and accommodate non-serializable parameters.

Property decorators receive only two parameters: the target object and the property key. They do not provide direct access to the property descriptor for an instance property, necessitating a different approach to manipulate or observe property behavior. A common tactic is to redefine property accessors using `Object.defineProperty`, thereby intercepting both get and set operations. This is particularly useful for enforcing invariants or for triggering side effects on property mutation. The example below illustrates a property decorator that enforces string length constraints:

```
function LimitLength(maxLength: number) {
    return function (target: any, propertyKey: string): void {
        let value: string;
        Object.defineProperty(target, propertyKey, {
            get: function() {
                return value;
            },
            set: function(newValue: string) {
                if (newValue.length > maxLength) {
                    throw new RangeError(`Value of ${propertyKey}
cannot exceed ${maxLength} characters.`);
                }
                value = newValue;
            },
            enumerable: true,
            configurable: true
        });
    };
}

class Message {
    @LimitLength(50)
    public content: string;

    constructor(content: string) {
        this.content = content;
    }
}
```

In this scenario, the `LimitLength` decorator redefines the `content` property in the `Message` class by providing custom getter and setter

183

functions. This pattern ensures that the length constraint is enforced
at each assignment, maintaining invariants even if the property is modified externally.

Combining method and property decorators within the same class further elevates the complexity and power of these constructs. In scenarios where both behaviors are interdependent, layered decorators must
be carefully organized to ensure that their operations do not conflict.
For instance, a property decorator that sanitizes input may need to run
before a method decorator that logs input parameters. While Type-
Script does not allow explicit control over decorator execution order
for different member types, disciplined design and explicit documentation of contracts are necessary to guarantee intended interactivity.

An advanced approach to property decorators involves integrating metadata reflection for richer introspection. Using the
reflect-metadata library, developers can store and later retrieve
metadata that describes property types, validation rules, or
transformation schemas. Such metadata, when combined with
a transformation pipeline, allows for sophisticated runtime data
validation. Consider the following example where a property
decorator leverages metadata to validate values:

```
import "reflect-metadata";

function ValidateByMetadata(target: any, propertyKey: string): void {
    let value: any;
    const type = Reflect.getMetadata("design:type", target,
    propertyKey);
    Object.defineProperty(target, propertyKey, {
        get: function() {
            return value;
        },
        set: function(newValue: any) {
            if (!(newValue instanceof type) && typeof newValue !==
        type.name.toLowerCase()) {
```

```
                    throw new TypeError(`Value of ${propertyKey} must be
        of type ${type.name}`);
                }
                value = newValue;
            },
            enumerable: true,
            configurable: true
        });
}

class Config {
    @ValidateByMetadata
    public timeout: number;

    @ValidateByMetadata
    public host: string;

    constructor(timeout: number, host: string) {
        this.timeout = timeout;
        this.host = host;
    }
}
```

Here, `ValidateByMetadata` retrieves the design type for a property at runtime and enforces that assigned values conform to this type. This technique opens the door to advanced, metadata-driven validation frameworks that scale efficiently across large codebases.

Additional advanced techniques include dynamically extending property behaviors. Developers may want to combine multiple property decorators or ensure that accessor modifications are idempotent. One trick is to store original descriptors in a weak map and allow decorators to chain their effects. In complex systems, it is beneficial to write decorators that merge with each other's metadata rather than overwriting it. For instance, a property may simultaneously require validation and sanitization. In such cases, composing decorators through higher-order functions ensures that each decorator's responsibilities are con-

185

tained and do not interfere with each other.

```
function ComposePropertyDecorators(...decorators: Array<(target: any,
    propertyKey: string) => void>) {
    return function(target: any, propertyKey: string) {
        decorators.forEach(decorator => decorator(target, propertyKey
    ));
    };
}


function Sanitize(target: any, propertyKey: string): void {
    let value: string;
    Object.defineProperty(target, propertyKey, {
        get: function() { return value; },
        set: function(newValue: string) {
            value = newValue.trim();
        },
        enumerable: true,
        configurable: true
    });
}


function ValidateNonEmpty(target: any, propertyKey: string): void {
    let value: string;
    Object.defineProperty(target, propertyKey, {
        get: function() { return value; },
        set: function(newValue: string) {
            if (newValue.trim() === '') {
                throw new Error(`${propertyKey} cannot be empty.`);
            }
            value = newValue;
        },
        enumerable: true,
        configurable: true
    });
}


class UserProfile {
    @ComposePropertyDecorators(Sanitize, ValidateNonEmpty)
    public username: string;

    constructor(username: string) {
        this.username = username;
    }
}
```

This composite decorator pattern demonstrates the integration of multiple property concerns in a coordinated fashion. Each decorator is applied sequentially, reinforcing modular design and enabling sophisticated combinations without tangled code.

Finally, the interaction between method and property decorators introduces considerations about runtime performance and state consistency. Whenever decorators add persistent state, such as caching or metadata storage, developers must be alert to memory usage patterns and lifecycle events. Complex decorators should be instrumented with profiling hooks and tested in isolation under various scenarios. Attention to detail in this area avoids memory leaks and ensures that decorator-induced side effects remain predictable and manageable.

By leveraging the inherent modularity of method and property decorators, advanced TypeScript developers are endowed with powerful tools to manage cross-cutting concerns. The techniques illustrated—ranging from execution wrapping and caching to metadata-driven validation and composite decoration—demonstrate a high level of control over both function invocation and state mutation. These approaches pave the way for creating robust, maintainable, and scalable applications by tightly integrating developer intent with runtime behavior, ultimately enabling codebases that are both expressive and resilient.

## 4.4 Leveraging Parameter Decorators

Parameter decorators in TypeScript provide a means of associating metadata with function parameters, enabling developers to gather insights or indirectly modify behavior at runtime by coupling with other decorator patterns. Unlike method or property decorators, parameter decorators only receive the target, the property key of the method, and the index of the parameter. They are primarily used to annotate parameters for later inspection by the method decorator or a dependency injection (DI) mechanism. Advanced applications of parameter decorators involve their combination with method decorators to implement behaviors such as runtime validation, logging of argument values, customized dependency resolution, or even dynamic transformation of function arguments.

At their core, parameter decorators receive three arguments: the target object (which could be the constructor for a static member or the prototype for an instance member), the property key of the method, and the parameter index. This minimal interface restricts their ability to directly modify parameters, so the typical strategy is to store the associated metadata using reflection APIs. The `reflect-metadata` library is commonly used in this context. By annotating parameters with metadata, subsequent runtime logic in method decorators can retrieve these annotations and apply custom behavior when the method is invoked.

A simple yet instructive example is a parameter logging decorator that records the indices of parameters marked for logging. The metadata produced by the parameter decorator is later used by a method decorator to log the values passed to those parameters at runtime. Consider the following implementation:

```
// Parameter decorator to mark parameters for logging.
function LogParam(target: any, propertyKey: string, parameterIndex:
    number) {
    const existingLogParams: number[] = Reflect.getOwnMetadata('
    log_params', target, propertyKey) || [];
    existingLogParams.push(parameterIndex);
    Reflect.defineMetadata('log_params', existingLogParams, target,
```

```
        propertyKey);
}


// Method decorator retrieves metadata about parameters and logs
    their values.
function LogParameters(target: any, propertyKey: string, descriptor:
    PropertyDescriptor) {
    const originalMethod = descriptor.value;
    descriptor.value = function (...args: any[]) {
        const indices: number[] = Reflect.getOwnMetadata('log_params
    ', target, propertyKey) || [];
        indices.forEach(index => {
            console.log(`Parameter at index ${index} in ${propertyKey
    } called with value:`, args[index]);
        });
        return originalMethod.apply(this, args);
    };
    return descriptor;
}


class ExampleService {
    @LogParameters
    performAction(@LogParam id: number, @LogParam name: string, flag:
      boolean): void {
        console.log('Action performed.');
    }
}
```

In the example above, the LogParam decorator attaches metadata indicating which parameter indices need to be logged. The method decorator LogParameters subsequently retrieves this metadata at runtime and logs the corresponding argument values. Although parameter decorators are unable to alter the parameter values directly, when combined with a method decorator, they enable runtime behaviors that depend on the parameter values.

Advanced scenarios may require complex manipulation of parameters, such as enforcing custom validation rules or transforming input data. Since parameter decorators cannot alter the method parameter list, the

design pattern used involves storing transformation or validation callbacks in the metadata. The method decorator then checks for these
callbacks and applies them to the relevant parameters before executing
the original method. The following example demonstrates a validation
mechanism, where parameters marked with a validation decorator are
automatically checked against custom validator functions:

```
type ValidatorFunction = (arg: any) => boolean;

function ValidateParam(validator: ValidatorFunction) {
    return function (target: any, propertyKey: string, parameterIndex
    : number) {
        // Retrieve existing validators for the method parameter.
        const validators: Map<number, ValidatorFunction[]> =
            Reflect.getOwnMetadata('validators', target, propertyKey)
    || new Map();
        if (!validators.has(parameterIndex)) {
            validators.set(parameterIndex, []);
        }
        validators.get(parameterIndex)!.push(validator);
        Reflect.defineMetadata('validators', validators, target,
    propertyKey);
    };
}

function ValidateParameters(target: any, propertyKey: string,
    descriptor: PropertyDescriptor) {
    const originalMethod = descriptor.value;
    descriptor.value = function (...args: any[]) {
        const validators: Map<number, ValidatorFunction[]> =
            Reflect.getOwnMetadata('validators', target, propertyKey)
    || new Map();
        for (const [index, funcs] of validators.entries()) {
            funcs.forEach(validator => {
                if (!validator(args[index])) {
                    throw new Error(`Validation failed for parameter
    at index ${index} in method ${propertyKey}.`);
                }
            });
        }
        return originalMethod.apply(this, args);
    };
```

```
    return descriptor;
}

// Example usage of the validation parameter decorators.
class DataProcessor {
    @ValidateParameters
    processData(
        @ValidateParam((arg: any) => typeof arg === 'number' && arg >
      0) amount: number,
        @ValidateParam((arg: any) => typeof arg === 'string' && arg.
      length > 3) description: string
    ): void {
        console.log('Data processed:', amount, description);
    }
}
```

In this snippet, the `ValidateParam` decorator accepts a validator function that is stored in the metadata for the given parameter index. The method decorator `ValidateParameters` retrieves the constructed metadata map and applies each validator function to the corresponding argument upon method invocation. This design pattern decouples the validation logic from the business logic of the method, maintaining clean separation of concerns while providing runtime safety guarantees.

Another critical use case for parameter decorators is in dependency injection (DI) frameworks. By annotating constructor or method parameters with a specific token or key indicating the dependency to be injected, the DI container can automatically resolve and inject the required dependencies at runtime. Advanced implementations of DI frameworks use parameter decorators to register metadata essential for dependency resolution. A robust implementation often leverages the TypeScript `reflect-metadata` library to capture the design-time types of parameters. An illustrative example is shown below:

```
function Inject(token: any) {
```

```
    return function (target: any, propertyKey: string | symbol,
    parameterIndex: number) {
        const existingInjectedParameters: Map<number, any> =
            Reflect.getOwnMetadata('inject_tokens', target,
    propertyKey) || new Map();
        existingInjectedParameters.set(parameterIndex, token);
        Reflect.defineMetadata('inject_tokens',
    existingInjectedParameters, target, propertyKey);
    };
}


// A method decorator that performs dependency injection based on
    parameter metadata.
function ProcessInjection(target: any, propertyKey: string,
    descriptor: PropertyDescriptor) {
    const originalMethod = descriptor.value;
    descriptor.value = function (...args: any[]) {
        const injectedParams: Map<number, any> =
            Reflect.getOwnMetadata('inject_tokens', target,
    propertyKey) || new Map();
        injectedParams.forEach((token, index) => {
            // Simplistic resolution: the token is directly used as
    the value.
            // In production, this would call a container's
    resolution method.
            args[index] = token;
        });
        return originalMethod.apply(this, args);
    };
    return descriptor;
}


class Service {
    @ProcessInjection
    execute(
        @Inject('DependencyA') depA: any,
        @Inject('DependencyB') depB: any
    ): void {
        console.log('Injected dependencies:', depA, depB);
    }
}
```

Here, the `Inject` decorator attaches tokens to method parameters, and the `ProcessInjection` decorator uses those tokens to replace the parameters with the corresponding dependencies. In a more robust DI framework, the token resolution would involve consulting an IoC container to provide instances based on these tokens. This pattern not only decouples dependency management from application logic but also leverages TypeScript's strong typing when integrated with appropriate generic constraints and metadata reflection.

Advanced scenarios in leveraging parameter decorators include combining multiple parameter annotations to perform more complex transformations on function arguments. For example, one may wish to simultaneously perform logging, validation, and injection on a single parameter by storing multiple metadata points. To achieve this, a composite parameter decorator can aggregate metadata from several sources and be processed by a combined method decorator. Such composition requires careful metadata management, ensuring that each annotation's intent remains isolated yet accessible. A composite approach may be realized as follows:

```
function ComposeParamDecorators(...decorators: ParameterDecorator[])
    {
    return function (target: any, propertyKey: string, parameterIndex
    : number) {
        decorators.forEach(decorator => decorator(target, propertyKey
    , parameterIndex));
    };
}

function LogAndValidate(validator: ValidatorFunction) {
    return ComposeParamDecorators(
        function (target: any, propertyKey: string, parameterIndex:
    number) {
            const loggedParams: number[] = Reflect.getOwnMetadata('
    log_params', target, propertyKey) || [];
            loggedParams.push(parameterIndex);
            Reflect.defineMetadata('log_params', loggedParams, target
    , propertyKey);
```

```
        },
        ValidateParam(validator)
    );
}

class ComplexService {
    @ValidateParameters
    @LogParameters
    complexOperation(
        @LogAndValidate((arg: any) => typeof arg === 'number' && arg
    % 2 === 0) evenNumber: number,
        @Inject('ConfigValue') config: any
    ): void {
        console.log('Complex operation with', evenNumber, config);
    }
}
```

In this design, ComposeParamDecorators applies multiple decorators
to a single parameter. The composite LogAndValidate decorator integrates logging and validation seamlessly, allowing the method decorators ValidateParameters and LogParameters to operate on combined
metadata. This layering provides a high degree of modularity and
scalability, which is essential in large codebases where cross-cutting
concerns need to be managed elegantly.

Performance considerations are paramount when using parameter decorators in high-frequency or resource-constrained applications. The
use of reflection APIs and metadata storage can introduce overhead
if not managed properly. It is advisable to cache metadata lookups,
minimize the use of deep object traversals, and consider lazy evaluation strategies where possible. Profiling tools should be employed in
production systems to identify and mitigate any potential performance
bottlenecks introduced by these decorators.

Advanced developers may also extend parameter decorators to integrate with compile-time validation tools. By coupling with static analy-

194

sis frameworks, metadata provided by parameter decorators can serve as auxiliary information for linters or type checkers, enhancing overall code quality. Furthermore, custom tooling can be developed to visualize parameter metadata across an application, aiding in debugging dependency graphs or pinpointing validation failures in complex method signatures.

The strategic use of parameter decorators, when paired with method decorators, creates a powerful mechanism for augmenting runtime behavior based solely on compile-time annotations. This synergy encapsulates key software principles such as separation of concerns, modularity, and maintainability while leveraging TypeScript's strong type system and reflective capabilities. As developers design distributed systems, enterprise applications, or frameworks, these advanced techniques enable a declarative approach towards runtime behavior modification, ultimately leading to cleaner, more resilient code systems that excel in both clarity and functionality.

## 4.5 Exploring Metadata Reflection in Type-Script

Metadata reflection in TypeScript provides an advanced mechanism for runtime type introspection and dynamic behavior modification by leveraging design-time type information. This capability, enabled by the reflect-metadata library, allows developers to attach, retrieve, and manipulate metadata for classes, methods, properties, and parameters. Such integration deepens the control over program behavior by linking static type declarations with runtime logic.

TypeScript's experimental support for decorators, when paired

with the `emitDecoratorMetadata` compiler option, ensures that
design-time information becomes available at runtime. The TypeScript
compiler automatically emits metadata for decorated constructs
using predefined keys such as `design:type`, `design:paramtypes`,
and `design:returntype`. This emitted metadata can be retrieved
using methods such as `Reflect.getMetadata` and modified
with `Reflect.defineMetadata`, forming the core of metadata
reflection. The following example illustrates the basic usage of
`reflect-metadata`:

```
import "reflect-metadata";

class Sample {
    constructor(public id: number, public name: string) {}
}

Reflect.defineMetadata("role", "admin", Sample);
console.log(Reflect.getMetadata("role", Sample)); // Outputs: admin
```

In the example above, custom metadata is defined for the `Sample` class
and later retrieved at runtime. When combined with decorators, this
process automates the annotation of runtime constructs with meaningful metadata. For instance, property decorators can extract the design
type of a property and log or validate assignments based on that type:

```
function Validate(target: any, propertyKey: string) {
    const type = Reflect.getMetadata("design:type", target,
     propertyKey);
    console.log(`Property ${propertyKey} is of type: ${type.name}`);
}

class Product {
    @Validate
    price: number;
}
```

In advanced scenarios, metadata reflection extends beyond simple

196

logging. Developers often embed configuration data, validation rules, or dependency injection tokens within metadata. The automatic emission of metadata for constructor parameters is particularly useful in dependency injection (DI) frameworks. By retrieving the `design:paramtypes` metadata, one can dynamically resolve and instantiate dependencies. Consider the following pattern:

```
function Injectable() {
    return function<T extends { new (...args: any[]): {} }>(
    constructor: T): T {
        const types = Reflect.getMetadata("design:paramtypes",
    constructor) || [];
        Reflect.defineMetadata("custom:inject", types, constructor);
        return constructor;
    };
}

@Injectable()
class Service {
    constructor(repository: any, logger: any) {}
}
```

Here, the `Injectable` decorator captures the design-time types of constructor parameters and attaches them as custom metadata. These types can later be used by a DI container to resolve dependencies, automating the wiring of large-scale systems.

Advanced applications of metadata reflection also involve merging and custom formatting of metadata. When multiple decorators contribute metadata to the same class member, careful management of metadata keys is required to avoid collisions. One effective technique is to adopt namespaced keys or even use `Symbols` to uniquely identify metadata entries. The following example demonstrates merging metadata from multiple decorators:

```
function MergeMetadata(key: string, value: any) {
    return function(target: any, propertyKey: string) {
```

```
        const existing = Reflect.getMetadata(key, target, propertyKey
    ) || {};
        const merged = Object.assign({}, existing, value);
        Reflect.defineMetadata(key, merged, target, propertyKey);
    };
}

class Config {
    @MergeMetadata("settings", { env: "production" })
    @MergeMetadata("settings", { version: "1.0.0" })
    endpoint: string;
}
```

In this snippet, two decorators merge their respective data under the
same metadata key settings. Such techniques allow for flexible aggregation of data from various sources, ensuring that the runtime view
accurately reflects multiple layers of configuration.

Performance considerations are paramount when working with metadata reflection. Frequent calls to Reflect.getMetadata may introduce
overhead in performance-critical paths. A common advanced trick is
to implement caching within the decorated object, thereby eliminating
redundant metadata lookups. For example:

```
function CachedMetadata(key: string) {
    return function(target: any, propertyKey: string) {
        const cacheKey = Symbol(`cache_${key}`);
        Object.defineProperty(target, propertyKey, {
            get: function() {
                if (!this[cacheKey]) {
                    this[cacheKey] = Reflect.getMetadata(key, target,
    propertyKey);
                }
                return this[cacheKey];
            },
            configurable: true
        });
    };
}
```

```
class Module {
    @CachedMetadata("config")
    config: any;
}
```

By caching metadata values on the first access, subsequent retrievals avoid redundant reflection calls, optimizing performance for high-frequency accessors.

Metadata reflection also plays a crucial role in building robust validation frameworks. A decorator can annotate class properties with validation rules that are then dynamically enforced at runtime. For instance, one can define custom validators and store them as metadata, later to be processed by a centralized validation engine:

```
type ValidatorFunction = (value: any) => boolean;

function ValidateProp(validator: ValidatorFunction, errorMsg: string)
    {
    return function(target: any, propertyKey: string) {
        const validators = Reflect.getMetadata("validators", target,
    propertyKey) || [];
        validators.push({ validator, errorMsg });
        Reflect.defineMetadata("validators", validators, target,
    propertyKey);
    };
}

class User {
    @ValidateProp((value: any) => typeof value === "string" && value.
    length > 0, "Name must be non-empty")
    name: string;
}
```

Advanced developers can design a middleware layer that scans class instances for attached validators, invoking them prior to critical operations. This pattern decouples validation logic from business logic, producing clean and maintainable architectures.

When constructing systems that leverage metadata reflection, it is essential to follow best practices for metadata key management and ordering. Because inheritance may cause metadata to be inherited or overridden in subclasses, a disciplined naming convention for metadata keys (potentially enforced via utility functions) is advisable. Using namespaced keys, such as `"myapp:config"`, minimizes conflicts across large codebases.

The orchestration of decorators and metadata reflection also provides a fertile ground for creating adaptive logging strategies. A logging decorator, for example, might retrieve type or parameter metadata to automatically enrich log messages with context. Such precision logging can be invaluable in distributed systems where dynamic behavior needs to be audited in real time.

Beyond runtime behavior, metadata reflection can assist in static analysis and tooling. By exposing design-time information through a unified API, developers can build custom code analyzers that validate consistency between design and implementation. Tools that extract metadata can generate documentation or enforce architectural constraints, ensuring that the written code adheres to expected patterns.

One subtle aspect of metadata reflection involves the initialization order of decorators. Since TypeScript applies decorators in a bottom-up sequence at declaration time, metadata may be overwritten or augmented by subsequent decorators. Advanced developers must be cautious in the design of decorator hierarchies; explicit ordering and clear documentation of metadata dependencies are critical to avoid subtle bugs.

An emerging advanced technique is to integrate metadata reflection with asynchronous initialization routines. Although the majority of metadata reflection occurs synchronously at declaration time, certain patterns—such as lazy dependency resolution in DI frameworks—can benefit from deferring the evaluation of a metadata lookup. Developers can design wrappers that perform asynchronous caching, ensuring that heavy computations or external resource lookups are performed only once during an object's lifecycle.

Finally, the evolution of metadata reflection in TypeScript encourages a shift toward more declarative programming paradigms. By embedding rich metadata directly within code constructs, developers create self-documenting modules that can be introspected and manipulated by external tools and runtime frameworks. This reflective capability permits the construction of adaptive systems where behavior can be modified without altering the underlying source code—a powerful technique for building scalable, maintainable applications.

Advanced programmers who master metadata reflection in TypeScript gain deep insights into the interplay between compile-time type systems and runtime behavior. The disciplined use of `reflect-metadata` not only simplifies dependency management and validation but also facilitates advanced logging, caching, and configuration management strategies. Through careful planning of metadata keys, performance optimizations, and adherence to strict decorator ordering, developers can produce sophisticated, resilient systems that leverage the full power of TypeScript's reflective capabilities.

## 4.6 Creating Custom Metadata with Reflect-metadata

The `reflect-metadata` library is a powerful tool that enables advanced TypeScript developers to create, retrieve, and manipulate custom metadata at runtime. This capability facilitates a wide array of use cases, such as building dependency injection containers, implementing sophisticated validation schemes, and enhancing logging solutions. In this section, we explore advanced techniques for designing custom metadata, managing metadata keys, and optimizing performance when handling metadata in large-scale TypeScript applications.

Custom metadata can be defined using `Reflect.defineMetadata` and later retrieved with `Reflect.getMetadata`. The flexibility provided by these functions permits the attachment of arbitrary values to classes, methods, properties, and parameters. A fundamental example is to annotate a class with configuration settings that can later be consumed by a runtime framework. Consider the following example:

```
import "reflect-metadata";

function Configurable(config: object) {
    return function<T extends { new (...args: any[]): {} }>(
    constructor: T): T {
        Reflect.defineMetadata("custom:config", config, constructor);
        return constructor;
    };
}


@Configurable({ endpoint: "https://api.example.com", timeout: 5000 })
class ApiService {
    // Implementation details
}

const config = Reflect.getMetadata("custom:config", ApiService);
console.log("ApiService config:", config);
```

In this snippet, the decorator `Configurable` attaches a configuration object to the class metadata under the key `"custom:config"`. Advanced usage of custom metadata extends beyond static configuration. Developers can dynamically update metadata in response to runtime conditions or merge metadata from multiple sources. One technique involves merging metadata entries when multiple decorators contribute to the same key. To ensure that metadata does not conflict, it is common to use namespaced keys or even `Symbols` as keys. The following example demonstrates a merge strategy:

```
function MergeMetadata(key: string, value: object) {
    return function(target: any, propertyKey?: string) {
        const existing = propertyKey
            ? Reflect.getMetadata(key, target, propertyKey) || {}
            : Reflect.getMetadata(key, target) || {};
        const merged = { ...existing, ...value };
        if (propertyKey) {
            Reflect.defineMetadata(key, merged, target, propertyKey);
        } else {
            Reflect.defineMetadata(key, merged, target);
        }
    };
}

class ServiceConfig {
    @MergeMetadata("custom:options", { retries: 3 })
    @MergeMetadata("custom:options", { cache: true })
    endpoint: string = "https://service.example.com";
}

const mergedConfig = Reflect.getMetadata("custom:options", new
    ServiceConfig(), "endpoint");
console.log("Merged Config:", mergedConfig);
```

By merging metadata, developers can combine data from separate decorator calls in a modular fashion. This approach is particularly beneficial in complex systems where multiple aspects (e.g., caching, security, and logging) contribute to the overall configuration of a property or class.

Another advanced strategy involves the use of metadata for dependency injection (DI). By tagging constructor parameters with custom metadata, a DI container can automatically resolve and instantiate required dependencies. The following example outlines a custom injection mechanism:

```
function Inject(token: any) {
    return function(target: any, propertyKey: string | symbol,
    parameterIndex: number) {
        const existingInjects: Map<number, any> = Reflect.
    getOwnMetadata("custom:inject_tokens", target, propertyKey) ||
    new Map();
        existingInjects.set(parameterIndex, token);
        Reflect.defineMetadata("custom:inject_tokens",
    existingInjects, target, propertyKey);
    };
}

class Logger {
    log(message: string) {
        console.log("[Logger]:", message);
    }
}

class Repository {
    // Repository implementation
}

class BusinessService {
    constructor(
        @Inject("Logger") private logger: Logger,
        @Inject("Repository") private repository: Repository
    ) {}

    performOperation() {
        this.logger.log("Operation performed.");
    }
}
```

```
// A hypothetical DI container function
function resolveDependencies<T>(target: { new(...args: any[]): T }):
  T {
    const paramTypes: any[] = Reflect.getMetadata("design:paramtypes
    ", target) || [];
    const injectTokens: Map<number, any> = Reflect.getMetadata("
    custom:inject_tokens", target) || new Map();
    const args = paramTypes.map((type, index) => {
        const token = injectTokens.get(index);
        // Replace directly with tokens or consult a container
    mapping (simplified resolution)
        return token === "Logger" ? new Logger() : token === "
    Repository" ? new Repository() : new type();
    });
    return new target(...args);
}

const serviceInstance = resolveDependencies(BusinessService);
serviceInstance.performOperation();
```

In the DI example above, custom tokens are stored as metadata on constructor parameters. The resolution function retrieves both design type metadata and custom injection tokens to instantiate the appropriate dependencies. This pattern decouples service definitions from instantiation logic, paving the way for inversion of control in applications.

Performance optimization is an important consideration when working with custom metadata, especially in high-performance applications. Metadata lookups may be cached to avoid repetitive calls to Reflect.getMetadata, which can be computationally expensive when performed frequently. An advanced technique is to implement caching at the module or class level, storing retrieved metadata in a closure. For instance:

```
function CachedMetadata(key: string) {
    return function(target: any, propertyKey?: string) {
        const cacheKey = Symbol(`cache:${key}`);
```

```
        const getter = function() {
            if (!this[cacheKey]) {
                this[cacheKey] = propertyKey
                    ? Reflect.getMetadata(key, target, propertyKey)
                    : Reflect.getMetadata(key, target);
            }
            return this[cacheKey];
        };
        if (propertyKey) {
            Object.defineProperty(target, propertyKey, { get: getter,
    configurable: true });
        } else {
            Object.defineProperty(target, key, { get: getter,
    configurable: true });
        }
    };
}


class CachedService {
    @CachedMetadata("custom:expensiveData")
    data: any;
}
```

In this code, the CachedMetadata decorator creates a getter that caches the metadata upon first access, eliminating repeated reflection overhead. Such optimizations are essential when decorators are applied to performance-critical properties or methods.

An advanced usage pattern involves integrating custom metadata into automated validation or transformation pipelines. For example, metadata may store validation rules associated with a class property, which are then processed by a centralized engine prior to business logic execution. Consider a scenario where each property is decorated with custom validation metadata:

```
type Validator = (value: any) => boolean;

function PropertyValidator(validator: Validator, message: string) {
    return function(target: any, propertyKey: string) {
```

```
        const validators: Array<{ validator: Validator, message:
    string }> =
            Reflect.getMetadata("custom:validators", target,
    propertyKey) || [];
        validators.push({ validator, message });
        Reflect.defineMetadata("custom:validators", validators,
    target, propertyKey);
    };
}

class UserProfile {
    @PropertyValidator((value: any) => typeof value === "string" &&
    value.length > 0, "Name must be provided")
    name: string;

    @PropertyValidator((value: any) => typeof value === "number" &&
    value > 0, "Age must be positive")
    age: number;

    constructor(name: string, age: number) {
        this.name = name;
        this.age = age;
    }
}

function validate(model: any): void {
    for (const propertyKey of Object.keys(model)) {
        const validators: Array<{ validator: Validator, message:
    string }> =
            Reflect.getMetadata("custom:validators", model,
    propertyKey) || [];
        for (const { validator, message } of validators) {
            if (!validator(model[propertyKey])) {
                throw new Error(`Validation error on ${propertyKey}:
    ${message}`);
            }
        }
    }
}

const user = new UserProfile("", -5);
try {
    validate(user);
} catch (error) {
    console.error("Validation failed:", error.message);
```

```
}
```

This example illustrates how custom metadata can decouple validation logic from the core application code. Each property is annotated with a validation function and an error message. The validation processing function iterates over model properties and evaluates the corresponding validators, simplifying the enforcement of complex business rules.

Integrating custom metadata with logging and diagnostic tools is another advanced technique. Metadata can be used to enhance log messages with additional context or to create detailed audit trails. For instance, custom metadata may store method-level performance metrics or trace identifiers that can be injected into log events:

```
function Trace(identifier: string) {
    return function(target: any, propertyKey: string, descriptor:
    PropertyDescriptor) {
        Reflect.defineMetadata("custom:trace", identifier, target,
    propertyKey);
        const originalMethod = descriptor.value;
        descriptor.value = function (...args: any[]) {
            const traceId = Reflect.getMetadata("custom:trace",
    target, propertyKey);
            console.log(`Trace ${traceId}: Entering ${propertyKey}`);
            const result = originalMethod.apply(this, args);
            console.log(`Trace ${traceId}: Exiting ${propertyKey}`);
            return result;
        };
        return descriptor;
    };
}

class AuditService {
    @Trace("Audit-1234")
    performAudit(details: any) {
        // Audit logic implementation
    }
}
```

```
const auditService = new AuditService();
auditService.performAudit({ event: "login", user: "admin" });
```

In this scenario, a custom trace identifier is embedded into the metadata of a method. The modified method logs entry and exit messages enriched with the trace identifier, facilitating detailed runtime analysis and debugging.

Overall, the creation and utilization of custom metadata using reflect-metadata empowers advanced developers to build applications that are both modular and adaptable. By leveraging custom metadata keys, merging disparate metadata contributions, caching for performance, and integrating with validation or logging pipelines, one can design systems that accurately reflect design-time intentions while adapting dynamically at runtime. The techniques discussed in this section represent sophisticated patterns that, when applied rigorously, yield codebases that are resilient, maintainable, and extensible.

## 4.7 Combining Decorators with Dependency Injection

Integrating decorators with dependency injection (DI) architectures provides a systematic and scalable approach to managing object creation, dependencies, and lifecycle concerns. In advanced TypeScript applications, decorators are not merely syntactic sugar but a core part of a comprehensive DI framework that leverages metadata reflection to automatically resolve and inject dependencies at runtime. This section delves into the advanced techniques of combining decorators with DI patterns, focusing on achieving modularity, extensibility, and efficient dependency resolution.

At the heart of DI is the inversion of control (IoC) principle, which shifts the creation and management of dependencies from the consumer code to a dedicated container. TypeScript's experimental decorator and metadata features, along with libraries such as `reflect-metadata`, facilitate this paradigm by automatically emitting design-time type information essential for resolving dependencies. A common approach is to annotate classes as services and mark their constructor parameters for injection. These decorators store injection tokens and design types as custom metadata, which the DI container reads during object instantiation.

A fundamental example is to annotate a service class with an @Injectable decorator and to annotate its constructor parameters using an @Inject decorator. Consider the following code:

```
import "reflect-metadata";

// Injectable decorator that marks a class as a candidate for DI.
function Injectable() {
    return function<T extends { new (...args: any[]): {} }>(target: T
    ): T {
        // Optionally register the class with a global container here

        Reflect.defineMetadata("custom:injectable", true, target);
        return target;
    };
}

// Inject decorator that attaches a token to constructor parameters.
function Inject(token: any) {
    return function(target: any, _propertyKey: string | symbol,
    parameterIndex: number) {
        const existingTokens: Map<number, any> = Reflect.getMetadata
    ("custom:inject_tokens", target) || new Map();
        existingTokens.set(parameterIndex, token);
```

```
        Reflect.defineMetadata("custom:inject_tokens", existingTokens
        , target);
    };
}


@Injectable()
class Logger {
    log(message: string): void {
        console.log("[Logger]:", message);
    }
}


@Injectable()
class UserRepository {
    findAll(): string[] {
        return ["Alice", "Bob", "Charlie"];
    }
}


@Injectable()
class UserService {
    constructor(
        @Inject("Logger") private logger: Logger,
        @Inject("UserRepository") private repository: UserRepository
    ) {}

    processUsers(): void {
        const users = this.repository.findAll();
        this.logger.log("Processing users: " + users.join(", "));
    }
}
```

In this example, the @Injectable decorator marks the classes as available for injection, while the @Inject decorator attaches custom tokens to the constructor parameters. These tokens facilitate the resolution of dependencies by the DI container. The container must be capable of reading both design-time types and custom injection metadata. An advanced DI container may implement caching, scoped lifecycles, and asynchronous resolution, but the core logic remains rooted in metadata reflection.

211

A simplified DI container function leverages the emitted metadata to
construct instances with their dependencies resolved. Consider the following implementation:

```
class DIContainer {
    private registry = new Map<any, any>();

    // Register a provider for a given token.
    register<T>(token: any, provider: { new(...args: any[]): T }):
    void {
        this.registry.set(token, provider);
    }

    // Resolve a dependency by inspecting metadata.
    resolve<T>(target: { new(...args: any[]): T }): T {
        // Retrieve design time types for constructor parameters.
        const paramTypes: any[] = Reflect.getMetadata("design:
paramtypes", target) || [];
        // Retrieve custom injection tokens, if provided.
        const injectTokens: Map<number, any> = Reflect.getMetadata("
custom:inject_tokens", target.prototype) || new Map();
        const args = paramTypes.map((type, index) => {
            let token = injectTokens.get(index) || type;
            const Provider = this.registry.get(token);
            if (!Provider) {
                throw new Error(`No provider registered for token: ${
token.toString()}`);
            }
            return this.resolve(Provider);
        });
        return new target(...args);
    }
}

const container = new DIContainer();
container.register("Logger", Logger);
container.register("UserRepository", UserRepository);
container.register(UserService, UserService);

const userServiceInstance = container.resolve(UserService);
userServiceInstance.processUsers();
```

This DI container uses both the design type metadata (automatically emitted when the `emitDecoratorMetadata` compiler option is enabled) and custom injection tokens defined by `@Inject`. The container recursively resolves dependencies, ensuring that the complete dependency graph of a service is constructed. This approach decouples dependency creation from consumer code, facilitating unit testing and promoting modularity.

One advanced skill in integrating decorators with DI is the ability to combine multiple decorators to enrich the service registration process. For example, a composite decorator may simultaneously mark a class as injectable, register it with the container, and attach additional metadata for configuration. By automating these tasks, developers reduce boilerplate and enforce consistency across the codebase. An example of a composite decorator is:

```
function Service(token?: string) {
    return function<T extends { new(...args: any[]): {} }>(target: T)
    : T {
        Reflect.defineMetadata("custom:injectable", true, target);
        if (token) {
            Reflect.defineMetadata("custom:service_token", token,
    target);
        }
        // Optionally, perform container registration here.
        return target;
    };
}

@Service("UserService")
class AdvancedUserService {
    constructor(
        @Inject("Logger") private logger: Logger,
        @Inject("UserRepository") private repository: UserRepository
    ) {}

    execute(): void {
        const users = this.repository.findAll();
        this.logger.log("Advanced processing for users: " + users.
    join(", "));
```

```
    }
}
```

Such composite decorators streamline service definitions by combining DI and configuration concerns. In larger systems, a well-defined set of decorators acting in concert with an IoC container reduces the probability of human error and simplifies the maintenance of dependency graphs.

An essential aspect of combining decorators with DI is managing the order of decorator execution. In TypeScript, decorators are applied in a bottom-up (last applied first) sequence. When multiple decorators annotate a class or its members, careful design is required to ensure that constructor injection metadata and type information are not inadvertently overwritten by subsequent decorators. One recommended trick is to use distinct metadata keys and clear naming conventions to isolate DI information from other cross-cutting concerns. For instance, consistently prefixing DI-related keys with `"custom:inject_"` minimizes conflicts and aids in debugging.

Caching strategies play a critical role in high-performance DI systems. As dependency graphs become complex, redundant metadata lookups can introduce overhead. Advanced practitioners can implement caching at various layers of the DI container. For example, caching resolved provider instances for singleton-scoped services or caching metadata lookups at the invocation level can dramatically reduce initialization time. The following example introduces a caching layer in the DI container:

```
class OptimizedDIContainer {
    private registry = new Map<any, any>();
    private singletonCache = new Map<any, any>();
```

```
register<T>(token: any, provider: { new(...args: any[]): T },
isSingleton: boolean = false): void {
    this.registry.set(token, { provider, isSingleton });
}

resolve<T>(target: { new(...args: any[]): T }): T {
    // Retrieve custom service token if defined.
    const serviceToken = Reflect.getMetadata("custom:
service_token", target) || target;
    // Check singleton cache.
    if (this.singletonCache.has(serviceToken)) {
        return this.singletonCache.get(serviceToken);
    }
    // Retrieve design param types and injection tokens.
    const paramTypes: any[] = Reflect.getMetadata("design:
paramtypes", target) || [];
    const injectTokens: Map<number, any> = Reflect.getMetadata("
custom:inject_tokens", target.prototype) || new Map();
    const args = paramTypes.map((type, index) => {
        const token = injectTokens.get(index) || type;
        const registration = this.registry.get(token);
        if (!registration) {
            throw new Error(`No provider registered for token: ${
token.toString()}`);
        }
        return this.resolve(registration.provider);
    });
    const instance = new target(...args);
    // Cache singleton instance.
    const registration = this.registry.get(serviceToken);
    if (registration && registration.isSingleton) {
        this.singletonCache.set(serviceToken, instance);
    }
    return instance;
    }
}

const optimizedContainer = new OptimizedDIContainer();
optimizedContainer.register("Logger", Logger, true);
optimizedContainer.register("UserRepository", UserRepository, true);
optimizedContainer.register(AdvancedUserService, AdvancedUserService)
    ;

const advancedService = optimizedContainer.resolve(
    AdvancedUserService);
```

215

```
advancedService.execute();
```

In this optimized DI container, a singleton cache ensures that services registered as singletons are instantiated only once. The container integrates both design-time metadata and custom injection tokens to resolve dependencies recursively while minimizing repetitive computation. Such performance optimizations are vital in large-scale systems where dependency graphs may be extensive.

Error handling is another critical dimension when combining decorators with DI. Advanced systems must gracefully handle cyclic dependencies and missing provider registrations. Developers can extend the basic DI container with cycle detection algorithms and meaningful error messages that incorporate metadata information. For instance, tracking the dependency resolution path in case of failure aids in debugging complex dependency graphs.

Furthermore, integrating decorators with DI promotes testability. By decoupling service definitions from instantiation logic, unit tests can swap implementations with mocks or stubs easily. Advanced techniques include designing decorators that automatically register test doubles in a dedicated testing container or allow selective overriding of provider registrations. Such practices foster a clean separation between production and test environments and enable automated testing pipelines that assert the correct wiring of dependencies.

Combining decorators with dependency injection ultimately leads to a highly modular, maintainable, and scalable software architecture. Advanced TypeScript developers leverage custom decorators to declaratively specify dependencies, configure service lifecycles, and encapsulate cross-cutting concerns. Through meticulous design of metadata keys, careful management of decorator ordering, and performance enhancements via caching, the integration of DI and decorators forms the backbone of robust enterprise applications. This approach not only simplifies dependency management but also facilitates code reuse, easier testing, and dynamic configuration adjustments in response to runtime conditions.

# 5

# Chapter 5: Leveraging Modules and Namespaces

*This chapter addresses the organization of TypeScript code using modules and namespaces. It clarifies their differences and showcases best practices for exporting, importing, and dynamic module loading. Additionally, it covers module resolution strategies and the combination of modules with namespaces, emphasizing modular design for maintainable and scalable applications.*

## 5.1 Essentials of TypeScript Modules

TypeScript modules extend the capabilities of standard JavaScript modules by incorporating static type checking, generic programming constructs, and compile-time error detection that fundamentally alter the way code is structured and maintained in large-scale applications. A primary distinction lies in the ability of TypeScript to perform rigorous type analysis during compilation, a feature absent in traditional JavaScript. This analysis ensures that the exported entities from one module are used with precise type expectations in another, thereby mitigating runtime errors that may arise from type mismatches.

In TypeScript, the module is essentially a file with at least one top-level import or export statement. This design enforces encapsulation by isolating variables and types within module boundaries, preventing inadvertent pollution of the global namespace. Unlike JavaScript, where module boundaries are often enforced only by convention or by the runtime environment (such as ECMAScript 6 modules in modern browsers), TypeScript's module system ensures that any misalignment between the module interface and its consumer is flagged at compile time. For example, consider a module that exports a type-safe function:

```
export function computeArea(radius: number): number {
    return Math.PI * radius * radius;
}
```

When this module is imported elsewhere, the type information is preserved due to the TypeScript compiler's rigorous checking, ensuring that any consumer of computeArea passes a valid argument type. This static verification is particularly beneficial in collaborative environments where modules are developed concurrently with well-defined interfaces. The import, reflecting similar precision, is defined as follows:

```
import { computeArea } from './geometry';

// Correct usage based on the type contract.
let area: number = computeArea(5);
```

The strict type system forces a deliberate coupling between the module's interface and its usage, thereby reducing the possibility

220

of subtle bugs that might otherwise go unnoticed until runtime in plain JavaScript. Moreover, TypeScript modules facilitate integration with modern build tools and bundlers through configurable module resolution strategies. The TypeScript compiler options such as `moduleResolution`, `baseUrl`, and `paths` grant advanced programmers fine-grained control over how modules interrelate, resolve, and are bundled, especially when following non-trivial dependency graphs.

One significant difference from conventional JavaScript modules is that TypeScript's module system supports module augmentation, a technique that allows developers to extend existing modules. This capability is indispensable when working with libraries that may need dynamic extension or when incorporating polyfills without altering the original source code. Augmentation is achieved through declaration merging, enabling the extension of existing module interfaces while preserving type safety. Consider the following example that augments a module with an additional function:

```
declare module './geometry' {
    export function computeCircumference(radius: number): number;
}

import { computeCircumference } from './geometry';

// The new function must conform to the module's expected type
    interface.
let circumference: number = computeCircumference(5);
```

This extension approach, available only in TypeScript's module system, contrasts with JavaScript where such dynamic augmentation often requires manual interventions that risk breaking invariants of the codebase.

Additionally, the interplay between TypeScript modules and ambient
module declarations results in a robust mechanism for incorporating
external libraries.   When using legacy JavaScript libraries, a corresponding declaration file can be crafted to represent the API surface
with type annotations.   This method allows advanced programmers
to integrate disparate ecosystems while maintaining full compile-time
checking. Consider a declaration file for a third-party library:

```
// geometry-lib.d.ts
declare module 'geometry-lib' {
    export function calculateVolume(radius: number, height: number):
    number;
}
```

When this library is used within a TypeScript module, the type declarations enforce a contract that mirrors the expected JavaScript behavior,
allowing developers to catch erroneous API usages prior to runtime.

Another advanced implementation detail rests in the fact that Type-
Script modules compile down to different module systems based on
compiler configuration. Developers can target CommonJS for Node.js
environments, AMD for browsers with asynchronous loading requirements, or ES6 modules for modern JavaScript engines.   Each target
influences how the module wrapper code is generated.   For example,
targeting CommonJS, the compiled module acquires the form:

```
// Generated JavaScript for a CommonJS module.
"use strict";
Object.defineProperty(exports, "__esModule", { value: true });
exports.computeArea = void 0;
function computeArea(radius) {
    return Math.PI * radius * radius;
}
exports.computeArea = computeArea;
```

Conversely, if targeting ES6 modules, the output adheres to the stan-

222

dardized module syntax, which is natively recognized by modern browsers. This flexibility in output format enables advanced programmers to align the module structure with the requirements of the deployment environment and leverage ecosystem-specific optimizations such as tree-shaking.

Furthermore, advanced techniques in modular design using Type-Script involve the use of import type and conditional imports that allow for more granular load-time optimizations. The import type syntax ensures that only type information, and not executable code, is imported. This separation is crucial for reducing bundle sizes and eliminating dead code in production builds. For example:

```
import type { Config } from './config';

function loadConfig(): Config {
    // Module logic to load the configuration object.
}
```

This approach is particularly beneficial in large codebases where dependency graphs become complex and efficient tree-shaking is a priority. The compiler can strip type-only imports in the compiled JavaScript, optimizing the runtime performance without sacrificing type safety.

Another nuance of the TypeScript module system is the introduction of namespaces in tandem with modules when the use case calls for internal logical grouping within a module. Although namespaces are generally reserved for organizing code in a manner analogous to internal modules, they can be integrated within module files to provide secondary levels of abstraction. While multiple techniques exist for code organization, the integration of namespaces must be approached with caution, ensuring that ambiguities in type resolution are avoided. The advanced programmer is advised to restrict the use of namespaces to situations where encapsulation of related members is necessary within a module, as modern ECMAScript modules already provide sufficient structure for independently distributed components.

Moreover, TypeScript enables explicit control over export visibility through the use of `export default` alongside named exports. The decision to export defaults or named exports can have implications on code readability, maintainability, and the resolution of circular dependencies. When designing libraries intended for consumption across various projects, a careful balance between default and named exports can considerably enhance the interface's resilience. Consider the following export semantics:

```
export default class Shape {
    constructor(public name: string) {}
}

export function computePerimeter(dimensions: number[]): number {
    return dimensions.reduce((acc, curr) => acc + curr, 0);
}
```

This approach allows consumers to import the default class and the function separately, thereby leveraging static analysis to detect discrepancies in module usage.

Advanced developers should also examine module resolution strategies when dealing with monorepos or complex directory structures. The configuration of the `tsconfig.json` file, including the use of the `paths` and `baseUrl` properties, facilitates the abstraction of deep module hierarchies into simpler alias paths. This practice not only improves code readability but also enhances maintainability across large projects. An exemplary configuration is as follows:

```
{
    "compilerOptions": {
        "baseUrl": "./src",
        "paths": {
            "@core/*": ["core/*"],
            "@utils/*": ["utils/*"]
        }
    }
}
```

Through these mappings, advanced programmers can reference deeply nested modules in a concise and understandable manner, thereby improving the modular organization of the code.

Overall, the principles embraced by TypeScript modules, when compared to traditional JavaScript modules, offer a more robust system for code organization. The introduction of compile-time type checking, module augmentation, and customizable resolution strategies transforms the development process into one that emphasizes both safety and scalability. Advanced programming practices in TypeScript are inherently geared towards constructing maintainable, scalable architectures where type integrity is preserved across module boundaries and code reuse is maximized.

The rigorous structuring enforced by TypeScript modules, combined with carefully crafted compiler options, puts power in the hands of developers who must manage large, distributed codebases. Embracing these advanced techniques in module design is imperative for achieving optimal performance and ensuring that the codebase adheres to stringent quality standards while remaining flexible in the face of evolving project requirements.

## 5.2   Exporting and Importing in TypeScript

Within large-scale systems, the explicit control over export and import operations in TypeScript drives modularity, decoupling, and maintainability.  Advanced developers leverage both the syntactical nuances and the underlying type system to enforce clean component boundaries and predictable dependency graphs. Fundamental to this is the deliberate creation and consumption of module interfaces, managed by the distinction between named exports, default exports, and the more recent type-only imports.

TypeScript offers two primary mechanisms for making module features public: named exports and default exports. With named exports, every exported member is explicitly referenced, promoting clarity in module dependencies.  The static type checker enforces explicit contracts between module consumers and producers, ensuring that each export fits a predefined interface. For instance, consider the following module that encapsulates several utility functions:

```
export function parseInput(input: string): number[] {
    return input.split(',')
                .map(token => parseInt(token, 10))
                .filter(num => !isNaN(num));
}

export function formatOutput(data: number[]): string {
    return data.map(num => num.toString()).join(';');
}

export interface ProcessingOptions {
    delimiter: string;
    ignoreErrors: boolean;
}
```

The corresponding consumer can selectively import only the necessary members, which improves code comprehension and bundler efficiency:

```
import { parseInput, ProcessingOptions } from './dataUtils';

const rawData: string = "12,7,42,invalid";
const numbers: number[] = parseInput(rawData);

const options: ProcessingOptions = { delimiter: ",", ignoreErrors:
    true };
```

In contrast, default exports cater to modules that expose a primary functionality or a core class. Although default exports allow for more concise import statements, they inherently reduce the explicitness of the exported contract by making the binding name arbitrarily chosen by the importer. Advanced patterns often favor named exports for better tree-shaking and clearer static analysis, yet default exports remain useful in encapsulating a single primary concern. An illustrative default export may look like:

```
export default class DataProcessor {
    constructor(private options: { threshold: number }) {}

    process(data: number[]): number[] {
        return data.filter(num => num > this.options.threshold);
    }
}
```

Consumers import this default module without requiring braces, thereby fostering a succinct representation of the module's intention:

```
import DataProcessor from './DataProcessor';

const processor = new DataProcessor({ threshold: 10 });
const processedData = processor.process([5, 15, 25]);
```

Advanced projects frequently involve complex dependency patterns that necessitate precise control over import behavior. This extends to re-exporting patterns, where modules aggregate exports from multiple components. Re-exporting consolidates disparate functionalities into a coherent API surface, essential for library authors and large monorepos. For example, re-exporting from several modules:

```
export { parseInput, formatOutput, ProcessingOptions } from './
    dataUtils';
export { default as DataProcessor } from './DataProcessor';
```

This pattern simplifies the consumer's import path and abstracts internal module organization, but it requires careful type propagation to preserve the integrity of the contracts.

The type system's static analysis shines when interacting with advanced import scenarios. The use of `import type` stands out as a critical performance and architectural consideration. By segregating type-only imports from value imports, the TypeScript compiler eliminates unneeded runtime components while maintaining full type-checking capabilities. A typical use-case appears as follows:

```
import type { ProcessingOptions } from './dataUtils';

function configure(options: ProcessingOptions): void {
    // runtime manipulation does not include type specifications.
}
```

This separation ensures that the eventual JavaScript output contains only the necessary code, thereby streamlining bundle size and load performance—an essential consideration in projects with tight constraints on runtime overhead.

Furthermore, conditional exports provide a mechanism to adapt to differing environments or feature flags. Advanced configurations might

228

include exporting different implementations based on compile-time conditions using techniques such as dynamic imports or discriminated unions in combination with module resolution strategies. An implementation schema might be defined as:

```
declare const ENVIRONMENT: 'development' | 'production';

export let Logger: { log: (message: string) => void };

if (ENVIRONMENT === 'development') {
    Logger = {
        log: (message: string) => console.debug('[DEBUG]', message)
    };
} else {
    Logger = {
        log: (message: string) => { /* minimal logging in production
    */ }
    };
}
```

When deploying across multiple environments, such explicit export logic ensures that a single API adapts dynamically, balancing the need for diagnostic verbosity during development and performance in production systems.

Advanced users frequently encounter circular dependencies in complex systems. By refactoring the module boundaries into isolated interfaces and leveraging barrel files (index files that re-export selected module content), developers can mitigate circular dependency issues. Barrel files re-export multiple modules from a single access point:

```
// In src/components/index.ts
export { ComponentA } from './ComponentA';
export { ComponentB } from './ComponentB';
export { ComponentC } from './ComponentC';
```

A consumer module then relies on this consolidated index, thereby decoupling direct dependency relationships:

```
import { ComponentA, ComponentB } from './components';
```

This re-export strategy not only simplifies the import paths but also aids in the identification and resolution of inadvertent circular dependencies when paired with TypeScript's type-checking across module boundaries.

A further layer of sophistication is attributed to asynchronous module loading, particularly important in performance-sensitive scenarios such as large web applications. TypeScript supports dynamic import() expressions to asynchronously load modules at runtime, which is crucial for code-splitting and lazy-loading strategies. The dynamic import syntax returns a promise that resolves to the module's exports, enabling developers to conditionally load code only when necessary:

```
async function loadAnalyticsModule() {
    const { Analytics } = await import('./analytics');
    const analytics = new Analytics();
    analytics.trackEvent('page_view');
}
```

Developers must ensure that dynamic importing is complemented by precise type annotations. One approach involves creating an interface that describes the module's shape and using type assertions after dynamic imports:

```
interface AnalyticsModule {
    Analytics: new () => { trackEvent: (event: string) => void };
}

async function loadAnalyticsModule(): Promise<AnalyticsModule> {
    return import('./analytics') as Promise<AnalyticsModule>;
}
```

This pattern guarantees that even dynamically loaded modules adhere to the established type contracts, preserving the benefits of static analysis across asynchronous boundaries.

The choice between various export/import paradigms inevitably impacts bundler behavior. Tree-shaking, a technique supported by bundlers such as Webpack and Rollup, fundamentally relies on static import/export statements that are analyzable at compile-time. Selecting named over default exports may yield improved dead code elimination, particularly when combined with TypeScript's module resolution configurations in the `tsconfig.json` file:

```
{
    "compilerOptions": {
        "module": "ES6",
        "target": "ES6",
        "esModuleInterop": true,
        "strict": true
    }
}
```

The aforementioned configuration empowers the bundler to remove unused code segments, resulting in finer-grained optimization without compromising the reliability of the type system. Moreover, advanced modifications such as conditional polyfills based on export states allow libraries to remain lean while offering extended functionalities in supporting environments.

Equally important is the handling of ambient modules and external type declarations. When integrating non-TypeScript libraries, declaration files provide a seamless bridge by delineating external module interfaces. Such declarations are inherently imported using ambient module syntax:

```
// custom-library.d.ts
```

```
declare module 'custom-library' {
    export function initialize(config: object): void;
    export const version: string;
}
```

Consuming these ambient modules follows the same import patterns, yet requires vigilance in maintaining alignment between the declaration file and the underlying JavaScript implementation.

Expert practices in exporting and importing underscore the necessity of consistency and predictability. Developers are encouraged to adopt module patterns that favor explicit interfaces, leverage type-only imports wherever possible, and be acutely aware of bundler implications. Combining static export patterns with dynamic import constructs yields systems that are both rigorously verifiable at compile-time and adaptive at runtime. These strategies establish a robust and scalable framework for component-based architectures in TypeScript.

Persistent attention to these nuanced practices ensures that module boundaries remain well-defined, dependencies are clearly articulated, and the overall system architecture adheres to the highest standards of type safety and performance. The deliberate orchestration of export and import strategies across modules directly translates into more maintainable, testable, and efficient codebases in real-world applications.

## 5.3   Understanding Module Resolution

TypeScript's module resolution process stands as a critical aspect of dependency management in large-scale applications. The resolution algorithm bridges the gap between module specifiers and the cor-

232

responding files on disk. Advanced developers can fine-tune this process through configuration settings such as baseUrl, paths, and moduleResolution in the tsconfig.json file, ensuring that module dependencies are efficiently discovered and correctly linked. By understanding the nuances of the Node and Classic resolution strategies, programmers can preemptively resolve conflicts and optimize the dependency graph, particularly in environments with complex directory structures or legacy codebases.

The moduleResolution compiler option supports two primary strategies: "node" and "classic". The Node strategy emulates the resolution algorithm defined in Node.js, supporting features like index resolutions and package configuration files (package.json). In contrast, the Classic strategy, which pre-dates the standardization of ECMAScript modules, follows a simpler logic that may not suffice for projects requiring interoperability with Node.js packages. The choice between these strategies can heavily impact both the build process and runtime behavior.

TypeScript's Node resolution starts by translating module specifiers into file paths. When an import statement such as:

```
import { Utility } from 'lib/utility';
```

is encountered, the compiler searches for a file lib/utility.ts or lib/utility.d.ts relative to the base directory. If the file is not found, it then examines lib/utility/index.ts or lib/utility/index.d.ts. This behavior, crucial for maintaining compatibility with Node modules, is governed by internal heuristics that prioritize the existence of explicit type declarations over JavaScript files, thereby enforcing type safety across module boundaries.

The role of the `baseUrl` configuration property acts as an anchor point
to simplify module specifiers by reducing relative paths. By setting
a `baseUrl`, developers allow for absolute imports that improve code
clarity and maintainability. For example, consider the following configuration:

```
{
    "compilerOptions": {
        "baseUrl": "./src"
    }
}
```

With this configuration, an import such as:

```
import { Helper } from 'utils/helper';
```

will resolve to `./src/utils/helper.ts` rather than relying on overly
complex relative path expressions like `../../utils/helper`. This
practice simplifies refactoring, especially in monorepos or deeply
nested project structures.

Equally impactful is the `paths` mapping, which allows developers to
create aliasing for module paths. This feature is particularly useful for
abstracting away directory hierarchies and for enabling polymorphic
module resolution where multiple implementations are available. The
following example demonstrates advanced usage in a `tsconfig.json`
file:

```
{
    "compilerOptions": {
        "baseUrl": "./src",
        "paths": {
            "@core/*": ["core/*"],
            "@features/*": ["features/*"],
            "*": ["types/*", "*"]
        }
    }
}
```

```
}
```

In this setup, a module import can leverage the alias @core to suc-
cinctly reference core functionalities, enabling a level of abstraction
that decouples the consumer code from concrete directory structures.
When combined with a rigorous folder organization, such mappings
can significantly reduce the cognitive burden during code navigation
and refactoring.

Beyond basic aliasing, advanced scenarios include using multi-pattern
paths to provide fallback options. The last mapping in the previous example ("*: ["types/*", "*"]) ensures that if a module is not found
under the types directory, the resolver can fall back to the default location. Such hierarchical lookup patterns mitigate issues that arise when
a project is transitioning from legacy JavaScript to TypeScript, allowing
incremental adoption of type annotations.

The behavior of module resolution is also affected by the presence of
declaration files. When a TypeScript project emits declaration files
(.d.ts), these files guide the resolution process, ensuring that type
information is correctly propagated even if the implementation code
is stripped from the final bundle. In projects where libraries are consumed by both TypeScript and JavaScript consumers, maintaining accurate declaration files is paramount. Advanced developers often integrate automated scripts to generate and validate declaration files, ensuring consistency between the runtime behavior and the static type
system.

Interoperability between modules written in TypeScript and those written in JavaScript is achieved by leveraging ambient declarations and
the allowJs compiler option. The allowJs setting allows TypeScript

to resolve JavaScript modules as first-class citizens. When combined
with checkJs, the compiler enforces type-checking on JavaScript code,
thereby reducing integration friction in hybrid codebases. An advanced configuration might look like:

```
{
    "compilerOptions": {
        "allowJs": true,
        "checkJs": true,
        "moduleResolution": "node",
        "baseUrl": "./src"
    }
}
```

This configuration ensures that JavaScript files are seamlessly integrated into the TypeScript module resolution process while still benefiting from static analysis and error detection.

Circular dependencies present another challenge in module resolution.
While TypeScript's static analysis can detect and warn about circular
imports, advanced techniques such as reorganizing code to utilize interface segregation and using barrel files can mitigate these issues. Barrel files, which re-export modules from a centralized index, provide a
single point of reference for multiple modules. A typical barrel file
might appear as:

```
// In src/modules/index.ts
export * from './moduleA';
export * from './moduleB';
export * from './moduleC';
```

This pattern not only simplifies imports by abstracting away the underlying directory structure but also minimizes the risk of circular dependencies by ensuring that modules are referenced indirectly rather than
through intertwined local paths.

236

Dynamic module resolution is another sophisticated feature facilitated by TypeScript. The dynamic `import()` syntax enables runtime module loading, which is particularly beneficial for implementing lazy loading in large applications. Modules can be loaded asynchronously, reducing the upfront cost of application initialization and deferring loading of code until it is explicitly needed. An advanced dynamic import might be structured as:

```
async function loadModule(moduleName: string) {
    try {
        const module = await import(`./modules/${moduleName}`);
        return module;
    } catch (error) {
        console.error("Module loading failed:", error);
        throw error;
    }
}
```

In performance-critical systems, combining dynamic imports with prefetching strategies and runtime metrics can lead to significant improvements in load times. Analysis tools can be employed to generate dependency graphs that highlight the most frequently accessed modules, thereby informing decisions on which modules to load eagerly versus lazily.

TypeScript's configuration options also afford developers control over module resolution via custom plugin systems integrated with build tools such as Webpack or Rollup. These plugins can extend the standard resolution logic, implementing domain-specific heuristics or integrating with non-standard file formats. Developers who require such customizations must ensure that the resolution behavior remains deterministic and that the augmented resolution logic is well-documented and consistently maintained.

Performance profiling of the module resolution process is another advanced topic. In large projects, the time taken by the compiler to resolve modules can impact the overall build time. Techniques such as incremental compilation and caching resolved modules are crucial. The TypeScript compiler supports incremental builds, which cache previous resolution results, thus reducing recompilation times. Configuring the project for incremental builds can be done by setting:

```
{
    "compilerOptions": {
        "incremental": true,
        "tsBuildInfoFile": "./.tsbuildinfo"
    }
}
```

Such settings ensure that subsequent builds leverage cached output, thereby optimizing the developer feedback loop in large codebases.

Advanced dependency management also benefits from understanding how module resolution interacts with third-party libraries. Libraries published on npm often use a combination of main, module, and types fields in their package.json files to guide the resolution process. TypeScript inspects these fields to determine which file to import. For instance, the module field should point to an ES6 module version of the package, while the types field directs TypeScript to the corresponding declaration file. A typical package configuration may be:

```
{
    "name": "advanced-lib",
    "main": "lib/index.js",
    "module": "es/index.js",
    "types": "lib/index.d.ts"
}
```

By aligning library configurations with TypeScript's module resolution expectations, developers can ensure that third-party modules integrate seamlessly with their applications, preserving both runtime behavior and type safety.

The combination of these advanced module resolution strategies empowers developers to construct modular, highly maintainable systems. Precision in configuring module paths, aliasing, and resolution strategies directly translates into reduced build times, improved performance, and enhanced clarity of the codebase. Mastery of these detailed techniques is essential for developers tasked with maintaining large-scale applications where dependency management is as critical as algorithmic performance.

Understanding and fine-tuning TypeScript's module resolution process is not only a matter of efficiency but also an exercise in enforcing clean architectural boundaries. The balance between explicit configuration and the inherent flexibility of dynamic imports ensures that the dependency graph remains both robust and performant. By leveraging these advanced techniques, engineers can achieve a harmonious blend of type safety, maintainability, and runtime efficiency in their sophisticated TypeScript projects.

## 5.4 Namespaces vs Modules: Key Differences

Namespaces and modules present two distinct paradigms for organizing code in TypeScript, each with unique trade-offs and applications. At a high level, namespaces encapsulate related functionality within a single global context, whereas modules encapsulate functionality within file boundaries that are exported and imported explicitly. Advanced practitioners must understand the intricate differences, particularly concerning scope control, dependency management, and the evolution of JavaScript module standards, in order to choose the most appropriate mechanism for organizing complex codebases.

Namespaces, historically known as internal modules, were designed to overcome limitations of the global namespace in early JavaScript. They allow for logical organization by wrapping code within a named block, effectively avoiding name collisions. A typical namespace declaration is as follows:

```
namespace Geometry {
    export interface Shape {
        area(): number;
    }

    export class Circle implements Shape {
        constructor(private radius: number) {}
        area(): number {
            return Math.PI * this.radius * this.radius;
        }
    }
}
```

In this example, the `Geometry` namespace provides a container for related classes and interfaces. These members are attached to a common global object, necessitating explicit export keywords to expose only intended members while hiding implementation details. Because namespaces merge in the global scope, declaration merging plays a critical role when extending or combining functionality, which can be both powerful and challenging. Advanced usage can leverage this capability to extend the same namespace across multiple files via reference tags, but this approach requires careful management of file inclusion order and can lead to maintenance challenges in modular applications.

Modules, by contrast, follow the ECMAScript 2015 (ES6) standard, where each file represents its own module with its own scope. This design inherently avoids polluting the global namespace. Modules mandate explicit exporting of members and importing by other modules, thereby enforcing well-defined dependencies. An equivalent example using modules is presented as:

```
export interface Shape {
    area(): number;
}

export class Circle implements Shape {
    constructor(private radius: number) {}
    area(): number {
        return Math.PI * this.radius * this.radius;
    }
}
```

A module-based approach improves code isolation since each file introduces a new scope, and dependencies are clearly expressed via import and export statements. For large-scale systems, this leads to better maintainability, as the inter-dependencies are more explicit and the build tools can optimize code-splitting and lazy-loading strategies through static analysis.

One of the most critical differences between namespaces and modules is the way they are resolved at compile time and runtime. Namespaces are compiled into JavaScript constructs that maintain the structure of a single global object, typically a nested object literal. This static structure limits scalability in modern development environments because it does not map effectively to runtime systems that rely on module loaders such as CommonJS or AMD. Conversely, modules integrate seamlessly with modern bundlers like Webpack, Rollup, or the Node.js module loader, ensuring that dependencies are dynamically loaded and optimized at runtime. This integration allows advanced developers to leverage tree-shaking techniques, where unused code is eliminated from the final bundle during the build process.

Additionally, module systems support asynchronous loading through dynamic import() expressions, which are beyond the capabilities of namespaces. For example, advanced dynamic import usage appears as:

```
async function loadShape() {
    const module = await import('./ShapeModule');
    const circle = new module.Circle(5);
    console.log(circle.area());
}
```

Namespaces do not support this asynchronous paradigm because they rely on a synchronous script loading model. This limitation makes modules significantly more attractive when designing applications that require performance optimizations, such as code-splitting and lazy-loading of components on demand.

Another key consideration is the evolution of language standards. Modules have become the de facto standard due to ECMAScript's evolution, and most modern browsers and execution environments have native support for ES modules. This ubiquitous support leads to more consistent behavior across various platforms. Namespaces, while still supported by TypeScript for backward compatibility, do not have corresponding native runtime support in JavaScript. This divergence means that leveraging namespaces can introduce additional complexity when interoperating with external tools that expect a module-based structure. Advanced developers must weigh the benefits of a more modern module system against legacy concerns when integrating with older codebases that rely on namespaces.

Type safety plays a role in both approaches but is often more rigorously

enforced in module-based design. Since modules enforce strict boundaries and require explicit import paths, the TypeScript compiler can
provide better context-specific diagnostic information, flagging inconsistencies and circular dependencies that might otherwise be obscured
in a namespace-driven approach. Consider the following subtle issue
arising in a namespace scenario:

```
namespace Utilities {
    export function helper(): void { /* implementation */ }
}

namespace Tools {
    // Implicitly relying on the global presence of Utilities
    export function run() {
        Utilities.helper();
    }
}
```

When these namespaces are merged, a misconfiguration or accidental
reordering of script inclusion could lead to runtime errors that are difficult to diagnose. In a module-based system, such errors are minimized
because each module explicitly specifies its dependencies:

```
import { helper } from './utilities';

export function run(): void {
    helper();
}
```

This explicit dependency declaration reduces the risk of missing or mis-
aligned dependencies, thus strengthening code robustness.

Furthermore, modules enhance code refactoring capabilities. Since
modules are file-centric, tooling support for refactoring is more mature
and effective. Tools like Visual Studio Code and WebStorm can reliably
update import paths, detect unused exports, and offer automatic mod-

ule resolution. For advanced practitioners, this capability translates into reduced friction when reorganizing or restructuring large codebases. In contrast, refactoring namespaces often involves more manual intervention and global search-and-replace operations, particularly when the codebase spans multiple files that rely on ambient declarations.

Namespaces can still offer advantages in scenarios where a collection of functionalities must be bundled into a single file and executed as a cohesive unit, particularly in isolated environments or when interacting with legacy systems. For instance, applications that need to be delivered as a single self-contained script may benefit from the namespace pattern because it consolidates the code into one global object. However, the trade-off is the loss of modular benefits such as asynchronous loading, dynamic dependency resolution, and tree shaking.

From an architectural standpoint, mixing namespaces and modules is generally discouraged unless there is a compelling reason to do so. The presence of both paradigms in a single project can lead to confusion and inconsistent code patterns. Advanced developers should enforce a unified module strategy whenever possible, migrating legacy namespaces into module files to capitalize on modern build systems and runtime optimizations. When a dual approach is unavoidable, careful layering is required: internal namespaces may be used within a module to organize related constructs, but the module boundary should encapsulate the entire public interface.

Consider the scenario of creating a library intended for consumption both in Node.js and in the browser. By using modules, the library author can export a well-defined interface that behaves predictably in both environments. Internal helper functions and types can be organized using a namespace within the module file without leaking to the global scope:

```
namespace InternalHelpers {
    export function computeFactor(x: number): number {
        return x * x;
    }
}

export function enhancedCompute(x: number): number {
    return InternalHelpers.computeFactor(x) + 10;
}
```

This design leverages the organizational benefits of namespaces while retaining the overall modular structure. Such hybrid approaches allow advanced developers to enjoy the strengths of both paradigms when absolute separation is required.

Performance implications also diverge between namespaces and modules. Modules, by virtue of their explicit dependency declarations, can assist bundlers in performing dead-code elimination more effectively, reducing overall bundle size and improving runtime performance. This is particularly significant in large applications where every kilobyte of the final bundle counts. Namespaces, on the other hand, aggregate code into a single global context, making it harder for static analysis tools to trim unused code. For developers optimizing for performance at scale, the module system is a far superior choice.

In summary, the primary differences between namespaces and modules hinge on scope management, dependency clarity, runtime efficiency, and tooling support. Modules provide strict encapsulation, asynchronous loading, modern language compatibility, and performance optimizations while namespaces offer simplicity in scenarios dominated by single-file or legacy applications. Advanced TypeScript development increasingly favors modules for their alignment with EC-

MAScript standards and superior integration with modern development workflows. Adopting a module-centric approach facilitates scalable code architecture, allowing developers to deliver robust, maintainable, and optimized applications in complex real-world environments.

## 5.5   Combining Modules with Namespaces

In advanced TypeScript applications, the coexistence of modules and
namespaces can be strategically employed to benefit from the strengths
unique to each paradigm. Modules offer fine-grained control over file
boundaries, external dependency management, and seamless integration with modern bundlers and dynamic import strategies. In contrast,
namespaces provide a mechanism to logically group related functionality within a module, facilitating internal organization and controlled
visibility. By combining these approaches, developers can achieve a
high degree of compartmentalization in large-scale codebases, balancing robust external modularity with flexible internal organization.

One common pattern is to encapsulate internally coherent collections
of helper functions, types, and interfaces within a namespace that re-
sides in a module file. This design pattern isolates advanced implementations behind a well-defined module boundary while using the
namespace to group related constructs that are not intended for external exposure. An example of this method is illustrated in the following
sample module:

```
namespace Internal {
    export interface IDataProcessor {
        process(input: any): any;
    }
```

```
export class DefaultProcessor implements IDataProcessor {
    process(input: any): any {
        // Complex grid partitioning logic or data transformation
        return input;
    }
}

export function validateData(data: any): boolean {
    // Perform rigorous checks across multiple fields
    return data !== null && typeof data === 'object';
}
}

export class DataManager {
    private processor: Internal.IDataProcessor;

    constructor() {
        // The internal namespace encapsulates essential algorithms
        this.processor = new Internal.DefaultProcessor();
    }

    public handleData(data: any): any {
        if (Internal.validateData(data)) {
            return this.processor.process(data);
        }
        throw new Error('Invalid data provided');
    }
}
```

In this architecture, DataManager exists as the exported public API of the module, while the Internal namespace houses implementation details that are not directly exposed. This approach enforces a clear separation between the public interface and the internal workings, thereby facilitating future refactoring and optimization without changing the external contract.

Advanced usage of combining namespaces with modules includes leveraging conditional compilation and selective export strategies. By carefully choosing which parts of a namespace are re-exported from

the module, developers can provide a comprehensive API surface
while keeping sensitive or experimental implementations private. For
instance, the following pattern introduces a private utility within a
namespace and selectively re-exports only its safe interface:

```
namespace Utils {
    interface Logger {
        log(message: string): void;
    }

    class ConsoleLogger implements Logger {
        log(message: string): void {
            console.log(`[INFO]: ${message}`);
        }
    }

    // Private logging function for diagnostic purposes
    export function logDebug(message: string): void {
        const logger: Logger = new ConsoleLogger();
        logger.log(message);
    }
}

// Expose only the safe API to consumers
export const LoggerAPI = {
    debug: Utils.logDebug
};
```

In this example, the Utils namespace encapsulates both the concrete
ConsoleLogger and its associated debugging function. Only the safe
abstraction LoggerAPI is exposed through the module's export, preventing accidental misuse of internal implementations while still leveraging namespace-based compartmentalization.

Combining modules with namespaces also plays a vital role in managing large enterprise codebases where teams may work concurrently
on overlapping domains. By architecting each module as a cohesive
unit that internally organizes sub-components via namespaces, devel-

248

opment teams can enforce strict boundaries at the module level while allowing internal teams latitude to structure their code logically. A practical scenario involves developing a shared library for data visualization in which each module represents a domain, and internal namespaces separate utilities, core algorithms, and configuration settings. Consider the design of a charting module:

```typescript
namespace ChartUtils {
    export function calculateAxisScale(data: number[]): number {
        // Advanced calculation based on statistical measures
        return Math.max(...data) / 10;
    }
}

namespace Renderers {
    export class SVGRenderer {
        render(data: number[]): string {
            // Generate an SVG representation of the chart
            return `<svg><!-- SVG chart rendering of data: ${data.
    join(', ')} --></svg>`;
        }
    }

    export class CanvasRenderer {
        render(data: number[]): HTMLCanvasElement {
            // Create and return a canvas element with the chart
    drawn
            const canvas = document.createElement('canvas');
            // Canvas drawing code
            return canvas;
        }
    }
}

export class Chart {
    private scale: number;
    private renderer: Renderers.SVGRenderer | Renderers.
    CanvasRenderer;

    constructor(data: number[], rendererType: 'svg' | 'canvas' = 'svg
    ') {
        this.scale = ChartUtils.calculateAxisScale(data);
```

```
        this.renderer = rendererType === 'svg'
            ? new Renderers.SVGRenderer()
            : new Renderers.CanvasRenderer();
    }

    render(data: number[]): string | HTMLCanvasElement {
        return this.renderer.render(data);
    }
}
```

Here, the module serves as the boundary encapsulating charting capabilities, while the namespaces `ChartUtils` and `Renderers` organize the
functionality into logical clusters that can be developed, maintained,
and optimized independently. Such separation in design minimizes
the risk of collisions and simplifies testing by isolating different aspects
of the implementation.

Another powerful technique involves using namespaces for declaration merging within module files. Declaration merging is common
when extending third-party libraries or building plugin architectures.
By augmenting existing module declarations using namespaces, developers can introduce additional type information or helper functions
without modifying the external API surface. An example of this technique is shown below:

```
import * as React from 'react';

namespace ReactExtensions {
    export interface Component<P = {}, S = {}> extends React.
    Component<P, S> {
        trackRender: () => void;
    }
}

export class TrackedComponent<P = {}, S = {}> extends React.Component
    <P, S> implements ReactExtensions.Component<P, S> {
    trackRender(): void {
        console.debug('Component rendered:', this.constructor.name);
```

```
    }

    render(): React.ReactNode {
        this.trackRender();
        return super.render();
    }
}
```

In this scenario, the namespace ReactExtensions is used to enrich React's component type declaration with additional functionality. This extension, confined to the module, empowers developers to enforce best practices such as render tracking without altering the underlying React library. Such hybrid arrangements enable clean, maintainable augmentation of external libraries while keeping the additional functionality modular and self-contained.

For large-scale applications, the sophistication of module-plus-namespace design can be further enhanced by employing automated build tools and static analysis. Tools such as ESLint and TypeScript's own compiler diagnostics can enforce naming conventions and detect unintended global leaks. Moreover, bundlers like Webpack take advantage of explicit module boundaries for tree-shaking, while namespaces act merely as an organizational tool that does not impact the generated bundle structure. A well-organized codebase that exploits both systems facilitates incremental builds and enables smoother integration with continuous integration pipelines.

In practice, the decision to combine modules with namespaces should be guided by the desire to achieve a balance between internal cohesion and external decoupling. Within a module, namespaces allow developers to logically group helper methods, internal configurations, and private implementation details. Meanwhile, the module boundary itself provides clear, explicit contracts for dependency injection and exter-

251

nal usage. This dual-layer strategy can be particularly useful in plugin architectures where the core functionality must remain stable, while various internal enhancements or extensions evolve independently.

For example, consider a plugin system for a framework where each plugin is delivered as a module and internal functionalities of the plugin are organized in a namespace. The following example demonstrates such an approach:

```
namespace PluginInternals {
    export interface PluginConfiguration {
        enableFeatureX: boolean;
        threshold: number;
    }

    export function loadDefaultConfig(): PluginConfiguration {
        return { enableFeatureX: true, threshold: 5 };
    }

    export class PluginHelper {
        static initialize(config: PluginConfiguration): void {
            // Initialization logic using the config
            console.debug('Initializing with:', config);
        }
    }
}

export class CustomPlugin {
    private config: PluginInternals.PluginConfiguration;

    constructor(config?: Partial<PluginInternals.PluginConfiguration
    >) {
        // Merge supplied configuration with default settings
        this.config = { ...PluginInternals.loadDefaultConfig(), ...
    config };
        PluginInternals.PluginHelper.initialize(this.config);
    }

    execute(): void {
        // Core plugin functionality exposed as part of the module
        API
        console.log('Plugin execution with config:', this.config);
```

```
      }
   }
```

This modular approach isolates plugin-specific configuration and helper routines within a namespace, while presenting a clear and lean API to the consumers of the plugin. By doing so, it becomes easier to manage version increments, enforce backward compatibility, and decouple plugin internals from the core framework.

In summary, combining modules with namespaces provides an effective strategy for compartmentalizing code in large-scale applications. By leveraging modules for explicit dependency management and external interaction, and namespaces for internal organization, advanced developers can achieve both robust encapsulation and flexible internal structuring. This dual approach encourages clear architectural boundaries, facilitates incremental enhancements, and simplifies both testing and maintenance across ambitious TypeScript projects.

## 5.6 Dynamic Module Loading

Dynamic module loading in TypeScript is an advanced technique that directly addresses the challenges of optimizing performance and flexibility in complex applications. By deferring the loading of modules until runtime, developers can reduce initial load times, optimize resource utilization, and enable adaptive behavior based on runtime conditions. This section delves into the underlying mechanics of dynamic module loading, best practices for its implementation, and insights into integrating it with modern bundlers and build systems.

The foundation of dynamic module loading rests on the ECMAScript `import()` function, which returns a promise that resolves to the module's exports. This asynchronous approach enables the deferment of module loading until the moment the functionality is required. In TypeScript, dynamic imports are fully supported and benefit from static type-checking when combined with appropriate type assertions. An elementary dynamic import is illustrated below:

```
async function loadUtilities() {
    const utilitiesModule = await import('./utilities');
    utilitiesModule.performComplexCalculation();
}
```

When employing dynamic module loading, advanced developers should pay special attention to caching and dependency ordering. Since dynamic imports return promises, it is possible to cache these promises to avoid redundant requests. A typical strategy is to maintain a local cache of loaded modules, enabling re-use of already fetched code and reducing the number of network requests or file system accesses in server-side environments.

```
const moduleCache: { [key: string]: Promise<any> } = {};

function loadModule(modulePath: string): Promise<any> {
    if (!moduleCache[modulePath]) {
        moduleCache[modulePath] = import(modulePath);
    }
    return moduleCache[modulePath];
}
```

This caching mechanism is essential in scenarios where multiple conditional branches or user interactions invoke the same module. Caching ensures that the module is fetched and evaluated only once, reducing overhead and potential inconsistencies that may arise due to multiple evaluations of the same code.

254

Advanced integration with bundlers such as Webpack or Rollup leverages dynamic imports for code splitting. Code splitting allows a bundler to separate the codebase into smaller chunks, which can be loaded on demand rather than bundling the entire application into a single file. A dynamic import used in this context might be written as:

```
// Webpack-specific dynamic import for code splitting
async function loadFeatureModule(featureName: string) {
    const featureModule = await import(
        /* webpackChunkName: "feature-[request]" */
        `./features/${featureName}`
    );
    return featureModule;
}
```

Including special comments such as webpackChunkName instructs Webpack to name the generated chunk appropriately, which is useful during debugging as well as for cache management on the client side.

One challenge that arises with dynamic module loading is the management of dependencies and side effects. Modules may perform initialization routines when loaded, and the order of module loading might affect application state. Advanced developers are encouraged to segregate initialization logic from module definition by encapsulating stateful operations in functions that can be triggered explicitly. For example:

```
export function initializeFeature(config: FeatureConfig): void {
    // Stateful initialization logic
    console.info('Initializing feature with config:', config);
}
```

The consumer of such a module should then dynamically import and explicitly call the initialization function only when the feature is required:

```
async function activateFeature(featureName: string, config:
    FeatureConfig) {
    const featureModule = await import(`./features/${featureName}`);
    featureModule.initializeFeature(config);
}
```

Advanced usage also involves conditional dynamic loading where the
decision to load a module depends on runtime parameters or environmental factors. This pattern is critical when supporting multiple environments or feature toggling. A robust implementation might involve
checking a configuration object and then dynamically importing the
corresponding module:

```
interface FeatureToggle {
    [featureName: string]: boolean;
}

const featureToggles: FeatureToggle = {
    analytics: true,
    experimental: false,
};

async function loadConditionalFeature(featureName: string) {
    if (featureToggles[featureName]) {
        const feature = await import(`./features/${featureName}`);
        return feature;
    } else {
        console.warn(`Feature ${featureName} is disabled.`);
        return null;
    }
}
```

The asynchronous nature of dynamic imports introduces new patterns
in error handling and timing management. Advanced designs often
incorporate fallback mechanisms using either native promise chaining
or helper libraries such as RxJS. Detailed error handling ensures that
failure to load a module does not bring down the entire application.

For example:

```
async function safeLoadModule(modulePath: string) {
    try {
        const module = await import(modulePath);
        return module;
    } catch (error) {
        console.error(`Error loading module ${modulePath}:`, error);
        // Optionally load a fallback or return a default
    implementation
        return { default: () => console.warn('Fallback executed') };
    }
}
```

Furthermore, advanced scenarios involve coordination between statically imported modules and dynamically loaded ones. In these architectures, static imports are reserved for core functionality, and dynamic imports handle peripheral or rarely used features. This division
can be orchestrated through a central module loader that abstracts both
mechanisms behind a unified interface. A simplified version of such a
loader would be:

```
import { coreFunctionality } from './core';

class ModuleLoader {
    private cache: { [key: string]: Promise<any> } = {};

    load(modulePath: string): Promise<any> {
        if (!this.cache[modulePath]) {
            this.cache[modulePath] = import(modulePath);
        }
        return this.cache[modulePath];
    }

    async executeDynamicFeature(featureName: string): Promise<void> {
        const featureModule = await this.load(`./features/${
    featureName}`);
        if (featureModule && featureModule.execute) {
            featureModule.execute();
        } else {
            console.warn(`Feature ${featureName} does not expose an
```

```
    execute method.`);
      }
   }
}


export const loader = new ModuleLoader();
```

This abstraction promotes a clean separation of concerns and simplifies error handling, caching, and performance diagnostics. The integration of static type-checking with dynamic behavior is one of TypeScript's unique strengths. By leveraging import type in conjunction with dynamic imports, developers can ensure that the shape of dynamically imported modules is predictable without incurring any runtime cost:

```
import type { AnalyticsModule } from './analytics';

async function loadAnalytics(): Promise<AnalyticsModule> {
    return import('./analytics') as Promise<AnalyticsModule>;
}
```

This technique improves the developer experience by allowing rich auto-completion and type safety even in dynamic contexts, which is particularly important when the imported module has a complex API surface.

Dynamic module loading also necessitates careful consideration during testing and debugging. Unit tests should account for asynchronous behavior, which may require the use of mocks or specialized testing frameworks that support asynchronous assertions. Integration tests, in particular, must verify that modules are loaded, initialized, and cached as expected. Tools such as Jest offer robust support for mocking dynamic imports through manual mocks or by intercepting import() calls, thereby allowing a controlled test environment.

Finally, performance profiling of dynamically loaded modules is essential in large-scale applications. Modern browsers and Node.js provide diagnostics tools to monitor network requests, resource loading times, and execution performance. Techniques such as prefetching—where modules are hinted to be loaded before they are requested—can be employed by using link preload strategies or bundler-specific configurations. An example of prefetching in Webpack might include:

```
// Webpack prefetching hint
import(
    /* webpackPrefetch: true */
    './features/optionalFeature'
);
```

Prefetching can significantly improve perceived application responsiveness by loading modules in the background during idle time.

Dynamic module loading in TypeScript elevates application performance and flexibility by delaying the loading of non-critical code until it is needed. The effective use of caching, error handling, and sophisticated bundler integration is critical for advanced applications. Techniques such as conditional loading, abstraction via centralized module loaders, and the combination of static type-checking with asynchronous imports empower developers to build highly responsive and scalable architectures. By adhering to these best practices and leveraging the available tooling, advanced developers can optimize both the runtime performance and maintainability of modern TypeScript applications.

# 5.7   Refactoring Code with Modular Design

Refactoring legacy or monolithic codebases into a modular architecture requires a systematic approach that addresses separation of concerns, dependency isolation, and clear API boundaries. Advanced refactoring involves identifying logical groupings of functionality, extracting them into discrete modules, and leveraging TypeScript's strong type system to enforce contracts between these modules. A key concept is to decompose the application's core logic into reusable, independently testable components while minimizing coupling. This section examines strategies to achieve refined modular design in existing codebases, focusing on practical techniques, transition patterns, and the subtleties of TypeScript's module system.

The first step in the refactoring process is to analyze the current codebase and identify natural boundaries. In many legacy systems, functionality is often conflated within large files or interdependent global objects. Advanced developers should begin by mapping out dependencies and isolating components that exhibit strong cohesion. One effective approach is to use dependency graphs generated by static analysis tools that track import paths. Once the core functionalities are identified, start re-organizing them into self-contained modules. For instance, consider the following fragmented code snippet that handles data processing and presentation aspects intermixed in a single file:

```
class DataHandler {
    process(rawData: string): any {
        // Parsing and validation logic
        const parsed = JSON.parse(rawData);
        // Additional processing logic mixed with presentation
    formatting
        return {
            processedData: parsed.data.map((item: any) => item.value
```

```
        * 2),
                html: `<div>${parsed.title}</div>`
            };
        }
    }
```

Refactoring would separate processing logic from presentation, leading to distinct modules. One module can focus on data transformation, and another on rendering output. The refactored code might appear as follows:

```
export namespace DataProcessing {
    export function parseAndTransform(rawData: string): number[] {
        const parsed = JSON.parse(rawData);
        return parsed.data.map((item: any) => item.value * 2);
    }
}

export namespace Presentation {
    export function renderTitle(title: string): string {
        return `<div>${title}</div>`;
    }
}
```

This refactoring not only improves maintainability by decoupling responsibilities but also facilitates targeted unit testing. Modules become isolated and can be independently evolved. The use of namespaces within modules, as shown above, remains a viable tool for grouping closely related functions while keeping the public API succinct.

When starting to refactor into modules, it is important to ensure that the new modules maintain compatibility with the existing code. TypeScript's ability to interoperate with JavaScript is an asset in incremental refactoring. Developers can use allowJs and checkJs options in tsconfig.json to gradually introduce TypeScript modules into a largely untyped JavaScript codebase. An example configuration might be:

```
{
    "compilerOptions": {
        "allowJs": true,
        "checkJs": true,
        "module": "ES6",
        "target": "ES6",
        "baseUrl": "./src",
        "paths": {
            "@app/*": ["app/*"]
        }
    },
    "include": ["src/**/*"]
}
```

The presence of explicit path mappings and base URL configurations
streamlines refactoring by allowing legacy code to gradually reference
new module paths. Advanced developers often use barrel files—a
technique where a module index re-exports selected submodules—to
consolidate imports and minimize refactoring disruption. A barrel file
might be structured as follows:

```
// In src/utils/index.ts
export * from './dataProcessing';
export * from './presentation';
```

With barrel files in place, refactoring becomes less intrusive because
consumers need only update a single import reference. The gradual adoption of modular design techniques minimizes the risk associated with extensive rewrites and introduces TypeScript's compile-time
checks gradually into the workflow.

Another powerful strategy is to adopt a layered approach to refactoring. Begin with the core logic that does not depend on external interfaces, moving towards more peripheral modules. Core functionality is
often the ideal candidate for relocation into pure modules. For exam-

ple, if a legacy system's business logic is entangled with UI code, isolating business rules into a separate module permits the application to evolve on multiple fronts independently. Consider an inline validation function deeply embedded within a view component:

```
function validateData(input: any): boolean {
    // Embedded business rules along with UI error handling
    if (!input || typeof input !== 'object') {
        alert('Invalid data');
        return false;
    }
    return input.id !== undefined;
}
```

An advanced refactoring strategy would extract the validation logic into its own module, while the UI layer is responsible only for displaying errors. The refactored modules could be organized as follows:

```
export module Validators {
    export function validateData(input: any): boolean {
        return input !== null && typeof input === 'object' && input.
    id !== undefined;
    }
}

export module UILogger {
    export function showError(message: string): void {
        // Replace alert with a more robust UI mechanism
        console.error(message);
    }
}
```

The decoupled modules allow for independent scaling. For instance, the business logic module can later be enhanced with additional rules or swapped out as requirements evolve, without necessitating changes in the UI layer.

In refactoring large codebases, it is also critical to address cross-cutting concerns such as logging, error handling, and configuration management through the use of shared modules. By creating centralized utilities, these concerns can be refactored out of individual components and into common libraries. For example, a logging utility might be refactored as follows:

```
export module Logger {
    export function logInfo(message: string): void {
        console.info(`[INFO]: ${message}`);
    }

    export function logError(message: string): void {
        console.error(`[ERROR]: ${message}`);
    }
}
```

Such utilities become essential building blocks in a modular design, promoting reusability and consistency across the application. Advanced techniques might include dependency injection to dynamically provide different logging implementations based on the environment, making the system flexible and testable.

Addressing circular dependencies is another advanced challenge encountered during modular refactoring. Oftentimes, as modules are extracted from a monolith, latent circular dependencies emerge that were previously masked by a shared global scope. Tools like madge can aid in detecting these issues. Once identified, the solution typically involves restructuring dependencies—either by introducing intermediary modules to decouple relationships or by adopting inversion of control patterns. An example of breaking a circular dependency is by refactoring two interdependent modules into one or introducing an abstract interface:

```
// Before refactoring: ModuleA and ModuleB rely on each other
// After refactoring: Introduce a common interface
```

```
export interface IDataProvider {
    getData(): any;
}

export module DataModule {
    export class Provider implements IDataProvider {
        getData(): any {
            // Implementation logic
        }
    }
}
```

Using interfaces ensures that concrete dependencies are injected at run-time, reducing static coupling among modules. Advanced developers should also consider patterns such as event-driven architectures or message buses to further decouple module interactions.

Progressive refactoring requires rigorous testing at every stage. Unit tests, integration tests, and end-to-end tests must be refactored in tandem with code to ensure that each module's contract is preserved. Utilizing TypeScript's type system effectively, developers can define strict interfaces and use mocks or stubs to simulate module behaviors during testing. A sample unit test for a refactored module might look as follows:

```
import { DataProcessing } from '../utils/dataProcessing';
import { expect } from 'chai';

describe('DataProcessing Module', () => {
    it('should correctly transform raw data', () => {
        const rawData = '{"data":[{"value":5},{"value":10}]}';
        const result = DataProcessing.parseAndTransform(rawData);
        expect(result).to.deep.equal([10, 20]);
    });
});
```

Maintaining a comprehensive test suite during refactoring instills confidence in the modular design and facilitates further enhancements. Advanced techniques involve using continuous integration pipelines to run tests automatically, ensuring that every module conforms to the defined contracts.

Finally, performance considerations should not be overlooked during refactoring. Modular design introduces new boundaries that can affect startup times, module loading, and runtime performance. Profiling tools and static analysis can be used to optimize module boundaries and ensure that refactoring does not inadvertently degrade performance. Techniques like lazy loading—previously discussed—can be employed to defer the initialization of non-critical modules until needed, thus balancing maintainability against performance overhead.

In practice, refactoring code with modular design is an iterative process, with incremental migration from legacy structures to a refined, loosely coupled architecture. Advanced developers are advised to focus on creating clear, small, disposable modules with well-defined interfaces. By leveraging TypeScript's type system, dynamic module loading capabilities, and sophisticated refactoring tools, a codebase can evolve into a modular, maintainable, and scalable enterprise-grade system.

# 6

# Chapter 6: Harnessing TypeScript with React and Redux

*This chapter explores integrating TypeScript with React and Redux, enhancing type safety in components, props, and state management. It examines advanced patterns with Hooks, ensuring robust applications, and covers the integration of Redux for type-safe actions, reducers, and stores. Additionally, it addresses creating typed selectors, middleware, and best practices for testing, ensuring code quality and performance.*

# 6.1   Type Safety in React with TypeScript

TypeScript fundamentally augments React application development by introducing a robust static type system that prohibits a range of runtime errors. This static analysis enforces contracts throughout component interfaces, props, state objects, and even dynamic properties such as render function returns. Advanced programmers gain granular control over type definitions by utilizing interfaces, generics, union and intersection types, and mapped types, thereby reducing the potential for type mismatches and ensuring that changes propagate safely through the codebase.

Advanced use cases often dictate the need for higher-order components (HOCs) and render props that accommodate varying component types. The TypeScript compiler validates that properties passed into components match the declared contract, resulting in early detection of errors without execution. For example, the following code snippet demonstrates a generic button component that accepts a callback and an associated data payload. The callback signature enforces both the event type and the generic data type, ensuring type consistency between the component and its usage context.

```
import React from 'react';

interface ButtonProps<T> {
    onClick: (event: React.MouseEvent<HTMLButtonElement>, data: T) =>
      void;
    data: T;
    label: string;
}

function GenericButton<T>({ onClick, data, label }: ButtonProps<T>) {
    return (
        <button
            onClick={(e) => {
```

```
              onClick(e, data);
        }}
    >
        {label}
    </button>
  );
}

export default GenericButton;
```

The above example leverages generics to make the component agnostic to the type of payload it handles. This technique is particularly potent for ensuring that all usages of such components are type-safe, even when they operate with varying data types. Extensive integration of generics, especially in multi-layered component hierarchies, avoids the pitfalls of untyped hooks and render prop patterns where mismatches might otherwise occur.

Another significant benefit is when type inference interacts with advanced React patterns. For instance, the employment of discriminated unions can be used effectively in conjunction with TypeScript's control flow analysis to refine the code paths based on the type of prop passed. Consider an abstract data renderer that can adaptively present different interfaces based on discriminative properties:

```
import React from 'react';

interface CircleData {
    kind: 'circle';
    radius: number;
}

interface SquareData {
    kind: 'square';
    side: number;
}

type ShapeData = CircleData | SquareData;
```

269

```typescript
interface ShapeRendererProps {
    shape: ShapeData;
}

const ShapeRenderer: React.FC<ShapeRendererProps> = ({ shape }) => {
    switch (shape.kind) {
        case 'circle':
            return <div>Circle with area: {Math.PI * shape.radius **
    2}</div>;
        case 'square':
            return <div>Square with area: {shape.side ** 2}</div>;
    }
};

export default ShapeRenderer;
```

In this example, TypeScript enforces that each branch of the switch statement correctly handles properties specific to the variant of ShapeData. This pattern precludes the possibility of runtime errors due to neglected properties or misinterpretation of the shape type. Advanced development further benefits from such techniques when scaling up to large applications with hundreds of discriminated unions.

Static type checking extends into React's state management as well. Integrating TypeScript types into the React useState hook ensures that state transitions adhere strictly to defined types. By meticulously annotating the state with types, developers can prevent direct mutations that lead to unpredictable UI behavior. Consider an example where a component manages a state object with several fields:

```typescript
import React, { useState } from 'react';

interface User {
    id: number;
    username: string;
    email: string;
```

270

```
}

const UserProfile: React.FC = () => {
    const [user, setUser] = useState<User | null>(null);

    const updateEmail = (newEmail: string) => {
        if (user) {
            setUser({ ...user, email: newEmail });
        }
    };

    return (
        <div>
            {user ? (
                <>
                    <h2>{user.username}</h2>
                    <p>{user.email}</p>
                    <button onClick={() => updateEmail('new@example.
    com')}>Change Email</button>
                </>
            ) : (
                <div>No user loaded</div>
            )}
        </div>
    );
};

export default UserProfile;
```

Through precise type annotations, any attempt to set an inappropriate state value or inadvertently mutate the state object is detected at compile time. This paradigm is fundamental to modern React development, where applications are built upon predictable state transitions and the immutability principle.

Furthermore, the combination of React and TypeScript is particularly beneficial in the context of context providers and consumer components. By defining context value types explicitly, the propagation of state data through deeply nested components becomes transparent and reliable. Consider an example of a global theme context:

```
import React, { createContext, useContext } from 'react';

interface Theme {
    primaryColor: string;
    secondaryColor: string;
    background: string;
}

const defaultTheme: Theme = {
    primaryColor: '#1976d2',
    secondaryColor: '#dc004e',
    background: '#ffffff',
};

const ThemeContext = createContext<Theme>(defaultTheme);

const ThemeProvider: React.FC<{ theme: Theme }> = ({ theme, children
    }) => (
    <ThemeContext.Provider value={theme}>
        {children}
    </ThemeContext.Provider>
);

const useTheme = (): Theme => {
    const context = useContext(ThemeContext);
    if (!context) {
        throw new Error('useTheme must be used within a ThemeProvider
    ');
    }
    return context;
};

export { ThemeProvider, useTheme };
```

By explicitly typing the `ThemeContext`, the provider assures that all consuming components benefit from enforced consistency. If a component attempts to read or write an unmatched property, TypeScript communicates the error during the development phase. This pattern yields a significant reduction in runtime exceptions, as component contracts are systematically validated.

Delving deeper into advanced patterns, strong type safety in React with TypeScript becomes indispensable when implementing component composition patterns. Particularly, when building polymorphic components that can render different HTML elements based on a as prop, robust type inference is required to propagate intrinsic element attributes alongside custom props. Such implementations often require the definition of props that merge custom types with the element's native attributes. An advanced implementation might look as follows:

```
import React from 'react';

type AsProp<C extends React.ElementType> = {
    as?: C;
};

type PolymorphicRef<C extends React.ElementType> =
    React.ComponentPropsWithRef<C>['ref'];

type PropsToOmit<C extends React.ElementType, P> = keyof (AsProp<C> &
    P);

type PolymorphicComponentProps<
    C extends React.ElementType,
    Props = {}
> = React.PropsWithChildren<Props & AsProp<C>> &
    Omit<React.ComponentPropsWithoutRef<C>, PropsToOmit<C, Props>> &
    {
        ref?: PolymorphicRef<C>;
    };

function PolymorphicButton<C extends React.ElementType = 'button'>(
    { as, children, ...restProps }: PolymorphicComponentProps<C, {
    variant: string }>
) {
    const Component = as || 'button';
    return <Component {...restProps}>{children}</Component>;
}
```

```
export default PolymorphicButton;
```

This pattern utilizes advanced TypeScript utility types and conditional type inference to ensure that intrinsic HTML attributes specific to the rendered element C are correctly merged with custom properties. Consequently, the compiler cross-checks every prop against both the element's native properties and the explicitly declared custom ones. This level of detail yields a flexible and type-secure component design capable of adapting to diverse rendering contexts.

Even in scenarios of dynamic component data exchange, the use of advanced type constructs, such as mapped types and conditional types, adds an extra layer of safety and expressiveness to React applications. For example, a higher-order component (HOC) that injects additional props into its wrapped component must reconcile the prop types of both the HOC and the child component. This is typically achieved by intersecting the types and then omitting conflicting keys through utility types provided by TypeScript. In such cases, each transformation maintains a strict type invariant that eliminates classically encountered errors in component property propagation.

Optimizations at the build time provided by TypeScript further include dead code elimination and tree shaking when combined with modern bundlers. The static representation of types allows tools to remove unused code paths and optimize memory footprints without compromising runtime behavior. Advanced configurations in the tsconfig.json file, such as strictNullChecks and noImplicitAny, compound these benefits by enforcing comprehensive type information across the entire React project.

Developers who leverage TypeScript with React also appreciate the

274

role of integrated development environments (IDEs) that harness these type declarations to offer intelligent code completion, refactoring tools, and contextual warnings. The synergy between robust type annotations and advanced tooling translates to an environment where refactoring large codebases is streamlined, making the system more maintainable and free from inadvertent regressions.

Through precise typing of complex component hierarchies, conditional rendering logic, and polymorphic patterns, TypeScript instills high confidence in the correctness of React applications. This comprehensive type safety not only accelerates the development process but also facilitates large-scale collaboration, where misunderstandings about component contracts can result in intricate bugs. By ensuring that every prop, external library interface, and custom hook adheres to defined types, the overall system becomes resilient, extensible, and easier to validate through both compile-time checks and rigorous testing suites.

## 6.2 Defining Props and State with TypeScript

In React applications, explicit type definitions for component props and state mitigate the risk of runtime errors and yield predictable behaviors during refactoring. Utilizing TypeScript's advanced type system, developers can define nuanced contracts that precisely capture the intended structure and constraints of both props and state. This section presents advanced techniques and patterns for annotating React components, enabling the creation of robust and maintainable systems.

Explicitly typed component props are typically declared using inter-

face or type aliases. Interfaces are particularly useful for defining
reusable contracts that describe the shape of an object, while union and
intersection types enable the expression of more complex relationships.
Consider a component that requires multiple optional and dependent
props; clearly distinguishing these variations avoids ambiguity in component usage. An advanced example is provided below:

```
interface BaseProps {
    id: string;
    visible?: boolean;
}

interface DataProps {
    data: {
        name: string;
        value: number;
    };
}

interface CallbackProps {
    onSelect: (id: string, value: number) => void;
}

// Composing props by merging multiple interfaces provides modularity
        and reuse.
type ComponentProps = BaseProps & DataProps & CallbackProps;

const AdvancedComponent: React.FC<ComponentProps> = ({
    id,
    visible = true,
    data,
    onSelect,
}) => {
    const handleClick = () => onSelect(id, data.value);
    return visible ? (
        <div id={id} onClick={handleClick}>
            <h3>{data.name}</h3>
            <p>{data.value}</p>
        </div>
    ) : null;
};
```

```
export default AdvancedComponent;
```

In the above example, merging interfaces using the intersection operator (&) creates a composite type that encapsulates both inherent and additive responsibilities of the component. Advanced programmers may further refine types using generics, which allow components to be parameterized by the types of their data. For instance, one may design components that can display polymorphic data types, ensuring at compile time that all operations conform to the expected type constraints.

```
interface WithDataProps<T> {
    data: T;
    renderData: (data: T) => JSX.Element;
}

function DataDisplay<T>({ data, renderData }: WithDataProps<T>): JSX.
    Element {
    return <div>{renderData(data)}</div>;
}

// Usage with a complex object type.
interface User {
    id: number;
    username: string;
    email: string;
}

const renderUser = (user: User): JSX.Element => (
    <div>
        <h4>{user.username}</h4>
        <p>{user.email}</p>
    </div>
);

const user: User = { id: 1, username: 'advanced_user', email: '
    user@example.com' };

<DataDisplay data={user} renderData={renderUser} />;
```

State management in React is equally enhanced by TypeScript. When using the useState hook or class component state, explicitly annotating state types prevents accidental type mismatches and helps maintain immutable data patterns. Particularly, when state is composite or nested, the use of discriminated unions or mapped types allows for granular control over state transitions.

Consider a functional component that fetches and processes asynchronous data. By defining a discriminated union for the state, the component can represent distinct states such as loading, success, or failure with explicit type checking.

```
// Discriminated union for asynchronous state management.
interface LoadingState {
    status: 'loading';
}

interface SuccessState<T> {
    status: 'success';
    data: T;
}

interface ErrorState {
    status: 'error';
    error: Error;
}

type AsyncState<T> = LoadingState | SuccessState<T> | ErrorState;

function useAsyncData<T>(fetcher: () => Promise<T>): AsyncState<T> {
    const [state, setState] = React.useState<AsyncState<T>>({ status:
      'loading' });

    React.useEffect(() => {
        fetcher()
            .then((data) => setState({ status: 'success', data }))
            .catch((error) => setState({ status: 'error', error }));
    }, [fetcher]);

    return state;
}
```

```
interface User {
    id: number;
    name: string;
    email: string;
}

const UserComponent: React.FC = () => {
    const state = useAsyncData<User>(() =>
        fetch('/api/user').then((res) => res.json())
    );

    switch (state.status) {
        case 'loading':
            return <div>Loading...</div>;
        case 'success':
            return <div>{state.data.name} ({state.data.email})</div>;
        case 'error':
            return <div>Error: {state.error.message}</div>;
    }
};
```

Expressing state as a discriminated union ensures that every branch of a conditional statement within the component is strictly typed. This pattern eliminates the risk of performing operations on invalid state shapes and provides a clear contract for the expected data structure at each point in the component lifecycle.

For class components, TypeScript enables the declaration of state types directly on the component class. While functional components are prevalent in recent React development, understanding class-based patterns remains relevant in legacy codebases. In class components, state is typically annotated as a generic parameter to the React.Component type, as demonstrated below:

```
interface CounterProps {
    initialCount?: number;
}
```

```
interface CounterState {
    count: number;
}


class Counter extends React.Component<CounterProps, CounterState> {
    static defaultProps: Partial<CounterProps> = {
        initialCount: 0,
    };

    constructor(props: CounterProps) {
        super(props);
        this.state = { count: props.initialCount! };
    }

    increment = (): void => {
        this.setState((prevState) => ({ count: prevState.count + 1 })
    );
    };

    render(): JSX.Element {
        return (
            <div>
                <span>Count: {this.state.count}</span>
                <button onClick={this.increment}>Increment</button>
            </div>
        );
    }
}
```

Annotating props and state values in class components covers the complete component lifecycle, ensuring that every state transition is validated. For critical applications where state composition is intricate, advanced techniques such as immutability helpers in combination with
TypeScript's type system can be applied to enforce predictable state
mutations while preserving type safety.

A crucial component in advanced React development is writing custom hooks that encapsulate stateful logic. Advanced hooks often combine multiple internal states and side effects, and proper typing of both

input parameters and returned state can prevent subtle bugs. For example, a custom hook that manages form state with validation can be defined as follows:

```
interface FormField<T> {
    value: T;
    error?: string;
}


type FormState<T> = {
    [K in keyof T]: FormField<T[K]>;
};


function useForm<T extends Record<string, any>>(initialValues: T): [
    FormState<T>,
    <K extends keyof T>(field: K, value: T[K], error?: string) =>
    void
] {
    const [formState, setFormState] = React.useState<FormState<T>>(()
    => {
        const state = {} as FormState<T>;
        for (const key in initialValues) {
            state[key] = { value: initialValues[key] };
        }
        return state;
    });

    const updateField = React.useCallback(
        <K extends keyof T>(field: K, value: T[K], error?: string) =>
        {
            setFormState((prev) => ({
                ...prev,
                [field]: { value, error },
            }));
        },
        []
    );

    return [formState, updateField];
}
```

This generic hook encapsulates a mutable form state and provides

281

a type-safe mechanism to update individual fields. By leveraging
mapped types, the hook ensures that every property in the form state
corresponds directly to a key in the initial object, and modifications
remain type-consistent.

Another advanced technique involves the combination of type inference and higher-order components (HOCs) to automatically inject
typed props. By defining a wrapper that enhances a component
with additional properties, developers can leverage TypeScript's utility
types to preserve and extend the original component's prop definitions.
An illustrative example is as follows:

```
type WithLoadingProps = { loading: boolean };

function withLoading<P>(
    Component: React.ComponentType<P>
): React.FC<P & WithLoadingProps> {
    return ({ loading, ...props }: P & WithLoadingProps) => {
        if (loading) {
            return <div>Loading...</div>;
        }
        return <Component {...(props as P)} />;
    };
}

interface DataDisplayProps {
    data: string;
}

const DataDisplay: React.FC<DataDisplayProps> = ({ data }) => (
    <div>Data: {data}</div>
);

const EnhancedDataDisplay = withLoading(DataDisplay);

<EnhancedDataDisplay loading={false} data="Advanced type-safe data"
    />;
```

This pattern permits the seamless injection of additional properties into an existing component while preserving original prop types. The use of generics and intersection types in the HOC guarantees that the consuming component adheres to a rigorous type contract.

Maintaining strict type definitions for props and state greatly simplifies refactoring. When component interfaces evolve, TypeScript's compiler flags discrepancies immediately, thereby reducing the likelihood of latent bugs. Moreover, advanced integrations with IDEs that leverage TypeScript's type system provide real-time feedback, intelligent auto-completion, and context-aware refactoring tools, all of which enhance developer productivity.

Precision in the definition of props and state is a cornerstone of reliable React applications. By utilizing discriminated unions, generics, mapped types, and higher-order component patterns, advanced development practices reduce runtime uncertainty and ensure that all components operate within well-defined contracts. The adoption of these techniques contributes implicitly to the overall maintainability and scalability of large-scale applications, as type definitions serve as living documentation that evolves with the codebase.

## 6.3 Leveraging TypeScript for Functional Components

TypeScript significantly enhances the reliability and scalability of functional components in React by providing a robust system for type checking and inference. In functional components, the absence of class-based state management shifts the developer's focus to hooks and function return types, all of which can be rigorously typed using TypeScript. This section examines advanced techniques for leveraging TypeScript in functional components, including generics, advanced hook interactions, conditional types, and optimized composition patterns.

One key advantage of functional components is the ability to create stateless and stateful components as pure functions. By defining function signatures with explicit input and output types, one can delineate component contracts with precision. The conventional usage of the React.FC type provides a baseline of type safety but may also introduce limitations, particularly when dealing with generics or higher-order functions. Advanced programmers often define components as plain functions with explicit return types to circumvent default prop children inference or to integrate with advanced generics. For example, a functional component with generic properties may be defined as follows:

```
interface ListProps<T> {
    items: T[];
    renderItem: (item: T, index: number) => JSX.Element;
}

function ListComponent<T>({ items, renderItem }: ListProps<T>): JSX.
    Element {
    return (
        <ul>
            {items.map((item, index) => (
                <li key={index}>{renderItem(item, index)}</li>
            ))}
        </ul>
    );
}

export default ListComponent;
```

The use of generics in the functional component above creates a highly reusable list component that accommodates any data type. This pattern enforces type correctness for the items array and the renderItem callback, ensuring that both operate on the same inferred type. A further refinement is to specify that keys for list items follow a stricter validation by enforcing a type constraint in cases where a unique identifier is required, thereby eliminating potential runtime errors.

TypeScript's support for advanced hook patterns contributes to more predictable state management within functional components. Custom hooks can now leverage generics and advanced type inference to encapsulate complex behavior. For example, consider a custom hook that synchronizes an asynchronous process with component state. The hook can be typed to accept a generic asynchronous function and model its state as a discriminated union:

```typescript
type AsyncStatus = 'idle' | 'pending' | 'fulfilled' | 'rejected';

interface AsyncResult<T> {
    status: AsyncStatus;
    data?: T;
    error?: Error;
}

function useAsync<T>(asyncFunction: () => Promise<T>): AsyncResult<T>
    {
    const [state, setState] = React.useState<AsyncResult<T>>({ status
    : 'idle' });

    React.useEffect(() => {
        let isMounted = true;
        setState({ status: 'pending' });
        asyncFunction()
            .then((data) => {
                if (isMounted) {
                    setState({ status: 'fulfilled', data });
                }
            })
            .catch((error) => {
                if (isMounted) {
                    setState({ status: 'rejected', error });
                }
            });
```

```
        return () => {
            isMounted = false;
        };
    }, [asyncFunction]);

    return state;
}
```

In the above custom hook, the discriminated union type
AsyncResult<T> explicitly distinguishes between various states of
the asynchronous operation. Functional components that consume
this hook benefit from exhaustive type checking on the resulting state,
ensuring that conditional branches handling errors, data display, or
idle states are correctly managed.

Another advanced technique involves the integration of memoization
and context separation in functional components. Combining Type-
Script with React.memo or custom comparison functions can enforce
stable component identities and prevent unnecessary re-renders. Since
React.memo relies on shallow comparison by default, advanced type
annotations paired with utility functions help guarantee that component properties remain stable and correctly typed even as component
hierarchies expand. An example of a memoized functional component
with specific prop type requirements is shown below:

```
interface ProfileProps {
    id: number;
    name: string;
    email: string;
    lastUpdated: Date;
}

const ProfileCard: React.FC<ProfileProps> = React.memo(({ id, name,
    email, lastUpdated }) => {
    return (
        <div>
            <h3>{name}</h3>
```

```
            <p>{email}</p>
            <small>Last Updated: {lastUpdated.toLocaleString()}</</
     small>
        </div>
     );
}, (prevProps, nextProps) => {
    return (
        prevProps.id === nextProps.id &&
        prevProps.name === nextProps.name &&
        prevProps.email === nextProps.email &&
        prevProps.lastUpdated.getTime() === nextProps.lastUpdated.
     getTime()
     );
});


export default ProfileCard;
```

The explicit function signature provided by TypeScript in the case above ensures that all properties passed to `ProfileCard` meet the expected types. The use of a custom comparison function within `React.memo` reinforces the integrity of the component by verifying deep equality for properties that are non-primitive, such as `Date` objects.

An area where functional components significantly benefit from Type-Script is in the definition of event handlers. When handling events in React, particularly synthetic events, pairing them with strong type definitions reduces the ambiguity of event object properties and their associated handlers. For instance, when defining a complex form control component, one can enforce type-safe event handling as demonstrated:

```
interface TextInputProps {
    value: string;
    onChange: (value: string, event: React.ChangeEvent<
     HTMLInputElement>) => void;
    placeholder?: string;
}
```

```
const TextInput: React.FC<TextInputProps> = ({ value, onChange,
    placeholder }) => {
    const handleChange = (event: React.ChangeEvent<HTMLInputElement>)
    => {
        onChange(event.target.value, event);
    };

    return (
        <input
            type="text"
            value={value}
            onChange={handleChange}
            placeholder={placeholder}
        />
    );
};

export default TextInput;
```

This pattern demonstrates how explicit typing of events and callback
functions enhances predictability and prevents common pitfalls associated with type coercion or accidental mutation of event objects. Additionally, the callback signature clearly communicates the relationship
between input value and event origin, reinforcing component contracts
during refactoring.

Another advanced application of TypeScript in functional components
involves the implementation of polymorphic components. In functional design, components are increasingly designed to be flexible with
regards to the underlying HTML elements they render. By introducing
a generic as prop and amalgamating intrinsic element attributes with
custom props, one ensures that the resulting component provides a
fully typed interface irrespective of the rendered element type. An advanced implementation strategy is illustrated below:

```
type AsProp<C extends React.ElementType> = {
    as?: C;
```

```
};

type MergeProps<C extends React.ElementType, P> =
    React.ComponentPropsWithRef<C> & P;

interface PolymorphicComponentProps<C extends React.ElementType, P>
    extends AsProp<C> {
    props?: MergeProps<C, P>;
}

function PolymorphicText<C extends React.ElementType = 'span'>(
    { as, props }: PolymorphicComponentProps<C, { color: string }>
): JSX.Element {
    const Component = as || 'span';
    return <Component style={{ color: props.color }} {...props} />;
}

export default PolymorphicText;
```

Through the integration of advanced generics and intersection types, functional components gain the versatility to render multiple intrinsic element types while preserving a consistent and robust type contract. Such techniques are particularly advantageous in design systems where components must adapt to various UI contexts dynamically.

TypeScript further supports the refinement of component behavior by facilitating complex conditional types and utility types such as `Partial`, `Required`, and `Pick`. These utilities enable functional components to adapt or narrow prop interfaces based on component configuration or contextual requirements. In scenarios where components render with optional sections or lazy-loaded content, conditional types can enforce logic that adapts the component's expected data shape. For instance, consider a component that conditionally requires additional metadata when a certain flag is set:

```
interface BaseCardProps {
    title: string;
```

```
    content: string;
}

interface DetailedCardProps extends BaseCardProps {
    metadata: {
        createdAt: Date;
        updatedAt: Date;
    };
}

type CardProps<T extends boolean> = T extends true ?
    DetailedCardProps : BaseCardProps;

function Card<T extends boolean>({ title, content, ...rest }:
    CardProps<T>): JSX.Element {
    return (
        <div className="card">
            <h3>{title}</h3>
            <p>{content}</p>
            {'metadata' in rest && (
                <div className="metadata">
                    <small>Created: {rest.metadata.createdAt.
    toLocaleString()}</small>
                    <small>Updated: {rest.metadata.updatedAt.
    toLocaleString()}</small>
                </div>
            )}
        </div>
    );
}
```

The conditional type CardProps<T> allows the component to adapt its
expected properties based on a type flag, ensuring that critical metadata is included only when necessary. This level of precision aids developers in maintaining clear distinctions between lightweight and enriched components in complex user interfaces.

Advanced techniques in leveraging TypeScript within functional components also extend to rigorous error handling and exhaustive checks.
By employing TypeScript's never type in switch statements or condi-

tional branches, developers can enforce that all potential states are considered. This is particularly useful when rendering components based on discriminated unions, ensuring that unforeseen states trigger compiler errors rather than subtle runtime issues.

Functional components that combine these advanced patterns benefit from enhanced maintainability and scalability. Comprehensive typing not only aids in documenting the intended behavior but also integrates seamlessly with modern development tools, resulting in improved auto-completion, refactoring safety, and static analysis. By carefully architecting component contracts and using TypeScript to its fullest extent, developers can build complex, reliable, and scalable applications that adapt to evolving project requirements without compromising on code quality.

## 6.4 Advanced Patterns with Hooks in TypeScript

React Hooks, when combined with TypeScript's strong typing, serve as a powerful toolset for managing complex state and side effects in functional components. In advanced applications, hooks are leveraged not only for basic state transitions or side effect management but also for constructing intricate data flows, dynamic dependencies, and performance optimizations. This section delves into several advanced patterns that exploit TypeScript's generics, discriminated unions, and conditional types to create custom hooks with robust type guarantees.

The design of custom hooks with TypeScript starts with creating generic abstractions that can handle multiple state scenarios. A common requirement in advanced applications is the need for a hook managing asynchronous operations, including cancellation, error handling, and state resets. Consider a hook that wraps asynchronous calls with cancellation support to handle race conditions. Type definitions can be derived from discriminated union types representing different states of an asynchronous operation. The following code snippet demonstrates a type-safe custom hook called useCancellableAsync:

```
type AsyncStatus = 'idle' | 'loading' | 'success' | 'error';
interface AsyncState<T> {
    status: AsyncStatus;
    data?: T;
    error?: Error;
}

function useCancellableAsync<T>(asyncFunction: () => Promise<T>, deps
    : any[]): AsyncState<T> {
    const [state, setState] = React.useState<AsyncState<T>>({ status:
    'idle' });
    const abortControllerRef = React.useRef<AbortController | null>(
    null);

    React.useEffect(() => {
        abortControllerRef.current?.abort();
        const controller = new AbortController();
        abortControllerRef.current = controller;

        setState({ status: 'loading' });
        asyncFunction()
            .then((data) => {
                if (!controller.signal.aborted) {
                    setState({ status: 'success', data });
                }
            })
            .catch((error) => {
                if (!controller.signal.aborted) {
                    setState({ status: 'error', error });
                }
            });

        return () => {
            controller.abort();
```

```
        };
    }, deps);

    return state;
}
```

The above hook makes extensive use of TypeScript's capability to enforce correctness in state transitions. The `AsyncState<T>` discriminated union delineates distinct render states for consumers of the hook, enabling exhaustive type checking in switch statements or conditionals. By employing a `useRef` to hold an abort controller instance, this pattern prevents stale or overlapping asynchronous operations, a common pitfall in complex component hierarchies.

Another advanced hook pattern involves dynamic dependency management using custom hooks for interdependent states. For example, consider a scenario where multiple asynchronous resources must be fetched based on dynamic criteria, with each resource influencing the others. A custom hook that orchestrates this behavior can be built using a combination of `useEffect` and `useReducer`. The following example illustrates a custom hook using a reducer to manage multi-step asynchronous state:

```
type FetchAction<T> =
    | { type: 'FETCH_INIT' }
    | { type: 'FETCH_SUCCESS'; payload: T }
    | { type: 'FETCH_FAILURE'; error: Error };

function fetchReducer<T>(state: AsyncState<T>, action: FetchAction<T
    >): AsyncState<T> {
    switch (action.type) {
        case 'FETCH_INIT':
            return { status: 'loading' };
        case 'FETCH_SUCCESS':
            return { status: 'success', data: action.payload };
        case 'FETCH_FAILURE':
            return { status: 'error', error: action.error };
```

```
        default:
            return state;
    }
}

function useChainedFetch<T>(fetcher: () => Promise<T>, deps: any[]):
    AsyncState<T> {
    const [state, dispatch] = React.useReducer(fetchReducer, { status
    : 'idle' } as AsyncState<T>);

    React.useEffect(() => {
        dispatch({ type: 'FETCH_INIT' });
        fetcher()
            .then((data) => dispatch({ type: 'FETCH_SUCCESS', payload
    : data }))
            .catch((error) => dispatch({ type: 'FETCH_FAILURE', error
    }));
    }, deps);

    return state;
}
```

Here, the reducer pattern not only segments the state machine into manageable transitions but also facilitates integration with multiple asynchronous operations that might depend on shared state. By coupling the reducer with TypeScript's detailed type annotations, the hook provides compile-time assurances that each state transition is handled appropriately and that all possible states are covered.

Memoization is another critical pattern in advanced hook usage. Leveraging hooks like useMemo and useCallback with TypeScript ensures that expensive computations or frequently re-instantiated functions are optimized without sacrificing type safety. In complex components, where dependencies and recalculations are intertwined, a properly typed memoization protocol reduces computational overhead and prevents unintentional re-renders. The following code snippet demonstrates a custom hook for memoizing a derived value based on deep

294

dependency comparison:

```
function useDeepMemo<T>(factory: () => T, deps: any[]): T {
    const memoizedValue = React.useRef<T>();
    const signalRef = React.useRef<string>();

    const currentSignal = JSON.stringify(deps);
    if (signalRef.current !== currentSignal) {
        memoizedValue.current = factory();
        signalRef.current = currentSignal;
    }

    return memoizedValue.current as T;
}
```

The `useDeepMemo` hook uses JSON stringification as a dependency comparison mechanism, which, while simple, illustrates the technique for creating custom memoization patterns in situations where shallow equality is insufficient. Developers can substitute more sophisticated deep comparison algorithms as needed.

Complex state updates within a single component often benefit from hooks that group related state variables into a single cohesive object. A custom hook that wraps `useReducer` for form handling is one such advanced pattern. It allows for granular field-level updates while ensuring that the overall form state remains consistent. In this example, mapped types are employed to create a strongly typed form state:

```
type FieldState<T> = {
    value: T;
    error?: string;
};

type FormState<T> = {
    [K in keyof T]: FieldState<T>;
};

function useFormState<T extends Record<string, any>>(initialValues: T
    ): [
```

```
    FormState<T>,
    <K extends keyof T>(field: K, value: T[K], error?: string) =>
    void,
    () => void
] {
    const [state, setState] = React.useState<FormState<T>>(() => {
        const formState = {} as FormState<T>;
        for (const key in initialValues) {
            formState[key] = { value: initialValues[key] };
        }
        return formState;
    });

    const updateField = React.useCallback(
        <K extends keyof T>(field: K, value: T[K], error?: string):
    void => {
            setState((prev) => ({
                ...prev,
                [field]: { value, error }
            }));
        },
        []
    );

    const resetForm = React.useCallback((): void => {
        setState((prev) => {
            const resetState = {} as FormState<T>;
            for (const key in prev) {
                resetState[key] = { value: (initialValues as T)[key]
    };
            }
            return resetState;
        });
    }, [initialValues]);

    return [state, updateField, resetForm];
}
```

This hook illustrates strong coupling between a complex object's shape
and its state representation, using mapped types to enforce that every
field in the initial values is reflected in the state. The design guarantees
that any update performed via the update function maintains the type

integrity of individual fields.

Advanced interactions between hooks can also be orchestrated using context-specific patterns. For instance, when multiple components need to access and modify shared state, combining context providers with custom hooks offers an effective solution. A custom hook that provides access to context state and dispatch functions can be implemented with rigorous typing:

```
interface GlobalState {
    count: number;
    user?: { id: string; name: string };
}

type GlobalAction =
    | { type: 'increment' }
    | { type: 'setUser'; user: { id: string; name: string } };

const GlobalStateContext = React.createContext<GlobalState |
    undefined>(undefined);
const GlobalDispatchContext = React.createContext<React.Dispatch<
    GlobalAction> | undefined>(undefined);

function globalReducer(state: GlobalState, action: GlobalAction):
    GlobalState {
    switch (action.type) {
        case 'increment':
            return { ...state, count: state.count + 1 };
        case 'setUser':
            return { ...state, user: action.user };
        default:
            return state;
    }
}

const GlobalProvider: React.FC = ({ children }) => {
    const [state, dispatch] = React.useReducer(globalReducer, { count
    : 0 });
    return (
        <GlobalStateContext.Provider value={state}>
            <GlobalDispatchContext.Provider value={dispatch}>
                {children}
```

```
            </GlobalDispatchContext.Provider>
         </GlobalStateContext.Provider>
     );
};

function useGlobalState(): GlobalState {
    const context = React.useContext(GlobalStateContext);
    if (context === undefined) {
        throw new Error('useGlobalState must be used within a
        GlobalProvider');
    }
    return context;
}

function useGlobalDispatch(): React.Dispatch<GlobalAction> {
    const context = React.useContext(GlobalDispatchContext);
    if (context === undefined) {
        throw new Error('useGlobalDispatch must be used within a
        GlobalProvider');
    }
    return context;
}
```

Integrating context with hooks in this manner not only adheres to a predictable state pattern but also leverages TypeScript to catch any misuse of the state management system at compile time. It enforces that all consuming components operate within the approved contracts, ensuring that state and dispatch functions remain synchronized.

Advanced hook patterns in TypeScript also embrace error boundaries and side effect encapsulation. By designing hooks that expose controlled interfaces for error handling and cleanup, developers can minimize side effects that propagate through component hierarchies. For example, consider a custom hook designed for a subscription-based data provider, which automatically unsubscribes when the component unmounts:

```
function useSubscription<T>(subscribe: (callback: (data: T) => void)
```

```
=> () => void): T | undefined {
const [data, setData] = React.useState<T | undefined>(undefined);

React.useEffect(() => {
    const unsubscribe = subscribe(setData);
    return () => {
        unsubscribe();
    };
}, [subscribe]);

return data;
}
```

In this hook, TypeScript confirmation that the subscription function returns a cleanup function enforces a strict contract between the consumer and the data provider. This reduces memory leaks and unintended side effects in large-scale applications with multiple asynchronous data channels.

Advanced patterns with hooks in TypeScript empower developers to build modular, maintainable, and scalable applications by providing a strongly typed foundation for complex state management and side effects. Comprehensive type annotations enforced by TypeScript ensure that interactions between state transitions, asynchronous operations, and component renders remain deterministic and free of subtle runtime errors. This meticulous approach, in turn, simplifies debugging and accelerates iterative development in high-stakes production environments.

## 6.5  Integrating Redux with TypeScript

The integration of Redux with TypeScript raises the level of type safety across state management by ensuring that every action creator, re-

299

ducer, and store interaction adheres to explicit type contracts. Using TypeScript with Redux involves constructing a sound type system that encompasses action types, payload shapes, state invariants, and middleware interactions while ensuring that the entire flow from action dispatch to state update is type-safe. This section explores advanced patterns for integrating Redux with TypeScript, discusses the challenges of statically typing Redux's unidirectional data flow, and provides useful coding examples for robust integration.

A key challenge when integrating Redux with TypeScript is ensuring that every action is correctly typed. Actions are represented as objects with a type property, and advanced applications often utilize discriminated unions to encapsulate distinct actions. A conventional approach is to define a set of action type constants and corresponding interfaces for each action. For example, consider the following definition of actions for a simple counter module:

```typescript
export enum CounterActionTypes {
    INCREMENT = 'INCREMENT',
    DECREMENT = 'DECREMENT',
    SET_VALUE = 'SET_VALUE'
}

interface IncrementAction {
    type: CounterActionTypes.INCREMENT;
}

interface DecrementAction {
    type: CounterActionTypes.DECREMENT;
}

interface SetValueAction {
    type: CounterActionTypes.SET_VALUE;
    payload: number;
}

export type CounterActions = IncrementAction | DecrementAction |
    SetValueAction;
```

300

By leveraging TypeScript's discriminated unions, each action type is uniquely identified by its type field, facilitating exhaustive checking in reducers, which ensures that every possible action is handled. In advanced scenarios where the payload structures are more complex, the use of generics for action creators can abstract repeated patterns, reducing boilerplate and reinforcing type consistency.

Reducer functions represent the core of the Redux data flow, where state transitions occur based on dispatched actions. The following reducer example demonstrates a type-safe approach for handling the previously defined counter actions:

```
export interface CounterState {
    count: number;
}

const initialState: CounterState = {
    count: 0
};

export function counterReducer(
    state: CounterState = initialState,
    action: CounterActions
): CounterState {
    switch (action.type) {
        case CounterActionTypes.INCREMENT:
            return { ...state, count: state.count + 1 };
        case CounterActionTypes.DECREMENT:
            return { ...state, count: state.count - 1 };
        case CounterActionTypes.SET_VALUE:
            return { ...state, count: action.payload };
        default:
            // Using exhaustive type checking ensures future changes
    are caught.
            return state;
    }
}
```

Within this reducer, the switch statement is enforced by TypeScript to

cover all cases of CounterActions. Failure to handle one of the actions
can be emphasized by using an additional helper function that asserts
the exhaustiveness of the switch statement, making the addition of new
actions less error-prone. Advanced practitioners often incorporate utility types or helper functions to assert unreachable code paths, for example:

```
function assertUnreachable(x: never): never {
    throw new Error("Unexpected object: " + x);
}
```

In complex applications, multiple reducers are typically combined using Redux's combineReducers function. When integrating TypeScript,
it becomes critical to derive the overall application state and ensure that
each reducer's state slice is correctly inferred. For instance, consider an
application that aggregates multiple modules:

```
import { combineReducers } from 'redux';
import { counterReducer, CounterState } from './counterReducer';
import { userReducer, UserState } from './userReducer';

export interface AppState {
    counter: CounterState;
    user: UserState;
}

export const rootReducer = combineReducers<AppState>({
    counter: counterReducer,
    user: userReducer
});
```

Here, explicit definitions for AppState guarantee that the store maintains a coherent and strongly typed representation, where each slice
of state is clearly defined. With explicit types in place, any changes to
shape within either CounterState or UserState will trigger compile-
time errors in components or middleware referencing the global state.

Store creation is another critical aspect where type safety can be enforced. By leveraging TypeScript's type annotations with Redux's `createStore` function, developers can leverage the benefits of auto-completion, inferred action types, and safe dispatch implementations. An advanced store creation might incorporate middleware for asynchronous side effects, such as `redux-thunk` or `redux-saga`. Consider a store configuration that includes thunk middleware:

```
import { createStore, applyMiddleware } from 'redux';
import thunk, { ThunkAction } from 'redux-thunk';
import { rootReducer, AppState } from './rootReducer';
import { CounterActions } from './counterReducer';

export type AppThunk<ReturnType = void> = ThunkAction<
    ReturnType,
    AppState,
    unknown,
    CounterActions
>;

const store = createStore(rootReducer, applyMiddleware(thunk));

export default store;
```

In this configuration, the `AppThunk` type provides a blueprint for asynchronous action creators. Leveraging TypeScript's generics not only enforces proper action dispatching but also aids in type inference within middleware, which might otherwise be a source of subtle bugs. Advanced developers can combine multiple middleware types and utilize custom middleware signatures to enforce strict contracts on side effects and state transitions.

The generation of type-safe action creators is another area where advanced patterns can reduce boilerplate while maintaining rigorous type contracts. Utilizing factory functions to create actions improves consistency and reduces human error. By encapsulating each action creator within a strict type, developers can create utility functions that automatically enforce the shape of each action. For example:

```
export const increment = (): IncrementAction => ({
    type: CounterActionTypes.INCREMENT
});

export const decrement = (): DecrementAction => ({
    type: CounterActionTypes.DECREMENT
});

export const setValue = (value: number): SetValueAction => ({
    type: CounterActionTypes.SET_VALUE,
    payload: value
});
```

The benefits of type-safe action creators extend further when integrating with asynchronous operations. A common pattern is the implementation of thunks that dispatch multiple actions based on asynchronous logic. The following example demonstrates an asynchronous thunk to fetch some data and then dispatch an action to update the store:

```
import { Dispatch } from 'redux';

interface FetchDataSuccessAction {
    type: 'FETCH_DATA_SUCCESS';
    payload: { data: string[] };
}

interface FetchDataFailureAction {
    type: 'FETCH_DATA_FAILURE';
    payload: { error: string };
}

type DataActions = FetchDataSuccessAction | FetchDataFailureAction;

export const fetchData = (): AppThunk => async (dispatch: Dispatch<
    DataActions>) => {
    try {
        const response = await fetch('/api/data');
```

```
        const data = await response.json();
        dispatch({
            type: 'FETCH_DATA_SUCCESS',
            payload: { data }
        });
    } catch (error) {
        dispatch({
            type: 'FETCH_DATA_FAILURE',
            payload: { error: error.message }
        });
    }
};
```

This thunk is fully typed using the `AppThunk` type, ensuring that any component that dispatches `fetchData` receives the appropriate typed action throughout the asynchronous flow. Advanced developers can further refine thunks to handle cancellation tokens, retries, or other asynchronous challenges while preserving the overall type contract.

Type inference plays a crucial role in connecting Redux and TypeScript. When reducers and action creators are designed with precise types, the TypeScript compiler can automatically detect mismatches or unhandled cases. An advanced integration might involve higher-order reducers that dynamically build new reducers from factory functions while maintaining strict type integrity. For example, a factory function can create reducers for multiple entities while sharing common logic:

```
type EntityActions<T> =
    | { type: 'ADD_ENTITY'; payload: T }
    | { type: 'REMOVE_ENTITY'; payload: { id: string } };

function createEntityReducer<T>(key: string) {
    const initialState: Record<string, T> = {};

    return function entityReducer(
        state = initialState,
        action: EntityActions<T>
    ): Record<string, T> {
```

305

```
    switch (action.type) {
        case 'ADD_ENTITY':
            // Enforce payload structure for dynamic keys.
            return { ...state, [key]: action.payload };
        case 'REMOVE_ENTITY': {
            const { [action.payload.id]: removed, ...rest } =
state;
            return rest;
        }
        default:
            return state;
    }
};
}
```

Such factories reduce duplication and ensure that any changes to base
logic are correctly typed and immediately propagate across the entire
application. Strong typing across these patterns also aids in writing
unit tests where strict type contracts prevent inadvertent changes in
logic that could compromise application state integrity.

Advanced patterns in middleware development further enhance the
Redux ecosystem in TypeScript. Custom middleware can be typed to
accept a strictly defined store and dispatch function, thereby enforcing
runtime invariants via compile-time checks. An example of a logging
middleware with explicit types is:

```
import { Middleware, AnyAction } from 'redux';
import { AppState } from './rootReducer';

export const loggerMiddleware: Middleware<{}, AppState> = store =>
    next => (action: AnyAction) => {
    console.log('Dispatching:', action);
    const result = next(action);
    console.log('Next state:', store.getState());
    return result;
};
```

Such middleware is both flexible and statically checked so that any modification in AppState or action types surfaces immediately in development environments. Advanced developers may also implement middleware for complex scenarios such as batching actions, handling offline states, or integrating with external logging services—all while preserving strict type contracts.

Integrating Redux with TypeScript ultimately empowers developers to create large-scale applications with a predictable and verifiable state flow. The explicit type annotations across actions, reducers, and stores not only enforce correctness during development but also provide comprehensive documentation that evolves with the codebase. This interplay between Redux's unidirectional data flow and TypeScript's static analysis significantly reduces runtime errors, improves refactoring safety, and streamlines collaborative development across complex codebases.

## 6.6   Creating Typed Selectors and Middleware

In sophisticated Redux architectures, the correctness and efficiency of state management rely on strongly typed selectors and middleware. Typed selectors provide a type-safe mechanism for extracting portions of the global state, while custom middleware enables controlled interception and transformation of actions. Both patterns rely on advanced TypeScript features to ensure consistency, minimize runtime errors, and streamline maintenance in large-scale applications.

Typed selectors are functions that derive data from the global state. When written in TypeScript, selectors not only abstract state access but also enforce that the returned data adheres precisely to expected types.

A common pattern is to define the overall state interface and then create selectors that target specific slices. For instance, assume an application state defined as follows:

```
interface UserState {
    id: string;
    name: string;
    email: string;
}

interface CounterState {
    count: number;
}

export interface AppState {
    user: UserState;
    counter: CounterState;
}
```

A typical typed selector extracts the user's email from the state. The function signature explicitly returns a string, allowing the TypeScript compiler to guarantee that any consumer of the selector can rely on the expected type:

```
export const selectUserEmail = (state: AppState): string => state.
    user.email;
```

Beyond simple selections, selectors often perform memoization to prevent unnecessary recalculations. Advanced practitioners typically use libraries such as Reselect, which facilitate the creation of memoized selectors with strict type definitions. An advanced implementation might resemble:

```
import { createSelector } from 'reselect';

const selectUser = (state: AppState) => state.user;
const selectCounter = (state: AppState) => state.counter.count;
```

```
export const selectUserWithCounter = createSelector(
    [selectUser, selectCounter],
    (user, counter) => ({
        id: user.id,
        name: user.name,
        email: user.email,
        counter
    })
);
```

In this example, the typed selectors `selectUser` and `selectCounter` act as input selectors, while the output selector consolidates data through the use of Reselect's `createSelector` function. Type inference ensures that the return object exactly matches the desired structure and that any changes in the underlying state shape will automatically surface as errors during compilation. Advanced usage of selectors may involve parameterized selectors. In such cases, generic types combined with higher-order functions yield selectors capable of adapting to dynamic query parameters. Consider a function that retrieves a user by a dynamic identifier:

```
export const makeSelectUserById = () => createSelector(
    [
        (state: AppState) => state.user,
        (_: AppState, userId: string) => userId
    ],
    (user, userId) => user.id === userId ? user : null
);
```

Here, the selector is parameterized by `userId` and returns either a valid `UserState` or `null`. Leveraging such patterns in large applications can centralize and abstract complex state queries, ensure code reuse, and enforce data consistency across the application.

Beyond selectors, custom middleware provides another avenue for enhancing Redux's capabilities via typed implementations. Middleware

intercepts actions before they reach reducers, enabling useful patterns
such as logging, analytics, error handling, and asynchronous processing. In a strongly typed environment, middleware must be defined
with explicit types for state, actions, and the next dispatch function. A
basic example of a logging middleware is presented below:

```
import { Middleware, AnyAction } from 'redux';
import { AppState } from './rootReducer';

export const loggerMiddleware: Middleware<{}, AppState> = store =>
    next => (action: AnyAction) => {
    console.log('Dispatching Action:', action);
    const result = next(action);
    console.log('New State:', store.getState());
    return result;
};
```

This middleware demonstrates how typing ensures that
`store.getState()` returns an object conforming to `AppState`.
Consequently, any modification to the global state structure surfaces
as a compile-time error, reinforcing the contract between action
processing and state transitions. Advanced middleware patterns
include side-effect management, error recovery, and transformation of
actions before reaching reducers. For instance, consider middleware
that handles actions with a `promise` property, dispatching subsequent
actions on resolution or rejection:

```
import { Middleware, Dispatch, AnyAction } from 'redux';

interface PromiseAction extends AnyAction {
    promise?: Promise<any>;
    onSuccess?: (result: any) => AnyAction;
    onError?: (error: any) => AnyAction;
}

export const promiseMiddleware: Middleware<{}, AppState> = store =>
    next => (action: PromiseAction) => {
    if (!action.promise) {
```

```
            return next(action);
    }
    action.promise
        .then((result) => {
            if (typeof action.onSuccess === 'function') {
                store.dispatch(action.onSuccess(result));
            }
        })
        .catch((error) => {
            if (typeof action.onError === 'function') {
                store.dispatch(action.onError(error));
            }
        });
    return next(action);
};
```

By embedding optional promise, onSuccess, and onError properties into the action interface, middleware can intercept and handle asynchronous operations while preserving type integrity. The middleware distinguishes between standard actions and promise-based actions, ensuring that the appropriate handler is dispatched based on the asynchronous outcome.

Advanced integrations also involve chaining middleware and selectors, where middleware may inject additional properties into actions that selectors later interpret. For example, a middleware that enriches actions with metadata can help selectors derive context-dependent values. Consider a middleware that adds a timestamp to qualifying actions:

```
export interface TimestampedAction extends AnyAction {
    meta?: {
        timestamp: number;
    };
}

export const timestampMiddleware: Middleware<{}, AppState> = store =>
    next => (action: TimestampedAction) => {
```

311

```
const enhancedAction = {
    ...action,
    meta: {
        ...action.meta,
        timestamp: Date.now()
    }
};
return next(enhancedAction);
};
```

Selectors then can safely assume that actions carry timestamp metadata. For example, a selector retrieving the most recent dispatch time might use the enhanced metadata:

```
export const selectLastActionTimestamp = (state: AppState, action:
    TimestampedAction): number | undefined => {
    return action.meta ? action.meta.timestamp : undefined;
};
```

Leveraging TypeScript's structural typing, middleware that enriches actions will interact harmoniously with selectors that expect specific metadata. This combination provides a robust mechanism for auditing, performance measurement, or conditional logic in downstream components.

The interactions between typed selectors and middleware become even more relevant when handling derived state calculations. For instance, selectors can extract data that has been modified by middleware, such as accumulated analytics events or error reports. Packaging these patterns into utility libraries and custom hooks further promotes reusability. Advanced developers may encapsulate selection logic inside a custom hook that combines multiple selectors, leveraging Reselect's memoization for performance optimization:

```
import { useSelector } from 'react-redux';
import { AppState } from './rootReducer';
```

```
export const useEnrichedUserData = () => {
    return useSelector((state: AppState) => {
        const user = state.user;
        const email = user.email.toLowerCase();
        return {
            ...user,
            email
        };
    });
};
```

In this pattern, one selector derives a transformed version of the user email, applying business logic directly within the selector's scope. Such integrations yield components that are self-contained and that expose only the data they need. Moreover, by using TypeScript annotations throughout, refactoring selector logic becomes safer and more predictable.

Advanced patterns extend beyond basic middleware and selectors to include error-handling middleware that interacts with error selectors. When errors are caught within middleware, a central error state can be updated and later retrieved by components that display error messages. A type-safe implementation might include an error action, reducer, and corresponding selector:

```
export enum ErrorActionTypes {
    SET_ERROR = 'SET_ERROR',
    CLEAR_ERROR = 'CLEAR_ERROR'
}

interface SetErrorAction {
    type: ErrorActionTypes.SET_ERROR;
    payload: string;
}

interface ClearErrorAction {
    type: ErrorActionTypes.CLEAR_ERROR;
```

```
}

export type ErrorActions = SetErrorAction | ClearErrorAction;

export interface ErrorState {
    message: string | null;
}

const initialErrorState: ErrorState = {
    message: null
};

export function errorReducer(
    state: ErrorState = initialErrorState,
    action: ErrorActions
): ErrorState {
    switch (action.type) {
        case ErrorActionTypes.SET_ERROR:
            return { message: action.payload };
        case ErrorActionTypes.CLEAR_ERROR:
            return { message: null };
        default:
            return state;
    }
}

export const selectErrorMessage = (state: AppState): string | null =>
    state.error.message;
```

Middleware that intercepts failed actions can dispatch a SET_ERROR action, updating the global error state. Components then rely on the selectErrorMessage selector, complete with a clear contract provided by TypeScript. This model centralizes error handling and contributes to a predictable data flow.

Typed selectors and middleware, when effectively combined, contribute to an application's robustness by ensuring that all interactions with the Redux store are well-defined and validated at compile time. By utilizing advanced TypeScript features such as generics, discriminated unions, and utility types, developers can create modular components that scale with the complexity of the application, reduce runtime exceptions, and enhance developer productivity. The development of thorough, well-typed selector and middleware libraries becomes a cornerstone of maintainable codebases in enterprise-level React and Redux applications.

## 6.7 Testing React and Redux Applications in TypeScript

The integration of comprehensive testing strategies with TypeScript in React and Redux applications not only verifies dynamic behavior but also enforces the static contracts established by the type system. Advanced testing methodologies leverage TypeScript's precision to improve code reliability and facilitate effective refactoring. Rigorously testing both presentational and container components, as well as Redux reducers, actions, and middleware, requires a synthesis of unit, integration, and end-to-end testing approaches that align tightly with the application's type definitions.

Type-safe unit tests serve as the foundation of a robust testing suite. Using libraries such as Jest and React Testing Library in conjunction with TypeScript makes it possible to verify component contracts defined by strongly typed interfaces and discriminated unions. The following example demonstrates a unit test for a functional component that is designed to receive a specific set of typed props. In this case, the UserProfile component expects a User object and a callback function for updating user details:

```
import React from 'react';
```

315

```
import { render, fireEvent } from '@testing-library/react';
import UserProfile from '../components/UserProfile';

interface User {
    id: number;
    name: string;
    email: string;
}

const mockUser: User = {
    id: 1,
    name: 'Test User',
    email: 'test@example.com'
};

describe('UserProfile Component', () => {
    it('renders user details correctly and handles update', () => {
        const onUpdate = jest.fn();
        const { getByText, getByRole } = render(
            <UserProfile user={mockUser} onUpdate={onUpdate} />
        );

        expect(getByText(/Test User/)).toBeTruthy();
        expect(getByText(/test@example.com/)).toBeTruthy();

        const updateButton = getByRole('button', { name: /Update User
/ });
        fireEvent.click(updateButton);
        expect(onUpdate).toHaveBeenCalledWith(mockUser);
    });
});
```

This test not only confirms that the component renders the provided
user information correctly but also asserts that the callback adheres
to the expected function signature as determined by the component's
TypeScript definitions. By matching the static types with the runtime
behavior, tests become an additional layer of documentation in the
codebase.

Redux's unidirectional data flow introduces unique challenges and opportunities for testing. With the aid of TypeScript, actions, reducers, and middleware can be thoroughly verified. For instance, Redux reducers benefit from exhaustive testing to ensure that each action transitions the state correctly. Consider a reducer that handles a simple counter state and its associated actions:

```
import { counterReducer, CounterState } from '../reducers/
    counterReducer';
import { CounterActionTypes } from '../actions/counterActions';

describe('counterReducer', () => {
    const initialState: CounterState = { count: 0 };

    it('increments the count', () => {
        const action = { type: CounterActionTypes.INCREMENT };
        const newState = counterReducer(initialState, action);
        expect(newState.count).toBe(1);
    });

    it('decrements the count', () => {
        const action = { type: CounterActionTypes.DECREMENT };
        const newState = counterReducer({ count: 1 }, action);
        expect(newState.count).toBe(0);
    });

    it('sets the count to a specific value', () => {
        const action = { type: CounterActionTypes.SET_VALUE, payload:
    5 };
        const newState = counterReducer(initialState, action);
        expect(newState.count).toBe(5);
    });
});
```

Each test case here leverages TypeScript's exhaustiveness to guarantee that the reducer logic comprehensively covers every action type. The use of discriminated unions in the action definitions provides a compiler-enforced contract that minimizes the risk of unhandled cases. Furthermore, the tests serve to verify that state transitions remain consistent as component requirements evolve.

Middleware testing extends these ideas to cover asynchronous and side-effectful operations. Custom middleware, such as one handling promise-based actions or logging, must be validated against expected side effects. For example, a test for a promise-based middleware that intercepts actions with a `promise` property would simulate asynchronous behavior and assert that the proper success or failure actions are dispatched:

```
import configureMockStore from 'redux-mock-store';
import thunk from 'redux-thunk';
import { AnyAction } from 'redux';
import { promiseMiddleware } from '../middleware/promiseMiddleware';

const middlewares = [thunk, promiseMiddleware];
const mockStore = configureMockStore(middlewares);

describe('promiseMiddleware', () => {
    it('dispatches onSuccess action when promise resolves', async ()
    => {
        const store = mockStore({});
        const successAction = { type: 'SUCCESS_ACTION', payload: '
result' };
        const asyncAction: AnyAction = {
            type: 'ASYNC_ACTION',
            promise: Promise.resolve('result'),
            onSuccess: (result: string) => successAction
        };

        await store.dispatch(asyncAction);
        const actions = store.getActions();
        expect(actions).toContainEqual(successAction);
    });

    it('dispatches onError action when promise rejects', async () =>
    {
        const store = mockStore({});
        const failureAction = { type: 'FAILURE_ACTION', payload: '
error' };
        const asyncAction: AnyAction = {
            type: 'ASYNC_ACTION',
            promise: Promise.reject(new Error('error')),
            onError: (error: Error) => failureAction
```

318

```
    };

    await store.dispatch(asyncAction);
    const actions = store.getActions();
    expect(actions).toContainEqual(failureAction);
  });
});
```

By leveraging mock stores and asynchronous testing strategies, mid-dleware tests simulate the dispatch chain and verify that metadata attached to actions, such as promise outcomes, conforms to declared types and business logic. It is essential that tests fail early when the middleware's logic deviates from expected behavior, a condition enforced by TypeScript when combined with robust unit tests.

Integration tests further unify the testing of React components with Redux state management. Using providers to bind components to the Redux store ensures that type-safe interactions propagate through the rendering tree. An advanced integration test might connect a container component to the Redux store using the `Provider` pattern and verify that state selections and dispatches occur as expected:

```
import React from 'react';
import { render, fireEvent, waitFor } from '@testing-library/react';
import { Provider } from 'react-redux';
import configureStore from 'redux-mock-store';
import ContainerComponent from '../containers/ContainerComponent';
import { AppState } from '../reducers/rootReducer';

const mockStore = configureStore([]);

describe('ContainerComponent integration test', () => {
    let store;
    let initialState: AppState;

    beforeEach(() => {
        initialState = {
            counter: { count: 2 },
```

```
        user: {
            id: '123',
            name: 'Integration Tester',
            email: 'integration@example.com'
        }
    };
    store = mockStore(initialState);
});

it('renders container with state and dispatches actions correctly
', async () => {
    const { getByText, getByRole } = render(
        <Provider store={store}>
            <ContainerComponent />
        </Provider>
    );

    expect(getByText(/Integration Tester/)).toBeTruthy();
    expect(getByText(/2/)).toBeTruthy();

    const incrementButton = getByRole('button', { name: /
Increment/ });
    fireEvent.click(incrementButton);

    await waitFor(() =>
        expect(store.getActions()).toEqual(
            expect.arrayContaining([
                { type: 'INCREMENT' }
            ])
        )
    );
});
});
```

This integration test wraps the container component with a Redux
Provider using a mock store, ensuring that the state shape adheres to
the AppState interface. The test verifies that both the rendered output
and the subsequent dispatched actions match the expected sequence
and type definitions. The emphasis on type correctness throughout
the integration aids in preempting bugs that could propagate in production.

320

End-to-end tests complement unit and integration tests by validating that the entire application behaves as expected in a production-like environment. Tools such as Cypress can be configured with TypeScript to generate end-to-end test cases that interact with the real store and components. Although the primary goal of end-to-end testing is not granular type verification, ensuring that the UI interactions invoke the correct Redux flows adds another layer of confidence. A typical end-to-end test might simulate a user journey that triggers complex Redux logic and then assert that the user interface reflects the transformed state:

```
describe('E2E Testing of Redux Flow', () => {
    it('navigates through the app and updates state accordingly', ()
    => {
        cy.visit('/');
        cy.get('button').contains('Login').click();
        cy.get('[data-testid="welcome-message"]').should(
            'contain.text',
            'Welcome, Integration Tester'
        );
        cy.get('button').contains('Logout').click();
        cy.get('[data-testid="login-form"]').should('be.visible');
    });
});
```

Best practices for testing in a TypeScript environment extend to leveraging static analysis ahead of test execution. TypeScript's compiler flags type mismatches even before tests are run, thereby reducing false positives. Advanced continuous integration pipelines integrate both static type checks (using `tsc --noEmit`) and runtime tests so that discrepancies between the intended and actual shapes of actions, state, or component props are caught early in the development cycle.

Moreover, sophisticated tests integrate code coverage tools (e.g., Istanbul) with TypeScript source maps, ensuring that both synthesized code from TypeScript and its intended logic are adequately exercised. Coupled with snapshot testing for components that render complex dynamic content, teams can enforce that unexpected changes in UI rendering are detected immediately. Using React Testing Library's built-in assertions, developers can measure snapshots not only for markup consistency but also for compliance with accessibility standards—a crucial consideration in production-grade applications.

In practice, employing dependency injection for asynchronous operations or external APIs in both component tests and Redux actions enhances testability. Abstracting away real API calls in favor of mocks, stubs, or using libraries such as MSW (Mock Service Worker) lets developers simulate network interactions while preserving the type-check boundaries defined in the application. For example, a test for a component that fetches user data might replace the real fetch function with a mock that returns a predetermined response, ensuring that the component's logic and side effects are controlled and observable.

Testing React and Redux applications in TypeScript, therefore, demands a multi-layered approach that combines rigorous unit testing, integration tests with mock stores, and end-to-end scenarios designed to simulate real user flows. Advanced techniques such as ensuring exhaustive action type checking in reducers, leveraging memoized selectors, mocking middleware interactions, and integrating static type analysis into continuous integration pipelines all contribute to a robust testing ecosystem. This paradigm not only safeguards code quality and reliability but also reinforces the internal contracts specified by TypeScript across the codebase, ensuring that scaling and refactoring efforts remain controlled and predictable.

# 7

# Chapter 7: Building Robust APIs with TypeScript

*This chapter focuses on developing resilient APIs using TypeScript, empha-*
*sizing design principles and integration with Node.js and Express. It guides*
*on creating type-safe endpoints, data validation, and secure authentication.*
*The chapter also covers handling asynchronous operations, versioning, and*
*comprehensive documentation, ensuring scalable and efficient API solutions.*

## 7.1  Design Principles for TypeScript APIs

Robust and scalable API design with TypeScript requires a disciplined
approach that integrates static type checking, advanced type system
features, and modern software engineering principles. TypeScript's
expressive type system allows for creating precise contracts between
different layers of an application, reducing runtime errors while facili-

tating refactoring and extension. This section elaborates on the fundamental design concepts that underpin robust TypeScript APIs, focusing on advanced techniques that exploit generics, utility types, immutability, and modularity.

A core tenet of API design is defining explicit contracts. It is imperative to leverage TypeScript interfaces and types to create formalized definitions of API inputs and outputs. This explicit contract definition facilitates consumer understanding, prevents data misinterpretation, and reduces coupling between modules. Using union types, intersection types, and conditional types provide superior flexibility to express complex shapes in data structures. Consider the following example that leverages discriminated unions to enforce state transition invariants in an API context:

```
interface PendingRequest {
    status: 'pending';
    createdAt: Date;
}

interface ApprovedRequest {
    status: 'approved';
    approvedAt: Date;
    approvedBy: string;
}

interface RejectedRequest {
    status: 'rejected';
    rejectedAt: Date;
    reason: string;
}

type RequestState = PendingRequest | ApprovedRequest |
    RejectedRequest;

function handleRequest(req: RequestState): void {
    switch (req.status) {
        case 'pending':
            // Process pending request details
```

```
            break;
        case 'approved':
            // Process approved request details
            break;
        case 'rejected':
            // Process rejected request details
            break;
        default:
            // Exhaustiveness check
            const _exhaustive: never = req;
            return _exhaustive;
    }
}
```

In the example above, careful attention to the discriminated property status enables both the compiler and developer to reason about state transitions reliably, ensuring that new states are incorporated systematically.

Another advanced design principle is the utilization of generics to abstract common functionality and enforce type consistency. Generic types enable developers to write utility functions and classes that operate over a variety of types while preserving precise type constraints. The power of generics can be illustrated in pagination, filtering, or mapping API responses. The following code snippet demonstrates an API response wrapper that harnesses generics to enforce a consistent structure:

```
interface ApiResponse<T> {
    success: boolean;
    data: T;
    error?: string;
}

function wrapResponse<T>(data: T): ApiResponse<T> {
    return {
        success: true,
        data
```

```
    };
}

const users = [{ id: 1, name: 'Alice' }, { id: 2, name: 'Bob' }];
const response = wrapResponse(users);
```

This approach enforces that all responses adhere to the prescribed structure at compile-time, thereby reducing potential runtime inconsistencies when changes occur in underlying data types.

Modularity is essential in designing APIs that scale horizontally. Dividing business logic into finely grained modules and employing dependency inversion helps in managing complexity. Design strategies such as the repository pattern and domain-driven design (DDD) have considerable implications when combined with TypeScript's static type checking. In well-architected APIs, modules have explicit contracts. As a best practice, one should isolate types close to the domain of their use. For example, consider a Domain Service that works with user entities:

```
interface User {
    id: number;
    username: string;
    email: string;
}

interface UserRepository {
    findById(id: number): Promise<User | null>;
    create(user: Partial<User>): Promise<User>;
}

class UserService {
    constructor(private repository: UserRepository) {}

    async getUserDetails(id: number): Promise<User> {
        const user = await this.repository.findById(id);
        if (!user) {
            throw new Error('User not found');
```

326

```
        }
        return user;
    }
}
```

By employing patterns like repository and service abstractions, one can unit test and refine each component independently. Using TypeScript to enforce method contracts within these abstractions results in cleaner boundaries and a codebase more amenable to long-term maintenance.

TypeScript's advanced type transformations, available via utility types, elevate the design of APIs. The `Partial`, `Required`, `Pick`, and `Omit` utility types enable precise transformations of interfaces, particularly useful in scenarios where API endpoints allow partial updates. For instance, when implementing a patch update for a resource, the following pattern can be applied:

```
interface Profile {
    id: number;
    username: string;
    bio: string;
    avatarUrl: string;
}

function updateProfile(id: number, updates: Partial<Profile>):
    Promise<Profile> {
    // Implementation that merges the partial update with current
    profile state
    // and persists to the database.
    return fetchProfileFromDB(id).then(currentProfile => ({
        ...currentProfile,
        ...updates
    }));
}
```

Using the `Partial` utility guarantees that the updates parameter only contains fields that are optionally specified, ensuring that API consumers are not forced to provide complete objects during an update operation.

To achieve robustness, error handling must be addressed at the architectural level by clearly distinguishing between operational and programmer errors. Incorporating custom error classes with precisely declared fields helps developers to programmatically distinguish error types during failure scenarios. For example:

```
class ApiError extends Error {
    public readonly statusCode: number;
    public readonly isOperational: boolean;
    constructor(message: string, statusCode = 500, isOperational =
    true) {
        super(message);
        this.statusCode = statusCode;
        this.isOperational = isOperational;
        Object.setPrototypeOf(this, new.target.prototype);
    }
}

function processApiRequest(data: any): void {
    if (!data) {
        throw new ApiError('Data payload is missing', 400);
    }
    // Further processing
}
```

This hierarchical error handling mechanism augments API robustness by separating recoverable operation errors from critical failures, thereby enabling systematic error logging and consistent client responses.

Immutable design has a profound impact on API consistency, especially in concurrent and asynchronous environments. TypeScript supports immutability through the enforcement of readonly properties and the use of libraries designed to enforce persistent data structures.

Leveraging immutable objects ensures that the internal state of an API is never inadvertently mutated. Mark elements as `readonly` in the type declarations to prevent state modifications post-construction. In a concurrency scenario, employ immutable techniques as demonstrated below:

```
interface Config {
    readonly apiUrl: string;
    readonly timeout: number;
}

const defaultConfig: Config = {
    apiUrl: 'https://api.example.com',
    timeout: 5000
};

function updateConfig(config: Config, updates: Partial<Config>):
    Config {
    return { ...config, ...updates };
}

const newConfig = updateConfig(defaultConfig, { timeout: 10000 });
```

Immutable patterns mitigate race conditions and inadvertent side effects, attributes that are indispensable to API scalability and security. The discrete separation of state control simplifies debugging and improves predictability within large-scale systems.

When designing APIs with TypeScript, special emphasis should be placed on the consistent use of asynchronous programming patterns. Promises, async/await, and concurrency control are fundamental components of modern API design. Leveraging async/await syntax combined with proper error handling and type-checking results in APIs that are both responsive and reliable. An advanced technique involves the creation of higher-order functions that automatically wrap asynchronous functions in predictable error handlers. For instance:

```
function asyncHandler<T extends (...args: any[]) => Promise<any>>(fn:
    T) {
    return function(...args: Parameters<T>): Promise<ReturnType<T>> {
        return fn(...args).catch(err => {
            // Log the error or transform it if necessary
            console.error('Async Handler Error: ', err);
            throw new ApiError('Internal Server Error', 500, true);
        });
    };
}


// Usage within an API endpoint:
const fetchData = asyncHandler(async (id: number): Promise<string> =>
    {
    // Simulate asynchronous operation
    if (id <= 0) {
        throw new Error('Invalid ID');
    }
    return 'Data fetched successfully';
});
```

This pattern standardizes asynchronous error handling, reducing boilerplate code and enhancing readability while preserving sophisticated error propagation strategies.

Furthermore, design strategies for scaling APIs often involve partitioning the system into microservices. TypeScript's robust type system is particularly beneficial in a microservices architecture by providing consistency across service boundaries. Define shared contracts as separate packages or modules and employ automated contract testing to ensure compatibility. Refining these contracts incrementally in lockstep with service evolution ensures long-term sustainability.

A final consideration is the integration of runtime type-checking with static type guarantees. While TypeScript guarantees compile-time type safety, runtime validation ensures data integrity at the boundaries of untyped interactions. Combining static types with runtime validation

330

libraries such as `io-ts` or `zod` guarantees that external data adheres to expected interfaces. This pattern is illustrated by the following example using zod:

```
import { z } from 'zod';

const UserSchema = z.object({
    id: z.number(),
    username: z.string(),
    email: z.string().email()
});

type User = z.infer<typeof UserSchema>;

async function createUser(input: unknown): Promise<User> {
    const parsed = UserSchema.parse(input);
    // Proceed with the guarantee that parsed conforms to User
    return parsed;
}
```

Integrating runtime validation preserves type safety across external boundaries and provides an additional security net against malformed data, thereby ensuring that API endpoints remain robust under diverse operational conditions.

Collectively, these advanced design principles and patterns coalesce into a framework that reinforces the robustness and scalability of Type-Script APIs. The deliberate emphasis on explicit contracts, modularity, generic programming, immutable patterns, and rigorous error handling transforms the codebase into maintainable and predictable software suited for production environments with high scalability demands.

## 7.2    Using TypeScript with Node.js and Express

Integrating TypeScript into a Node.js and Express environment introduces a rigorous type layer over asynchronous JavaScript, enabling
compile-time guarantees that increase code clarity and maintainability.
The inherent flexibility of Express is complemented by TypeScript's
static type system, which together facilitate advanced error handling,
middleware composition, and modular routing strategies. In this section, advanced techniques and patterns are examined to illustrate the
construction of high-performance, scalable APIs with a strong emphasis on type safety.

One of the primary steps is ensuring a precise configuration
in `tsconfig.json`.    Advanced setups not only target modern
ECMAScript standards but also enforce strict null checks and implicit
type inferences. An exemplary configuration might appear as follows:

```
{
  "compilerOptions": {
    "target": "ES2020",
    "module": "commonjs",
    "strict": true,
    "esModuleInterop": true,
    "forceConsistentCasingInFileNames": true,
    "skipLibCheck": true,
    "outDir": "./dist",
    "resolveJsonModule": true
  },
  "include": ["src"]
}
```

This configuration forms the groundwork for a hardened TypeScript
project and ensures that expressive type contracts are enforced uniformly, thereby reducing runtime errors when integrating Express
routes with business logic.

Express applications benefit significantly from TypeScript's explicit typing of request and response objects. Customizing middleware to extend the default types allows for the inclusion of properties that are later accessed in downstream processes. The following snippet demonstrates how one can augment the Express request interface:

```
import * as express from 'express';

declare global {
  namespace Express {
    interface Request {
      user?: { id: number; role: string };
    }
  }
}
```

This augmentation enforces type safety across middleware layers that depend on the authenticated user's metadata, ensuring that each subsequent handler can safely access the user property without redundant type assertions.

Middleware design in an Express/TypeScript environment benefits from the use of generic functions to enforce error-handling semantics. Wrapping asynchronous routes with a higher-order function that guarantees proper error propagation eliminates repetitive try/catch blocks. Consider the advanced pattern shown below:

```
import { Request, Response, NextFunction } from 'express';

function asyncMiddleware<T extends (...args: any[]) => Promise<void
    >>(fn: T) {
  return (req: Request, res: Response, next: NextFunction): void => {
    fn(req, res, next).catch(next);
  };
}

// Example usage in a route
app.get('/data', asyncMiddleware(async (req: Request, res: Response)
```

```
    => {
  const data = await fetchDataFromService();
  res.json({ success: true, data });
}));
```

By abstracting asynchronous error handling, the code remains both concise and robust, ensuring that exceptions are centrally caught and processed, thereby safeguarding against unhandled rejections.

Organizing the application into modular routers further enhances maintainability. Advanced routing techniques capitalize on dependency injection, ensuring express routers are cleanly separated from business logic. Each router might be implemented as a self-contained module that exports a configured router instance with well-defined TypeScript interfaces guiding the contract between layers. An example of a modular router is provided below:

```
import { Router, Request, Response } from 'express';
import { UserService } from '../services/UserService';

const router = Router();
const userService = new UserService();

router.get('/:id', async (req: Request, res: Response) => {
  const id = parseInt(req.params.id, 10);
  if (isNaN(id)) {
    res.status(400).json({ error: 'Invalid user ID' });
    return;
  }
  try {
    const user = await userService.findUserById(id);
    if (!user) {
      res.status(404).json({ error: 'User not found' });
      return;
    }
    res.json({ data: user });
  } catch (error) {
    res.status(500).json({ error: 'Internal Server Error' });
  }
```

```
});

export default router;
```

The use of TypeScript not only enforces parameter type validation but also ensures that the asynchronous interactions with the service layer are predictable. Moreover, advanced use of dependency injection frameworks can be explored to manage service instances with greater granularity, reducing global state and enhancing testability.

Error handling in a TypeScript-based Express API can be refined by designing custom error classes that encapsulate HTTP-specific metadata. By extending the native `Error` object, one can incorporate status codes and operational flags. This approach allows error middleware to introspect error objects and respond appropriately. A robust error class might be defined as follows:

```
export class HttpError extends Error {
  public statusCode: number;
  public isOperational: boolean;

  constructor(message: string, statusCode: number = 500,
    isOperational: boolean = true) {
    super(message);
    this.statusCode = statusCode;
    this.isOperational = isOperational;
    Object.setPrototypeOf(this, HttpError.prototype);
  }
}
```

Integrating this custom error class within middleware ensures a consistent pattern for error responses:

```
import { Request, Response, NextFunction } from 'express';
import { HttpError } from './HttpError';

function errorHandler(err: HttpError, req: Request, res: Response,
    next: NextFunction) {
```

```
const status = err.statusCode || 500;
const message = err.isOperational ? err.message : 'Internal server
    error';
res.status(status).json({ error: message });
}

app.use(errorHandler);
```

TypeScript's advanced type utilities further promote refined control over request handling. One trick is to use generics to parameterize request handlers with expected input and output data types. This design clarifies the intended structure of incoming request bodies and outgoing responses. An example of this advanced technique is:

```
import { RequestHandler } from 'express';

interface CreateUserRequest {
  username: string;
  email: string;
  password: string;
}

interface CreateUserResponse {
  id: number;
  username: string;
  email: string;
}

const createUserHandler: RequestHandler<{}, CreateUserResponse,
    CreateUserRequest> = async (req, res, next) => {
  try {
    const { username, email, password } = req.body;
    const newUser = await userService.createUser({ username, email,
    password });
    res.json({ id: newUser.id, username: newUser.username, email:
    newUser.email });
  } catch (err) {
    next(err);
  }
};
```

336

By specifying request and response types, developers reduce ambiguity and facilitate smoother integration with automated documentation and testing tools. This is particularly beneficial when working with large teams and evolving API contracts.

The adoption of code quality tools is indispensable in a production-grade Node.js and Express project written in TypeScript. Tools such as ESLint, Prettier, and TypeScript's own tsc enforce coding standards while external type-checking workflows detect anomalies early. Configuring ESLint for a TypeScript project might include plugins specifically designed for enhanced type analysis:

```
module.exports = {
  parser: '@typescript-eslint/parser',
  plugins: ['@typescript-eslint'],
  extends: [
    'eslint:recommended',
    'plugin:@typescript-eslint/recommended'
  ],
  rules: {
    // Custom rules for advanced usage
    '@typescript-eslint/no-unused-vars': ['error']
  }
};
```

Such tool configurations prevent subtle bugs that could arise from dynamic language pitfalls, enhancing the overall robustness of the codebase.

Integration testing in an Express application benefits greatly from TypeScript, as the defined interfaces allow mock implementations of external services to adhere strictly to intended contracts. Utilizing dependency injection, developers can replace real database or network calls with mock stubs that simulate responses. For example, consider the following test setup that replaces a user repository for a particular

337

route:

```
import * as request from 'supertest';
import app from '../src/app';
import { UserRepository } from '../src/repositories/UserRepository';

jest.mock('../src/repositories/UserRepository');

const mockedUserRepository = UserRepository as jest.MockedClass<
    typeof UserRepository>;

describe('GET /users/:id', () => {
  it('should return 200 and valid user data for a known user', async
    () => {
    mockedUserRepository.prototype.findById.mockResolvedValue({
      id: 1,
      username: 'testuser',
      email: 'test@example.com'
    });
    const response = await request(app).get('/users/1');
    expect(response.status).toBe(200);
    expect(response.body.data).toHaveProperty('username', 'testuser')
    ;
  });
});
```

Using typed mocks ensures that any deviation from the expected interface is detected at compile time, thus increasing confidence in integration tests during refactoring and rapid iterations.

Advanced patterns also include the utilization of asynchronous iteration and streaming in Express endpoints. When receiving large payloads or interacting with long-running operations, TypeScript can enforce contracts over event streams. Combining Express's middleware
with Node.js streams requires careful type composition. The following
sample demonstrates an endpoint that streams file data:

```
import * as fs from 'fs';
import { Request, Response } from 'express';
```

338

```
app.get('/stream/:filename', (req: Request, res: Response) => {
  const filepath = `/data/${req.params.filename}`;
  const fileStream = fs.createReadStream(filepath);
  fileStream.on('error', (err) => {
    res.status(500).json({ error: 'File stream error' });
  });
  res.type('application/octet-stream');
  fileStream.pipe(res);
});
```

Here, TypeScript's integration with Node.js core modules enforces consistency across async operations, while explicit stream typing aids debugging and ensures correct content negotiation.

The deliberate fusion of TypeScript's static type system with the dynamic capabilities of Node.js and Express facilitates a development workflow where the API's behavior is both predictable and efficient. Emphasizing explicit contracts, middleware abstraction, rigorous error handling, and thorough integration testing creates an environment primed for advanced API development. This marriage of technologies supports scalable, maintainable, and high-performance back-end systems suitable for demanding production scenarios.

## 7.3  Implementing Type-safe API Endpoints

Implementing type-safe API endpoints requires leveraging TypeScript's static type analysis to enforce precise and expressive contracts between clients and servers. The objective is to eliminate latent type inconsistencies and runtime errors by accurately describing the shape, structure, and constraints of data exchanged between endpoints. Advanced programmers can achieve this by integrating advanced type constructs such as generics, discriminated unions, and

339

conditional types into the endpoint design. This section delves into explicit strategies to construct API endpoints that guarantee reliability and improve developer productivity.

One approach to achieving type safety is to partition the API layer into input validation, business logic, and output transformation. Each stage is rigorously typed to ensure data integrity at every transition. The input payload, often received as an untyped object, must be validated and transformed into a well-defined structure. Consider the following pattern combining static types with runtime checks:

```
import { Request, Response, NextFunction } from 'express';
import { z } from 'zod';

// Define a schema using zod for runtime validation
const CreateUserSchema = z.object({
  username: z.string().min(3),
  email: z.string().email(),
  password: z.string().min(8)
});

type CreateUserPayload = z.infer<typeof CreateUserSchema>;

async function createUser(req: Request, res: Response, next:
    NextFunction) {
  try {
    // Validate input and infer type
    const payload: CreateUserPayload = CreateUserSchema.parse(req.
    body);
    // Business logic processing with strict types
    const user = await userService.createUser(payload);
    res.status(201).json({ id: user.id, username: user.username });
  } catch (error) {
    next(error);
  }
}
```

By coupling runtime validation with compile-time type inference, this design minimizes discrepancies between the anticipated and actual request payloads, ensuring that subsequent business logic can operate with full confidence in the data structure.

Another central concept is the use of discriminated unions to model different API responses based on business logic outcomes. Leveraging a common discriminant property, endpoints can return varied response types that are guaranteed to follow predetermined contracts. For instance, consider an endpoint that either returns a successful user retrieval or an error message:

```
type SuccessResponse<T> = {
  status: 'success';
  data: T;
};

type ErrorResponse = {
  status: 'error';
  error: string;
};

type ApiResponse<T> = SuccessResponse<T> | ErrorResponse;

async function getUser(req: Request, res: Response, next:
    NextFunction) {
  const userId: number = parseInt(req.params.id, 10);
  try {
    const user = await userService.findUserById(userId);
    if (!user) {
      const errorResponse: ErrorResponse = { status: 'error', error:
      'User not found' };
      res.status(404).json(errorResponse);
      return;
    }
    const successResponse: SuccessResponse<typeof user> = { status: '
    success', data: user };
    res.status(200).json(successResponse);
  } catch (error) {
    next(error);
  }
}
```

Discriminated unions enable the compiler to narrow types based on the response status, allowing consumers to handle each scenario in a type-safe manner. This pattern establishes a robust contract for API consumers, who can programmatically discriminate between errors and successes without resorting to runtime type assertions.

Generics improve endpoint reusability and flexibility by abstracting over similar patterns within the API layer. Developers can define generic functions for common response wrapping, pagination logic, or error handling, ensuring that the endpoints adhere to consistent typing throughout the codebase. The following example demonstrates a generic response wrapper function:

```
interface ApiResponseWrapper<T> {
  payload: T;
  timestamp: number;
}

function wrapResponse<T>(data: T): ApiResponseWrapper<T> {
  return { payload: data, timestamp: Date.now() };
}

// Usage in an endpoint
async function listUsers(req: Request, res: Response, next:
    NextFunction) {
  try {
    const users = await userService.getAllUsers();
    res.json(wrapResponse(users));
  } catch (error) {
    next(error);
  }
}
```

This generic design facilitates consistency across endpoints, reduces code duplication, and ensures that the API responses are wrapped in a standardized manner.

Advanced endpoint design also requires careful consideration of asynchronous patterns. TypeScript's type system can capture nuances in asynchronous operations using Promise types. Wrapping endpoints in higher-order functions to standardize error handling across asynchronous calls is a recognized best practice. Consider a higher-order function designed to centralize promise error handling:

```
function asyncRouteHandler<T extends (...args: any[]) => Promise<void
    >>(
  routeHandler: T
): (...args: Parameters<T>) => void {
  return (req, res, next) => {
    routeHandler(req, res, next).catch(next);
  };
}

// Endpoint definition with enhanced type safety
app.post('/create-user', asyncRouteHandler(async (req: Request, res:
    Response) => {
  const payload: CreateUserPayload = CreateUserSchema.parse(req.body)
    ;
  const user = await userService.createUser(payload);
  res.status(201).json({ id: user.id, username: user.username });
}));
```

This pattern reduces boilerplate code while ensuring that all asynchronous errors are consistently captured and routed into Express's centralized error handling mechanism. By strictly enforcing the return types of asynchronous functions, developers can ensure that every endpoint's eventual resolution adheres to predefined contracts.

Another refined technique is integrating type-safe middleware for authentication and authorization. Custom Express middleware can be designed to assert user roles and authentication states with advanced type predicates. Augmenting the Request interface allows middleware to attach precise user objects that subsequent endpoints depend on without repetitive type assertions. An exemplary middleware logic is illustrated below:

```
import { Request, Response, NextFunction } from 'express';

interface AuthenticatedUser {
  id: number;
  username: string;
  roles: string[];
}

declare global {
  namespace Express {
    interface Request {
      user?: AuthenticatedUser;
    }
  }
}

function ensureAuthenticated(req: Request, res: Response, next:
    NextFunction): void {
  if (req.user) {
    next();
  } else {
    res.status(401).json({ error: 'Authentication required' });
  }
}
```

With robust type definitions in place, endpoints that depend on user data can assume the availability of specific properties, making it possible to avoid repetitive null checks and reducing error surfaces. Endpoints built on these premises enhance reliability and simplify the development process.

Type-safe API endpoints also benefit from strict contract definitions for request parameters and query strings. Using TypeScript's intersection and utility types, one can combine multiple sources of parameters into a single, coherent type. An example of this technique is demonstrated below:

```
import { RequestHandler } from 'express';
```

```
interface PaginationParams {
  page: number;
  limit: number;
}

interface FilterParams {
  search?: string;
}

type ListUsersQuery = PaginationParams & FilterParams;

const listUsers: RequestHandler<{}, any, any, ListUsersQuery> = async
    (req, res, next) => {
  const { page, limit, search } = req.query;
  try {
    const { users, total } = await userService.listUsers({ page,
    limit, search });
    res.json({ users, total, page, limit });
  } catch (error) {
    next(error);
  }
};
```

This approach not only reinforces the integrity of query parameters
but also facilitates automated documentation generation tools, such as
Swagger or OpenAPI, by providing explicit type contracts that accurately describe the endpoint's expectations.

Advanced error handling is inseparable from the deployment of type-
safe endpoints. Custom error types can encapsulate domain-specific
errors and are extended to represent granular error states. A robust error model might distinguish between validation errors, authentication
failures, and system-level exceptions:

```
class ValidationError extends Error {
  public readonly statusCode: number = 422;
  constructor(message: string) {
    super(message);
    Object.setPrototypeOf(this, ValidationError.prototype);
```

```
   }
}

class AuthError extends Error {
  public readonly statusCode: number = 401;
  constructor(message: string) {
    super(message);
    Object.setPrototypeOf(this, AuthError.prototype);
  }
}
```

Endpoints can then selectively throw these errors based on strict type checks. For example, the user creation endpoint may validate inputs against business rules and throw a `ValidationError` if constraints are violated. This not only improves error traceability but also allows middleware to distinguish error types and generate detailed error responses accordingly.

When implementing type-safe API endpoints, it is essential to consider the entire lifecycle of the request-response pattern. Combining static types with runtime validations ensures that all transformations are traceable and predictable. Advanced applications may integrate automated testing with strongly-typed mocks that mimic the behavior of external services. Using dependency injection, one can substitute production implementations with these mocks during tests:

```
import * as request from 'supertest';
import app from '../src/app';
import { UserService } from '../src/services/UserService';

jest.mock('../src/services/UserService');

const mockedUserService = UserService as jest.MockedClass<typeof
    UserService>;

describe('POST /create-user', () => {
  it('should return 201 on successful user creation', async () => {
    const newUser = { id: 1, username: 'advanceduser', email: '
```

```
    user@example.com' };
    mockedUserService.prototype.createUser.mockResolvedValue(newUser)
    ;

    const payload = {
      username: 'advanceduser',
      email: 'user@example.com',
      password: 'StrongPass123'
    };

    const response = await request(app).post('/create-user').send(
    payload);
    expect(response.status).toBe(201);
    expect(response.body).toEqual({ id: newUser.id, username: newUser
    .username });
  });
});
```

Type checking at both compile-time and test-time enforces strict compliance with API contracts, which is pivotal in preventing regressions during refactoring and iterative development.

The application of these advanced methods, from explicit payload validation, discriminated unions for response types, and generic response wrappers, to refined middleware extensions, creates an ecosystem where API endpoints are inherently type-safe. This discipline not only accelerates development cycles through improved autocomplete, navigation, and refactorability but also elevates the overall quality and maintainability of the APIs. The integration of advanced error strategies and strong testing practices further solidifies these endpoints as robust components in a large-scale system, making the codebase resilient to unexpected input and behavior while significantly reducing production issues.

## 7.4   Validating and Transforming API Data

Ensuring the accuracy and consistency of data throughout an API's lifecycle is critical to maintaining data integrity and system reliability. Advanced techniques for data validation and transformation involve both compile-time assurances and runtime checks. Static type analysis in TypeScript minimizes many classes of errors; however, external inputs, particularly those that originate from uncontrolled sources, demand rigorous runtime validation. An effective strategy employs schema validation libraries such as zod or io-ts, which permit the definition of declarative data schemas that can auto-generate TypeScript types while performing robust validation.

A typical approach begins with the definition of immutable schemas that describe the shape and constraints of expected data. These schemas serve as a single source of truth. For example, the zod library allows the declaration of complex schema objects and supports nested validations, refinements, and transformations. The following code defines a schema for a user object and illustrates how to compose these validations:

```
import { z } from 'zod';

const UserSchema = z.object({
  id: z.number().int().nonnegative(),
  username: z.string().min(3).max(30),
  email: z.string().email(),
  createdAt: z.preprocess(arg => {
    if (typeof arg === 'string' || arg instanceof Date) return new
    Date(arg);
  }, z.date())
});

type User = z.infer<typeof UserSchema>;
```

In this example, the z.preprocess function enables transformation of input data before running the main schema checks. This is especially useful when needing to normalize different representations of the same data format, such as dates provided in multiple formats. Advanced users can leverage such transformations to guarantee type integrity while allowing for flexible input formats.

Beyond singular validations, advanced data transformation involves altering the structure of data to fit a required output model. APIs often need to convert complex domain objects into simplified DTOs (Data Transfer Objects) or view models that are optimized for consumption by clients. Transformation pipelines can be built using chained functions that map, filter, and restructure data appropriately. Consider the following utility that transforms a validated user object into a client-readable DTO:

```
const UserDTO = UserSchema.transform(user => ({
  userId: user.id,
  name: user.username,
  emailAddress: user.email,
  memberSince: user.createdAt.toISOString()
}));

type UserDTO = z.infer<typeof UserDTO>;
```

This pattern leverages the transformation capabilities provided by schema libraries to produce domain-specific output. Notably, such an approach ensures that any modifications to the source object structure necessitate an update in a single location, thereby reducing the risk of data inconsistencies over time.

Modular schema definitions are critical to maintaining readability and reusability in large codebases. Complex API endpoints often require the validation and transformation of deeply nested data structures. By

349

composing smaller, reusable schemas into larger ones, developers can handle complex data formats without redundancy. For instance, an API endpoint that handles order processing might combine customer and product schemas:

```
const ProductSchema = z.object({
  productId: z.number().int().nonnegative(),
  name: z.string(),
  price: z.number().positive()
});

const OrderSchema = z.object({
  orderId: z.number().int().nonnegative(),
  customer: UserSchema,
  items: z.array(ProductSchema).min(1),
  orderDate: z.date(),
  status: z.enum(['pending', 'shipped', 'delivered'])
});

type Order = z.infer<typeof OrderSchema>;
```

Here, the reuse of UserSchema and the creation of ProductSchema encapsulate domain logic specific to each sub-component while maintaining a consistent validation strategy across the API. Such modularity is particularly beneficial in microservice architectures, where services share common data contracts.

Handling optional fields and union types is a frequent requirement in robust API designs. TypeScript naturally accommodates union and optional types; when combined with schema libraries, developers can leverage composability to manage multiple data shapes under a single validation construct. For example, consider an endpoint that accepts a payload which could represent either a new user registration or a user update:

```
const NewUserSchema = UserSchema.omit({ id: true, createdAt: true }).
    extend({
```

```
  password: z.string().min(8)
});

const UpdateUserSchema = UserSchema.partial();

const UserPayloadSchema = z.union([NewUserSchema, UpdateUserSchema]);

type UserPayload = z.infer<typeof UserPayloadSchema>;
```

In this snippet, the use of `omit` and `partial` utility methods from zod permits the creation of variant schemas that accommodate different API endpoint scenarios. The union of these schemas ensures that a single endpoint can flexibly handle multiple input compositions while providing explicit error messages when a payload does not conform to any expected structure.

Performance considerations are also paramount when integrating validation logic into high-throughput API endpoints. Excessive use of runtime schema validations can potentially introduce latency. Advanced strategies include caching compiled schema validators and applying validation selectively based on the request context. In some cases, transforming the input stream into a parsed schema object prior to dispatch can offload validation work from the critical request path. For example, a middleware architecture could be implemented to validate and cache incoming requests:

```
import { Request, Response, NextFunction } from 'express';

function validationMiddleware<T>(schema: z.ZodSchema<T>) {
  return (req: Request, res: Response, next: NextFunction) => {
    try {
      // Parse and transform the request body
      req.body = schema.parse(req.body);
      next();
    } catch (err) {
      res.status(422).json({ error: err.errors });
    }
```

```
    };
  }

  // Usage in an Express route
  app.post('/user', validationMiddleware(NewUserSchema), async (req:
      Request, res: Response) => {
    const userData = req.body as z.infer<typeof NewUserSchema>;
    const newUser = await userService.createUser(userData);
    res.status(201).json(newUser);
  });
```

The middleware pattern centralizes the validation logic while minimizing the redundant parsing of request bodies within each business logic module. Developers should also consider asynchronous validation strategies where external factors, such as database lookups or remote service checks, are integrated into the validation pipeline.

For data transformation, developers can also apply functional programming techniques to streamline and simplify transformation chains. Combining map, filter, and reduce functions with immutability guarantees allows for concise data manipulation that preserves the original payload. Consider a transformation function that cleanses and restructures a list of user records:

```
  function transformUserList(users: ReadonlyArray<User>): Array<UserDTO
      > {
    return users
      .filter(user => user.email.endsWith('@example.com'))
      .map(user => ({
        userId: user.id,
        name: user.username,
        emailAddress: user.email,
        memberSince: user.createdAt.toISOString()
      }));
  }
```

Utilizing TypeScript's readonly arrays ensures that data is not inadvertently modified during transformation. Such patterns are instrumental in maintaining a predictable state throughout the data pipeline, which is particularly important in concurrent and asynchronous API environments.

Error handling in the validation and transformation stages must be both granular and informative. When a schema fails validation, detailed error messages should be propagated to inform API consumers of the exact data discrepancies. Schema libraries generally provide structured error objects that enumerate the failing constraints. Advanced error handling may include logging mechanisms and automated alerts for recurring validation issues. For example:

```
try {
  const validatedData = OrderSchema.parse(rawData);
  // Proceed with business logic using validatedData
} catch (error) {
  // Log detailed error information for later analysis
  console.error('Data validation error:', error.errors);
  throw new Error('Invalid order data provided');
}
```

In scenarios where data transformation introduces subtle discrepancies, developers can incorporate unit tests that capture edge cases. Automated testing with frameworks like Jest, integrated with TypeScript's type checking, ensures that any modifications in the transformation logic trigger a rigorous test suite, thereby preventing regression issues.

Moreover, advanced developers may explore compile-time schema generation techniques. Tools exist which can automatically generate zod or io-ts schemas based on database models or OpenAPI specifications. This automation reduces manual coding efforts and aligns the API's runtime checks with its static types. Such techniques ensure that any evolution in the underlying data models is immediately reflected

353

in the validation and transformation layers, promoting a self-healing codebase.

When working in distributed systems, consistency across services becomes critical; hence, shared validation libraries or common schema packages can be leveraged. By publishing a validation package internally, multiple microservices can use the exact same data contracts, ensuring uniform data handling and reducing the risk of inconsistencies. This approach also simplifies versioning and dependency management, allowing teams to enforce backward compatibility and integrate automatic updates into continuous integration pipelines.

The combination of static type guarantees and runtime validations creates a robust barrier against data anomalies. Advanced transformation pipelines not only normalize data but also enrich it by computing derived properties or filtering out redundant information. The techniques outlined in this section help establish a disciplined data processing strategy that guarantees consistency and improves maintainability across API boundaries. This disciplined approach ultimately mitigates integration errors and enhances the overall resilience of the API-based ecosystem.

## 7.5   Managing Authentication and Authorization

Robust security in TypeScript-based APIs hinges on the careful orchestration of authentication and authorization mechanisms. Advanced implementations require blending sound cryptographic practices with TypeScript's precise type system to enforce rigorous contracts across security boundaries. In this section, we explore strategies for securely implementing authentication, token verification, and role-based access control, using modern libraries, statically typed middleware, and advanced error handling to create resilient and maintainable security layers.

Central to most modern APIs is the use of JSON Web Tokens (JWT), which offer a stateless, compact mechanism for securely transmitting identity and claims. When integrating JWT, developers must ensure that tokens are correctly issued, validated, and that their payload adheres to strict structural definitions. By leveraging libraries such as jsonwebtoken with TypeScript, one can define custom type guards and schema decoders to sanitize token payloads. The following snippet exemplifies a strictly typed JWT verification function:

```
import jwt, { JwtPayload } from 'jsonwebtoken';

interface CustomJwtPayload extends JwtPayload {
  userId: number;
  roles: string[];
}

const verifyToken = (token: string, secretKey: string):
    CustomJwtPayload => {
  const decoded = jwt.verify(token, secretKey) as CustomJwtPayload;
  if (!decoded.userId || !Array.isArray(decoded.roles)) {
    throw new Error('Invalid token payload');
  }
  return decoded;
};
```

Here, the function leverages TypeScript's type assertion in conjunction with runtime checks to ensure that essential properties exist. Integrating these checks mitigates risks posed by malformed tokens and prevents unauthorized access that might arise from type ambiguity.

Middleware functions form the backbone of authorization checks in Express applications. By extending the Express Request interface via declaration merging, developers can safely attach authenticated user details for downstream handlers. The following illustrates a custom middleware to extract and attach token claims:

```
import { Request, Response, NextFunction } from 'express';

declare global {
  namespace Express {
    interface Request {
      auth?: CustomJwtPayload;
    }
  }
}

const authenticate = (secretKey: string) => {
  return (req: Request, res: Response, next: NextFunction): void => {
    const authHeader = req.headers.authorization;
    if (!authHeader) {
      res.status(401).json({ error: 'Authorization header missing' })
      ;
      return;
    }
    const token = authHeader.split(' ')[1];
    try {
      req.auth = verifyToken(token, secretKey);
      next();
    } catch (error) {
      res.status(401).json({ error: 'Invalid token' });
    }
  };
};
```

By embedding type information directly within the request lifecycle, this middleware ensures that subsequent handlers can safely access the auth property without repeated validation, thus reducing boilerplate code and centralizing error handling.

Beyond verifying token integrity, advanced authorization involves role-based access control (RBAC), where endpoints are selectively accessible based on user roles and permissions. TypeScript's robust type system allows for the definition of distinct role types, such that the access control logic is both explicit and maintainable. Consider the following interface that defines various roles within an application:

```
type UserRole = 'admin' | 'editor' | 'viewer';

interface CustomJwtPayload extends JwtPayload {
  userId: number;
  roles: UserRole[];
}
```

Building upon this, a role-checking middleware function inspects the token claims for required roles and denies access if the claims do not align with expected privileges. The snippet below illustrates a generic middleware factory for role-based authorization:

```
const authorize = (requiredRoles: UserRole[]) => {
  return (req: Request, res: Response, next: NextFunction): void => {
    if (!req.auth || !req.auth.roles) {
      res.status(403).json({ error: 'Access forbidden: no
      authentication details' });
      return;
    }
    const hasRole = requiredRoles.some(role => req.auth!.roles.
    includes(role));
    if (!hasRole) {
      res.status(403).json({ error: 'Access forbidden: insufficient
      privileges' });
      return;
    }
    next();
  };
};
```

This function not only enforces the required permissions but also provides clear error messages, aiding both debugging and auditing processes. The use of higher-order functions in this context exemplifies how TypeScript's generics and advanced type constructs can enhance control flow while preserving comprehensibility.

For APIs that demand more granular authorization, attribute-based access control (ABAC) may be necessary. ABAC mechanisms evaluate multiple facets of a request, such as user attributes, resource metadata, and environmental context. Implementing ABAC can involve combining several middleware functions that examine these aspects in isolation before synthesizing a final authorization decision. A simplified example involves comparing a user's ID with the resource owner's ID:

```
const authorizeOwnership = (getResourceOwnerId: (req: Request) =>
    number) => {
  return (req: Request, res: Response, next: NextFunction): void => {
    const ownerId = getResourceOwnerId(req);
    if (!req.auth || req.auth.userId !== ownerId) {
      res.status(403).json({ error: 'Access forbidden: resource
      ownership mismatch' });
      return;
    }
    next();
  };
};
```

When combined with RBAC or other policy engines, this middleware precisely tailors access control based on dynamic conditions. Such an approach benefits from TypeScript's ability to enforce function contracts and accurately capture transformations that occur as data flows through these layers.

Security best practices dictate that private keys and secrets used for signing and verifying tokens should be managed with utmost care. Environment variables, external secret management systems, or secure vaults can safeguard these assets. TypeScript's integration with configuration management libraries permits strong typing for configuration values and helps avoid misconfiguration. For instance, a configuration module might be defined as follows:

```
interface Config {
  jwtSecret: string;
  tokenExpiry: string;
  issuer: string;
}

const config: Config = {
  jwtSecret: process.env.JWT_SECRET as string,
  tokenExpiry: process.env.TOKEN_EXPIRY || '1h',
  issuer: process.env.JWT_ISSUER || 'myapi'
};


export default config;
```

Such structures enforce that essential parameters are present at compile time, reducing functional errors caused by missing or misconfigured environment variables.

Another area of concern is the secure storage and handling of authentication tokens on the client side. Although beyond the immediate scope of APIs, server-side considerations include mechanisms to mitigate token replay attacks and unauthorized token usage. Implementing token blacklisting or rotating refresh tokens are advanced techniques that can be incorporated within authentication controllers. Developers may create a token management service that interacts with a caching layer such as Redis. A simplified token revocation function looks as follows:

```
import Redis from 'ioredis';

const redisClient = new Redis();

const revokeToken = async (token: string, expiry: number): Promise<
    void> => {
  await redisClient.set(token, 'revoked', 'EX', expiry);
};

const isTokenRevoked = async (token: string): Promise<boolean> => {
```

```
  const result = await redisClient.get(token);
  return result === 'revoked';
};
```

Integrating token revocation checks into the authentication middle-ware furthers the security posture of the API by ensuring that tokens rendered invalid by an administrative action are not accepted.

Integrating third-party identity providers using protocols such as OAuth2 or OpenID Connect (OIDC) is another sophisticated strategy for authentication. When using libraries like `passport`, advanced Type-Script definitions allow for strict integration of external user profiles into local type definitions. The following snippet outlines how Pass-port strategies might be typed and integrated into an Express middle-ware stack:

```
import passport from 'passport';
import { Strategy as JwtStrategy, ExtractJwt, VerifiedCallback } from
    'passport-jwt';

const jwtOptions = {
  jwtFromRequest: ExtractJwt.fromAuthHeaderAsBearerToken(),
  secretOrKey: config.jwtSecret,
  issuer: config.issuer
};

passport.use(new JwtStrategy(jwtOptions, (payload: CustomJwtPayload,
    done: VerifiedCallback) => {
  if (payload && payload.userId) {
    return done(null, payload);
  }
  return done(null, false);
}));

const passportAuthenticate = passport.authenticate('jwt', { session:
    false });

app.get('/secure-route', passportAuthenticate, (req: Request, res:
    Response) => {
```

```
    res.json({ message: 'Secure data accessed' });
});
```

This integration demonstrates how authentication logic can be externalized while preserving type safety and ensuring that the local application's expectations align with externally provided tokens. Passport's strategy pattern allows for flexibility in swapping out authentication strategies without impacting the core business logic, provided that type contracts are consistently enforced.

Error handling and logging add further dimensions to securing authentication and authorization systems. Structured logging of authentication attempts—both successful and failed—provides valuable insights during forensic analysis. Advanced setups might involve middleware that tracks the status of each request and correlates it with user activity. Care should be taken to avoid logging sensitive information while still providing adequate context for troubleshooting.

A comprehensive approach to managing authentication and authorization in TypeScript-based APIs involves combining strong type enforcement with modular, composable middleware, vigilant token handling, and adherence to security best practices. This multifaceted strategy not only mitigates security risks but also enhances developer productivity by providing clear, enforceable contracts throughout the codebase. Advanced type definitions and runtime validations ensure that authentication data—ranging from token payloads to role claims—remains consistent and trustworthy as it permeates the API architecture.

## 7.6 Asynchronous API Operations with Type-Script

Efficiently handling asynchronous operations is fundamental to building high-performance APIs, particularly in environments where concurrent request processing is a central requirement. TypeScript, with its expressive type system and native support for modern asynchronous patterns, facilitates the creation of APIs that remain highly responsive even under heavy load. This section delves into advanced patterns and techniques for managing asynchronous operations and concurrency within API request processing, focusing on optimizing response times, enhancing error handling, and ensuring predictable behavior in concurrent environments.

Advanced asynchronous control flow in TypeScript typically relies on the `async`/`await` syntax, which provides a clear, linear style for managing promises. While this syntactic sugar simplifies writing asynchronous code, experienced developers must handle subtleties such as error propagation, cancellation, and resource management. Consider the following advanced pattern that wraps asynchronous operations with custom error handling, ensuring that unhandled rejections are funneled into a centralized error handler:

```
function asyncHandler<T extends (...args: any[]) => Promise<any>>(fn:
    T) {
  return (...args: Parameters<T>): Promise<ReturnType<T>> => {
    return fn(...args).catch((err: unknown) => {
      // Advanced error handling: log error details, set metrics, etc
      .
      console.error('Async operation error:', err);
      throw err;
    });
  };
}
```

```
// Usage in an Express route:
app.get('/items', asyncHandler(async (req, res) => {
  const items = await itemService.fetchLatestItems();
  res.status(200).json({ data: items });
}));
```

Utilizing higher-order functions for error handling not only centralizes error logic but also improves the observability of asynchronous failures. Advanced users should consider integrating this pattern with monitoring systems to capture detailed timing and error metrics.

Actions that depend on multiple asynchronous operations can benefit significantly from concurrent execution. Developers often leverage `Promise.all` to run several independent operations in parallel, reducing the total response time. However, this pattern may require careful error aggregation and resource management when dealing with a large number of concurrent promises. An advanced approach might involve using a concurrency limiter, as demonstrated below:

```
async function fetchDataInBatches<T>(
  operations: (() => Promise<T>)[],
  concurrency: number
): Promise<T[]> {
  const results: T[] = [];
  let index = 0;

  async function worker(): Promise<void> {
    while (index < operations.length) {
      const current = index++;
      try {
        const result = await operations[current]();
        results[current] = result;
      } catch (error) {
        // Optional: Collect or log individual errors
        console.error(`Error in operation ${current}:`, error);
        throw error;
      }
    }
  }
```

```
  }

  const workers = Array.from({ length: concurrency }, () => worker())
    ;
  await Promise.all(workers);
  return results;
}

// Example usage: fetching details for multiple user IDs concurrently
const operations = userIds.map((id) => async () => await userService.
    fetchUserDetails(id));
const users = await fetchDataInBatches(operations, 5);
```

This controlled concurrency pattern prevents overwhelming the system while still achieving parallel execution. Developers can fine-tune the concurrency limit based on system resources and expected load, ensuring that the API remains responsive.

Streaming is another powerful technique for efficiently handling large payloads or long-running asynchronous operations. Node.js provides native stream support, and when combined with TypeScript, these patterns can be strongly typed for increased safety. Using streams to process or transform data incrementally can prevent memory bloat and improve the responsiveness of data-heavy endpoints. The following example illustrates how to implement a streaming API endpoint that transforms file data on the fly:

```
import * as fs from 'fs';
import { Request, Response } from 'express';

app.get('/download/:filename', (req: Request, res: Response) => {
  const filepath = `/files/${req.params.filename}`;
  const fileStream = fs.createReadStream(filepath);

  fileStream.on('error', (err) => {
    res.status(500).json({ error: 'File reading error' });
  });
```

```
// Set type and other headers before piping
res.setHeader('Content-Type', 'application/octet-stream');
fileStream.pipe(res);
});
```

Beyond basic streaming, more advanced operations may involve transforming streams, such as compressing data or parsing CSV inputs in real time. Libraries that support stream transformations, when used with TypeScript, provide strict input-output type guarantees that are critical in complex data processing pipelines.

Another aspect of asynchronous API operations is managing long-running tasks or operations with heavy I/O. Offloading such tasks to background workers or job queues is an advanced strategy that decouples processing from immediate user responses. In a TypeScript-based API, integrating a job queue like Bull or Agenda can be enhanced through strict type definitions of jobs and their payloads. Consider the following example that enqueues a heavy processing task and immediately returns a job ID to the client:

```
import Queue from 'bull';

interface ProcessJobData {
  userId: number;
  inputData: string;
}

const processQueue = new Queue<ProcessJobData>('processQueue');

app.post('/process', async (req, res) => {
  const { userId, inputData } = req.body;
  try {
    const job = await processQueue.add({ userId, inputData });
    res.status(202).json({ jobId: job.id });
  } catch (err) {
    res.status(500).json({ error: 'Job enqueue failed' });
  }
});
```

This pattern minimizes blocking by returning control to the client immediately while executing the heavy operation asynchronously in the background. When integrated with real-time notification mechanisms (e.g., web sockets), APIs can update clients on job progress while preserving system responsiveness.

Handling race conditions and ensuring data consistency in concurrent environments is a significant concern in asynchronous programming. Optimistic concurrency control and atomic operations using database transactions can be combined with asynchronous API logic. For instance, using a transactional query with an ORM that supports TypeScript, such as TypeORM or Prisma, ensures that multiple concurrent operations do not corrupt shared state:

```typescript
import { getManager } from 'typeorm';

app.post('/update-item', async (req: Request, res: Response) => {
  const { itemId, updateData } = req.body;
  try {
    await getManager().transaction(async (transactionalEntityManager)
      => {
      const item = await transactionalEntityManager.findOne(Item,
    itemId);
      if (!item) {
        throw new Error('Item not found');
      }
      // Apply updates in a safe transaction
      transactionalEntityManager.merge(Item, item, updateData);
      await transactionalEntityManager.save(item);
    });
    res.status(200).json({ success: true });
  } catch (error) {
    res.status(400).json({ error: error.message });
  }
});
```

By leveraging transactional semantics and commit protocols, developers can prevent data races and ensure that asynchronous operations maintain consistency despite concurrent modifications.

The integration of cancellation tokens for asynchronous operations is another advanced technique that enhances system responsiveness. In complex systems, it becomes necessary to cancel long-running requests based on user actions or system timeouts. Libraries such as `AbortController` from the Node.js API can be used in conjunction with TypeScript to propagate cancellation signals across asynchronous boundaries. An advanced use-case involves wrapping an asynchronous fetch operation with cancellation support:

```
async function fetchDataWithTimeout(url: string, timeout: number):
    Promise<Response> {
  const controller = new AbortController();
  const id = setTimeout(() => controller.abort(), timeout);

  try {
    const response = await fetch(url, { signal: controller.signal });
    return response;
  } catch (err) {
    if (err.name === 'AbortError') {
      throw new Error('Request timed out');
    }
    throw err;
  } finally {
    clearTimeout(id);
  }
}
```

Integrating cancellation logic into your asynchronous operations prevents wasted resources on requests that no longer need to complete, thereby improving overall system efficiency.

TypeScript's type inference, when combined with asynchronous patterns, can enforce strict contracts at every stage of request processing. Advanced developers should take full advantage of this by defining explicit interfaces for asynchronous operations, including the input parameters and eventual output. This not only improves code readability but also facilitates integration with automated testing frameworks and static analysis tools. For instance, defining a service interface for asynchronous data retrieval enhances contract reliability:

```
interface DataService {
  fetchData(query: string): Promise<DataRecord[]>;
}

class ApiDataService implements DataService {
  async fetchData(query: string): Promise<DataRecord[]> {
    // Asynchronously retrieve data from the datastore
    const records = await dataRepository.find({ where: { query } });
    return records;
  }
}
```

This approach reinforces modular design principles and ensures that asynchronous operations across the API remain interchangeable and testable.

Parallelism within a single request can be further optimized by employing a pattern known as fan-out/fan-in, where multiple asynchronous tasks are initiated in parallel and their results aggregated once all tasks complete. This pattern can be particularly beneficial when an API endpoint depends on data from several microservices. The advanced pattern is illustrated as follows:

```
async function aggregateData(userId: number): Promise<AggregatedData>
   {
  const [profile, activity, recommendations] = await Promise.all([
    userService.fetchUserProfile(userId),
    activityService.fetchUserActivity(userId),
    recommendationService.fetchRecommendations(userId)
  ]);
  return { profile, activity, recommendations };
}

app.get('/dashboard/:userId', asyncHandler(async (req, res) => {
```

```
const userId = parseInt(req.params.userId, 10);
const data = await aggregateData(userId);
res.status(200).json({ data });
}));
```

Implementing fan-out/fan-in efficiently minimizes latency by performing independent operations concurrently and reducing the number of sequential waits that can degrade API responsiveness.

In summary, handling asynchronous operations and concurrency in TypeScript-based APIs involves a multifaceted approach that includes centralized error handling, controlled concurrency, stream processing, job queue integration, transactional operations, and cancellation support. Leveraging TypeScript's static type checks alongside modern asynchronous patterns leads to APIs that are not only resilient under load but also maintain code clarity and predictability. Advanced developers benefit from these techniques by improving system throughput, reducing latency, and ensuring that multiple asynchronous operations can be orchestrated reliably in a highly concurrent production environment.

# 7.7  Versioning and Documentation of APIs

Establishing a coherent strategy for versioning and documenting APIs is vital for ensuring long-term maintainability and seamless integration with external systems. For advanced developers, this process involves crafting explicit versioning policies that accommodate both backward compatibility and progressive evolution, while also employing automated documentation generation tools that integrate with the static type system provided by TypeScript.

A well-defined versioning strategy protects consumers of an API from unintended breaking changes. A common method is URL-based versioning, where the version number is embedded in the endpoint path. For example, endpoints might be structured as `/v1/resource` versus `/v2/resource`. This approach allows multiple versions of endpoints to coexist, and clients can choose which version to consume. Advanced implementations may involve using request headers or media type negotiation for version control. In header-based versioning, the API expects a custom header (e.g., `X-API-Version`) or relies on the Accept header to dictate the desired version. Consider the following Express middleware snippet that routes requests based on the API version indicated in a query parameter:

```
import { Request, Response, NextFunction } from 'express';

function versionRouter(req: Request, res: Response, next:
    NextFunction): void {
  const version = req.query.version;
  if (version === 'v2') {
    req.url = `/v2${req.url}`;
  } else {
    req.url = `/v1${req.url}`;
  }
  next();
}

app.use(versionRouter);
```

This middleware illustrates how to direct requests dynamically to the appropriate versioned endpoints, ensuring that the underlying service logic can evolve independently for each version without compromising existing clients.

Semantic Versioning (SemVer) plays a crucial role in conveying the nature and scope of changes made to an API. By following the major.minor.patch format, API designers can signal breaking API changes, backward-compatible enhancements, or bug fixes. When a breaking change is introduced (a major version increment), it is essential to deprecate the previous version gradually. Deprecation notices should be communicated clearly through documentation, response headers, or within the API payload. Implementing a deprecation header in Express can be done as follows:

```
app.use((req: Request, res: Response, next: NextFunction) => {
  if (req.url.startsWith('/v1/')) {
    res.setHeader('X-API-Deprecation', 'This API version is
    deprecated and will be removed on 2024-12-31.');
  }
  next();
});
```

By incorporating a dedicated deprecation header, developers inform API consumers about outdated endpoints and encourage migration to newer, more robust versions.

Documentation of APIs is as integral to the ecosystem as versioning. Clear, precise, and comprehensive documentation facilitates efficient collaboration and smooth integration, minimizing ambiguities that could lead to misinterpretation or errors. Documentation tools like Swagger/OpenAPI, Apiary, and Postman Collections are popular choices in the industry. Leveraging tools such as swagger-jsdoc or openapi-generator allows dynamic generation of API documentation directly from TypeScript source code. When TypeScript interfaces are used to define request and response payloads, these definitions can be automatically mapped into API documentation, ensuring that the documentation remains in sync with the actual implementation.

Annotating API endpoints with JSDoc comments is an effective method of providing detailed documentation that is easily consumed by automated tools.  A well-documented endpoint might look like this:

```
/**
 * @openapi
 * /v1/users/{id}:
 *   get:
 *     summary: Retrieve a user by their unique identifier
 *     description: Returns user details for a given user ID. The
     user must exist,
 *                       otherwise a 404 error is returned.
 *     parameters:
 *       - in: path
 *         name: id
 *         required: true
 *         schema:
 *           type: integer
 *         description: Numeric identifier of the user.
 *     responses:
 *       200:
 *         description: Successful retrieval of user details.
 *         content:
 *           application/json:
 *             schema:
 *               $ref: '#/components/schemas/User'
 *       404:
 *         description: No user found with the provided ID.
 */
app.get('/v1/users/:id', async (req: Request, res: Response, next:
    NextFunction) => {
  try {
    const userId = parseInt(req.params.id, 10);
    const user = await userService.getUserById(userId);
    if (!user) {
      res.status(404).json({ error: 'User not found' });
      return;
    }
    res.status(200).json(user);
  } catch (error) {
    next(error);
  }
});
```

This level of detail in the annotations ensures that the generated documentation is both informative and unambiguous. It highlights the expected input, potential errors, and output structure, which is essential for external developers consuming the API.

Integrating automated documentation generation into the build and deployment pipelines is a sophisticated strategy that reduces manual overhead and keeps the documentation current. Tools such as Swagger UI can be embedded directly into the API portal, providing interactive documentation that enables developers to test and explore endpoints. Configuration of Swagger in a TypeScript-based Express application might appear as follows:

```
import swaggerUi from 'swagger-ui-express';
import swaggerJSDoc from 'swagger-jsdoc';

const swaggerOptions = {
  definition: {
    openapi: '3.0.0',
    info: {
      title: 'Advanced API',
      version: '1.0.0',
      description: 'A highly versioned and documented API for
    advanced usage'
    },
    servers: [
      { url: 'https://api.example.com/v1' },
      { url: 'https://api.example.com/v2' }
    ]
  },
  apis: ['./src/routes/*.ts'],
};

const swaggerSpec = swaggerJSDoc(swaggerOptions);
app.use('/docs', swaggerUi.serve, swaggerUi.setup(swaggerSpec));
```

This configuration enables the API to deliver live, interactive documentation tailored to different endpoints and versions. By referencing paths in the source code, the documentation automatically reflects any changes, ensuring consistency between the codebase and the documentation.

Version control of API documentation itself is crucial, particularly when major changes are introduced. Maintaining separate documentation instances for each version—either physically via separate directories or logically through version-controlled branches—provides clarity and prevents confusion among API consumers. A versioned documentation structure might be implemented by serving different Swagger specifications based on the endpoint:

```
import express from 'express';
const docsV1 = express.Router();
const docsV2 = express.Router();

// Assume swaggerSpecV1 and swaggerSpecV2 are pre-generated specs for
    each version
docsV1.use('/', swaggerUi.serve, swaggerUi.setup(swaggerSpecV1));
docsV2.use('/', swaggerUi.serve, swaggerUi.setup(swaggerSpecV2));

app.use('/docs/v1', docsV1);
app.use('/docs/v2', docsV2);
```

Such an approach allows stakeholders to compare different iterations of the API and to plan migrations accordingly.

Beyond interactive documentation, a robust API should also provide comprehensive change logs and migration guides that accompany major version updates. These documents outline breaking changes, deprecation timelines, and step-by-step instructions for migrating from one API version to another. Integrating versioned API change logs into automated documentation frameworks ensures that developers always have access to the historical evolution of the API. Tools that extract commit messages and compile change logs into formatted documentation, such as conventional changelog generators, can be integrated as part of the continuous integration process.

Finally, rigorous testing and validation of both versioned endpoints and their documentation should be part of the development lifecycle. Automated tests using frameworks like Jest, coupled with contract testing tools such as Pact or Dredd, verify that each API version adheres strictly to its documented interface. Ensuring that documentation is not only accurate but also actionable reduces integration friction and improves developer confidence.

In summary, best practices for API versioning and documentation merge robust design principles with the benefits of TypeScript's static type system and automated toolchains. From dynamic version routing and semantic versioning to comprehensive, interactive documentation generation and change management, these strategies enable the development of APIs that are both resilient and developer-friendly. Advanced techniques, including dual version support, deprecation headers, and automated pipelines for documentation, result in a cohesive ecosystem where external systems can integrate seamlessly while internal teams maintain a clear path for future evolution.

# 8

# Chapter 8: Optimizing Type-Script for High-performance Applications

*This chapter delves into optimizing TypeScript for high-performance applications, addressing code profiling, advanced compiler options, and efficient data structures. It explores the use of Web Workers, memory optimization techniques, lazy loading, code splitting, and caching strategies. These practices collectively enhance application responsiveness and scalability.*

## 8.1 Profiling and Analyzing TypeScript Code

When examining performance bottlenecks within TypeScript applications at scale, it is imperative to employ both dynamic profiling techniques and static analysis tools to monitor execution flow, memory allocation, and asynchronous event distribution. The intricacy of TypeScript's transpilation process combined with runtime JavaScript execution requires the developer to instrument code paths and analyze the resulting metrics with high fidelity. Advanced programmers must integrate multiple levels of profiling—from low-level CPU sampling to high-resolution memory snapshots—in order to accurately isolate performance anomalies and throughput constraints.

A critical step in this process is the instrumentation of key functional areas for precise timing measurements. Utilizing the `perf_hooks` module in Node.js allows for sub-millisecond resolution timing through the `performance.now()` API. This precision aids in measuring short-duration events, particularly when evaluating the overhead introduced by abstraction layers inherent in TypeScript. An advanced technique involves wrapping critical routines with a high-resolution timer function as shown in the following code snippet:

```
import { performance } from 'perf_hooks';

function measureExecutionTime<T>(func: () => T): { result: T, time:
    number } {
    const start = performance.now();
    const result = func();
    const time = performance.now() - start;
    return { result, time };
}

const computation = () => {
    let sum = 0;
    for (let i = 0; i < 1e6; i++) {
        sum += Math.sqrt(i);
    }
    return sum;
};

const { result, time } = measureExecutionTime(computation);
console.log(`Result: ${result}, Execution Time: ${time.toFixed(3)}ms
```

378

```
`);
```

This pattern alleviates the need for external profilers in early stages of micro-benchmarking and allows developers to isolate expected computational delays. Nevertheless, isolated microbenchmarks rarely capture the full spectrum of performance challenges, especially in asynchronous I/O or event-driven paradigms commonly encountered in modern TypeScript applications.

Subsequent analysis requires integration with the V8 inspector modules to enable comprehensive CPU profiling and heap analysis. V8's inspector protocol provides mechanisms for real-time monitoring of JavaScript execution and memory allocation. By programmatically invoking the inspector session through Node.js, one can gather detailed execution traces that capture function call frequencies, hot paths, and memory leaks. Consider the following advanced example that initiates a CPU profiling session:

```
import inspector from 'inspector';
import fs from 'fs';

const session = new inspector.Session();
session.connect();

session.post('Profiler.enable', () => {
    session.post('Profiler.start', () => {
        // Insert operations to be profiled.
    });
});

setTimeout(() => {
    session.post('Profiler.stop', (err, { profile }) => {
        if (err) {
            throw new Error(`Profiler stop error: ${err}`);
        }
        fs.writeFileSync('profile.cpuprofile', JSON.stringify(profile
    ));
```

```
    session.disconnect();
    console.log('CPU profile captured and saved to profile.
 cpuprofile');
  });
}, 15000);
```

The generated .cpuprofile file can subsequently be inspected using Chrome DevTools or other performance analysis platforms that
accept the format.   Advanced users can correlate call graph data
from these profiles with TypeScript source maps to trace performance
degradation back to the original code.   This approach bridges the
gap between the transpiled JavaScript and the high-level TypeScript
constructs, thereby providing more actionable insights during performance regression studies.

Deep analysis of asynchronous operations warrants particular attention.   Profiling tools must account for the concurrency model of
JavaScript, wherein asynchronous functions, promises, and event loop
delays can obscure actual processing time. Employing the built-in performance timeline API in conjunction with browser developer tools
can highlight the jitter and latencies introduced by callback queues. In
Node.js, one may monitor event loop delays using external modules
such as toobusy-js or custom instrumentation via setImmediate to
simulate a heartbeat across event loop cycles.

Additionally, integrating manual instrumentation for asynchronous
functions can provide valuable insights into promise resolution latencies. By instrumenting the entry and exit points of async functions,
developers can measure the duration between scheduling and execution. For instance, one may incorporate a middleware-like approach in
frameworks or utilities where asynchronous service calls are prevalent.
Consider the following pattern:

```
async function instrumentedAsyncFunction<T>(fn: () => Promise<T>):
    Promise<T> {
    const start = performance.now();
    const result = await fn();
    const time = performance.now() - start;
    console.log(`Async function executed in ${time.toFixed(3)}ms`);
    return result;
}

async function fetchData(): Promise<any> {
    // Simulate asynchronous operation, e.g., database access or
    network request.
    return new Promise(resolve => setTimeout(() => resolve({ success:
    true }), 200));
}

instrumentedAsyncFunction(fetchData).then(data => {
    // Process data after profiling.
    console.log('Fetched Data:', data);
});
```

This formulation not only captures quantitative execution metrics but also establishes a baseline for identifying non-linear performance degradation in asynchronous pipelines. Sophisticated analysis should consider aggregated statistics over multiple invocations to recognize sporadic spikes attributable to external conditions such as I/O contention or resource throttling.

Memory profiling is equally critical when addressing performance bottlenecks. TypeScript applications, especially those with dynamic object creation or heavy use of closures, can be susceptible to memory leaks and heap bloat. Developers should acquire heap snapshots at strategic intervals during application execution and utilize tools such as Chrome's Heap Profiler or Node's built-in diagnostic reports to identify unintended memory retention. The analysis must focus on dominant retention paths, particularly in scenarios where garbage collection

381

is inadvertently delayed. Advanced commands can be scripted to periodically capture these snapshots, enabling automated trend analysis. For instance:

```
import v8 from 'v8';
import fs from 'fs';

function captureHeapSnapshot(snapshotFile: string): void {
    const snapshotStream = v8.getHeapSnapshot();
    const fileStream = fs.createWriteStream(snapshotFile);
    snapshotStream.pipe(fileStream);
    fileStream.on('finish', () => {
        console.log(`Heap snapshot saved to ${snapshotFile}`);
    });
}

captureHeapSnapshot('heap_snapshot.heapsnapshot');
```

Performance degradation resulting from uncollected garbage or circular references can be deduced when comparing multiple heap snapshots. Identifying persistent allocations across iterations can reveal subtle memory leaks, particularly in long-running applications. Developers must be adept at using these snapshots in tandem with source maps to pinpoint problematic constructs in the original TypeScript code.

Another advanced aspect involves the analysis of compiler optimizations and the impact of TypeScript's transpilation settings on runtime performance. Although TypeScript itself is a superset and does not impose runtime overhead beyond that of JavaScript, certain compiler flags can influence how code is structured post-transpilation. Fine-tuning settings such as `target`, `module`, and `downlevelIteration` will affect performance in critical loops and asynchronous contexts. Static code analysis tools and linters can be configured to flag patterns that lead to inadvertent performance penalties, such as excessive use of polymorphic functions or dynamically typed constructs that inhibit V8's inline caching.

Furthermore, leveraging source maps during profiling sessions ensures that the abstracted TypeScript code is correlated with the precise locations within transpiled output. Advanced developers should ensure that the build process retains source map information accurately to facilitate efficient reverse mapping from production profiles to the source code. This integration often involves configuring build tools like Webpack or Rollup with appropriate source map directives, ensuring that optimization steps do not obfuscate the mapping integrity.

Instrumentation frameworks can augment the profiling process by injecting tracing calls that capture function entry and exit events, enabling a fine-grained view of the call stack. Custom instrumentation frameworks can be layered upon existing logging solutions to embed trace identifiers that persist through asynchronous calls, thereby elucidating the causal chains that underlie sporadic performance issues. This is particularly useful in distributed environments where asynchronous service interactions contribute to overall latency. Inlined trace information should be suppressed or conditionally compiled in production releases to avoid performance overhead when not under diagnostic evaluation.

In environments where performance must be measured under production-like loads, the adoption of sampling profilers and statistical analysis becomes critical. Advanced machine profiling often employs statistical sampling to minimize the intrusiveness of instrumentation. While sampling profilers provide coarser granularity, their impact on performance is minimal compared to heavy instrumentation. The trade-off between sampling frequency and overhead is a critical design decision that advanced practitioners must evaluate based on application characteristics.

Through the systematic use of these profiling techniques—ranging from microbenchmarking isolated code segments to comprehensive CPU and heap profiling—practitioners are empowered to not only detect performance anomalies but also to quantify the efficacy of subsequent optimizations. This multi-faceted approach, which encompasses synchronous and asynchronous execution, memory management, and compiler insight, is essential for producing and maintaining high-performance TypeScript applications that scale reliably under demanding workloads.

## 8.2   Optimizing Compilation and Build Processes

Advanced TypeScript projects demand a build pipeline that minimizes compilation overhead while maintaining rigorous type safety and code correctness. The evolution of modern build architectures necessitates the adoption of incremental compilation, fine-tuning of TypeScript compiler options, and integration with specialized build tools—each contributing to reduced turnaround times and enhanced developer productivity.

A fundamental technique for optimizing the TypeScript compilation process lies in the proper configuration of the `tsconfig.json`. Enabling the `incremental` flag introduces a build cache that stores information about previous compilations, thereby avoiding redundant work on unchanged files. The following configuration snippet illustrates a setup that leverages incremental compilation along with composite projects that enable project references:

```
{
  "compilerOptions": {
    "target": "ES2020",
    "module": "ESNext",
    "strict": true,
    "incremental": true,
    "composite": true,
    "skipLibCheck": true,
    "esModuleInterop": true,
    "baseUrl": "./",
    "paths": {
      "@app/*": ["src/app/*"]
    }
  },
  "include": ["src"],
  "exclude": ["node_modules", "dist"]
}
```

The integration of project references allows the build system to partition code into discrete, interdependent modules. This modularity aids both in maintaining clean separation between application layers and in leveraging parallelism during compilation. Advanced builds utilize tools such as `tsc --build` which orchestrate the incremental build process across project boundaries, thereby dramatically reducing full recompilation times for large repositories.

Complex build pipelines often require the coordination of multiple tools. Integrating TypeScript with bundlers like `Webpack` or `Rollup` demands careful orchestration between the TypeScript compiler and the bundler's own asset transformation processes. Loaders such as `ts-loader` and `babel-loader` can introduce additional overhead if not correctly configured. An advanced trick involves deferring type checking to a dedicated process using plugins like `fork-ts-checker-webpack-plugin`. This separation allows the bundler to focus on code transformation and tree shaking, while

a parallel process validates type integrity.  Consider the following
advanced webpack.config.js snippet:

```
const path = require('path');
const ForkTsCheckerWebpackPlugin = require('fork-ts-checker-webpack-
    plugin');

module.exports = {
  mode: 'production',
  entry: './src/index.ts',
  module: {
    rules: [
      {
        test: /\.ts$/,
        use: [
          {
            loader: 'ts-loader',
            options: {
              transpileOnly: true,
              experimentalWatchApi: true,
              // Add additional performance options here
            }
          }
        ],
        exclude: /node_modules/
      }
    ]
  },
  resolve: {
    extensions: ['.ts', '.js']
  },
  plugins: [
    new ForkTsCheckerWebpackPlugin({
      async: false,
      typescript: {
        configFile: path.resolve(__dirname, 'tsconfig.json')
      }
    })
  ],
  output: {
    filename: 'bundle.js',
    path: path.resolve(__dirname, 'dist')
  }
};
```

The separation of type checking and code transformation harnesses the full potential of multi-core processors, reducing build latency and mitigating the overhead associated with synchronous type checking processes. Incremental builds are further optimized by leveraging file system watchers that only recompile on detected changes. Advanced developers should consider integrating tools like `tsc-watch` or employing custom scripts in continuous integration pipelines.

Customizing the transpilation process can also yield significant performance improvements. Alternatives to the default TypeScript compiler, such as `esbuild` or `SWC`, offer near-instantaneous build speeds by reusing common optimization techniques from lower level compilers written in systems languages like Go or Rust. These tools do not perform full type checking but can be seamlessly integrated into the development workflow for rapid iteration. For example, employing `esbuild` with TypeScript support involves a straightforward build script:

```
const esbuild = require('esbuild');

esbuild.build({
  entryPoints: ['src/index.ts'],
  bundle: true,
  outfile: 'dist/bundle.js',
  platform: 'node',
  target: ['node14'],
  tsconfig: 'tsconfig.json',
  incremental: true,
  sourcemap: true,
}).catch(() => process.exit(1));
```

While these tools expedite the bundling process, maintaining comprehensive type safety remains paramount. A balanced approach involves using `esbuild` or `SWC` in development iterations, followed by full `tsc` checks in pre-commit or continuous integration environments. This dual-strategy leverages rapid feedback loops on code changes, while

ensuring that the end product conforms to strict type standards before
deployment.

The integration of caching mechanisms further enhances build speed.
Compiler caching, when correctly configured, prevents unnecessary
recompilation of unchanged modules. In build systems where caching
is externally managed, such as through the use of `Bazel` or `Nx`, the build
pipeline is abstracted to determine dependency changes at a granular
level.    Advanced users can annotate their code with metadata indicating immutable assets. This explicit declaration prompts the build
system to reuse cached artifacts, thereby significantly reducing compilation times.  For instance, Bazel's build rules for TypeScript can be
configured to cache outputs using remote caching techniques. Custom
build rules should ensure that environments are reproducible and that
cache invalidation policies are strictly enforced based on input modifications.

Parallelization is indispensable in reducing overall build time. Modern build systems distribute compilation tasks across available CPU
cores.  Advanced configurations using TypeScript's project references
inherently facilitate parallel builds.  Additionally, bundlers like Webpack provide thread loaders—such as `thread-loader`—which offload
expensive loaders to worker threads.  The following snippet demonstrates this strategy:

```
module.exports = {
  module: {
    rules: [
      {
        test: /\.ts$/,
        use: [
          {
            loader: 'thread-loader',
            options: {
              workers: 2
```

```
        }
      },
      {
        loader: 'ts-loader',
        options: {
          transpileOnly: true
        }
      }
    ],
    exclude: /node_modules/
  }
  ]
 }
};
```

Thread loaders allow CPU-intensive tasks such as TypeScript transpilation to be concurrently executed, leveraging multi-threading capabilities inherent in modern architectures. However, the implementation must balance the overhead of thread spawning against the performance gains achieved. Fine-grained benchmarking of worker thread performance is essential to ascertain the optimal number of threads for a given hardware environment.

Incremental builds can also benefit from selective recompilation strategies. When managing large monorepos or highly modularized codebases, the build system should detect dependency graphs and isolate those modules that have undergone changes. This selective recompilation requires advanced dependency analysis both at the source code level and through configuration files. Developers can manually specify file dependency graphs or rely on third-party tools that integrate with the compiler's internal change detection mechanisms. Automated dependency injection, paired with advanced cache invalidation algorithms, ensures that only a minimal subset of files are recompiled upon changes.

Further optimization is achieved by scrutinizing compiler flags that influence output code quality versus build performance. The selective disabling of features such as `strictNullChecks` or targeting higher ECMAScript versions can reduce transpilation overhead, albeit at a potential cost of reduced type safety or compatibility. In certain scenarios where performance is critical, maintaining a lean `tsconfig.json` that only enables necessary checks can yield measurable improvements. Advanced developers must balance these flags with the requirements of the application domain, ensuring that performance gains do not compromise the code's integrity.

Analyzing build performance through profiling and instrumentation is as critical as runtime profiling. Integration of build-time analyzers, such as `webpack-bundle-analyzer`, provides insights into bundle composition and module weight. By examining the bundle structure, developers can identify and optimize dependency bloat, remove dead code, and leverage tree shaking more effectively. Profiling build times at a granular level—identifying which plugins or loaders introduce latency—enables targeted optimizations. This introspection is particularly valuable when adopting new libraries or when the build process itself becomes a bottleneck in continuous integration pipelines.

Consolidating build processes via robust scripting and automation ensures consistent build environments and reduces human error. Advanced build scripts, typically written in Node.js or Bash, orchestrate multi-step build processes, incorporating steps such as code linting, testing, and artifact generation. Leveraging task runners like `gulp` or `npm scripts` in conjunction with dependency graph analyzers can automate the entire workflow. The automated decision-making process based on code changes not only expedites development but also ensures that production builds are reproducible and compliant with predefined quality metrics.

Effective optimization of TypeScript's compilation and build processes is a confluence of targeted compiler configurations, selective caching, parallel execution, and continuous profiling. Each layer of the build system—from the `tsconfig.json` to the bundler and beyond—presents opportunities for fine-grained control and performance refinement. Advanced practitioners combine these techniques to achieve an optimal build process that is both swift and robust, ensuring that development velocity is maintained without sacrificing code quality.

## 8.3 Efficient Data Structures and Algorithms

Optimizing TypeScript applications extends beyond runtime profiling and compilation techniques; selecting the appropriate data structures and algorithms is foundational to ensuring high-performance code execution. Advanced practitioners must critically assess the trade-offs between time complexity, space utilization, and the nuances of TypeScript's type system when engineering solutions for real-world problems. A rigorous analysis of data structures—requiring fine control over generics, immutability, and algorithmic design—directly translates into reduced computational overhead and improved application scalability.

The inherent challenges with traditional JavaScript arrays prompt the exploration of alternative paradigms. While arrays in TypeScript offer dynamic resizing and built-in methods, careful evaluation of algorithmic patterns reveals scenarios where alternative structures yield superior performance. For example, when constant-time lookups and insertions are critical, the native Map and Set objects, designed for key-value and unique collections respectively, become indispensable. Their underlying implementations are generally optimized for hash-based access, thus mitigating the need for iterative searches. Consider the following advanced usage of Map with generics for a caching layer, designed to avoid recalculation of expensive function calls:

```typescript
type ExpensiveComputation = (input: number) => number;

class Memoizer {
  private cache = new Map<number, number>();

  constructor(private compute: ExpensiveComputation) {}

  public run(input: number): number {
    if (this.cache.has(input)) return this.cache.get(input)!;
    const result = this.compute(input);
    this.cache.set(input, result);
    return result;
  }
}

const computeFactorial: ExpensiveComputation = function factorial(n:
    number): number {
  if (n <= 1) return 1;
  return n * factorial(n - 1);
};

const memoizedFactorial = new Memoizer(computeFactorial);
console.log(memoizedFactorial.run(5));
```

The above structure not only exemplifies efficient memoization techniques but also highlights the use of TypeScript's type system to enforce function signatures and invariant cache key mappings. The meticulous design of such an algorithm contributes to dramatic reductions in redundant computations, particularly in recursive and dynamic programming scenarios.

392

A more advanced consideration involves the implementation of tree data structures for ordered data processing and hierarchical problem solving. Binary search trees (BSTs) offer logarithmic time complexity for insertion, deletion, and lookup operations under balanced conditions. However, the maintenance of balance is non-trivial, and naive implementations can deteriorate to linear time operations. Advanced algorithms such as AVL trees or red-black trees resolve these issues by enforcing balancing constraints via rotations during insertions and deletions. TypeScript's support for classes and generics simplifies the construction of such data structures while maintaining type safety. The following code demonstrates an AVL tree insertion mechanism with type-parameterized nodes:

```typescript
class AVLNode<T> {
  public height: number;
  public left: AVLNode<T> | null = null;
  public right: AVLNode<T> | null = null;

  constructor(public value: T) {
    this.height = 1;
  }
}

class AVLTree<T> {
  private root: AVLNode<T> | null = null;

  private getHeight(node: AVLNode<T> | null): number {
    return node ? node.height : 0;
  }

  private updateHeight(node: AVLNode<T>): void {
    node.height = 1 + Math.max(this.getHeight(node.left), this.
     getHeight(node.right));
  }

  private rotateRight(y: AVLNode<T>): AVLNode<T> {
    const x = y.left!;
    y.left = x.right;
    x.right = y;
```

```
    this.updateHeight(y);
    this.updateHeight(x);
    return x;
}

private rotateLeft(x: AVLNode<T>): AVLNode<T> {
    const y = x.right!;
    x.right = y.left;
    y.left = x;
    this.updateHeight(x);
    this.updateHeight(y);
    return y;
}

private getBalance(node: AVLNode<T>): number {
    return this.getHeight(node.left) - this.getHeight(node.right);
}

public insert(value: T): void {
    this.root = this._insert(this.root, value);
}

private _insert(node: AVLNode<T> | null, value: T): AVLNode<T> {
    if (!node) return new AVLNode(value);
    if (value < node.value) node.left = this._insert(node.left, value
     );
    else node.right = this._insert(node.right, value);

    this.updateHeight(node);
    const balance = this.getBalance(node);

    if (balance > 1 && value < (node.left as AVLNode<T>).value) {
        return this.rotateRight(node);
    }
    if (balance < -1 && value > (node.right as AVLNode<T>).value) {
        return this.rotateLeft(node);
    }
    if (balance > 1 && value > (node.left as AVLNode<T>).value) {
        node.left = this.rotateLeft(node.left!);
        return this.rotateRight(node);
    }
    if (balance < -1 && value < (node.right as AVLNode<T>).value) {
        node.right = this.rotateRight(node.right!);
        return this.rotateLeft(node);
    }
```

394

```
      return node;
  }
}

const tree = new AVLTree<number>();
tree.insert(10);
tree.insert(20);
tree.insert(30);
```

Exemplary implementations such as the above demand a thorough understanding of both algorithmic principles and JavaScript engine optimizations. Advanced programmers not only implement these data structures but also conduct extensive benchmarking to validate that the theoretical time complexity is realized in practice. Profiling aspects such as memory consumption during frequent rotations and potential hot spots in recursive function calls are critical to ensuring that balancing overhead does not offset the benefits of logarithmic search and update times.

Parallel to custom data structure design is the adoption of algorithmic paradigms that utilize efficient processing pipelines. Techniques such as divide-and-conquer and dynamic programming are particularly useful in TypeScript when algorithm performance is bounded by recursion or overlapping subproblems. For instance, a well-crafted dynamic programming solution for the longest common subsequence problem must effectively manage both time and space complexity while managing state in an idiomatic TypeScript fashion. Code organization and immutability guarantee that side effects are minimized, allowing for consistent, repeatable computation:

```
function longestCommonSubsequence<T>(a: T[], b: T[]): T[] {
  const dp: T[][] = Array.from({ length: a.length + 1 }, () => []);
  for (let i = 0; i <= a.length; i++) {
    for (let j = 0; j <= b.length; j++) {
      if (i === 0 || j === 0) {
```

```
        dp[i][j] = [] as T[];
      } else if (a[i - 1] === b[j - 1]) {
        dp[i][j] = dp[i - 1][j - 1].concat(a[i - 1]);
      } else {
        dp[i][j] = dp[i - 1][j].length > dp[i][j - 1].length ? dp[i -
      1][j] : dp[i][j - 1];
      }
    }
  }
  return dp[a.length][b.length];
}

const seq1 = [1, 3, 4, 1, 2, 8];
const seq2 = [3, 4, 1, 2, 1, 7];
console.log(longestCommonSubsequence(seq1, seq2));
```

Building on the previous sections that emphasized profiling and build optimizations, the systematic profiling of algorithmic implementations becomes instrumental in validating theoretical improvements. Refined instrumentation of the algorithm's critical path using fine-grained timers—such as those provided by the perf_hooks library—allows developers to verify that optimizations lead to actual performance gains in production scenarios.

Moreover, the considerations extend to leveraging TypeScript's functional programming capabilities, such as immutability and higher-order functions, without incurring performance penalties. Advanced implementations often require that operations on data structures avoid deep copying or unnecessary reallocation of memory. Structural sharing techniques, borrowed from persistent data structure theories, can be implemented to ensure that modifications are efficient. Utilizing libraries that implement immutable data structures natively (while ensuring they are type-safe with TypeScript) can yield significant performance benefits in multi-threaded or reactive environments where state consistency is paramount.

396

Integrating algorithm design patterns with TypeScript's union and intersection types results in a system where invariants are enforced at
compile time, thereby reducing runtime checks and eliminating classes
of errors. For instance, when dealing with heterogeneous collections,
discriminated unions serve to constrain state transitions and guarantee
that algorithms operate correctly on dynamic data types. Advanced
sorting algorithms, such as quicksort or mergesort, can be generically
implemented in TypeScript while leveraging these type constraints to
ensure algorithmic correctness across diverse datasets.

```typescript
function mergeSort<T>(array: T[], compare: (a: T, b: T) => number): T
    [] {
  if (array.length <= 1) return array;
  const middle = Math.floor(array.length / 2);
  const left = mergeSort(array.slice(0, middle), compare);
  const right = mergeSort(array.slice(middle), compare);

  return merge(left, right, compare);
}

function merge<T>(left: T[], right: T[], compare: (a: T, b: T) =>
    number): T[] {
  const result: T[] = [];
  while (left.length && right.length) {
    if (compare(left[0], right[0]) <= 0) result.push(left.shift()!);
    else result.push(right.shift()!);
  }
  return result.concat(left, right);
}

const numbers = [34, 7, 23, 32, 5, 62];
console.log(mergeSort(numbers, (a, b) => a - b));
```

In high-performance applications where sorting large datasets is routine, ensuring that comparisons are optimized and that intermediate
allocations are minimized can yield substantial performance benefits.
Frequently, inline comparison logic paired with static analysis of the
code can lead to aggressive optimization by modern JavaScript engines.

Developers must therefore be judicious in their algorithm design—
ensuring that the cost of abstraction does not eclipse the benefits of
a clean and maintainable code base.

Advanced algorithmic solutions also embrace parallelism and asynchronous processing. When faced with inherently combinatorial or
computationally expensive tasks—such as graph traversal, pathfind-
ing, or large-scale data aggregation—TypeScript developers can exploit concurrency models using Web Workers or asynchronous functions. Partitioning the workload into concurrent jobs ensures maxi-
mal utilization of available CPU cores. Implementing concurrent algorithms in TypeScript involves careful orchestration of Promises and
shared memory, requiring a precise understanding of task dependencies and potential race conditions. Strategies such as work stealing and
task queues further optimize performance by dynamically balancing
load across workers.

Harnessing efficient data structures and algorithms in TypeScript is
a continuous process of evaluation, benchmarking, and refinement.
Metrics collected during operation should influence iterative design
decisions—leading developers to refactor code, adopt new data structures, or modify algorithmic approaches based on measurable performance gains. This adaptive approach not only improves immediate
application responsiveness but also contributes to the long-term maintainability of the codebase.

This format is compliant with the necessary guidelines and should
compile without LaTeX errors.

## 8.4 Enhancing Application Performance with Web Workers

High-performance TypeScript applications increasingly rely on offloading heavy computations from the main thread to achieve responsiveness in user interfaces and to ensure smooth interaction with real-time data processing routines. Advanced developers face the challenge of integrating Web Workers into complex TypeScript ecosystems while maintaining type safety, efficient message passing, and minimal serialization overhead. Exploiting Web Workers requires a thorough knowledge of message-driven architectures, transferable objects, and the intricacies of concurrency models in the JavaScript runtime environment.

One advanced technique is to encapsulate computationally intensive tasks within dedicated Web Worker scripts rather than attempting to perform synchronous operations on the main thread. In TypeScript, this encapsulation can be achieved by splitting the application logic into separate modules where the worker scripts are strictly typed and run in an isolated context. Developers must consider the limitations imposed by the worker environment; for instance, DOM manipulation is unavailable, and the API subset is constrained. The following example demonstrates how to create a dedicated worker for performing matrix operations that require significant computational resources:

```
/// worker/mathWorker.ts
const ctx: Worker = self as any;

function multiplyMatrices(a: number[][], b: number[][]): number[][] {
  const result: number[][] = [];
  for (let i = 0; i < a.length; i++) {
    result[i] = [];
    for (let j = 0; j < b[0].length; j++) {
```

399

```
    let sum = 0;
    for (let k = 0; k < a[0].length; k++) {
      sum += a[i][k] * b[k][j];
    }
    result[i][j] = sum;
  }
}
return result;
}

ctx.addEventListener('message', (event: MessageEvent) => {
  const { matrixA, matrixB } = event.data as { matrixA: number[][];
    matrixB: number[][] };
  const result = multiplyMatrices(matrixA, matrixB);
  ctx.postMessage({ result });
});
```

This worker script encapsulates a matrix multiplication routine while
adhering to TypeScript's strict typing conventions. Ensuring type correctness in both the input parameters and the output results is crucial
when interfacing with other modules. On the main thread, development of a robust worker management module is essential. This module
should facilitate dynamic creation, error handling, and termination of
workers while abstractly handling the communication details. A typical implementation might involve a worker wrapper class that provides promises to handle asynchronous responses:

```
/// src/workerManager.ts
export class WorkerManager<T, U> {
  private worker: Worker;

  constructor(workerScript: string) {
    this.worker = new Worker(workerScript);
  }

  public send(data: T): Promise<U> {
    return new Promise((resolve, reject) => {
      const handleMessage = (event: MessageEvent) => {
        resolve(event.data as U);
        this.worker.removeEventListener('message', handleMessage);
```

```
    };

    const handleError = (error: ErrorEvent) => {
      reject(error);
      this.worker.removeEventListener('error', handleError);
    };

    this.worker.addEventListener('message', handleMessage);
    this.worker.addEventListener('error', handleError);
    this.worker.postMessage(data);
  });
}

public terminate(): void {
  this.worker.terminate();
}
}
```

Such an abstraction not only enforces a consistent interface for communicating with workers but also ensures that asynchronous message passing integrates well with Promise-based workflows. Advanced error recovery strategies involve timeout mechanisms, heartbeat signals to monitor worker health, and logic to restart workers if they become unresponsive. In systems performing repetitive data processing, these mechanisms help maintain system resilience while maximizing performance gains.

An important aspect of advanced Web Worker usage is the reduction of message passing overhead through the use of transferable objects. Transferring large data buffers between the main thread and the worker can otherwise lead to significant serialization costs due to structured cloning. Modern browsers support transferring ownership of ArrayBuffer objects, thereby eliminating the need for deep copies. When structured data such as typed arrays is involved, developers should ensure that data is passed via the transfer parameter of postMessage. The following example highlights this technique:

401

```
/// worker/dataWorker.ts
const ctx: Worker = self as any;
ctx.addEventListener('message', (event: MessageEvent) => {
  const dataBuffer = event.data as ArrayBuffer;
  // Perform intensive computations on the transferred buffer.
  const view = new Float64Array(dataBuffer);
  let sum = 0;
  for (let i = 0; i < view.length; i++) {
    sum += view[i];
  }
  ctx.postMessage({ sum });
});
```

```
/// src/main.ts
import { WorkerManager } from './workerManager';

const data = new Float64Array(1e6).fill(1.23);
const buffer = data.buffer;
const manager = new WorkerManager<ArrayBuffer, { sum: number }>('
    worker/dataWorker.js');

manager.send(buffer).then(response => {
  console.log(`Computed sum: ${response.sum}`);
}).catch(error => {
  console.error('Worker error:', error);
});
```

Ensuring that workers are effectively utilized to offload CPU-bound tasks involves careful orchestration of both the main thread's scheduling and worker lifecycle management. Advanced techniques include the use of shared buffers and Atomics to synchronize data among multiple workers when a high degree of parallelism is required. In scenarios where multiple workers need to coordinate their progress on a shared dataset, implementing a shared memory model using SharedArrayBuffer can reduce communication latency and improve throughput. Yet, such implementations necessitate a meticulous approach to avoid race conditions and ensure memory safety. Consider

an example where a pool of workers is used to calculate partial sums
from a shared array:

```
/// worker/partialSumWorker.ts
const ctx: Worker = self as any;

ctx.addEventListener('message', (event: MessageEvent) => {
  const { sab, start, end } = event.data as { sab: SharedArrayBuffer;
      start: number; end: number };
  const sharedArray = new Float64Array(sab);
  let partialSum = 0;
  for (let i = start; i < end; i++) {
    partialSum += sharedArray[i];
  }
  ctx.postMessage({ partialSum });
});
```

```
/// src/parallelSum.ts
import { WorkerManager } from './workerManager';

function parallelSum(data: Float64Array, numWorkers: number): Promise
    <number> {
  const segmentLength = Math.ceil(data.length / numWorkers);
  const sab = new SharedArrayBuffer(data.buffer.byteLength);
  new Float64Array(sab).set(data);
  const promises: Promise<{ partialSum: number }>[] = [];

  for (let i = 0; i < numWorkers; i++) {
    const start = i * segmentLength;
    const end = Math.min(start + segmentLength, data.length);
    const manager = new WorkerManager<{ sab: SharedArrayBuffer; start
    : number; end: number }, { partialSum: number }>('worker/
    partialSumWorker.js');
    promises.push(manager.send({ sab, start, end }));
  }

  return Promise.all(promises).then(results => results.reduce((acc,
    res) => acc + res.partialSum, 0));
}

const data = new Float64Array(1e6).fill(1.0);
parallelSum(data, 4).then(total => {
  console.log(`Total sum: ${total}`);
```

```
}).catch(err => {
  console.error('Error in parallel sum computation:', err);
});
```

Leveraging SharedArrayBuffer improves performance by eliminating multiple copies of data between threads; however, developers must be aware of potential pitfalls introduced by concurrent access. The appropriate use of synchronization primitives and atomic operations is a hallmark of an advanced design in concurrent programming within TypeScript-enabled applications.

In addition to manual thread management and data transfer optimizations, advanced applications increasingly adopt abstraction layers that simplify the integration of Web Workers. Libraries such as Comlink abstract the messaging layer by proxying function calls, allowing developers to write asynchronous code that closely resembles synchronous logic. Using such abstractions reduces boilerplate, minimizes error-prone message serialization code, and drives productivity. However, advanced scenarios might demand custom domain-specific protocols, such as specialized serialization methods or custom scheduling algorithms, to better align with specific performance requirements. Evaluating the trade-offs between built-in libraries and custom implementations is an essential decision for architects developing high-performance TypeScript applications.

Furthermore, performance diagnostics in a multi-threaded environment must incorporate robust monitoring and profiling techniques. Developers need to instrument both the main thread and workers to capture detailed metrics on execution duration, data transfer latency, and resource utilization. Profiling tools should be extended to correlate events from multiple threads. Logging frameworks that support asynchronous logging across workers can facilitate centralized monitoring and provide insight into potential bottlenecks that are not immediately apparent from single-threaded analysis.

Advanced techniques also include the dynamic scaling of worker pools. Instead of statically allocating a fixed number of workers, adaptive algorithms can monitor the workload and adjust the number of active workers based on current load and system capabilities. This dynamic management requires careful insertion of control logic within the worker manager, ensuring that the creation and termination of workers do not themselves become a bottleneck. Fine-tuning such systems is essential in environments where performance constraints are stringent and system responsiveness directly impacts user experience.

Employing Web Workers within TypeScript applications ultimately demands a balance between isolation, communication overhead, and computational load distribution. Advanced developers must incorporate type-safe patterns, message-passing optimizations, and concurrency control mechanisms to maximize performance benefits while ensuring maintainability of complex codebases. This multifaceted approach to leveraging Web Workers consolidates computational intensity away from the main thread and harnesses modern multi-core architectures to drive scalable, high-performance applications.

## 8.5 Minimizing Memory Usage with TypeScript

Advanced applications developed in TypeScript require careful management of memory usage to ensure robust performance under pressure. Memory consumption can be minimized through a series of targeted strategies, including optimizing garbage collection behavior, reducing object allocation frequency, leveraging structural sharing, and applying design patterns that proactively mitigate memory leaks. An in-depth understanding of JavaScript's memory model, combined with TypeScript's type system, enables developers to adopt precise techniques that result in more efficient runtime behavior and lower memory footprints.

A significant aspect of memory optimization is the reduction of excessive object allocations. High-frequency creation of transient objects, particularly in tight loops or recursive functions, places undue strain on the garbage collector. Advanced strategies include avoiding unnecessary object encapsulation and reusing existing data structures through pooling. Object pooling is particularly effective when managing a large number of similar objects that experience brief lifespans. The following example demonstrates a minimal object pool implementation tailored for a custom data type:

```typescript
interface PooledObject {
  reset(): void;
}

class ObjectPool<T extends PooledObject> {
  private pool: T[] = [];

  constructor(private factory: () => T, private maxSize: number =
    100) {}

  acquire(): T {
    return this.pool.length > 0 ? this.pool.pop()! : this.factory();
  }

  release(obj: T): void {
    obj.reset();
    if (this.pool.length < this.maxSize) {
      this.pool.push(obj);
    }
  }
}

// Example usage with a sample class that implements PooledObject.
```

```
class DataBuffer implements PooledObject {
  data: number [];

  constructor(size: number = 1024) {
    this.data = new Array(size);
  }

  reset(): void {
    this.data.fill(0);
  }
}

const pool = new ObjectPool((() => new DataBuffer(1024));
const buffer = pool.acquire();
// Execute operations using buffer
pool.release(buffer);
```

This approach avoids repeated allocations and deallocations by recycling objects. Care must be taken to ensure that pooled objects do not retain stale references, which could inadvertently increase memory usage. Moreover, using the reset() method to clear data helps to minimize the memory footprint while ensuring that released objects are in a predictable state for reuse.

Another cornerstone of memory optimization is the strategic use of immutable data structures. Immutable objects simplify state management and reduce the likelihood of unintended side effects leading to memory leaks. Libraries such as immutable.js or native implementations using structural sharing via persistent data structures provide immutable collections that minimize memory overhead when compared to deep copies. TypeScript's advanced type system further enhances these benefits by statically guaranteeing that immutability constraints are respected. For instance, when managing large configurations in a multi-threaded environment, immutable objects ensure that concurrent accesses remain free of race conditions while avoiding multiple object instantiations.

Memory profiling in TypeScript applications must incorporate detailed measurement of garbage collection (GC) activity. The periodic and non-deterministic nature of GC in modern JavaScript engines can be a performance bottleneck if not properly managed. Instrumenting GC events with tools such as Chrome DevTools, Node.js's `--trace-gc` flag, or specialized libraries that capture heap snapshots is critical. Advanced developers utilize periodic snapshots to compare object retention graphs, thereby identifying memory leaks as well as redundant data that remains in scope past its useful lifetime.

Efficient memory management also involves careful handling of closure references. Closures capture their surrounding state, and inadvertent retention of variables can lead to increased memory consumption. Developers must minimize the use of heavy inner functions that capture large objects. Instead, restructuring code to pass only necessary parameters prevents excessive memory retention. The following example highlights a common pitfall with closures and a refactored solution:

```
// Problematic usage: Closure capturing entire context.
function heavyComputation(data: number[]) {
  const largeBuffer = new Array(1000000).fill(0);
  return data.map(item => {
    // The closure captures 'largeBuffer' though it's unnecessary.
    return item + largeBuffer.length;
  });
}

// Optimized usage: Explicit parameter passing.
function computeWithBuffer(data: number[], bufferLength: number) {
  return data.map(item => item + bufferLength);
}

const data = [1, 2, 3, 4];
const result = computeWithBuffer(data, 1000000);
```

In the refactored version, the inner function no longer creates an implicit reference to a large buffer, thereby reducing the impact on memory when the function is executed repeatedly.

Effective memory management also encompasses the strategic use of weak references. WeakMaps and WeakSets allow developers to associate data with objects without preventing their garbage collection. This is particularly valuable when caching auxiliary metadata that should not extend the lifetime of the data being cached. By utilizing weak collections, the system ensures that memory is autonomously reclaimed once the primary objects are no longer in use. An advanced example illustrating this pattern is the implementation of a memoization utility that leverages a WeakMap:

```
function memoize<T extends object, R>(fn: (arg: T) => R): (arg: T) =>
    R {
  const cache = new WeakMap<T, R>();

  return (arg: T) => {
    if (cache.has(arg)) {
      return cache.get(arg)!;
    }
    const result = fn(arg);
    cache.set(arg, result);
    return result;
  };
}

// Sample usage with an object input
const processData = memoize((obj: { value: number }) => obj.value *
    2);
const input = { value: 42 };
console.log(processData(input));
```

The use of WeakMap ensures that if the `input` object becomes unreachable, its corresponding memoized result is also eligible for garbage collection. Such tactics assist in managing caches in memory-constrained

409

environments without leading to inadvertent memory retention.

Beyond micro-level optimizations, memory usage can benefit from architectural design decisions that promote efficient data management. Employing techniques such as lazy initialization defers expensive allocations until they are strictly necessary. Lazy loading design patterns, which are commonly paired with code splitting and dynamic imports, reduce the initial memory footprint of an application. Advanced developers can combine these patterns with fine-grained control over the garbage collection through explicit nullification of unneeded references. The following code snippet illustrates lazy initialization:

```typescript
class ExpensiveResource {
  private resource: number[] | null = null;

  getResource(): number[] {
    if (this.resource === null) {
      this.resource = new Array(1000000).fill(Math.random());
    }
    return this.resource;
  }

  releaseResource(): void {
    this.resource = null;
  }
}

const resourceManager = new ExpensiveResource();
const resourceData = resourceManager.getResource();
// Use resourceData in computations
resourceManager.releaseResource();
```

By deferring allocation until demand arises and explicitly releasing resources when they are no longer needed, the overall memory footprint is reduced and more predictable. This methodology becomes critical in applications where memory is a premium and unpredictable allocation patterns can lead to performance degradation due to frequent

410

garbage collection pauses.

TypeScript developers also benefit from modular programming practices that separate memory-intensive operations into discrete modules.
Splitting code into smaller chunks reduces the scope of memory retention errors, aids in identifying memory leaks via systematic profiling, and permits isolated garbage collection of transient modules.
Such modularization, when documented by rigorous type annotations,
also simplifies the static analysis of potential memory pitfalls. Static
code analyzers and linters integrated into the build pipeline can flag
common memory mismanagement patterns, such as unintentional closures, unused variables, or cycles in object graphs that prevent garbage
collection.

Optimizing memory usage frequently entails trade-offs between performance and memory consumption. While caching and object reuse
significantly reduce the runtime overhead of frequent allocations, they
require careful invalidation policies to prevent stale data accumulation.
Moreover, a balance must be struck between the granularity of memoization and the risk of cache thrashing. Advanced developers must
calibrate these aspects using empirical data obtained from robust profiling and thorough benchmarking. Instrumenting code with custom
memory usage metrics and periodic logging can illuminate trends and
pinpoint areas for further optimization.

The nuanced interplay between garbage collection, object lifecycle
management, and design patterns in TypeScript applications necessitates a holistic approach to memory minimization. By leveraging object pools, avoiding unnecessary closures, utilizing weak references,
and implementing lazy loading strategies, advanced developers can
construct applications that not only perform efficiently but also maintain a lean memory footprint over extended periods. Continual mon-

itoring, profiling, and iterative refinement of these techniques ensure that as applications grow in scale and complexity, memory usage remains within acceptable parameters, thereby supporting both performance and maintainability in production environments.

## 8.6    Implementing Lazy Loading and Code Splitting

Optimizing resource loading and application startup times can be achieved effectively through the implementation of lazy loading and code splitting strategies. Advanced developers must carefully design application architecture to defer non-critical module loading, thereby reducing the initial bundle size and expediting interactive times. This section presents an in-depth examination of various techniques, including dynamic imports, bundler optimizations, and runtime module management in a TypeScript context.

Lazy loading involves deferring imports of modules until they are actually needed. Instead of eagerly loading all code at startup, the application can initiate requests for components or libraries only when they are required by user interaction or runtime conditions. The TypeScript support for ECMAScript dynamic imports enables code splitting, where modules are segmented into distinct bundles generated by the build tool. A canonical example using dynamic import syntax is as follows:

```
async function loadModule(): Promise<void> {
  const { heavyFunction } = await import('./heavyModule');
  heavyFunction();
}
```

In this example, the module heavyModule is not bundled with the main application bundle, but is instead loaded on-demand. This strategy reduces the main bundle size and improves the perceived startup performance. Developers must ensure proper error handling and timeout mechanisms when using dynamic imports to accommodate network latency and potential failures.

Building on this foundation, configuring a bundler such as Webpack can further enhance the efficiency of lazy loading. Webpack supports code splitting via magic comments that provide granular control over chunk naming and prioritization. The following snippet demonstrates an advanced configuration for a lazy-loaded module:

```
async function loadComponent(): Promise<void> {
  const { default: MyComponent } = await import(
    /* webpackChunkName: "myComponent" */
    './components/MyComponent'
  );
  // Render or initialize MyComponent as needed.
  MyComponent.init();
}
```

The use of the /* webpackChunkName: "myComponent" */ directive instructs Webpack to name the resulting chunk accordingly, which facilitates debugging and cache management. Advanced developers can combine such techniques with code splitting configuration in the build process to monitor chunk size, dependency trees, and identify redundant modules. Plugins like webpack-bundle-analyzer further assist in visualizing the bundle composition and evaluating the impact of lazy loading on overall bundle performance.

Another advanced technique involves the implementation of route-based code splitting in single-page applications (SPAs). Frameworks such as Angular, React, or Vue support lazy loading of modules directly via their routing mechanisms. In TypeScript, route definitions can be augmented with dynamic import statements to load modules on an as-needed basis. The following React example illustrates a higher-order component that defers the loading of a feature module:

```
import * as React from 'react';

function lazyLoader<T>(importFunc: () => Promise<{ default: T }>):
    React.ComponentType {
  return React.lazy(importFunc);
}

const FeatureModule = lazyLoader(() =>
  import(/* webpackChunkName: "featureModule" */ './features/
    FeatureModule')
);

export const AppRouter: React.FC = () => (
  <React.Suspense fallback={<div>Loading...</div>}>
    <FeatureModule />
  </React.Suspense>
);
```

The combination of React.lazy with the React.Suspense component creates a robust pattern for route-based lazy loading, depreciating the initial rendering time while displaying appropriate fallback content. The advanced integration of these techniques requires mapping the dependency graph carefully to ensure that shared modules, such as utilities and common libraries, are not redundantly loaded in multiple chunks. In this context, setting up common or vendor chunks serves as a pivotal practice in minimizing resource duplication.

Beyond conventional lazy loading, advanced builders often implement prefetching and preloading strategies to improve user experience. When deploying a sophisticated application, certain chunks can be preloaded based on predicted user behavior to ensure that

414

the transition is smooth. Utilizing Webpack's `PrefetchPlugin` and `PreloadPlugin` allows developers to specify resources that should be prefetched in idle time or immediately prioritized. An example of preloading a module is illustrated below:

```
<link rel="preload" as="script" href="featureModule.bundle.js">
```

In addition, embedding prefetch hints in dynamic import statements using magic comments facilitates asynchronous preloading. Consider the following variant:

```
async function preloadModule(): Promise<void> {
  await import(
    /* webpackPreload: true, webpackChunkName: "preloadedModule" */
    './modules/PreloadedModule'
  );
}
```

Preloading strategies must be applied judiciously to avoid overloading the network while still capitalizing on the available idle processing time. Advanced developers should analyze real user metrics to determine the optimal balance between lazy loading and prefetching, ensuring that the preloading mechanism does not lead to wasteful resource consumption.

Integration of lazy loading into an application's lifecycle requires a carefully thought-out fallback strategy. For instance, error boundaries or retry logic should be implemented to handle scenarios where dynamically imported modules might fail. Timeout mechanisms, circuit breakers, and logging offer the necessary robustness when loading external modules asynchronously. A robust implementation might include:

```
async function safeLoad<T>(importFunc: () => Promise<{ default: T }>,
    timeout = 3000): Promise<T | null> {
```

```
let timer: number;
try {
  const result = await Promise.race([
    importFunc(),
    new Promise<never>((_, reject) => timer = window.setTimeout(()
    => reject(new Error('Timeout')), timeout))
  ]);
  clearTimeout(timer);
  return result.default;
} catch (err) {
  console.error('Module failed to load:', err);
  return null;
}
}
```

This wrapper employs a timeout mechanism ensuring that delays in module loading do not lead to blocked threads or suboptimal user experiences. Equally, fallback UIs or alternative modules can be injected in cases where a module fails to load within the defined timeframe. The practice facilitates a resilient application architecture that prioritizes performance and reliability.

Advanced applications may also use dependency injection to manage lazy-loaded modules. By leveraging dependency injection frameworks, such as InversifyJS in a TypeScript environment, developers can manage module instantiation in a lazy fashion while maintaining clear separation of concerns. The design patterns involved in dependency injection support inversion of control, which is complementary to code splitting. An example of configuring a dependency injection container with dynamic module resolution is as follows:

```
import 'reflect-metadata';
import { Container, injectable } from 'inversify';

const container = new Container();

interface IService {
```

```
  execute(): void;
}

@injectable()
class RealService implements IService {
  execute(): void {
    console.log('Service executed.');
  }
}

container.bind<IService>('IService').toDynamicValue(async () => {
  const module = await import(/* webpackChunkName: "RealService" */
    './services/RealService');
  return new module.RealService();
}).inSingletonScope();

// Resolving the service dynamically
async function resolveService() {
  const service = await container.getAsync<IService>('IService');
  service.execute();
}

resolveService();
```

Such an architecture leverages the lazy loading paradigm within a comprehensive dependency injection system, resulting in optimized startup times and controlled resource initialization. This pattern is especially useful in large-scale applications where multiple services need to be conditionally loaded.

It is also crucial to understand the trade-offs inherent in lazy loading and code splitting. While such techniques reduce initial load times, they can introduce latency when deferred modules are eventually needed. Profiling and monitoring the performance impact of lazy loading, through tools like Webpack's bundle analyzer, become critical in fine-tuning these trade-offs. Profiling tools should measure not only the size and load time of individual chunks but also the cumulative impact on time-to-interactive metrics. Analyzing user flow and prioritizing modules that are critical for initial engagement ensures that the benefits of a lean initial bundle do not become offset by runtime delays.

Streamlining the integration of lazy loading and code splitting within TypeScript also demands strict adherence to type safety. Dynamic imports return promises whose resolution must be managed by careful type annotations. This ensures that developers and tooling can maintain compile-time validation despite the asynchronous nature of module loading. The consistent use of interfaces and generics in dynamic import scenarios reduces runtime errors and improves maintainability in large codebases.

Finally, experimentation and iterative refinement are essential. Advanced practitioners must continuously refine their build configurations, integrate feedback from profiling sessions, and adapt their lazy loading strategies based on user engagement metrics. The ultimate goal is to craft an application that is resilient to performance bottlenecks related to resource loading while maintaining a coherent and maintainable code structure.

Integrating these techniques into a cohesive strategy requires a combination of sound architectural principles, detailed profiling, and proactive management of edge cases. Advanced developers can transform the user experience by ensuring that resources are loaded on demand without overwhelming the initial load process. This comprehensive approach not only optimizes resource utilization but also sets the foundation for building scalable, high-performance TypeScript applications.

## 8.7 Leveraging Advanced Caching Techniques

Advanced caching techniques are pivotal for reducing application latency and enhancing perceived performance in complex TypeScript applications. In high-throughput environments, intelligent caching not only accelerates response times but also alleviates backend load by avoiding redundant computations and I/O operations. This section details the design and implementation of sophisticated caching strategies that encompass in-memory caching, distributed caching, and cache invalidation policies, all while leveraging TypeScript's powerful type system for robust and maintainable code.

Central to advanced caching is the design of an efficient in-memory cache structure that supports rapid lookups and expiry management. A common pattern is the implementation of a Least Recently Used (LRU) cache that automatically ejects stale items to manage memory footprint. The following code demonstrates an LRU cache in TypeScript; it employs generics for type safety and rigorous interface contracts to ensure consistency in key and value types:

```
interface CacheEntry<V> {
  value: V;
  timestamp: number;
}

class LRUCache<K, V> {
  private maxSize: number;
  private cache = new Map<K, CacheEntry<V>>();
  private ttl: number; // Time-to-live in milliseconds

  constructor(maxSize: number, ttl: number = 300000) {
    this.maxSize = maxSize;
    this.ttl = ttl;
  }

  private isExpired(entry: CacheEntry<V>): boolean {
```

```
    return (Date.now() - entry.timestamp) > this.ttl;
  }

  public get(key: K): V | undefined {
    const entry = this.cache.get(key);
    if (!entry) return undefined;
    if (this.isExpired(entry)) {
      this.cache.delete(key);
      return undefined;
    }
    // Refresh the key as most recently used.
    this.cache.delete(key);
    this.cache.set(key, { value: entry.value, timestamp: Date.now()
    });
    return entry.value;
  }

  public set(key: K, value: V): void {
    if (this.cache.has(key)) {
      this.cache.delete(key);
    } else if (this.cache.size >= this.maxSize) {
      // Evict least recently used.
      const lruKey = this.cache.keys().next().value;
      this.cache.delete(lruKey);
    }
    this.cache.set(key, { value, timestamp: Date.now() });
  }

  public delete(key: K): boolean {
    return this.cache.delete(key);
  }

  public clear(): void {
    this.cache.clear();
  }
}

const cache = new LRUCache<string, number>(100, 60000);
cache.set("answer", 42);
console.log(cache.get("answer"));
```

In scenarios where computation is expensive and results are deterministic, the use of memoization complements caching. Advanced memo-

ization functions can be implemented to cache the results of function calls, thereby preventing repeated evaluations of computationally intensive functions. The following example demonstrates a generic memoization utility in TypeScript using a Map and a custom resolver for function arguments:

```
function memoize<T extends (...args: any[]) => any>(fn: T, resolver?:
    (...args: any[]) => string): T {
  const cache = new Map<string, ReturnType<T>>();
  return function (...args: any[]): ReturnType<T> {
    const key = resolver ? resolver(...args) : JSON.stringify(args);
    if (cache.has(key)) {
      return cache.get(key)!;
    }
    const result = fn(...args);
    cache.set(key, result);
    return result;
  } as T;
}

function heavyComputation(n: number): number {
  // Simulate heavy computation.
  let result = 0;
  for (let i = 0; i < n; i++) {
    result += Math.sqrt(i);
  }
  return result;
}

const memoizedHeavyComputation = memoize(heavyComputation);
console.log(memoizedHeavyComputation(100000));
```

While in-memory caching remains a cornerstone in client-side applications, distributed caching becomes essential when scaling applications over multiple servers or across microservices architectures. Strategies such as cache-aside, write-through, and write-behind allow the application to synchronize in-memory caches with persistent data stores. Distributed caching platforms, like Redis or Memcached, are commonly integrated with server-side TypeScript applications using li-

421

braries that provide type-safe client interfaces.

For instance, a cache-aside pattern involves checking the cache for data
before querying a database. To implement this in a server-side Type-
Script context, one might design an asynchronous cache layer that returns promises. The following snippet illustrates an advanced cache-
aside implementation using a hypothetical Redis client:

```
import Redis from 'ioredis';
const redisClient = new Redis();

interface CacheOptions {
  ttl: number; // in seconds
}

async function cacheAside<T>(key: string, fetchFunc: () => Promise<T
    >, options: CacheOptions): Promise<T> {
  const cachedData = await redisClient.get(key);
  if (cachedData) {
    return JSON.parse(cachedData) as T;
  }
  const data = await fetchFunc();
  await redisClient.set(key, JSON.stringify(data), 'EX', options.ttl)
    ;
  return data;
}

async function getUserProfile(userId: string): Promise<{ name: string
    ; age: number }> {
  return await cacheAside(`user:${userId}`, async () => {
    // Fetch from database logic here.
    return { name: "Alice", age: 30 };
  }, { ttl: 3600 });
}

getUserProfile("user1").then(console.log);
```

Advanced caching strategies also require careful management of cache
invalidation and consistency. The choice of cache eviction policies and
TTL settings directly impacts the freshness of the cached data and the

overall performance profile of the application. For real-time applications or those with high update frequencies, a short TTL might be preferred, while static datasets can leverage longer TTLs to minimize cache misses. Tools for monitoring cache hit rates and latencies should be integrated into the application's operational dashboard, allowing developers to tune parameters in response to actual performance metrics.

Another sophisticated caching technique involves hierarchical caches that combine multiple levels of storage. For example, leveraging a small, fast in-memory cache as a first-level store, with a larger distributed cache as a secondary layer, can yield significant performance gains. This multi-tier caching approach minimizes latency for frequently accessed data while ensuring that less-common queries still benefit from a cached response. The following pseudocode illustrates the concept:

```
// Pseudocode illustrating hierarchical caching.
async function getHierarchicalData(key: string, fetchFunc: () =>
    Promise<any>, ttl: number): Promise<any> {
  let data = inMemoryCache.get(key);
  if (data !== undefined) return data;

  data = await distributedCache.get(key);
  if (data !== undefined) {
    inMemoryCache.set(key, data); // Promote to in-memory store.
    return data;
  }

  data = await fetchFunc();
  distributedCache.set(key, data, ttl);
  inMemoryCache.set(key, data);
  return data;
}
```

In this design, both caches are asynchronously coordinated; the in-

423

memory store serves as the fastest retrieval mechanism, while the distributed cache offers a fallback layer that can handle larger data volumes.

For applications requiring fine-grained control over cache content and structure, developers may implement custom caching layers that integrate with complex data models. For instance, a highly customizable cache manager might include methods for bulk invalidations, dependency-aware cache updates, and even real-time synchronization with backend data sources using event streams. Utilizing TypeScript's capabilities, such systems can be developed with strongly typed interfaces to ensure that all components of the caching layer adhere to rigorous contracts.

```
interface CacheManager<K, V> {
  get(key: K): Promise<V | undefined>;
  set(key: K, value: V, ttl?: number): Promise<void>;
  invalidate(key: K): Promise<void>;
  bulkInvalidate(keys: K[]): Promise<void>;
}

class AdvancedCacheManager<K, V> implements CacheManager<K, V> {
  private cacheStore = new Map<K, CacheEntry<V>>();

  async get(key: K): Promise<V | undefined> {
    const entry = this.cacheStore.get(key);
    if (entry && (Date.now() - entry.timestamp) < 300000) { // Fixed
    TTL for simplicity.
      return entry.value;
    }
    this.cacheStore.delete(key);
    return undefined;
  }

  async set(key: K, value: V, ttl: number = 300000): Promise<void> {
    this.cacheStore.set(key, { value, timestamp: Date.now() });
    // Custom logic to handle TTL expirations can be added.
  }

  async invalidate(key: K): Promise<void> {
```

```
    this.cacheStore.delete(key);
  }

  async bulkInvalidate(keys: K[]): Promise<void> {
    keys.forEach(key => this.cacheStore.delete(key));
  }
}
```

This class illustrates the construction of an advanced, custom caching layer that could be extended to include integration with external event sources (e.g., message queues, WebSocket streams) for real-time cache invalidation. By coupling the cache layer with operational metrics and alerts, advanced developers can ensure that cache staleness is minimized and that the system promptly recovers from inconsistency.

Caching not only reduces the latency of data retrieval operations but also enhances the overall perceived performance from the perspective of the end-user. It is crucial to utilize performance monitoring frameworks and logging mechanisms to capture and analyze cache hit ratios, response times, and memory usage patterns. Advanced APM (Application Performance Management) tools should be integrated to provide a cohesive view of how caching strategies impact both server and client performance.

Moreover, caching strategies must be revisited and refined iteratively. As application usage patterns change over time, dynamic adjustments in cache configuration—such as modifying TTLs, updating eviction policies, or even redistributing workloads between multiple cache tiers—require a data-driven approach. Advanced CI/CD pipelines should incorporate performance regression testing that specifically focuses on caching behaviors, ensuring that code changes do not inadvertently degrade cache performance.

Advanced caching techniques thus form an essential layer in a high-performance TypeScript application by reducing backend load, improving response times, and enabling scalable architectures. Through the judicious use of in-memory caches, memoization, distributed caching systems, and hierarchical cache designs, developers can achieve significant performance gains while maintaining rigorous type safety and adherence to architectural best practices.

9

# Chapter 9: Testing and Robust Error Handling in TypeScript

*This chapter examines methods for testing and error handling in TypeScript applications, emphasizing unit, integration, and end-to-end testing. It highlights the use of popular testing frameworks and advanced error handling techniques, such as error boundaries in React. Additionally, it covers logging and monitoring practices to ensure application resilience and quality.*

## 9.1   Setting Up a TypeScript Testing Environment

A robust testing environment for TypeScript applications demands careful consideration of tool selection, configuration management, and integration strategies that support rapid iteration while ensuring high code quality. In this section, we dissect the essential elements underlying an effective testing framework setup, detailing manual configuration of TypeScript compilers, test runners, and coverage analyzers. The approach described herein assumes familiarity with advanced build pipelines and continuous integration workflows.

The foundational element in this testing ecosystem is the compiler configuration defined in `tsconfig.json`. A nuanced configuration tailored for testing separates the specifications required for production compilation from those suited to rapid test iteration. An advanced configuration typically includes compiler options that support ESNext modules, incremental compilation, and detailed source mapping. This precision enables synchronous source map alignment between compiled and source code, crucial for accurate stack traces during test failures. An exemplary snippet is as follows:

```
{
  "compilerOptions": {
    "target": "es2020",
    "module": "commonjs",
    "lib": ["es2020", "dom"],
    "strict": true,
    "esModuleInterop": true,
    "sourceMap": true,
    "outDir": "./dist",
    "declaration": true,
    "incremental": true,
    "paths": {
```

428

```
      "@src/*": ["src/*"]
  }
 },
 "include": ["src/**/*.ts", "tests/**/*.ts"],
 "exclude": ["node_modules", "dist"]
}
```

This configuration not only enforces type safety but also leverages module resolution paths for cleaner imports. A further optimization involves utilizing `incremental` and `composite` options. These ensure that changes in individual modules only trigger recompilation for impacted segments, thus reducing overhead during rapid test cycles.

Test runners and frameworks, such as Jest, Mocha, and Jasmine, form the core of the testing environment. For TypeScript-centric projects, employing adapters like `ts-jest` or directly invoking `ts-node/register` is critical. Jest is broadly adopted for its out-of-the-box capabilities that include parallel test execution, snapshot testing, and native mocking solutions. Detailed configuration for Jest using `ts-jest` necessitates custom setup in a `jest.config.js` file. The code snippet below exemplifies a configuration optimized for TypeScript projects:

```
module.exports = {
  preset: 'ts-jest',
  testEnvironment: 'node',
  moduleNameMapper: {
    '^@src/(.*)$': '<rootDir>/src/$1'
  },
  globals: {
    'ts-jest': {
      tsconfig: 'tsconfig.json',
      diagnostics: {
        warnOnly: true
      }
    }
  },
```

```
transform: {
  '^.+\\.tsx?$': 'ts-jest'
},
collectCoverage: true,
coverageDirectory: 'coverage',
coverageReporters: ['json', 'lcov', 'text', 'clover']
};
```

This configuration leverages the strictness of TypeScript while allowing for graceful degradation via the `diagnostics.warnOnly` flag, ensuring that non-critical type warnings do not disrupt test processes. A similar strategy applies to Mocha, which can be extended with `ts-node/register` for immediate TypeScript execution. For instance, a `mocha.opts` file may include:

```
--require ts-node/register
--reporter spec
--recursive
--timeout 5000
tests/**/*.spec.ts
```

Complex applications may require integration with Babel for transpilation tasks where language features or polyfills are necessary. Configurations involving `babel-jest` or similar plugins require synchronization between Babel's presets and the TypeScript compiler options to avoid discrepancies. Advanced environments can merge Babel caching with incremental builds for performance efficiency. Developers must validate that Babel's configuration files harmonize with TypeScript's output, particularly when customizing the `targets` or introducing stage-x proposals.

Beyond the test runners, incorporating a type-aware linting mechanism into the testing pipeline enhances robustness. Tools such as ESLint, configured with `@typescript-eslint/parser`, not only highlight syntactic errors but can also enforce architectural guidelines. Integrating these linters into pre-commit hooks using Husky and lint-staged automates quality control, reducing erroneous commits into the repository. An advanced `.eslintrc.js` configuration file might resemble:

```
module.exports = {
  parser: '@typescript-eslint/parser',
  parserOptions: {
    project: './tsconfig.json'
  },
  plugins: ['@typescript-eslint'],
  extends: [
    'eslint:recommended',
    'plugin:@typescript-eslint/recommended',
    'plugin:@typescript-eslint/recommended-requiring-type-checking'
  ],
  rules: {
    '@typescript-eslint/no-unused-vars': ['error', {
    argsIgnorePattern: '^_' }],
    '@typescript-eslint/no-explicit-any': 'warn'
  }
};
```

Integrating such tooling supports a comprehensive testing strategy by preempting common pitfalls even before tests are executed. This coupling between static analysis and dynamic testing is particularly beneficial when targeting complex asynchronous operations or interfacing with external APIs.

Parallel execution of tests in larger projects necessitates advanced configuration optimizations. Tools such as Jest inherently support parallel testing by isolating test environments of individual files. However, balancing the number of workers, managing shared resource contention, and synchronizing fixture state become critical. Fine-tuning the maxWorkers parameter in Jest, for instance, allows precise control

431

over concurrency levels:

```
module.exports = {
  // Other configuration omitted for brevity...
  maxWorkers: "50%"
};
```

Furthermore, developers may benefit from custom test environments in Jest that simulate edge cases not easily achievable within general configurations. For example, setting up a custom environment that simulates global variables or overrides native functions can expose corner cases in error handling routines. Writing such environments involves extending Jest's `NodeEnvironment`, as shown below:

```
const NodeEnvironment = require('jest-environment-node');

class CustomTestEnvironment extends NodeEnvironment {
  async setup() {
    await super.setup();
    this.global.customVar = 'simulateGlobalState';
  }
  async teardown() {
    this.global.customVar = undefined;
    await super.teardown();
  }
  runScript(script) {
    return super.runScript(script);
  }
}

module.exports = CustomTestEnvironment;
```

Introducing custom environments furnishes developers with a sandbox that mimics production-specific conditions or replicates known bugs in isolation, thereby enhancing the observability of faults prior to release.

Instrumentation for capturing performance metrics and code coverage remains paramount in a testing environment that aspires to robustness. Coverage tools such as Istanbul (nyc) when used in conjunction with TypeScript require specific hooks to accurately map source code to instrumented code. Since transpiling TypeScript to JavaScript can obfuscate original source mappings, precise configuration is necessary in the nyc.config.js. A detailed configuration to reconcile these mappings might be:

```
module.exports = {
  extension: ['.ts', '.tsx'],
  include: ['src/**/*.ts'],
  exclude: ['tests/**/*.ts'],
  reporter: ['lcov', 'text'],
  all: true,
  sourceMap: true,
  instrument: true
};
```

Such instrumentation configurations leverage both Babel and TypeScript's source map generation, thereby ensuring that coverage reports accurately reflect the original source code. Additionally, configuring continuous integration servers to parse these reports is essential for maintaining historical trends in code quality and test effectiveness.

A comprehensive testing setup further extends to the use of containerization and virtualized environments to replicate production dependencies. Dockerizing the testing environment ensures consistency across multiple development machines and CI/CD pipelines. Crafting a minimal Dockerfile that encapsulates installation of the necessary dependencies, builds the TypeScript project, and runs specified test suites can be optimized for iterative testing:

```
FROM node:16-alpine
WORKDIR /app
COPY package*.json ./
RUN npm install
```

```
COPY . .
RUN npm run build
CMD ["npm", "test"]
```

This approach isolates the test suite from local configuration variances, ensuring that tests are reproducible and reliable. Advanced users may furthermore leverage multi-stage Docker builds to separate the compilation phase from the execution phase, thereby minimizing image size and reducing surface area for environmental inconsistencies.

Integration with continuous integration platforms such as GitHub Actions, GitLab CI, or Jenkins is critical for enforcing an unbroken chain of quality control. The configuration provided in YAML syntax defines a job that compiles TypeScript, runs linting, and executes tests with coverage analysis. A representative GitHub Actions workflow might include:

```
name: CI

on:
  push:
    branches: [ main ]
  pull_request:
    branches: [ main ]

jobs:
  test:
    runs-on: ubuntu-latest
    steps:
      - uses: actions/checkout@v2
      - name: Setup Node.js
        uses: actions/setup-node@v2
        with:
          node-version: 16
      - name: Install Dependencies
        run: npm ci
      - name: Run Lint and Tests
        run: npm run lint && npm run test
```

Production-grade pipelines rely upon such configurations to enforce code quality, and integration with artifact management systems ensures that testing artifacts and coverage reports are archived. Advanced configurations may include caching mechanisms for node_modules and the TypeScript build cache to further optimize build times and maintain operational efficiency.

A key nuance in configuring the testing environment involves ensuring that debugging is straightforward, even when tests fail due to subtle type mismatches or asynchronous code misbehavior. Configurations that enable inline source maps and advanced logging within the test runner are indispensable. Developers often temporarily augment test commands with verbose logging or tracing options:

```
// Example of augmenting Jest's verbosity dynamically in a test file
if (process.env.DEBUG_TESTS) {
  console.log("Debug mode enabled. Detailed information:")
}
```

The technical strategies described offer advanced solutions for integrating TypeScript testing into a modern development workflow. By combining tailored compiler configurations, dedicated test runner setups, detailed instrumentation for coverage, and seamless integration into containerized and CI environments, developers can achieve an environment that not only accelerates iteration but also significantly raises the threshold for code correctness. Such precision-oriented practices enhance maintainability and significantly mitigate regression risks as projects evolve.

## 9.2    Unit Testing with TypeScript

Advanced unit testing with TypeScript revolves around ensuring that each individual component or function operates correctly under a variety of conditions. Given TypeScript's static type system, developers are empowered to catch a range of errors at compile time; however, unit tests validate behavior at runtime and document precise design contracts. Detailed unit tests require judicious selection of test frameworks, careful configuration of module systems, and specialized techniques for mock management and dependency isolation.

Central to designing effective unit tests is the principle of isolation. In TypeScript projects, modules and functions should be tested individually without contingent dependencies from other modules or external services. This necessitates a disciplined application of dependency injection and interface abstraction. Advanced practitioners often design components such that dependencies are expressed via interfaces, allowing them to substitute concrete implementations with mocks or stubs during testing. Consider the following example:

```
export interface IDataProvider {
  fetchData(id: number): Promise<string>;
}

export class DataService {
  constructor(private provider: IDataProvider) {}

  async processData(id: number): Promise<string> {
    const data = await this.provider.fetchData(id);
    return data.trim().toUpperCase();
  }
}
```

The above design facilitates the injection of a mock IDataProvider instance during testing. By leveraging TypeScript interfaces, tests can verify the logic within `processData` without engaging in actual network calls or database queries. An accompanying test case using Jest with `ts-jest` might appear as follows:

```
import { DataService, IDataProvider } from '@src/services/DataService
  ';

describe('DataService.processData', () => {
  it('trims and converts fetched data to uppercase', async () => {
    const mockProvider: IDataProvider = {
      fetchData: async (id: number) => {
        return Promise.resolve('   sample data   ');
      }
    };

    const service = new DataService(mockProvider);
    const result = await service.processData(123);
    expect(result).toBe('SAMPLE DATA');
  });
});
```

In this test, the mock provider is implemented inline. However, advanced projects often incorporate utilities to automatically generate type-safe mocks. Tools such as `ts-auto-mock` or custom factories can enforce that mock objects adhere strictly to the underlying interface contracts. This eliminates potential errors where a mocked dependency might inadvertently omit a member, thereby increasing test reliability.

Unit tests for asynchronous functions must address the nuances of promise resolution and error propagation. Using async/await syntax in conjunction with Jest's built-in features provides clarity and determinism. When testing error handling, it is beneficial to simulate failures from dependencies in a controlled manner. An example is presented below:

```
it('throws an error when the dependency fails', async () => {
  const mockProvider: IDataProvider = {
    fetchData: async (id: number) => {
      return Promise.reject(new Error('Dependency failure'));
    }
  };

  const service = new DataService(mockProvider);
  await expect(service.processData(456)).rejects.toThrow('Dependency
    failure');
});
```

Here, the test leverages Jest's `rejects` matcher to assert that the promise correctly propagates an error when the underlying dependency fails. This pattern is essential to verify the robustness of error handling logic within unit-tested modules.

Mocking libraries such as Sinon can extend the capabilities of test suites by allowing fine-grained control over function invocation. Sinon enables the inspection of call counts, argument lists, and even the order of function invocations. For example, when verifying that a function is invoked with the correct parameters, a spy can be added to the dependency:

```
import sinon from 'sinon';

it('ensures fetchData is called with the correct identifier', async
    () => {
  const mock = {
    fetchData: async (id: number) => {
      return Promise.resolve('data');
    }
  };
  const spy = sinon.spy(mock, 'fetchData');

  const service = new DataService(mock);
  await service.processData(789);

  sinon.assert.calledOnce(spy);
```

```
sinon.assert.calledWithExactly(spy, 789);
});
```

The above snippet demonstrates the use of a Sinon spy to assert that the correct arguments are passed to a dependency. Integrating such techniques with TypeScript's type system further reinforces test coverage by ensuring that refactoring does not inadvertently modify function signatures.

Pure functions that are deterministic and side-effect free benefit from property-based testing. Libraries such as fast-check enable the generation of randomized input and verification of invariant properties over many iterations. Property-based tests are especially useful when conventional unit tests might miss edge cases hidden in the input domain. An advanced test for a function that reverses a string might be written as follows:

```
import * as fc from 'fast-check';

function reverseString(input: string): string {
  return input.split('').reverse().join('');
}

it('should reverse any string while preserving length', () => {
  fc.assert(
    fc.property(fc.string(), (s: string) => {
      const reversed = reverseString(s);
      return reversed.length === s.length && reversed === s.split('')
      .reverse().join('');
    })
  );
});
```

Property-based testing complements traditional unit tests by increasing the scenario coverage automatically via randomized inputs. This method does not substitute explicit unit tests; rather, it enriches the testing strategy by uncovering potentially hidden contract violations.

The addition of custom TypeScript types in test assertions enhances the clarity and precision of unit tests. Advanced usage includes leveraging generics to write reusable test helpers, ensuring consistency and reducing duplication. For instance, a generic test helper for verifying transformer functions can be defined as:

```
function testTransformer<T, U>(transformer: (input: T) => U, input: T
    , expected: U): void {
  expect(transformer(input)).toEqual(expected);
}

// Usage in a test case
it('transforms input correctly', () => {
  const transformer = (num: number) => (num * 2).toString();
  testTransformer<number, string>(transformer, 5, '10');
});
```

Defining such utility functions reduces boilerplate and ensures that test logic remains tightly coupled with the domain models defined in TypeScript interfaces and types.

Advanced unit testing also requires careful attention to the setup and teardown lifecycle of tests. For instance, if unit tests rely on global configuration or environmental variables, utilizing Jest's lifecycle hooks (beforeAll, afterAll, beforeEach, and afterEach) helps ensure a pristine test environment. Complex test scenarios may necessitate dynamic reconfiguration of the testing context, as in the following example:

```
let originalEnv: string | undefined;

beforeAll(() => {
  originalEnv = process.env.CUSTOM_FLAG;
  process.env.CUSTOM_FLAG = 'true';
});
```

```
afterAll(() => {
  process.env.CUSTOM_FLAG = originalEnv;
});

it('behaves differently when CUSTOM_FLAG is enabled', () => {
  // Context-specific logic executed based on process.env.CUSTOM_FLAG

  const result = someFunctionAffectedByEnv();
  expect(result).toMatch(/enabled/);
});
```

This pattern ensures that global state is correctly restored after tests execute, preventing cascading errors across test suites. Unit tests for functions that manipulate state or interact with singleton objects must pay attention to possible side effects and race conditions. Employing immutability where possible, or creating fresh instances before each test, reduces flakiness and improves reproducibility.

For modules implementing business logic with intricate state manipulation or asynchronous internal events, test double patterns such as stubs and fakes are indispensable. Developers can design fakes that mimic the behavior of a database connection or an external service while allowing for precise control over responses. This strategy avoids the overhead of real interactions during unit testing while preserving the fidelity of logic validation. An advanced fake implementation might simulate network latency or intermittent failures, thereby forcing the unit under test to execute alternative code paths. Often, these fakes are implemented as in-memory substitutes that adhere strictly to the corresponding interfaces.

Thorough unit testing also involves leveraging code coverage tools to identify untested paths. Advanced testing regimes integrate code coverage reports generated by Istanbul (nyc) or Jest's built-in cover-

age feature into their CI pipelines. TypeScript projects must ensure
that source maps are correctly processed so that coverage reports reflect original TypeScript files rather than transpiled JavaScript. A well-
annotated unit test suite will target edge cases, input validation, exception handling, and asynchronous event handling, thereby fostering a
resilient codebase that evolves in lock-step with domain requirements.

Maintaining an effective unit testing strategy in TypeScript projects demands both systematic design of testable units and a rigorous application of advanced testing techniques. Through careful use of dependency injection, type-safe mocking, property-based testing, and lifecycle management, advanced programmers can systematically isolate
and verify functionality. The resulting tests not only serve as robust
guards against regressions but also provide comprehensive documentation of expected behavior. This disciplined approach to unit testing
underpins reliable, maintainable code, ensuring that individual components fulfill their contracts in increasingly complex application architectures.

## 9.3   Integration and End-to-end Testing Strate-
gies

Modern TypeScript applications increasingly rely on a network of interdependent modules, microservices, and components. Advanced integration and end-to-end testing strategies are paramount to validating seamless interactions, verifying data flow across module boundaries, and confirming that system contracts remain intact under varied
conditions. Integration tests in the TypeScript ecosystem typically focus on the confluence of multiple modules, whereas end-to-end tests

simulate real-world operational workflows using sophisticated tooling and automation frameworks. Both techniques are critical to preemptively detecting subtle interface mismatches, concurrency issues, and environment-specific misconfigurations.

In designing integration tests, the inherent modularity of TypeScript applications is leveraged by composing tests that cover interactions beyond isolated functions. Integration tests validate collocation of several units working together. It is common practice to use established testing frameworks like Jest and Mocha in combination with libraries such as Supertest for HTTP endpoint validations or TypeORM's in-memory database capabilities. A typical integration test involving an API endpoint might integrate several layers of an application. Consider the following advanced integration test scenario that leverages a temporary in-memory database and mocks underlying authentication middleware:

```
import request from 'supertest';
import { createServer } from '@src/server';
import { Database } from '@src/db';
import { AuthMiddleware } from '@src/middleware/auth';

jest.mock('@src/middleware/auth', () => ({
  AuthMiddleware: jest.fn((req, res, next) => next())
}));

describe('API Integration: POST /api/resource', () => {
  let server: any;
  let db: Database;

  beforeAll(async () => {
    db = new Database({ type: 'sqlite', database: ':memory:' });
    await db.connect();
    server = createServer(db);
  });

  afterAll(async () => {
    await db.disconnect();
```

```
    });

  it('should persist new resources and return status 201', async ()
    => {
    const newResource = { name: 'Advanced', value: 42 };
    const response = await request(server)
      .post('/api/resource')
      .send(newResource)
      .set('Accept', 'application/json');

    expect(response.status).toBe(201);
    expect(response.body).toMatchObject(newResource);
  });
});
```

The preceding sample illustrates the orchestration of multiple system
components.  The in-memory SQLite database serves as a transient
persistence layer, while the authentication middleware is stubbed to
bypass authorization logic.  Advanced practitioners often encode environmental variability by abstracting test settings into configuration
files that align with production parameters, thereby minimizing dis-
parities that could lead to integration errors post-deployment.

For more sophisticated integration scenarios, dependency injection is
utilized to control and simulate services.  In a microservices architecture, an integration test might simulate a service failure or latency on
a dependency.  This investigation into fault tolerance requires injecting dummy instances that mimic network calls or third-party service
responses.  A representative pattern might involve the use of custom
factory functions that generate either live or simulated services on demand. For example:

```
import { ServiceA } from '@src/services/ServiceA';
import { ServiceB } from '@src/services/ServiceB';
import { createTestEnvironment } from '@src/testUtils/environment';

describe('ServiceA Integration with ServiceB', () => {
```

```
let serviceB: ServiceB;
let serviceA: ServiceA;

beforeEach(() => {
  // Create a controlled test environment where ServiceB can
  simulate latency or errors
  serviceB = createTestEnvironment<ServiceB>('ServiceB', {
    simulateLatency: 50, // milliseconds delay
    failureProbability: 0.05  // 5% chance to fail
  });
  serviceA = new ServiceA(serviceB);
});

it('should correctly handle sporadic failures from ServiceB', async
    () => {
  const attempts = 10;
  const results = await Promise.all(
    Array.from({ length: attempts }).map(() => serviceA.
    performOperation())
  );

  results.forEach(result => {
    expect(result).toBeDefined();
    // Detailed assertions based on fallback logic or error
    transformation
  });
});
});
```

In this paradigm, the integration test not only validates normal functioning but also examines resilience under adverse conditions. Simulating latency or intermittent failures provides critical insight into how error propagation is managed across service boundaries and ensures that timeouts, retries, and fallback procedures operate as designed.

End-to-end (E2E) testing takes a broader perspective by focusing on complete user workflows and the orchestration of entire systems, including front-end interfaces and back-end APIs. E2E tests in Type-Script environments often rely on dedicated frameworks such as Cypress, Playwright, or Selenium. Advanced configurations involve the integration of TypeScript with these tools to achieve type-safe interactions with DOM elements, coordinated state management, and verification of asynchronous behavior. When setting up Cypress for a TypeScript application, developers must configure both the TypeScript compiler and Cypress's internal modules. A typical `tsconfig.json` tailored for Cypress tests will include:

```
{
  "compilerOptions": {
    "types": ["cypress", "node"],
    "target": "es6",
    "lib": ["es6", "dom"],
    "strict": true
  },
  "include": ["cypress/**/*.ts"]
}
```

Advanced practitioners often go further by defining custom commands in Cypress to encapsulate common interactions and enable reusable testing constructs. For example, a custom command for authenticating a user might look like this:

```
Cypress.Commands.add('login', (username: string, password: string) =>
    {
  cy.request('POST', '/api/auth', { username, password })
    .its('body')
    .then((body) => {
      window.localStorage.setItem('authToken', body.token);
    });
});

// In a test file:
cy.login('advancedUser', 'complexPassword123');
cy.visit('/dashboard');
cy.get('.welcome-message').should('contain', 'Welcome, advancedUser')
    ;
```

Integrating TypeScript end-to-end tests into a comprehensive test suite demands meticulous orchestration and persistent cleanup. Advanced strategies include the use of isolated user accounts, database seeding, and network stubbing to simulate production data while avoiding repercussions on live environments. For example, manipulating network requests to simulate varying API responses can be achieved by intercepting calls at the browser level. A typical pattern in Cypress might involve:

```
cy.intercept('GET', '/api/user', (req) => {
  req.reply({
    statusCode: 200,
    body: { id: 1, name: 'Advanced Tester', role: 'admin' }
  });
}).as('getUser');

cy.visit('/profile');
cy.wait('@getUser');
cy.get('.profile-name').should('contain', 'Advanced Tester');
```

Combining integration and end-to-end tests offers the assurance that system interactions remain coherent from low-level API calls to full-scale user interactions. A refined testing strategy often involves embedding these tests in continuous integration pipelines, where each commit triggers an automated test run that covers unit, integration, and end-to-end tests. The automation framework should also support parallel execution of tests to reduce total run time, utilizing test orchestration tools and containerization to mimic distributed system configurations.

Sophisticated scenarios, such as testing progressive web applications (PWA) or single-page applications (SPA) with dynamic routing, require the deployment of headless browsers and advanced scripting. Tools like Playwright extend these capabilities with multi-language

447

support and dynamic context creation. An advanced Playwright test using TypeScript might include intricate state setup and teardown, as demonstrated below:

```typescript
import { chromium, Browser, Page } from 'playwright';

let browser: Browser;
let page: Page;

beforeAll(async () => {
  browser = await chromium.launch({ headless: true });
  const context = await browser.newContext();
  page = await context.newPage();
});

afterAll(async () => {
  await browser.close();
});

it('navigates through the onboarding flow', async () => {
  await page.goto('http://localhost:3000/onboarding');
  await page.fill('#firstName', 'TypeScript');
  await page.fill('#lastName', 'Expert');
  await page.click('#submit');
  await page.waitForSelector('.congratulation');
  const result = await page.locator('.congratulation').textContent();
  expect(result).toContain('Congratulations');
});
```

Beyond simulating user interactions, end-to-end tests should account for cross-browser discrepancies, varying network speeds, and mobile responsiveness. Leveraging emulation modes and advanced assertions to capture screen snapshots for regression analysis is an additional technique that supports comprehensive validation. Coupling these tests with continuous deployment strategies ensures that every system modification is evaluated against real-world usage scenarios, mitigating the risk of integration failures in production.

Advanced integration and end-to-end testing methodologies also rec-

448

ommend extensive logging and granular traceability. This entails capturing detailed logs at every testing stage and employing instrumentation to track API interactions, transaction IDs, and error propagation paths. Integrating these logs into centralized monitoring solutions simplifies the diagnosis of complex failures. Configuring tests to output structured JSON logs facilitates post-mortem analysis, even when tests are executed in isolated environments such as Docker containers or serverless CI nodes.

The discussed strategies furnish a rigorous framework for achieving high fidelity in integration and end-to-end testing. Developers harness controlled service simulations, network intercepts, advanced dependency injections, and headless browser automation to validate that TypeScript applications operate cohesively across all layers. These robust practices, when combined with efficient CI/CD pipelines, guarantee that system interactions, data flows, and user experiences remain consistent as the application evolves, thereby underpinning a resilient and production-ready software architecture.

## 9.4 Using TypeScript with Popular Testing Frameworks

Integrating TypeScript into established testing frameworks such as Jest, Mocha, and Jasmine demands careful configuration of transpilation, type checking, and runtime environments. Advanced practitioners must ensure that runtime environments preserve TypeScript's invariants while leveraging the sophisticated features of these frameworks. This section provides an in-depth analysis of the integration steps, performance optimizations, and non-trivial configuration patterns that harmonize TypeScript with these testing frameworks.

TypeScript integration with Jest is widely adopted due to Jest's comprehensive feature set, including snapshot testing, parallel execution, and built-in mocking capabilities. The primary adapter is ts-jest, which mediates between Jest and the TypeScript compiler, preserving type information and ensuring that advanced type assertions function without disruption. Configuring ts-jest requires careful coordination of compiler options and Jest settings. An exemplary jest.config.js tailored for a TypeScript project is given below:

```
module.exports = {
  preset: 'ts-jest',
  testEnvironment: 'node',
  globals: {
    'ts-jest': {
      tsconfig: 'tsconfig.json',
      diagnostics: {
        warnOnly: true
      }
    }
  },
  transform: {
    '^.+\\.tsx?$': 'ts-jest'
  },
  moduleNameMapper: {
    '^@src/(.*)$': '<rootDir>/src/$1'
  },
  collectCoverage: true,
  coverageDirectory: 'coverage',
  coveragePathIgnorePatterns: ['/node_modules/']
};
```

Advanced users will refine this configuration by toggling diagnostics options to control the verbosity of type warning outputs and by leveraging caching strategies to optimize incremental builds during continuous testing. Additionally, integrating custom matchers or leveraging Jest's custom test environments can substantially enhance the expressiveness of test suites.

The advanced use of Jest with TypeScript also involves managing asynchronous tests and subtle concurrency errors.  By wrapping asynchronous functions with `async/await` or using Jest's built-in done callback, developers can write robust tests that capture transient states or race conditions. For example, testing asynchronous data fetching with error handling might be implemented as follows:

```
describe('Async Data Fetching', () => {
  it('should reject with appropriate error message', async () => {
    await expect(fetchDataFunction('invalidID')).rejects.toThrowError
      ('Invalid ID');
  });
});
```

Here, the use of `rejects.toThrowError` ensures that the promise is properly asserted, while TypeScript's static analysis verifies that the expected error conforms to defined interface contracts.

The inclusion of Mocha as a testing framework in TypeScript projects introduces additional considerations due to its minimalistic design. Mocha relies on external tools for transpilation and module resolution.  Integration requires the use of `ts-node/register` to compile TypeScript on the fly, which can be achieved by configuring Mocha's command-line options in the `mocha.opts` or `.mocharc.js` file. A typical configuration is presented below:

```
// .mocharc.js
module.exports = {
  require: ['ts-node/register'],
  extension: ['ts'],
  spec: 'tests/**/*.spec.ts',
  timeout: 10000,
  recursive: true
};
```

Advanced Mocha configurations may include custom test reporters and parallel execution using tools like `mocha-parallel-tests`. In larger codebases, configuring global setup hooks becomes pivotal; advanced setups load environment variables, initialize database connections, or prepare in-memory caches before tests commence. For instance, an advanced test setup file could be structured as:

```
// tests/globalSetup.ts
import { initializeDatabase } from '@src/db';
import { loadEnv } from '@src/config';

before(async () => {
  loadEnv();
  await initializeDatabase({ inMemory: true });
});
```

TypeScript's strict type system aids in ensuring that these global configurations are consistent across test files, reducing runtime inconsistencies that might arise from misconfigured environments.

Jasmine, though less prevalent in some modern contexts, remains a powerful framework for behavior-driven development (BDD). When integrating TypeScript with Jasmine, similar strategies to Mocha are required; namely, dynamic transpilation through `ts-node/register` or pre-compilation. A common practice is to define a custom `jasmine.json` configuration file that designates the test files and compilation strategy. An example is shown below:

```
{
  "spec_dir": "tests",
  "spec_files": [
    "**/*[sS]pec.ts"
  ],
  "helpers": [
    "helpers/**/*.ts"
  ],
  "stopSpecOnExpectationFailure": false,
```

452

```
"random": false
}
```

For advanced Jasmine configurations, developers may define custom reporters that integrate seamlessly with TypeScript's verbose error outputs. Incorporating advanced reporter libraries, developers can output structured logs or integrate with external monitoring systems, thereby improving traceability in complex test suites.

Integrating TypeScript with these testing frameworks is further enriched by leveraging advanced language features such as decorators and generics within test utilities. For instance, creating a generic test fixture loader that automatically infers types from fixture files and maps them to test contracts greatly reduces boilerplate and enhances type safety:

```
import fs from 'fs';
import path from 'path';

export function loadFixture<T>(fixturePath: string): T {
  const data = fs.readFileSync(path.resolve(__dirname, fixturePath),
    'utf-8');
  return JSON.parse(data) as T;
}

// Usage in a test case:
interface UserFixture {
  id: number;
  name: string;
  role: string;
}

it('should match the user fixture structure', () => {
  const fixture = loadFixture<UserFixture>('fixtures/user.json');
  expect(fixture).toHaveProperty('id');
  expect(fixture.name).toEqual('Admin');
});
```

This pattern systematically enforces consistency between the mocked data and the expected schema, as TypeScript's static analysis catches discrepancies before runtime.

The continuous integration (CI) pipeline must also be configured to effectively run these tests. A robust CI configuration for TypeScript projects often caches compiled output or node modules, thereby reducing build times. Advanced CI configurations also run a dedicated type-checking job that executes `tsc --noEmit` concurrently with test suites to catch type errors that might interfere with runtime tests. An exemplary GitHub Actions workflow is as follows:

```
name: CI Pipeline

on:
  push:
    branches:
      - main
  pull_request:
    branches:
      - main

jobs:
  type-check:
    runs-on: ubuntu-latest
    steps:
      - uses: actions/checkout@v2
      - name: Install Dependencies
        run: npm ci
      - name: Type Check
        run: npm run type-check

  test:
    runs-on: ubuntu-latest
    needs: type-check
    steps:
      - uses: actions/checkout@v2
      - name: Install Dependencies
        run: npm ci
      - name: Run Jest Tests
        run: npm run test:jest
```

```
    - name: Run Mocha Tests
      run: npm run test:mocha
```

Advanced projects might separate test execution into parallel steps where each framework's tests are run in isolated environments, preventing resource contention and cross-interference.

Performance optimization is another critical consideration when using TypeScript with these testing frameworks. By developing a detailed understanding of TypeScript's incremental compilation, developers can adjust the tsconfig.json parameters specifically for test environments. For example, leveraging the skipLibCheck flag in test builds reduces compilation overhead without significant loss of type safety in iterative test development:

```
{
  "compilerOptions": {
    "target": "es2020",
    "module": "commonjs",
    "skipLibCheck": true,
    "strict": true,
    "sourceMap": true,
    "incremental": true,
    "outDir": "./build"
  },
  "include": ["src/**/*.ts", "tests/**/*.ts"],
  "exclude": ["node_modules"]
}
```

Advanced developers also rely on secondary caching mechanisms provided by ts-jest and related transformers, ensuring that repeated test executions in CI environments are as efficient as possible. This is especially crucial in monorepo setups where multiple packages share similar configuration strategies.

In addition to static configurations, dynamic test scenarios may require

455

runtime adjustments, such as switching test adapters based on environment variables. This design pattern can be implemented in a test bootstrap module that conditionally imports the appropriate testing configuration based on the execution context:

```
if (process.env.TEST_FRAMEWORK === 'mocha') {
  require('ts-node').register({ project: './tsconfig.test.json' });
} else if (process.env.TEST_FRAMEWORK === 'jasmine') {
  require('ts-node').register({ project: './tsconfig.jasmine.json' })
    ;
} else {
  // Default to Jest configuration for local runs
  require('ts-jest');
}
```

This dynamic strategy facilitates the simultaneous support of multiple testing frameworks within a single repository, minimizing overhead while ensuring that each framework operates with its optimal configuration.

A further nuance in integrating TypeScript with popular testing frameworks is managing module resolution. Modern projects often employ aliasing via paths in tsconfig.json to simplify imports. However, each testing framework needs to resolve these aliases consistently. In Jest, this is addressed with the moduleNameMapper configuration; in Mocha and Jasmine, webpack or other bundlers can be configured to support alias resolution. An exemplary webpack alias configuration might be:

```
module.exports = {
  resolve: {
    extensions: ['.ts', '.js'],
    alias: {
      '@src': path.resolve(__dirname, 'src/')
    }
  },
  module: {
```

```
rules: [
  {
    test: /\.ts$/,
    use: 'ts-loader',
    exclude: /node_modules/
  }
 ]
}
};
```

Supporting these custom aliases across testing frameworks reduces friction in code readability and maintainability while ensuring that test artifacts reflect production architectures accurately.

Integrating TypeScript with popular testing frameworks requires not only careful configuration but also a mindset focused on continuous improvement. By exploiting advanced configurations, adapting incremental builds, and dynamically switching environments, experienced developers can maintain a high level of test reliability and efficiency. These practices ensure that tests remain comprehensive, maintainable, and scalable as application complexity evolves while leveraging the powerful type system of TypeScript to catch errors at compile time and provide robust runtime assurances.

## 9.5 Advanced Error Handling Mechanisms

Advanced error handling in TypeScript extends beyond traditional try/catch blocks by leveraging the type system to create resilient applications that gracefully degrade under failure conditions. A sophisticated strategy involves defining hierarchical error classes, designing discriminated unions for error results, and integrating functional paradigms to ensure that error propagation is explicit, type-safe, and auditable at compile time.

A central technique is the creation of custom error classes. By extending the built-in `Error` type, developers can encapsulate contextual information and categorize errors according to domain, system, or operational layers. For example, consider the following implementation which defines a set of custom error types, each capable of carrying additional metadata:

```
class BaseError extends Error {
  public readonly timestamp: Date;
  constructor(message: string) {
    super(message);
    this.timestamp = new Date();
    Object.setPrototypeOf(this, new.target.prototype);
  }
}

export class NetworkError extends BaseError {
  constructor(public readonly statusCode: number, message?: string) {
    super(message || 'Network error occurred');
  }
}

export class DatabaseError extends BaseError {
  constructor(public readonly query: string, message?: string) {
    super(message || 'Database error occurred');
  }
}

export class ValidationError extends BaseError {
  constructor(public readonly field: string, message?: string) {
    super(message || 'Validation error occurred');
  }
}
```

In this design, each error class adds properties specific to its error domain. The use of `Object.setPrototypeOf` is necessary to maintain correct prototype linkage across transpilation boundaries. This pattern allows error handlers to perform type guards in a precise manner:

```
function handleError(error: unknown): void {
  if (error instanceof NetworkError) {
    console.error(`Network Error: ${error.message} (status: ${error.
    statusCode}) at ${error.timestamp}`);
  } else if (error instanceof DatabaseError) {
    console.error(`Database Error: ${error.message} (query: ${error.
    query}) at ${error.timestamp}`);
  } else if (error instanceof ValidationError) {
    console.error(`Validation Error: ${error.message} (field: ${error
    .field}) at ${error.timestamp}`);
  } else {
    console.error(`Unknown Error: ${String(error)}`);
  }
}
```

Transparently handling various error types is crucial for fault-tolerant systems. Beyond conventional error classes, techniques derived from functional programming paradigms can further improve error handling. One such method is the use of `Result` types or the `Either` monad, which encapsulate success and failure into a single return type, forcing the caller to acknowledge and explicitly handle errors. A minimal implementation of a `Result` type may be as follows:

```
type Result<T, E> = Success<T> | Failure<E>;

interface Success<T> {
  readonly type: 'success';
  readonly value: T;
}

interface Failure<E> {
  readonly type: 'failure';
  readonly error: E;
}

function success<T>(value: T): Result<T, never> {
  return { type: 'success', value };
}
```

```
function failure<E>(error: E): Result<never, E> {
  return { type: 'failure', error };
}

function isSuccess<T, E>(result: Result<T, E>): result is Success<T>
    {
  return result.type === 'success';
}

function isFailure<T, E>(result: Result<T, E>): result is Failure<E>
    {
  return result.type === 'failure';
}
```

This pattern forces a rigorous handling of error cases. For example, a
function that interacts with a remote API can return a `Result` type:

```
async function fetchData(url: string): Promise<Result<string,
    NetworkError>> {
  try {
    const response = await fetch(url);
    if (!response.ok) {
      return failure(new NetworkError(response.status, `Failed to
      fetch from ${url}`));
    }
    const data = await response.text();
    return success(data);
  } catch (err) {
    return failure(new NetworkError(0, 'Network exception occurred'))
      ;
  }
}
```

The caller is then required to inspect the result:

```
async function processData() {
  const result = await fetchData('https://api.example.com/data');
  if (isSuccess(result)) {
    console.log('Data received:', result.value);
  } else {
    handleError(result.error);
  }
```

```
}
```

By avoiding thrown exceptions, this design pattern minimizes unexpected control flow jumps and simplifies asynchronous error handling. Furthermore, adopting a functional approach can leverage libraries such as fp-ts to combine multiple operations using combinators like chain and map, streamlining error propagation in a composable manner.

Advanced error handling also considers the challenge of dealing with asynchronous operations where multiple error sources may converge. One common pitfall is that tail-call rejections in promise chains can be silently dropped. Therefore, practitioners introduce global error handling hooks and dedicated middleware. In Node.js environments, an unhandled promise rejection can be captured using:

```
process.on('unhandledRejection', (reason: unknown, promise: Promise<
    unknown>) => {
  console.error('Unhandled Rejection at:', promise, 'reason:', reason
    );
  // Optionally exit the process to avoid undefined behavior
});
```

Correct management of asynchronous errors can also be achieved by wrapping asynchronous operations with a utility function that standardizes error handling across the system:

```
async function safelyExecute<T>(fn: () => Promise<T>): Promise<Result
    <T, BaseError>> {
  try {
    const result = await fn();
    return success(result);
  } catch (err) {
    if (err instanceof BaseError) {
      return failure(err);
    }
    return failure(new BaseError(String(err)));
```

```
    }
}

// Usage example:
const result = await safelyExecute((() => performComplexTask());
if (isFailure(result)) {
  // Centralized error logging or recovery mechanism
  handleError(result.error);
} else {
  // Continue processing the result.value
}
```

Providing such wrappers around complex asynchronous logic not only
standardizes error handling but also assists in maintaining a consistent
error-reporting structure across diverse parts of an application.

Another advanced technique is the integration of contextual logging
within error handling routines. Rather than merely logging error messages, developers can augment the error context with trace identifiers,
metadata, and runtime environment details. This is especially useful
in distributed systems where correlating logs from disparate services
is crucial for diagnosing issues. One approach is to extend the custom
error classes to include contextual information:

```
interface Context {
  requestId?: string;
  userSession?: string;
  additionalData?: Record<string, unknown>;
}

class ContextualError extends BaseError {
  constructor(message: string, public readonly context: Context) {
    super(message);
  }
}

export class ServiceError extends ContextualError {
  constructor(message: string, context: Context) {
    super(message, context);
```

```
  }
}
```

Error handling functions can then be modified to extract and log context-specific data:

```
function advancedHandleError(error: unknown): void {
  if (error instanceof ContextualError) {
    console.error(`Error: ${error.message} at ${error.timestamp}`);
    console.error('Context:', JSON.stringify(error.context, null, 2))
    ;
  } else {
    console.error(`Unknown error: ${String(error)}`);
  }
}
```

When combined with structured logging frameworks, this approach facilitates end-to-end traceability in systems where errors may cascade through multiple layers and services.

Error recovery strategies themselves benefit from depth in TypeScript. A robust design does not only report errors but attempts partial recovery or fallback mechanisms without compromising the overall system consistency. One advanced technique is the use of retry strategies with exponential backoff for recoverable errors. A generic retry helper using asynchronous recursion is shown below:

```
async function retry<T>(
  fn: () => Promise<T>,
  attempts: number,
  backoff: number = 100
): Promise<Result<T, BaseError>> {
  try {
    const result = await fn();
    return success(result);
  } catch (err) {
    if (attempts === 1) {
      return failure(err instanceof BaseError ? err : new BaseError(
      String(err)));
```

```
    }
    await new Promise((resolve) => setTimeout(resolve, backoff));
    return retry(fn, attempts - 1, backoff * 2);
  }
}

// Example usage in a network request scenario:
const result = await retry(() => fetchData('https://api.example.com/
    data'), 3);
if (isFailure(result)) {
  advancedHandleError(result.error);
} else {
  console.log('Fetched data:', result.value);
}
```

The above implementation demonstrates how retries with exponential
backoff can be neatly encapsulated, providing resilience for transient
failures while ensuring that persistent errors are eventually escalated
appropriately.

TypeScript's advanced error handling practices are further
enhanced by compile-time guarantees. With the introduction of
the strictNullChecks compiler option and discriminated unions,
developers enforce exhaustive error handling patterns. For instance,
when implementing a function that returns a discriminated union,
the compiler will signal any unhandled cases:

```
type OperationResult =
  | { kind: 'success'; data: string }
  | { kind: 'error'; error: BaseError };

function processOperation(result: OperationResult): string {
  switch (result.kind) {
    case 'success':
      return result.data;
    case 'error':
      advancedHandleError(result.error);
      return 'default';
    default:
```

```
    // The compiler verifies that all cases are handled.
    throw new Error('Unhandled case');
  }
}
```

Leveraging these compile-time checks minimizes risks associated with unhandled error states and encourages developers to consider every possible execution branch explicitly.

The techniques outlined herein amplify the integrity of error propagation in TypeScript applications. By combining custom error hierarchies, functional error encapsulation, and strategic logging, advanced practitioners can design systems that anticipate failure modes and degrade gracefully. Integrating retry policies, comprehensive context capture, and exhaustive type-checking structures creates an error management framework that not only responds to anomalies but also provides critical insights for debugging and corrective maintenance. This holistic approach to error handling ultimately leads to resilient application architectures capable of operating reliably in complex, distributed environments.

## 9.6 Working with Error Boundaries in React

Advanced React applications require robust mechanisms to capture runtime errors in the UI, isolate them from the main rendering process, and provide a graceful recovery mechanism. Error boundaries in React are specialized components that implement the `componentDidCatch` lifecycle method (or its functional equivalents via hooks) to catch errors in descendant component trees. Leveraging TypeScript in this context not only ensures type safety but also enforces precise contracts for error payloads and recovery strategies. This section delves into advanced patterns for implementing error boundaries in React, their integration with application-level error handling, and sophisticated techniques for isolating UI errors without compromising user experience.

A foundational implementation of an error boundary in React involves extending the `React.Component` class and overriding the `componentDidCatch` method.    The following code illustrates an advanced error boundary component written in TypeScript.    It incorporates custom error state typing, contextual error logging, and a fallback UI that can propagate error reports back to a centralized monitoring system.

```typescript
import React, { ReactNode } from 'react';

interface ErrorBoundaryProps {
  children: ReactNode;
  fallback: ReactNode;
  onError?: (error: Error, errorInfo: React.ErrorInfo) => void;
}

interface ErrorBoundaryState {
  hasError: boolean;
  error?: Error;
  errorInfo?: React.ErrorInfo;
}

export class ErrorBoundary extends React.Component<ErrorBoundaryProps
    , ErrorBoundaryState> {
  constructor(props: ErrorBoundaryProps) {
    super(props);
    this.state = { hasError: false };
  }

  static getDerivedStateFromError(error: Error): Partial<
    ErrorBoundaryState> {
    // Update state to indicate error has been caught
    return { hasError: true, error };
  }
```

```
componentDidCatch(error: Error, errorInfo: React.ErrorInfo): void {
  // Optionally send the error to an external logging service
  if (this.props.onError) {
    this.props.onError(error, errorInfo);
  }
  this.setState({ error, errorInfo });
}

render(): ReactNode {
  if (this.state.hasError) {
    // Render fallback UI from props, preserving original styling
    and layout if needed
    return this.props.fallback;
  }
  return this.props.children;
}
}
```

In this implementation, TypeScript assists by statically verifying that the component handles children of type ReactNode and ensures that both error and errorInfo are captured correctly. The use of a fallback property, passed as a prop, allows developers to specify context-appropriate UI when an error occurs. The onError callback provides flexibility for logging mechanisms, enabling the integration of analytics or error monitoring services such as Sentry or LogRocket.

Further sophistication comes from designing error boundaries that differentiate error categories based on the context in which they occur. For example, in a complex application with multiple sections or modules, developers can craft distinct error boundaries that isolate errors within a particular domain of the UI. Consider a scenario in which different error boundaries are nested around high-risk components such as data visualizations or live data feeds. An advanced pattern is to create a higher-order component (HOC) that wraps any component with error handling capabilities. The following code shows an HOC that enhances any component with an error boundary using generics to preserve prop types:

```typescript
import React, { ComponentType, ReactNode } from 'react';

export function withErrorBoundary<P>(
  WrappedComponent: ComponentType<P>,
  fallback: ReactNode,
  onError?: (error: Error, errorInfo: React.ErrorInfo) => void
): ComponentType<P> {
  return class ErrorBoundaryHOC extends React.Component<P,
    ErrorBoundaryState> {
    constructor(props: P) {
      super(props);
      this.state = { hasError: false };
    }

    static getDerivedStateFromError(error: Error): Partial<
    ErrorBoundaryState> {
      return { hasError: true };
    }

    componentDidCatch(error: Error, errorInfo: React.ErrorInfo): void
    {
      if (onError) {
        onError(error, errorInfo);
      }
      this.setState({ error, errorInfo });
    }

    render(): ReactNode {
      if (this.state.hasError) {
        return fallback;
      }
      return <WrappedComponent {...this.props} />;
    }
  };
}
```

This HOC permits seamless integration of error boundaries in a modular fashion, allowing developers to compose error boundaries around specific components without modifying the underlying component code. The use of TypeScript generics ensures that prop types of the

468

wrapped component remain intact, leading to better maintainability and reusability.

Complex applications sometimes require error boundaries to perform context-sensitive logging and even incorporate user feedback. One advanced technique involves integrating error boundaries with React Context. By creating a centralized error reporting context, error boundaries can update global error states, trigger modal dialogs, or even allow users to submit additional information about the error. For example, consider a context that provides error reporting functions:

```
import React, { createContext, useContext } from 'react';

interface ErrorReportingContextType {
  reportError: (error: Error, errorInfo: React.ErrorInfo) => void;
}

export const ErrorReportingContext = createContext<
    ErrorReportingContextType>({
  reportError: () => {},
});

export const useErrorReporting = (): ErrorReportingContextType =>
    useContext(ErrorReportingContext);
```

Within an error boundary, the error reporting function can be invoked to synchronize error logs with centralized state management or external services:

```
import React from 'react';
import { useErrorReporting } from './ErrorReportingContext';

export class GlobalErrorBoundary extends React.Component<
    ErrorBoundaryProps, ErrorBoundaryState> {
  static contextType = ErrorReportingContext;
  context!: React.ContextType<typeof ErrorReportingContext>;

  componentDidCatch(error: Error, errorInfo: React.ErrorInfo): void {
    // Use contextual error reporting for centralized error
```

```
   management
  this.context.reportError(error, errorInfo);
  this.setState({ error, errorInfo, hasError: true });
}

render(): React.ReactNode {
  if (this.state.hasError) {
    // Optionally, render a fallback UI that includes a reset
    button for application recovery
    return (
      <div>
        <h2>Something went wrong.</h2>
        <button onClick={() => window.location.reload()}>Reload</
    button>
      </div>
    );
  }
  return this.props.children;
}
}
```

Integrating error boundaries with React Context provides an extensible mechanism for applications to adjust recovery strategies dynamically—in some cases, showing detailed error logs in a production dashboard, and in others, prompting users to provide supplemental error-relevant data.

Advanced error boundaries in React can also be equipped with features that allow for error recovery without necessitating a complete reload of the application. Techniques such as re-mounting a specific component subtree can be employed to attempt self-recovery. One strategy is to leverage a key prop to force a remount of child components. By adjusting a key based on a timestamp or a random value upon error detection, the application can effectively reset the component state. For example:

```
interface SelfRecoveringErrorBoundaryProps extends ErrorBoundaryProps
  {}
```

470

```
interface SelfRecoveringErrorBoundaryState extends ErrorBoundaryState
    {
  resetKey: number;
}


export class SelfRecoveringErrorBoundary extends React.Component<
  SelfRecoveringErrorBoundaryProps,
  SelfRecoveringErrorBoundaryState
> {
  constructor(props: SelfRecoveringErrorBoundaryProps) {
    super(props);
    this.state = { hasError: false, resetKey: Date.now() };
  }

  static getDerivedStateFromError(error: Error): Partial<
    SelfRecoveringErrorBoundaryState> {
    return { hasError: true };
  }

  componentDidCatch(error: Error, errorInfo: React.ErrorInfo): void {
    if (this.props.onError) {
      this.props.onError(error, errorInfo);
    }
    this.setState({ error, errorInfo });
  }

  handleReset = (): void => {
    this.setState({ hasError: false, resetKey: Date.now() });
  };

  render(): React.ReactNode {
    if (this.state.hasError) {
      return (
        <div>
          {this.props.fallback}
          <button onClick={this.handleReset}>Try Again</button>
        </div>
      );
    }
    // Using resetKey to force a fresh render of child components
    return <React.Fragment key={this.state.resetKey}>{this.props.
    children}</React.Fragment>;
  }
}
```

This component demonstrates a self-recovering pattern where a user can trigger the remount of a subtree to clear transient errors. The dynamic manipulation of the component key ensures that internal states are reinitialized, potentially resolving issues arising from ephemeral states or memory leaks.

Advanced error boundaries must also integrate with logging solutions. Complex UI applications demand detailed logs that not only capture error messages but also record stack traces, component hierarchies, and user interactions leading up to the error. Enhancing the logging features in an error boundary may involve serializing error information into structured logs that can be sent asynchronously to a backend logging service. This is particularly useful in production environments where capturing enough context during an error event is critical for troubleshooting and iterative improvements.

```
function logErrorToService(error: Error, errorInfo: React.ErrorInfo):
    void {
  const errorPayload = {
    message: error.message,
    stack: error.stack,
    componentStack: errorInfo.componentStack,
    time: new Date().toISOString(),
    // Additional metadata such as user ID, current route, etc.
  };
  // Asynchronously send errorPayload to a logging service (e.g.,
    Sentry, LogRocket)
  fetch('https://logging.service/api/errors', {
    method: 'POST',
    headers: { 'Content-Type': 'application/json' },
    body: JSON.stringify(errorPayload),
  });
}
```

By invoking such logging functions within the error boundary's `componentDidCatch` method, developers ensure that no error goes unnoticed even if it is ultimately masked by a fallback UI.

When integrating error boundaries into a large-scale React application, it is advisable to adopt a layered approach. Global error boundaries catch unforeseen errors at the highest level and prevent the entire application from crashing, while localized error boundaries isolate errors in specific sections, such as forms, dashboards, or interactive components. This segregation minimizes the impact of errors and allows for more granular recovery strategies. Advanced strategies include placing error boundaries within route components, ensuring that navigation and critical pages remain functional even if a specific sub-component fails.

The effective use of error boundaries in React, augmented by TypeScript, also benefits from a thorough suite of tests. Component-level tests should validate that error boundaries correctly catch errors, render fallback UIs, and trigger logging callbacks. Testing strategies using Enzyme or React Testing Library in combination with TypeScript assertions help guarantee that error boundaries behave as expected. An example unit test for an error boundary might confirm that a thrown error in a child component triggers the display of fallback content.

Integrating error boundaries into the React development workflow, with a strong emphasis on type safety and modular design, elevates the resilience of UI applications. By exploiting advanced patterns such as higher-order components, contextual error reporting, self-recovery through key remounts, and comprehensive logging, developers can establish a robust framework that not only isolates runtime errors but also facilitates proactive debugging and iterative refinement. This systematic approach to managing UI errors underpins a fault-tolerant application architecture capable of maintaining a seamless user experience even under adverse conditions.

473

## 9.7   Logging and Monitoring in TypeScript Applications

Advanced logging and monitoring are essential components for building resilient TypeScript applications. They enable developers to track performance, isolate subtle bugs, and observe system behaviors in production environments. In TypeScript applications, leveraging robust logging solutions is not merely about capturing exceptions; it involves creating a structured, context-rich trail of operational data that facilitates debugging and performance optimization across distributed systems. This section examines best practices, design patterns, and advanced techniques for implementing logging and monitoring, with detailed examples and configuration strategies.

A comprehensive logging solution in TypeScript begins with selecting an appropriate logging library that integrates with TypeScript's type system. Libraries such as Winston, Pino, and Bunyan are widely adopted in the Node.js ecosystem. When expanded upon with TypeScript, these libraries provide structured logging, strongly-typed log entry formats, and easy integration with third-party monitoring solutions. An advanced strategy involves creating an abstraction layer that encapsulates the chosen logging library, exposing a consistent interface that supports various logging levels and structured data.

The following example illustrates how to create a logging service using Winston and TypeScript. By defining a logger interface and a corresponding implementation, the application code can remain decoupled from the underlying logging library:

```
import winston, { format, transports, Logger as WinstonLogger } from
    'winston';
```

474

```typescript
export interface Logger {
  info(message: string, meta?: Record<string, unknown>): void;
  warn(message: string, meta?: Record<string, unknown>): void;
  error(message: string, meta?: Record<string, unknown>): void;
  debug(message: string, meta?: Record<string, unknown>): void;
}

class WinstonLoggingService implements Logger {
  private logger: WinstonLogger;

  constructor() {
    this.logger = winston.createLogger({
      level: 'debug',
      format: format.combine(
        format.timestamp(),
        format.printf(({ timestamp, level, message, ...meta }) => {
          const metaString = Object.keys(meta).length ? JSON.
    stringify(meta) : '';
          return `${timestamp} [${level}]: ${message} ${metaString}`;
        })
      ),
      transports: [
        new transports.Console({
          format: format.combine(
            format.colorize(),
            format.printf(({ timestamp, level, message, ...meta }) =>
    {
              const metaString = Object.keys(meta).length ? JSON.
    stringify(meta) : '';
              return `${timestamp} [${level}]: ${message} ${
    metaString}`;
            })
          )
        }),
        new transports.File({ filename: 'application.log' })
      ]
    });
  }

  info(message: string, meta: Record<string, unknown> = {}): void {
    this.logger.info(message, meta);
  }

  warn(message: string, meta: Record<string, unknown> = {}): void {
```

```typescript
    this.logger.warn(message, meta);
  }

  error(message: string, meta: Record<string, unknown> = {}): void {
    this.logger.error(message, meta);
  }

  debug(message: string, meta: Record<string, unknown> = {}): void {
    this.logger.debug(message, meta);
  }
}


export const logger: Logger = new WinstonLoggingService();
```

In this implementation, a structured log format is enforced, including timestamps, log levels, and additional metadata. The use of TypeScript interfaces ensures that every log message conforms to a predetermined shape, making it easier to filter and analyze log data downstream.

Beyond basic logging, incorporating contextual information is crucial for debugging and performance analysis in distributed systems. A common practice is to leverage correlation identifiers, such as request IDs and session tokens, so that log entries can be correlated across multiple services and asynchronous operations. Middleware in Express applications, for instance, can inject a unique request identifier into the logging context. An advanced example follows:

```typescript
import express, { Request, Response, NextFunction } from 'express';
import { v4 as uuidv4 } from 'uuid';
import { logger } from './loggingService';

declare global {
  namespace Express {
    interface Request {
      correlationId?: string;
    }
  }
}
```

476

```
function correlationIdMiddleware(req: Request, res: Response, next:
    NextFunction): void {
  req.correlationId = uuidv4();
  logger.info('Assigned new correlation ID', { correlationId: req.
    correlationId });
  next();
}

const app = express();
app.use(correlationIdMiddleware);

app.get('/data', (req: Request, res: Response) => {
  logger.debug('Handling /data request', { correlationId: req.
    correlationId });
  // Process the request
  res.send({ data: 'sample data' });
});

app.use((err: Error, req: Request, res: Response, next: NextFunction)
    => {
  logger.error('Unhandled error occurred', { correlationId: req.
    correlationId, error: err.message });
  res.status(500).send({ error: 'Internal Server Error' });
});
```

This middleware injects a UUID into every incoming request, which is then propagated and included in every subsequent log entry. Such a mechanism is invaluable for linking log entries that pertain to the same operational context, especially during debugging sessions for issues that span multiple microservices.

Integrating monitoring alongside logging elevates an application's observability. Advanced monitoring encompasses real-time performance tracking, health checks, and alert configurations that enable proactive incident management. Tools like Prometheus, Grafana, and OpenTelemetry facilitate the instrumentation of application metrics and traces. OpenTelemetry, for example, provides a unified context propagation and distributed tracing solution that integrates seamlessly

with TypeScript applications.  Instrumenting code with OpenTelemetry can offer insights into the performance of database queries, external
API calls, and internal function executions.

The following example demonstrates basic instrumentation using
OpenTelemetry in a TypeScript application:

```typescript
import { NodeTracerProvider } from '@opentelemetry/sdk-trace-node';
import { SimpleSpanProcessor } from '@opentelemetry/sdk-trace-base';
import { ConsoleSpanExporter } from '@opentelemetry/sdk-trace-base';
import { trace, context } from '@opentelemetry/api';

const provider = new NodeTracerProvider();
provider.addSpanProcessor(new SimpleSpanProcessor(new
    ConsoleSpanExporter()));
provider.register();

const tracer = trace.getTracer('my-application-tracer');

async function fetchData(url: string): Promise<string> {
  const span = tracer.startSpan('fetchData', {
    attributes: { url }
  });
  try {
    // Simulate fetching data
    await new Promise(resolve => setTimeout(resolve, 100));
    return 'fetched data';
  } catch (error) {
    span.recordException(error);
    throw error;
  } finally {
    span.end();
  }
}

async function processData(): Promise<void> {
  const ctx = trace.setSpan(context.active(), tracer.startSpan('
    processData'));
  await context.with(ctx, async () => {
    const data = await fetchData('https://api.example.com/data');
    logger.info('Data processed', { data });
  });
}
```

```
processData().catch(error => logger.error('Error in processData', {
    error: error.message }));
```

In this example, spans are created to measure and trace the execution of asynchronous operations. The traces can later be aggregated and visualized to pinpoint performance bottlenecks and error propagation paths. Coupled with a logging service that includes correlation IDs, such traces provide a complete view of the application's dynamic behavior.

Advanced monitoring should cover not only performance metrics but also error rates, latency, and resource utilization patterns. Implementing health checks and periodic metric emission into a time-series database enables proactive monitoring and alerting. For instance, integrating a health check endpoint in an Express application and pushing metrics to Prometheus might look as follows:

```
import express, { Request, Response } from 'express';
import client from 'prom-client';

const app = express();

// Create a Prometheus registry
const register = new client.Registry();
client.collectDefaultMetrics({ register });

// Define a custom metric
const httpRequestDurationMicroseconds = new client.Histogram({
    name: 'http_request_duration_ms',
    help: 'Duration of HTTP requests in ms',
    labelNames: ['method', 'route', 'code'],
    buckets: [50, 100, 200, 300, 400, 500]
});
register.registerMetric(httpRequestDurationMicroseconds);

app.get('/health', (req: Request, res: Response) => {
    res.status(200).send({ status: 'ok' });
```

```typescript
});

app.use((req: Request, res: Response, next) => {
  const start = Date.now();
  res.on('finish', () => {
    const duration = Date.now() - start;
    httpRequestDurationMicroseconds
      .labels(req.method, req.path, res.statusCode.toString())
      .observe(duration);
  });
  next();
});

app.get('/metrics', async (req: Request, res: Response) => {
  res.set('Content-Type', register.contentType);
  res.end(await register.metrics());
});

app.listen(3000, () => {
  logger.info('Server is running on port 3000');
});
```

The above example demonstrates integrating Prometheus metrics into
an Express application. It captures the duration of HTTP requests
and exposes a /metrics endpoint for scraping by monitoring systems.
When combined with detailed log entries, such metrics provide a mul-
tidimensional view of application performance and reliability.

Advanced logging and monitoring strategies benefit from
asynchronous log aggregation and external service integrations.
Cloud-based solutions such as ELK (Elasticsearch, Logstash, Kibana),
Datadog, or Splunk can ingest logs from multiple sources and
correlate them with distributed traces. Configuring a transport
in a logging library to send log entries directly to such platforms
ensures real-time visibility into system health. Complex configuration
examples may involve batch processing of logs and handling network
failures gracefully.

Another useful trick is implementing log sampling to reduce overhead in very high-throughput environments. Instead of logging every event, the system can be configured to log a representative percentage based on log level or event type. Advanced log processors can later expand these samples into statistically accurate representations for analysis.

Implementing advanced logging and monitoring in TypeScript applications requires a multi-layered approach. By building an abstraction over logging libraries, injecting context via middleware, integrating distributed tracing with OpenTelemetry, and exposing system metrics via Prometheus, developers create a robust framework for debugging and performance tracking. These practices not only facilitate rapid incident resolution but also enable continuous performance optimization in complex, distributed application environments.

**10**

# Chapter 10: Advanced Tooling and Practices for TypeScript Development

*This chapter explores advanced tooling and practices to enhance TypeScript development, covering setup with modern toolchains, task automation, and compiler configurations. It discusses integration with CI/CD pipelines and effective version control using Git. Additionally, it emphasizes the use of linters, formatters, and static analysis tools, promoting code quality, consistency, and efficiency in complex projects.*

## 10.1    Setting Up TypeScript Projects with Modern Toolchains

The integration of modern toolchains—specifically Webpack, Babel, and ESLint—forms the backbone of effective TypeScript project architectures in advanced development environments. The objective is to harmonize TypeScript's rigorous type system with the dynamic features of contemporary JavaScript ecosystems. This section delves into the detailed configuration and interplay among these tools, providing the experienced developer with practical insights, configuration patterns, and precision tuning to maximize build performance and code robustness.

At the core of this setup lies Webpack, an extensible module bundler that enables granular control over the build pipeline. It permits dynamic module resolution and code splitting that are essential when combining the static analysis benefits of TypeScript with runtime optimizations. A typical Webpack configuration for TypeScript projects requires explicit loader definitions to handle both .ts and .tsx files, along with a chain of transformations enabling Babel to transpile features unsupported in the target execution environment. The following configuration snippet illustrates a refined approach for integrating TypeScript with Webpack and Babel:

```
const path = require('path');

module.exports = {
  entry: './src/index.ts',
  output: {
    filename: 'bundle.js',
    path: path.resolve(__dirname, 'dist')
  },
  resolve: {
```

```
    extensions: ['.ts', '.tsx', '.js']
  },
  module: {
    rules: [
      {
        test: /\.tsx?$/,
        exclude: /node_modules/,
        use: [
          {
            loader: 'babel-loader',
            options: {
              cacheDirectory: true,
              presets: [
                ['@babel/preset-env', { targets: "defaults" }],
                '@babel/preset-typescript'
              ],
              plugins: ['@babel/plugin-transform-runtime']
            }
          }
        ]
      }
    ]
  },
  devtool: 'source-map'
};
```

This configuration demonstrates several critical aspects: file resolution order, loader chaining (ensuring Babel processes the TypeScript code), and the use of caching to accelerate rebuilds. The inclusion of source-map generation is also key for effective debugging and error tracing in production-grade applications.

Babel's role in this ecosystem extends beyond merely transpiling newer ECMAScript features. When used in conjunction with the TypeScript compiler (tsc), Babel assumes the responsibility of runtime transformation while delegating type checking to TypeScript's own mechanisms. This bifurcation of responsibilities permits faster builds when coupled with tools like fork-ts-checker-webpack-plugin to run type

checks in parallel. Advanced usage often leverages Babel's extensive
plugin ecosystem to introduce experimental language features or to enforce custom transformation logic. An exemplary Babel configuration,
typically placed in a `babel.config.js` file, is shown below:

```
module.exports = {
  presets: [
    ['@babel/preset-env', {
      targets: {
        esmodules: true,
      },
      debug: false,
      useBuiltIns: 'usage',
      corejs: 3,
    }],
    '@babel/preset-typescript'
  ],
  plugins: [
    '@babel/plugin-proposal-class-properties',
    '@babel/plugin-transform-runtime'
  ],
  comments: false,
  compact: true,
};
```

The configuration exploits the modularity of Babel presets, ensuring that the final output adheres to the targeted runtime environments. The deliberate disabling of comments and enabling of code
compaction reflect the pre-optimization steps for deployment, which
are crucial in advanced builds where every byte and cycle counts.

Beyond bundling and transpilation, maintaining a high code quality standard is paramount. ESLint, a versatile static analysis tool,
plays an essential role in enforcing consistent coding conventions
and catching semantic errors at an early stage. In TypeScript contexts, ESLint requires specific parser and plugin configurations to accurately understand the language syntax and semantics. The following

.eslintrc.js configuration represents an advanced setup tailored to a TypeScript project:

```
module.exports = {
  parser: '@typescript-eslint/parser',
  parserOptions: {
    ecmaVersion: 2020,
    sourceType: 'module',
    project: './tsconfig.json'
  },
  plugins: [
    '@typescript-eslint'
  ],
  extends: [
    'eslint:recommended',
    'plugin:@typescript-eslint/recommended',
    'prettier'
  ],
  rules: {
    '@typescript-eslint/no-unused-vars': ['error', {
    argsIgnorePattern: '^_' }],
    '@typescript-eslint/explicit-function-return-type': ['warn'],
    'no-console': 'off'
  },
  env: {
    browser: true,
    node: true,
    es6: true
  }
};
```

The configuration leverages the TypeScript parser and the corresponding plugin set to ensure a robust linting process. Specific rules, such as the one enforcing explicit function return types, embody advanced coding standards that contribute to maintainability and clarity in large code bases.

Fastidious integration of toolchain components demands a synchronization mechanism where configuration files co-evolve. For instance, ensuring that tsconfig.json aligns with both Babel and ESLint ex-

487

pectations is essential. An optimized `tsconfig.json` for such environments might look like this:

```
{
  "compilerOptions": {
    "target": "esnext",
    "module": "esnext",
    "jsx": "react",
    "strict": true,
    "esModuleInterop": true,
    "skipLibCheck": true,
    "noEmit": true,
    "sourceMap": true,
    "baseUrl": "./src",
    "paths": {
      "*": ["types/*"]
    }
  },
  "include": ["src/**/*"],
  "exclude": ["node_modules", "dist"]
}
```

The configuration purposefully sets `noEmit` to true, as Babel handles the transformation and emission of code. The alignment between these settings across multiple tools is imperative for avoiding type mismatches and ensuring a seamless incremental build process.

Efficient task sequencing within the build pipeline is another area where advanced developers can gain significant efficiency. By leveraging Webpack's plugin architecture, one can incorporate sophisticated features such as incremental builds, caching mechanisms, and code splitting strategies. Consider the integration of the `fork-ts-checker-webpack-plugin` to offload type checking into a parallel process, thereby significantly reducing build times:

```
const ForkTsCheckerWebpackPlugin = require('fork-ts-checker-webpack-
    plugin');

module.exports = {
```

```
// existing webpack configuration
plugins: [
  new ForkTsCheckerWebpackPlugin({
    async: false,
    typescript: {
      diagnosticOptions: {
        semantic: true,
        syntactic: true
      }
    }
  })
]
};
```

This integration demonstrates a sophisticated approach to balancing performance and type safety by decoupling linting and type checking from the main bundling process. The result is a more responsive development cycle that does not compromise on code integrity—a necessity for expert-level projects.

Attention to detail extends to the handling of source maps. Debugging optimized builds can be challenging, and hence, the configuration of accurate source-map generation deserves a detailed examination. Both Babel and Webpack support fine-grained source-map options, allowing developers to trade off build performance for improved debugging capabilities. When employing a combination of these tools, ensuring that inline source maps or separate map files are generated consistently is critical. A typical advanced configuration in Webpack might include:

```
module.exports = {
  // existing configuration options
  devtool: 'cheap-module-source-map',
  output: {
    // additional options to support source maps
    sourceMapFilename: '[file].map'
  }
};
```

This setting is particularly valuable in environments where debugging
is performed on minified output, a common scenario in production
deployments.

Efficiency in development is further amplified by the usage of caching
strategies across these tools.   Enabling filesystem caching in Babel
via the `cacheDirectory` option, as shown in the Webpack configuration, can dramatically reduce the turnaround time on subsequent
builds.   Equivalent caching mechanisms are available in Webpack itself through persistent caching strategies that store modules and dependency graphs between builds.

Moreover, developers may incorporate advanced logging and diagnostic capabilities to monitor and troubleshoot performance issues in the
build process.   Tools such as Webpack Bundle Analyzer can be integrated into the configuration to visualize bundle size and module dependencies.   An example command to run the analyzer could be encapsulated in an npm script:

```
{
  "scripts": {
    "analyze": "webpack --profile --json > stats.json && webpack-
    bundle-analyzer stats.json"
  }
}
```

The technical approach outlined here not only fosters a deeper understanding of the underlying mechanics but also equips the developer
with practical methods to optimize, debug, and maintain large-scale
TypeScript codebases.

Finally, incorporating these advanced configurations demands
disciplined project organization.    Directory and file structures
should reflect a modular approach where each segment of the

build process—TypeScript transpilation, Babel transformation, and ESLint static analysis—is decoupled for clarity and maintainability. Consistency across these configurations ensures that the pipeline remains robust even as project requirements evolve, making scaling and adaptation considerably more manageable.

The systematic alignment of these modern toolchains illustrates the importance of orchestration in managing a contemporary TypeScript project. By harnessing the full spectrum of available features from Webpack, Babel, and ESLint, developers can maintain rigorous standards of both type safety and runtime performance. This fusion of reliable static typing with dynamic build pipelines underpins the development of high-quality, production-ready applications while providing the tools necessary for optimizing build times and code quality in even the most demanding environments.

## 10.2 Automating Development with Task Runners

Advanced automation in development workflows leverages task runners to streamline repetitive processes, enforce consistency, and enhance productivity. In complex TypeScript projects, integrating task runners such as Gulp and npm scripts provides a flexible framework to orchestrate tasks including code transpilation, testing, bundling, linting, and deployment. The design of these workflows involves a deep understanding of task orchestration, asynchronous execution, stream processing, and environment configuration to fully exploit their capabilities.

A sophisticated usage of Gulp involves the creation of tasks that are

both compositional and modular. In Gulp, each task represents a unit
of work that can be combined either in series or in parallel. The advanced developer is expected to design robust pipelines by harnessing
Node.js streams, enabling the processing of large codebases with minimal memory overhead. An exemplary Gulp task to transpile Type-
Script files, followed by minification, demonstrates chaining operations with error propagation and logging:

```
const gulp = require('gulp');
const ts = require('gulp-typescript');
const sourcemaps = require('gulp-sourcemaps');
const terser = require('gulp-terser');
const plumber = require('gulp-plumber');
const notify = require('gulp-notify');

const tsProject = ts.createProject('tsconfig.json');

function buildScripts() {
  return gulp.src('src/**/*.ts')
    .pipe(plumber({ errorHandler: notify.onError("Error: <%= error.
    message %>") }))
    .pipe(sourcemaps.init())
    .pipe(tsProject())
    .pipe(terser({
      ecma: 2020,
      compress: { drop_console: true },
      mangle: true
    }))
    .pipe(sourcemaps.write('./maps'))
    .pipe(gulp.dest('dist'));
}

exports.build = gulp.series(buildScripts);
```

This task demonstrates advanced usage of Gulp plugins to integrate
error management via plumber and system notifications, along with
the use of sourcemaps to maintain traceability between transformed
and original code. The modular structure, achieved by configuring individual transformation streams, allows for fine-grained control over

each stage of the build process.

Beyond task composition, an advanced pipeline must account for performance optimization. This involves parallel execution where tasks are independent, and shallow watching of file changes to trigger minimal rebuilds. Gulp's capability to run tasks concurrently can be exploited using gulp.parallel, which is critical when integrating tasks like static analysis and asset optimization that do not depend on one another. For instance, consider the automation of style preprocessing alongside TypeScript compilation:

```
const sass = require('gulp-sass')(require('sass'));
const autoprefixer = require('gulp-autoprefixer');

function buildStyles() {
  return gulp.src('styles/**/*.scss')
    .pipe(sourcemaps.init())
    .pipe(sass({ outputStyle: 'compressed' }).on('error', sass.
    logError))
    .pipe(autoprefixer({ cascade: false }))
    .pipe(sourcemaps.write('./maps'))
    .pipe(gulp.dest('dist/styles'));
}

exports.default = gulp.parallel(buildScripts, buildStyles);
```

By segregating concerns, one can maintain high-performance build systems that leverage multicore architectures on modern development machines. Additionally, the inherent modularity of the Gulp ecosystem facilitates the creation of custom plugins when built-in transformations are inadequate. For example, a developer might create a custom stream transformer that analyzes TypeScript diagnostics in real-time and applies context-specific annotations to the output.

The integration of npm scripts in task automation complements Gulp by running tasks that do not require the overhead of a full task runner.

For many workflows, npm scripts provide an elegant solution for sequential task execution, environment variable management, and cross-platform support without the dependency on additional libraries. The package.json file is extended with scripts that encapsulate complex command-line operations. An advanced developer recognizes that npm scripts can orchestrate tasks provided by multiple tools and can invoke node-based APIs directly. A representative npm script configuration might be:

```
{
  "scripts": {
    "clean": "rimraf dist",
    "build:ts": "tsc --project tsconfig.json",
    "build:styles": "node-sass styles -o dist/styles --output-style
    compressed --source-map true",
    "bundle": "webpack --config webpack.prod.js",
    "lint": "eslint 'src/**/*.{ts,tsx}' --max-warnings 0",
    "test": "jest --config jest.config.js --runInBand",
    "prebuild": "npm run clean && npm run lint",
    "build": "npm run prebuild && npm run build:ts && npm run build:
    styles && npm run bundle",
    "watch": "concurrently \"npm run watch:ts\" \"npm run watch:
    styles\"",
    "watch:ts": "tsc --watch --project tsconfig.json",
    "watch:styles": "node-sass styles -o dist/styles --watch --output
    -style expanded --source-map true"
  }
}
```

This configuration demonstrates chaining multiple tasks, conditional execution, and concurrency, with the use of tools like rimraf for robust deletion of output directories and concurrently to manage parallel watching processes seamlessly. Incorporating such scripts into a CI/CD pipeline further automates testing and deployment, allowing for controlled integration of automated development tasks.

Advanced optimization also entails the coordination between Gulp and npm scripts. Developers can define npm scripts that invoke Gulp tasks, allowing the centralization of build commands. This hybrid approach benefits scenarios in which a project requires different modes of operation (e.g., development versus production) or when specific tasks, such as static analysis, are better handled outside of Gulp's streaming paradigm. An example command in the package.json might delegate to Gulp as follows:

```
{
  "scripts": {
    "gulp:build": "gulp build",
    "dev": "concurrently \"npm run gulp:build\" \"npm run watch\""
  }
}
```

In advanced environments, understanding error propagation and logging mechanisms within task runners is crucial. Gulp's plumber plugin, as seen earlier, can intercept errors to prevent process termination and emit detailed diagnostic messages. Coupled with advanced logging libraries that interface with real-time monitoring systems, this approach ensures that issues are captured early and are actionable. Tuning the verbosity of logs via environment variables can also be achieved by scripting conditional logic in Gulp tasks, scaling the output information depending on whether the code is in production or development mode.

Moreover, task runners can serve as an interface to more complex operations like parallel processing, caching results between builds, and dynamic dependency resolution. An advanced developer might integrate the file-system caching capabilities provided by plugins, ensuring that unchanged assets are not re-processed. This is achieved by applying checksum-based filtering within the task pipeline. For instance, one might leverage a caching plugin to conditionally bypass transformation streams:

```
const cache = require('gulp-cached');

function optimizedBuildScripts() {
  return gulp.src('src/**/*.ts')
    .pipe(cache('typescript'))
    .pipe(sourcemaps.init())
    .pipe(tsProject())
    .pipe(terser({
      ecma: 2020,
      compress: { drop_console: true },
      mangle: true
    }))
    .pipe(sourcemaps.write('./maps'))
    .pipe(gulp.dest('dist'));
}

exports.build = gulp.series(optimizedBuildScripts);
```

This strategic use of caching drastically reduces build times by eliminating redundant processing, particularly beneficial in large-scale projects with expansive codebases. Advanced users may combine this with file watchers that are sensitive to dependency graphs, ensuring that caches are invalidated appropriately and only the necessary subsets of the code are rebuilt.

On the subject of environment configuration, task runners empower developers to define behaviors for different build environments. This is typically achieved by parsing external configuration files or by injecting environment variables dynamically. Gulp tasks can reference these variables to conditionally adjust parameters—a practice that ensures that builds are reproducible across divergent environments. A well-structured configuration might query process.env.NODE_ENV and adjust optimization flags:

```
function conditionalMinify() {
  const isProduction = process.env.NODE_ENV === 'production';
```

```
return gulp.src('src/**/*.ts')
  .pipe(sourcemaps.init())
  .pipe(tsProject())
  .pipe(isProduction ? terser() : gulp.dest('dist'))
  .pipe(sourcemaps.write('./maps'))
  .pipe(gulp.dest('dist'));
}
```

The flexibility achieved by utilizing environment variables allows developers to embed multiple configurations in the same codebase, simplifying deployments across local, staging, and production environments without code duplication.

Advanced task automation also benefits from monitoring file changes beyond simple watching. Tools capable of incremental builds, such as gulp-watch, can integrate with file system events to trigger specific tasks only when files matching particular patterns change. This reduces the iteration cycle and helps in developing responsive build systems. Advanced configurations may include strategies for debouncing file events to prevent redundant invocations in high-change environments, ensuring that the task runner remains responsive under heavy modifications.

The utilization of npm scripts for continuous integration and testing also forms a critical aspect of development automation. Developers often embed logic to run test suites, static analysis, and lint checks as part of a pre-commit hook or CI pipeline. Leveraging cross-platform environment management tools and chaining commands as shown earlier in the npm scripts allows for a high degree of automation, thereby reducing manual intervention. The predictability of such scripts is essential when managing large teams and ensuring code consistency across diverse environments.

497

The orchestration of these advanced task runners necessitates periodic review and optimization. Detailed logging, performance profiling, and integration with real-time monitoring dashboards offer insight into the build pipeline's efficiency and stability. Developers are encouraged to employ tools such as `gulp-debug` to trace file events within streams and to instrument build tasks with custom timers, thereby identifying bottlenecks. This level of introspection, combined with iterative refinement of task sequences, is a hallmark of expert-level development practices.

The synthesis of these approaches—modular Gulp tasks, comprehensive npm scripts, conditional environment configurations, caching strategies, and detailed performance monitoring—underscores a mature automation strategy that scales with project complexity. By harnessing these tools judiciously, developers not only reduce repetitive manual processes but also enforce rigorous quality checks that are integral to maintaining the integrity and performance of modern TypeScript codebases.

## 10.3    Advanced TypeScript Compiler Options

In large-scale TypeScript projects, meticulous compiler configuration is paramount to harnessing both performance and code correctness. Advanced users must delve into nuanced settings that fine-tune typechecking, module resolution, and incremental compilation. By tailoring the `tsconfig.json` file, developers can leverage sophisticated options to achieve optimal compile-time behavior and robust errorchecking without sacrificing developer productivity.

Central to advanced TypeScript configuration is the judicious usage of the strict family of compiler flags. Enabling strictNullChecks, strictFunctionTypes, strictBindCallApply, noImplicitAny, and similar options ensures that subtle type errors are detected early. By moving the emphasis from runtime corrections to compile-time guarantees, developers achieve higher code integrity. For instance, the following tsconfig.json snippet illustrates a configuration that adopts these rigorous standards:

```
{
  "compilerOptions": {
    "target": "ES2020",
    "module": "ESNext",
    "strict": true,
    "noImplicitAny": true,
    "noImplicitThis": true,
    "strictNullChecks": true,
    "strictFunctionTypes": true,
    "strictBindCallApply": true,
    "forceConsistentCasingInFileNames": true,
    "esModuleInterop": true,
    "skipLibCheck": true,
    "sourceMap": true,
    "incremental": true,
    "baseUrl": "./src",
    "paths": {
      "@app/*": ["app/*"],
      "@lib/*": ["library/*"]
    }
  },
  "include": ["src/**/*"],
  "exclude": ["node_modules", "dist"]
}
```

Each flag enforces a tight contract between TypeScript's type system and the codebase, ensuring that type mismatches and potential runtime errors are caught during development. The incremental flag, in particular, enables faster rebuilds by storing information about previous compilations. Advanced configurations often merge the type-checking rigor with module aliasing mechanisms, as seen with the paths setting, to resolve modules more intuitively across large codebases.

One of the subtle aspects of advanced compiler configuration is managing module resolution. The `moduleResolution` flag can be set to `node` or `classic`; the former is typically preferred in projects that adhere to Node.js module semantics. However, the integration of custom path mappings and base directories introduces new dimensions of complexity. Advanced projects may also utilize the `resolveJsonModule` feature to import JSON files directly, enforcing type safety in data consumption. Consider the following snippet, which emphasizes these points:

```
{
  "compilerOptions": {
    "moduleResolution": "node",
    "resolveJsonModule": true,
    "allowSyntheticDefaultImports": true,
    "baseUrl": "./src",
    "paths": {
      "@config/*": ["config/*"]
    }
  }
}
```

This configuration enhances compatibility with Node.js libraries while integrating JSON imports into the type system. Advanced developers can combine these options with custom transformers during the build process to transform JSON data formats at compile time, further reducing runtime overhead.

Performance tuning is achieved by integrating complete control over output file generation and source maps. The `declaration` flag is invaluable for generating type declaration files (`.d.ts`), facilitating library development and strict API contracts. However, for performance-critical applications, generating declarations for large codebases might incur significant overhead. Advanced users may choose to conditionally enable this option within subprojects or during production releases only. Coupled with `composite` projects, developers can partition codebases into isolated builds which benefit from faster incremental builds and parallel processing. The following configuration highlights a composite project setup:

```
{
  "compilerOptions": {
    "composite": true,
    "declaration": true,
    "declarationMap": true,
    "emitDeclarationOnly": false,
    "incremental": true
  },
  "references": [
    { "path": "../core" },
    { "path": "../utils" }
  ]
}
```

This approach facilitates disparate teams working on different modules while preserving type consistency. Using project references also minimizes recompilation of unchanged modules, thereby reducing build times in continuous integration pipelines.

Optimizing error-checking strategies in TypeScript should not overlook the integration of third-party tools that augment the built-in diagnostics. Custom transformers paired with the TypeScript compiler API can perform code modifications during the compilation phase. For example, developers might write a transformer to enforce additional lint-like rules or generate metadata from annotated classes. The following pseudo-code illustrates how to integrate a custom transformer:

```
const ts = require('typescript');
```

```
const transformer = (context) => {
  return (sourceFile) => {
    // Perform source file modifications and custom diagnostics here
    return ts.visitNode(sourceFile, function visitor(node) {
      // Example: Inject logging into methods with a certain
      decorator
      return ts.visitEachChild(node, visitor, context);
    });
  };
};

const program = ts.createProgram(['src/index.ts'], {
  // Compiler options here...
});
const { emitSkipped, diagnostics } = program.emit(undefined,
    undefined, undefined, false, {
  before: [transformer]
});
if (emitSkipped) {
  console.error(ts.formatDiagnosticsWithColorAndContext(diagnostics,
    {
    getCurrentDirectory: ts.sys.getCurrentDirectory,
    getCanonicalFileName: fileName => fileName,
    getNewLine: () => ts.sys.newLine
  }));
}
```

This example, while abstract, encapsulates advanced techniques to integrate real-time code analysis directly into the compile process. Sophisticated error-checking may also involve manipulating the reporting behavior of the compiler. By leveraging flags such as --pretty and controlling diagnostic output via custom scripts, engineers can make the compile-time feedback loop more informative and actionable.

Additional advanced techniques involve targeting language heterogeneity where TypeScript outputs may ultimately need to interoperate with other languages or specialized deployment environments. The target and lib compiler options allow precise control over the JavaScript features available, ensuring that polyfills or down-level transformations are only applied when necessary. For instance, an enterprise-focused build might specify:

```
{
  "compilerOptions": {
    "target": "ES2017",
    "lib": ["es2017", "dom"],
    "downlevelIteration": true,
    "noEmitHelpers": true,
    "importHelpers": true
  }
}
```

The use of `downlevelIteration` ensures that constructs such as for-of loops over iterables are transformed efficiently, while `noEmitHelpers` coupled with `importHelpers` reduces bundle size by centralizing helper functions provided by `tslib`.

Error reporting can be further refined by employing `diagnostics`: `true` in development environments, which offers verbose output of compiler decisions and performance metrics. For example, integrating diagnostic information into automated build pipelines aids in identifying optimization opportunities during the compilation process. Advanced developers might write scripts that filter and correlate diagnostic messages to pinpoint recurring issues, a feature that not only accelerates debugging but also drives preventive maintenance across large codebases.

Furthermore, integrating TypeScript compiler options with advanced IDE features yields profound productivity gains. Modern editors like Visual Studio Code leverage `tsconfig.json` to power IntelliSense, refactoring, and in-editor diagnostics. By creating separate `tsconfig` files for dedicated purposes—such as one for tests, one for benchmarks, and one for production builds—teams can ensure that each subset of the project benefits from specialized configurations. Consider organizing the project with a base configuration and an extended test-specific configuration:

```
// tsconfig.base.json
{
  "compilerOptions": {
    "target": "ES2020",
    "module": "ESNext",
    "strict": true,
    "sourceMap": true,
    "esModuleInterop": true
  },
  "include": ["src/**/*"]
}

// tsconfig.test.json
{
  "extends": "./tsconfig.base.json",
  "compilerOptions": {
    "module": "CommonJS",
    "noEmit": false,
    "types": ["jest", "node"]
  },
  "include": ["test/**/*"]
}
```

This modular approach allows test suites to compile code with a different module system and include specialized type definitions, thereby isolating test behavior from production code paths. Advanced developers can script environment-specific builds that dynamically select the appropriate configuration file based on context.

The interplay between compiler settings and continuous integration is another domain for refined optimization. For build systems that support parallel or incremental builds, ensuring that the incremental option is activated is crucial. When combined with detailed logging mechanisms, incremental builds not only accelerate the compilation cycle but also generate logs that can be analyzed to detect performance regressions. Distributed build systems may also benefit from selectively enabling `tsBuildInfoFile` to centralize bottleneck information:

```
{
  "compilerOptions": {
    "incremental": true,
    "tsBuildInfoFile": "buildcache/tsconfig.tsbuildinfo"
  }
}
```

This configuration centralizes build metadata, allowing both local and remote build servers to reference the same cache, thereby reducing redundant type-checking and enhancing overall efficiency.

Advanced users must also reconcile the need for rigorous error checking with developer workflow fluidity. Tools such as `fork-ts-checker-webpack-plugin` decouple type-checking from the main process, enabling faster, asynchronous builds while still reporting detailed type errors. Coupling this plugin with advanced compiler flags allows for aggressive optimizations without compromising on code quality. A representative configuration snippet in a Webpack environment might appear as follows:

```
const ForkTsCheckerWebpackPlugin = require('fork-ts-checker-webpack-
    plugin');

module.exports = {
  // Other configuration properties
  plugins: [
    new ForkTsCheckerWebpackPlugin({
      async: false,
      typescript: {
        configFile: 'tsconfig.json',
        diagnosticOptions: {
          semantic: true,
          syntactic: true
        }
```

```
      }
    })
  ]
};
```

The advanced compiler options in TypeScript offer a rich palette of configurations for optimizing both developer efficiency and application robustness. Meticulous tuning of these options, combined with adaptive build strategies and comprehensive type-checking, forms the cornerstone of high-performance and scalable TypeScript codebases.

## 10.4  Integrating    TypeScript    with    CI/CD Pipelines

Integrating TypeScript build and test processes into continuous integration and deployment pipelines requires a thorough understanding of both the development ecosystem and the orchestration tools that execute builds in distributed environments. Advanced practitioners must design CI/CD workflows that maintain type safety, leverage caching, and optimize build times while ensuring that every commit passes a rigorous series of tests and quality checks.

One of the primary considerations is the segmentation of tasks within the CI pipeline. Tasks should be categorized into static analysis, code compilation, unit testing, integration testing, and deployment. A robust pipeline starts by installing dependencies, then proceeds to execute a series of build commands that have been heavily optimized via the TypeScript compiler options discussed earlier. For example, an advanced npm script setup might consolidate these steps as illustrated below:

```
{
  "scripts": {
    "ci:clean": "rimraf dist && rimraf buildcache",
    "ci:lint": "eslint 'src/**/*.{ts,tsx}' --max-warnings 0",
    "ci:build": "tsc --project tsconfig.json",
    "ci:test": "jest --runInBand --coverage",
    "ci:prepare": "npm run ci:clean && npm run ci:lint",
    "ci": "npm run ci:prepare && npm run ci:build && npm run ci:test"
  }
}
```

In this configuration, the separate tasks for cleaning previous builds, linting, building TypeScript files, and running tests enforce a high code quality standard. The use of `--runInBand` in the test command assures deterministic test execution in CI environments, particularly when parallelization may introduce non-determinism.

Advanced CI pipelines also take advantage of caching mechanisms. For large TypeScript codebases, reusing incremental build data from previous runs is critical. Configuring `tsc` with the `incremental` flag and specifying a centralized `tsBuildInfoFile` enables the CI job to detect unchanged modules and skip redundant type-checking. The following `tsconfig.json` snippet reflects such considerations:

```
{
  "compilerOptions": {
    "incremental": true,
    "tsBuildInfoFile": "./buildcache/tsconfig.tsbuildinfo",
    "strict": true,
    "target": "ES2020",
    "module": "ESNext",
    "sourceMap": true
  },
  "include": ["src/**/*"],
  "exclude": ["node_modules", "dist"]
}
```

Integrating these build strategies into a CI/CD system entails careful orchestration. Many teams deploy CI systems like GitHub Actions, CircleCI, or Jenkins to implement these strategies. A sophisticated GitHub Actions workflow for a TypeScript project could be structured as shown below:

```
name: CI Pipeline

on:
  push:
    branches:
      - main
  pull_request:
    branches:
      - main

jobs:
  build-and-test:
    runs-on: ubuntu-latest
    steps:
      - uses: actions/checkout@v2

      - name: Setup Node.js
        uses: actions/setup-node@v2
        with:
          node-version: '16'

      - name: Install dependencies
        run: npm ci

      - name: Run Lint and Build
        run: npm run ci:prepare && npm run ci:build

      - name: Run Tests with Coverage
        run: npm run ci:test

      - name: Upload Coverage Report
        uses: actions/upload-artifact@v2
        with:
          name: coverage-report
          path: coverage
```

This workflow leverages the caching and build optimizations described earlier. The use of npm ci ensures deterministic installations, while the separation of tasks into distinct steps aids in debugging and performance profiling. Including a step to upload the coverage report provides immediate feedback on code quality and test coverage.

In more complex environments, containerization further isolates the build process. Using Docker enables the CI system to run consistent environments across different platforms. A Dockerfile tailored for building TypeScript projects may include pre-cached dependency layers and a focus on minimizing rebuild times:

```
FROM node:16-alpine

WORKDIR /app

# Install dependencies and cache them
COPY package.json package-lock.json ./
RUN npm ci --production

# Copy source files and compile
COPY tsconfig.json .
COPY src/ ./src/
RUN npm run ci:build

# Running the tests
COPY test/ ./test/
CMD ["npm", "run", "ci:test"]
```

Integrating this Docker-based build into a CI system such as Jenkins can be accomplished through a Jenkins Pipeline (Jenkinsfile). Advanced users can script Jenkins to pull the latest source, build the Docker image, and run tests inside the container:

```
pipeline {
    agent any
```

```
stages {
  stage('Checkout') {
    steps {
      checkout scm
    }
  }
  stage('Install Dependencies') {
    steps {
      sh 'npm ci'
    }
  }
  stage('Build') {
    steps {
      sh 'npm run ci:build'
    }
  }
  stage('Test') {
    steps {
      sh 'npm run ci:test'
    }
  }
  stage('Docker Build') {
    steps {
      script {
        dockerImage = docker.build("my-app:${env.BUILD_ID}")
      }
    }
  }
  stage('Docker Test') {
    steps {
      script {
        dockerImage.inside {
          sh 'npm run ci:test'
        }
      }
    }
  }
}
post {
  always {
    archiveArtifacts artifacts: 'coverage/**', fingerprint: true
  }
  failure {
    echo 'Pipeline failed. Check build logs for diagnostics.'
  }
```

```
  }
}
```

This pipeline demonstrates sophisticated orchestration in a Jenkins environment. Notably, it leverages Docker to encapsulate the build environment, ensuring consistency across different build agents. Fine-tuning the pipeline to include artifact archiving and conditional failure notifications enhances both the reliability and maintainability of the CI/CD process.

Advanced CI/CD integration for TypeScript projects further entails using environment-specific configurations. Test environments may require different compiler options or additional type definitions (e.g., for testing libraries such as Jest). Configuring multiple tsconfig files (for instance, one for production and one for testing) ensures that each environment receives a tailored build process. An example directory structure might include tsconfig.json, tsconfig.prod.json, and tsconfig.test.json, with the following sample for testing:

```
{
  "extends": "./tsconfig.json",
  "compilerOptions": {
    "module": "CommonJS",
    "noEmit": false,
    "types": ["jest", "node"]
  },
  "include": ["test/**/*", "src/**/*"]
}
```

CI pipelines can then selectively invoke the appropriate configuration via npm scripts, allowing for dynamic adaptation of the build process depending on the environment. In these scenarios, setting the appropriate environment variable (e.g., NODE_ENV or TS_ENV) in the CI job influences the behavior of the build scripts.

A recurring challenge in CI/CD integration is ensuring that asynchronous operations complete reliably. For projects that use tools such as `fork-ts-checker-webpack-plugin` for parallel type-checking, developers must be cautious that asynchronous diagnostics do not escape the build stage. Configuring the plugin in synchronous mode for CI ensures that the build only passes once all type errors have been resolved:

```
const ForkTsCheckerWebpackPlugin = require('fork-ts-checker-webpack-
    plugin');

module.exports = {
  // Other Webpack configuration settings
  plugins: [
    new ForkTsCheckerWebpackPlugin({
      async: false,
      typescript: {
        configFile: 'tsconfig.json',
        diagnosticOptions: {
          semantic: true,
          syntactic: true
        }
      }
    })
  ]
};
```

This synchronization is critical in CI environments because it ensures that any type errors are reported immediately and cause the build to fail, preventing faulty code from progressing to production. Advanced logs from such builds can then be integrated into dashboards for monitoring purposes.

Parallelization of test execution is another area where advanced configuration can greatly reduce feedback cycles. Advanced CI systems can distribute tests across multiple nodes or containers. Strategies to achieve this include sharding the test suite or using test runners with built-in parallel execution capabilities. For example, when using Jest, setting the --maxWorkers option dynamically based on the number of available cores can be beneficial:

```
{
  "scripts": {
    "ci:test": "jest --maxWorkers=50%"
  }
}
```

In CI/CD systems, parallel test execution must be balanced with resource constraints. Intelligent scheduling and orchestration within the CI platform can further optimize test runtimes.

Integration with CI/CD pipelines is also greatly enhanced by automated deployment scripts. After successful builds and tests, pipelines often trigger a series of deployment tasks. These tasks might involve pushing Docker images to a container registry, updating Kubernetes deployments, or publishing to a CDN. Signing artifacts, verifying code integrity with checksums, and automating rollback procedures in case of deployment failures are advanced techniques that ensure the reliability of production releases. Advanced deployments often combine these strategies by interfacing with deployment-specific tools and APIs. Developers may incorporate deployment steps into the pipeline as follows:

```
- name: Deploy to Kubernetes
  if: github.ref == 'refs/heads/main'
  run: |
    kubectl apply -f k8s/deployment.yaml
    kubectl rollout status deployment/my-app-deployment
```

Automating such deployment steps ensures that every commit passing through the CI pipeline has a clear, repeatable path to production, with rollback mechanisms in place should any telemetry indicate a degraded state.

The integration of TypeScript with CI/CD pipelines emphasizes the transformation of development practices into continuous, automated processes capable of dynamically adapting to code changes. Leveraging efficient caching, precise environment configurations, and seamless interfacing with external build and deployment tools facilitates both rapid feedback cycles and stringent quality controls. Mastery of these techniques empowers advanced practitioners to scale build processes to meet the demands of modern, distributed development environments while maintaining uncompromised type safety and code integrity.

## 10.5   Effective Version Control Practices

Advanced version control for TypeScript projects requires a deep comprehension of Git's internal mechanisms and sophisticated workflows to manage evolution across a codebase characterized by rigid type contracts and complex dependency graphs. Leveraging Git effectively in such an environment involves not only branch management and commit hygiene but also the integration of automated hooks, submodule configuration, and a disciplined approach to merge and rebase strategies. The following discussion explores these topics in depth, offering nuanced configuration examples and actionable techniques that facilitate a high level of code integrity, traceability, and collaborative efficiency.

Effective branch management is foundational in enforcing clear development protocols. In TypeScript projects with robust compiler configurations, it is critical to ensure that merges do not introduce subtle type errors. A recommended strategy involves using a branching model similar to Git Flow, but augmented with strict branch protection rules. The use of feature branches for incremental changes, coupled with a dedicated integration branch, supports thorough code reviews and continuous integration testing before merging into the main branch. For example, an advanced Git workflow may include the following sequence:

```
git checkout -b feature/advanced-type-checking
```

This practice isolates experimental or incremental revisions while maintaining the stability of the production branch. Advanced users also integrate pre-push hooks to enforce linting, unit tests, and even TypeScript type-checking. The following sample .git/hooks/pre-push script ensures that only commits passing all validations are pushed to remote repositories:

```
#!/bin/bash
npm run lint && npm run test && npm run build:ts
if [ $? -ne 0 ]; then
    echo "Pre-push checks failed. Aborting push."
    exit 1
fi
```

Such hooks, often automated via tools like Husky, integrate code quality checks directly into the version control workflow, ensuring that advanced efforts in static typing and automated testing are preserved at all integration points.

Rebasing and merging strategies in advanced Git workflows directly impact the maintainability and clarity of the project history. In TypeScript projects, where refactoring and code propagation are frequent due to stricter type annotations, history clarity is paramount. Instead of traditional merge commits, which might obfuscate the progression of changes, advanced practitioners prefer an interactive rebase to lin-

515

earize commit history. This is especially valuable when integrating incremental updates that must be traced and audited over time. A typical
interactive rebase command is:

```
git rebase -i HEAD~10
```

Here, the developer can squash trivial commits, reword commit messages for clarity regarding type changes, and ensure that each commit
encapsulates a logically coherent change. This process aids in debugging, auditing, and a thorough understanding of how type definitions
evolve across the project.

Git's submodule and subtree mechanisms are indispensable when
managing multi-package TypeScript repositories or projects with
microservice-like architectures. Submodules allow for the separate
evolution of shared libraries or modules, each potentially compiled
with its own set of strict TypeScript configurations.   Integrating
submodules can be accomplished as shown:

```
git submodule add https://github.com/organization/typescript-library.
    git lib/tslib
git submodule update --init --recursive
```

This strategy ensures that certain core libraries, which might be compiled with their own tsconfig.json settings, are maintained independently while still being integrated into the primary repository. Subtree
merges offer an alternative for teams that require a more homogeneous
history between the main project and its components. Advanced users
choose between these approaches based on integration complexity, update frequency, and the necessity for isolated versioning.

Commit message discipline is another advanced consideration. Clear
commit messages facilitate the tracking of type changes, bug fixes, and

refactoring efforts, which is crucial in projects where incremental type safety improvements are made regularly. Conventionally, teams might adopt a commit message style compliant with tools such as Conventional Commits. An example commit message following this standard might be:

```
feat(core): enhance strict null checks on User module

BREAKING CHANGE: Refactored user model to enforce strict null
    invariants,
which requires changes in the consumer code.
```

This level of detail is essential for advanced practitioners who rely on automated changelogs, semantic versioning, and migration tools that parse commit histories to trigger deprecations or refactor recommendations.

Integrating Git with automated continuous integration (CI) pipelines further enforces best practices through scripted validation. Advanced developers frequently utilize commit hooks generated by frameworks like Husky to immediately run tests, lint checks, and type verifications. A representative package.json snippet that configures Husky for precommit checks is:

```
{
  "husky": {
    "hooks": {
      "pre-commit": "npm run lint && npm run test",
      "commit-msg": "commitlint -E HUSKY_GIT_PARAMS"
    }
  }
}
```

This configuration prevents faulty commits from entering the repository, thus serving as an automated gatekeeper for code quality. For projects with extensive type-based logic, such safeguards ensure that

517

refactoring or enhancements do not compromise the static analysis guarantees enforced by the TypeScript compiler.

Handling merge conflicts in TypeScript projects can be particularly challenging due to the interplay between code and type definitions. Advanced diff and merge tools such as git mergetool can be configured to respect coding standards and formatting rules, thereby minimizing manual intervention. Tools like VSCode or Beyond Compare integrated with custom merge drivers can intelligently handle differences in .ts files. Custom Git configuration can also specify merge strategies for particular file types:

```
# In .gitattributes
*.ts merge=typescript
```

Setting up a custom merge driver in the .gitconfig file allows differentiation between code changes and auto-generated declarations, thus preventing spurious merge conflicts in auto-generated or compiled TypeScript declaration files.

Tagging and versioning practices are crucial when distributing TypeScript libraries or applications that depend heavily on type integrity. Advanced users adhere to strict tagging protocols that coincide with semantic versioning. Annotated tags in Git capture snapshots of significant releases, ensuring that any regression in type safety or API behavior can be traced back to a specific commit. Creating an annotated tag is straightforward:

```
git tag -a v2.3.0 -m "Release version 2.3.0: improved type inference
    and stricter interface contracts."
git push origin v2.3.0
```

These tags become pivotal in automated deployment scripts and CI pipelines to trigger version-specific builds or rollbacks when anomalies are detected in production.

For teams working collaboratively on extensive TypeScript codebases, incorporating blame and annotate tools becomes crucial. Using commands like git blame or git annotate provides insights into the origins of type-related changes or refactoring efforts. Advanced developers script periodic reviews of such data to identify patterns or recurring issues, potentially leading to targeted training or refactoring initiatives. A sample command to inspect recent modifications might be:

```
git blame -L 100,200 src/models/User.ts
```

This granular approach affords developers a mechanism to audit type changes, verify consistency, and ensure that high-level architectural patterns are maintained.

Integrating Git with issue tracking systems further consolidates version control efforts. Linking commit messages with relevant issue IDs, by using syntax such as Fixes #123 in commit descriptions, facilitates traceability between code changes and the resolution of type-related or functional bugs. Advanced Git integrations with CI/CD systems can automatically update issue statuses upon successful merges, thereby creating a closed loop between version control and project management.

Revisiting the importance of repository organization, advanced version control practices demand clarity in directory structure and module separation. Monorepo strategies that combine multiple TypeScript projects under one roof can benefit from tools like Lerna or Yarn Workspaces. These facilitate coordinated dependency management, version bumping, and collective testing while preserving individual package histories. A typical Lerna configuration might include:

```
{
  "packages": [
    "packages/core",
    "packages/utils",
    "packages/api"
  ],
  "version": "independent"
}
```

This configuration allows each package to adopt its own version control strategies and upgrade schedules while benefiting from centralized dependency tracking and publication workflows.

Advanced practitioners also leverage Git bisect to isolate regressions introduced by type changes or refactoring. This tool remains invaluable when a bug is introduced in one commit among hundreds of changes. The following sequence illustrates the use of Git bisect:

```
git bisect start
git bisect bad HEAD
git bisect good v2.2.0
# Git identifies the first bad commit through a series of test
    iterations.
```

Complementing this with automated test scripts and diagnostic logging streamlines the iterative process of pinpointing regressions, especially in projects with rigorous type validations.

Collectively, these version control practices not only maintain code quality but also enhance team productivity and collaboration in TypeScript projects. By integrating advanced branching, commit hygiene, merge strategies, and automated checks into Git workflows, teams can ensure that each code integration maintains the strict type safety and performance standards demanded by modern TypeScript applications.

Such practices empower developers to manage complexity efficiently and to scale codebases without compromising on traceability, consistency, or development velocity.

## 10.6  Utilizing Code Linters and Formatters

Advanced development in TypeScript projects mandates a rigorous enforcement of coding standards to maintain code quality and consistency across diverse teams. Leveraging linters and formatters, such as TSLint and Prettier, is a proven strategy to automate style conformance and catch potential issues early in the development cycle. At this level, integration is not merely about running analysis tools, but about tuning them to the project's specific needs, embedding them in build pipelines, and even customizing rulesets to address domain-specific challenges.

A primary consideration is configuration granularity. TSLint, although largely replaced by ESLint with @typescript-eslint in modern workflows, still serves as a pedagogical example for setting up a static analysis tool tailored to TypeScript's intricacies. A highly-tuned TSLint configuration might incorporate strict settings for enforcing explicit access modifiers, consistent naming conventions, and prohibitions against certain anti-patterns that could compromise type safety. An example configuration in `tslint.json` can appear as follows:

```
{
  "defaultSeverity": "error",
  "extends": [
    "tslint:recommended"
  ],
  "rules": {
    "no-console": false,
    "indent": [true, "spaces", 2],
```

```
    "member-access": [true, "check-accessor", "check-constructor"],
    "no-inferrable-types": [true, "ignore-params"],
    "object-literal-sort-keys": false,
    "quotemark": [true, "single", "avoid-escape"],
    "semicolon": [true, "always"],
    "triple-equals": [true, "allow-null-check"],
    "interface-name": [true, "never-prefix"],
    "max-line-length": [true, 120],
    "no-unused-variable": [true, {"ignore-pattern": "^_"}],
    "naming-convention": [
      true,
      {
        "type": "default",
        "format": "camelCase"
      },
      {
        "type": "variable",
        "format": "camelCase"
      },
      {
        "type": "function",
        "format": "camelCase"
      }
    ]
  },
  "jsRules": {},
  "rulesDirectory": []
}
```

Customizing such rules allows developers to strike a balance between enforcing strict type correctness and enabling common development patterns. Modifications such as allowing console statements during development, ignoring unused variables with specific prefixes, and setting maximum line length are some examples that provide a practical balance in advanced usage.

Prettier, on the other hand, ensures stylistic consistency without interfering with the semantic correctness ensured by TypeScript's compiler and TSLint. The integration of Prettier is principally achieved through configuration files, command-line options, or IDE plugins that automatically format files on save. An advanced `.prettierrc` configuration might look as follows:

```
{
  "printWidth": 100,
  "tabWidth": 2,
  "useTabs": false,
  "semi": true,
  "singleQuote": true,
  "trailingComma": "all",
  "bracketSpacing": true,
  "arrowParens": "avoid",
  "endOfLine": "lf"
}
```

In advanced scenarios, integrating Prettier with TSLint (or ESLint in ecosystems that have migrated away from TSLint) can be achieved by utilizing the Prettier plugin for TSLint. This ensures that style issues are either flagged or automatically corrected before commits. Such integration not only enforces a common code style but also reduces cognitive overhead in manual formatting. Furthermore, using tools such as `lint-staged` in combination with Husky ensures that all code is formatted correctly prior to commits. A representative configuration might be:

```
{
  "husky": {
    "hooks": {
      "pre-commit": "lint-staged"
    }
  },
  "lint-staged": {
    "*.{ts,tsx}": [
      "prettier --write",
      "tslint --fix",
      "git add"
    ]
  }
}
```

```
}
```

This configuration prevents poorly formatted and non-compliant code from entering the repository by chaining auto-formatting and linting on staged files. Such pipelines are essential in large TypeScript projects where multiple developers work on interdependent modules and coding consistency is critical.

Beyond configuration, advanced practitioners must consider performance optimization and diagnostic capabilities when running these tools in large projects. For instance, running TSLint over a monorepo with thousands of files can be a resource-intensive process. Techniques such as caching lint results, running linters in parallel, or even splitting the linting process over independent CI nodes can alleviate performance bottlenecks. Parallel execution might be achieved using a command-line tool like `gulp-parallel` or using Node.js's cluster module to distribute tasks across multiple cores. A sample command to run linting in parallel could be:

```
npx concurrently "tslint -p tsconfig.json --format stylish" "prettier
    --check \"src/**/*.{ts,tsx}\""
```

Advanced integration into CI pipelines further extends the utility of linters and formatters. For example, in a Jenkins or GitHub Actions pipeline, incorporating steps that run these tools not only enforces code quality but also prevents integration of non-compliant code. An advanced GitHub Actions snippet might be:

```
name: Lint and Format

on:
  pull_request:
  push:
    branches:
```

```
      - main

jobs:
  format-and-lint:
    runs-on: ubuntu-latest
    steps:
      - name: Checkout Code
        uses: actions/checkout@v2

      - name: Install Dependencies
        run: npm ci

      - name: Check Prettier Format
        run: npx prettier --check "src/**/*.{ts,tsx}"

      - name: Run TSLint
        run: npx tslint -p tsconfig.json --format verbose
```

In high-stakes projects, failing these tests ensures that any deviations from the established code style are caught before merging. Advanced users can integrate these steps with environment variables to toggle between more relaxed or strict checks based on the branch or deployment stage.

Customization also extends to crafting bespoke linting rules. Projects with unique domain-specific requirements might need rules that go beyond the defaults provided by TSLint. Advanced developers can write custom rules in TypeScript that analyze the abstract syntax tree (AST) of source files before flagging issues. An elementary structure for a custom TSLint rule is as follows:

```
import * as Lint from 'tslint';
import * as ts from 'typescript';

export class Rule extends Lint.Rules.AbstractRule {
  public static FAILURE_STRING = 'Custom rule violation.';

  public apply(sourceFile: ts.SourceFile): Lint.RuleFailure[] {
    return this.applyWithWalker(new CustomWalker(sourceFile, this.
```

```
      getOptions()));
  }
}

class CustomWalker extends Lint.RuleWalker {
  public visitNode(node: ts.Node): void {
    // Analyze node and flag issues
    if (/* condition */) {
      this.addFailureAtNode(node, Rule.FAILURE_STRING);
    }
    super.visitNode(node);
  }
}
```

This level of customization enables teams to enforce project-specific conventions that might be crucial for maintaining consistent design patterns across a complex TypeScript codebase.

Developers should also consider the integration of linters and formatters with other code quality tools. Automated tools, such as static analysis for detecting potential performance issues or security vulnerabilities, may run concurrently. Coordinating these tools so that their outputs are aggregated into a unified dashboard is an advanced practice. Tools that provide IDE integration, such as Visual Studio Code extensions for TSLint and Prettier, ensure that developers receive feedback instantly, cultivating a culture of continuous improvement. Additionally, the configuration of file watchers that automatically re-lint or reformat changed files enhances productivity, especially in projects where incremental changes are frequent.

The synergy between linters, formatters, and the build system becomes particularly crucial in continuous integration pipelines. A typical advanced workflow involves equal emphasis on unit testing, type-checking by TypeScript, linting by TSLint, and formatting by Prettier. Coordinating these processes into a micro-service-oriented build can leverage tools like Webpack for bundling, while concurrently running quality tools as part of hooks. This unified strategy ensures that the codebase remains pristine at every stage of the development cycle.

Finally, disciplined version control of configuration files for both TSLint and Prettier is essential in complex projects. Treating these configuration files as first-class citizens in the repository, subject to code review and continuous testing, ensures that any modifications are deliberate and beneficial. Institutions should standardize the usage of configuration directories or even adopt meta-configurations that allow variations across project segments. The deployment of configuration validation scripts as part of CI further cements a culture of high code quality.

Utilizing code linters and formatters, when done at an advanced level, transcends the basic enforcement of style guidelines. It integrates into the fabric of the development workflow, aids in early detection of bugs, and upholds the rigor of TypeScript's type system. Mastery of these tools not only encourages consistency across diverse teams but also streamlines the code review process, allowing advanced developers to focus on architectural improvements while trusting that style and syntax remain uniformly managed.

## 10.7   Leveraging Static Analysis Tools

Advanced developers seeking to improve the robustness of TypeScript codebases must look beyond conventional linters and formatters to fully exploit static analysis tools. These tools perform deep inspections of source code by analyzing the abstract syntax trees (ASTs), control flow graphs, and data flow properties, allowing the identification of

subtle bugs and performance issues that may elude traditional compilation and runtime testing. By incorporating static analysis into the
development lifecycle, teams can detect unreachable code paths, identify dead code, enforce architectural constraints, and validate complex
type invariants prior to deployment.

Static analysis tools can be integrated seamlessly into both local development environments and CI/CD pipelines. Extending the baseline
capabilities of the TypeScript compiler, these tools often provide customizable diagnostics that target specific domains. For example, advanced static analyzers can scrutinize the consistency of dependency
injections in frameworks, ensure secure handling of untrusted inputs,
and flag patterns known to lead to memory leaks. A typical integration
involves combining tools such as SonarQube, CodeQL, or custom-built
analyzers using the TypeScript Compiler API.

An illustrative example is the use of CodeQL to query TypeScript code.
CodeQL allows developers to write queries that reveal intricate code
patterns. A simple query might identify all instances where a function
may throw an exception without proper error handling. An example
CodeQL snippet might look as follows:

```
import javascript

from FunctionCall fc, Method m
where m.getName() = "throw"
   and fc.getEnclosingCallable() = m
select m, "Unhandled exception might be raised here."
```

This query, although basic, demonstrates the power of static analysis in
identifying areas where error handling may be insufficient. Advanced
practitioners extend such queries to focus on domain-specific error conditions, performance bottlenecks, or security vulnerabilities.

For projects requiring bespoke analysis, building custom static analysis tools using the TypeScript Compiler API is a compelling approach. The API exposes the compiler's internal representation of source files, allowing advanced manipulation and validation of code. Developers can implement visitor patterns that traverse ASTs to enforce custom rules. Consider the following example of a custom static analysis tool that flags the usage of deprecated APIs:

```
import * as ts from 'typescript';

function findDeprecatedAPIs(fileNames: string[], options: ts.
    CompilerOptions): void {
  const program = ts.createProgram(fileNames, options);
  const checker = program.getTypeChecker();

  for (const sourceFile of program.getSourceFiles()) {
    if (!sourceFile.isDeclarationFile) {
      ts.forEachChild(sourceFile, visit);
    }
  }

  function visit(node: ts.Node): void {
    if (ts.isCallExpression(node)) {
      const signature = checker.getResolvedSignature(node);
      if (signature) {
        const decl = signature.getDeclaration();
        if (decl && ts.getJSDocDeprecatedTag(decl)) {
          const { line, character } = sourceFile.
    getLineAndCharacterOfPosition(node.getStart());
          console.warn(`Deprecated API call at ${sourceFile.fileName
    }:${line + 1}:${character + 1}`);
        }
      }
    }
    ts.forEachChild(node, visit);
  }
}

// Usage example:
findDeprecatedAPIs(['src/index.ts'], { target: ts.ScriptTarget.ES2020
    , module: ts.ModuleKind.ESNext });
```

This tool traverses the codebase, using the checker to locate calls to functions annotated with the JSDoc @deprecated tag. It not only enforces deprecation policies but also provides precise feedback pinpointing the location of deprecated usage, a crucial feature for mitigating technical debt in large projects.

Integrating static analysis with build systems enhances tolerance to the evolving codebase. For example, Webpack plugins and custom CI job steps can be devised to run static analysis passes as part of the build process. A Jenkins pipeline step that executes a custom static analyzer may be defined as follows:

```
pipeline {
  agent any
  stages {
    stage('Static Analysis') {
      steps {
        script {
          def result = sh(script: 'npm run static-analysis',
    returnStatus: true)
          if(result != 0) {
            error "Static analysis failed. Review the output for
    critical issues."
          }
        }
      }
    }
  }
}
```

In the above snippet, npm run static-analysis could be a custom script that executes static analysis using tools like ESLint with advanced rules, CodeQL, or custom TypeScript analyzers. By enforcing a build failure when critical issues are detected, teams ensure problems do not propagate to production.

Another advanced static analysis technique involves adopting formal verification methods to reason about TypeScript code. Although TypeScript remains an optionally typed language, efforts to integrate formal methods can yield significant benefits. For instance, employing model checking techniques in conjunction with static analysis can verify that state transitions in an application adhere to defined invariants. While this approach may involve additional tooling, its benefits for mission-critical applications justify the investment. Developers might integrate a model checker that correlates with static analysis findings to produce automated proofs of correctness for specific modules.

Combining static analysis results with metrics presents an additional layer of intelligence. Tools such as SonarQube aggregate results from multiple analyzers and present a unified dashboard that tracks code smells, vulnerabilities, and complexity measures. Advanced configuration of these tools allows teams to set thresholds that, when exceeded, trigger notifications or block deployments. Integration with Git hooks and CI dashboards ensures that quality metrics are visible at every stage of the development process.

Customization and extensibility are also significant aspects of leveraging static analysis tools. Advanced developers ought to develop custom rules and plugins tailored to the application's architectural patterns. For instance, in large monorepos or microservice architectures managed with Lerna or Yarn Workspaces, it is beneficial to enforce constraints that prevent prohibited dependencies between modules. A custom ESLint rule can detect and flag such unwanted imports, ensuring that each module adheres to the intended dependency graph. A simple example of an ESLint rule that restricts module boundaries might look like this:

```
module.exports = {
  meta: {
```

```
    type: 'problem',
    docs: {
      description: 'disallow cross-module imports',
      category: 'Best Practices'
    },
    schema: []
  },
  create: function (context) {
    return {
      ImportDeclaration(node) {
        const importPath = node.source.value;
        if (importPath.startsWith('../forbidden')) {
          context.report({
            node,
            message: 'Cross-module import detected: "{{path}}" is not
      allowed.',
            data: { path: importPath }
          });
        }
      }
    };
  }
};
```

Deploying such custom rules in a static analysis pipeline can automatically enforce architectural boundaries. When combined with automated CI checks and pre-commit hooks, these rules ensure that any violations are caught at the earliest possible stage.

Performance analysis is another advanced area where static analysis tools provide insight. By statically analyzing code paths, it is possible to identify frequently executed code sections and potential hotspots that could benefit from optimization. Tools that instrument code during the analysis phase can simulate runtime conditions and predict resource usage. Although not a substitute for runtime profiling, such static predictions help developers preemptively optimize algorithms or refactor inefficient structures. The integration of these predictions into automated reports can guide performance tuning efforts, especially in computation-intensive TypeScript applications.

Furthermore, static analysis tools facilitate security audits in Type-Script projects. A common use case is the identification of potential injection vulnerabilities or the misuse of APIs that handle sensitive data. Advanced static security analyzers scan for patterns that may lead to cross-site scripting (XSS) or SQL injection vulnerabilities, even when type safety is high. By mapping variable flow and checking for sanitization routines, these tools provide a safety net that transcends traditional code reviews. A configuration for a security-focused ESLint plugin might be as follows:

```
{
  "plugins": ["security"],
  "extends": ["plugin:security/recommended"],
  "rules": {
    "security/detect-object-injection": "error"
  }
}
```

This configuration ensures that potential security vulnerabilities are highlighted during static analysis, prompting immediate remediation before code deployment.

Sophisticated static analysis workflows also incorporate machine learning techniques to detect anomalous patterns in code. Advanced tools in this domain analyze historical commit data and code evolution trends to predict areas most likely to harbor bugs or security issues. While such tools are still emerging in the TypeScript sphere, early adoption in large-scale projects can yield insights that standard rule-based analyzers might miss. Integrating these insights into an automated dashboard provides continuous feedback on code health and guides targeted refactoring strategies.

Leveraging static analysis tools in advanced TypeScript projects is a multi-dimensional strategy that encompasses custom rule development, integration with CI/CD pipelines, performance and security analysis, and even formal verification techniques. These tools work synergistically with traditional type-checking and linting to enforce a rigorous quality standard. Advanced configurations, combined with continuous monitoring and tailored feedback, empower development teams to preemptively identify and rectify issues before they evolve into critical problems. Such a proactive approach not only improves code robustness and maintainability but also fosters a culture of continuous improvement and technical excellence within the development organization.

www.ingramcontent.com/pod-product-compliance
Lightning Source LLC
La Vergne TN
LVHW022332060326
832902LV00022B/3995

* 9 7 9 8 3 1 0 6 8 6 1 2 0 *